Pearson

Endorsement Statement from Pearson

In order to ensure that this resource offers high-quality support for the associated Pearson qualification, it has been through a review process by the awarding body. This process confirms that this resource fully covers the teaching and learning content of the specification or part of a specification at which it is aimed. It also confirms that it demonstrates an appropriate balance between the development of subject skills, knowledge and understanding, in addition to preparation for assessment.

Endorsement does not cover any guidance on assessment activities or processes (e.g. practice questions or advice on how to answer assessment questions), included in the resource nor does it prescribe any particular approach to the teaching or delivery of a related course.

While the publishers have made every attempt to ensure that advice on the qualification and its assessment is accurate, the official specification and associated assessment guidance materials are the only authoritative source of information and should always be referred to for definitive guidance.

Pearson examiners have not contributed to any sections in this resource relevant to examination papers for which they have responsibility.

Examiners will not use endorsed resources as a source of material for any assessment set by Pearson.

Endorsement of a resource does not mean that the resource is required to achieve this Pearson qualification, nor does it mean that it is the only suitable material available to support the qualification, and any resource lists produced by the awarding body shall include this and other appropriate resources.

'I'm blown away by this book. Packed with breadth and depth of content, it matches the specification scrupulously and is supplemented by clear exam guidance and examples. This must be the companion for everyone teaching or learning A-Level Politics – I cannot do without it.'

– **Benjamin De Jong**, Jewish Community Secondary School, London

'Another excellent publication from *Essentials*. The book's chapters on Feminism are particularly helpful to me in teaching Paper 2 as they break down a complex topic into easily digestible chunks. It looks at topics such as patriarchy from both the lens of general understanding, and from the specific feminist groups as per the exam specification. This really breaks down the unit for students and teachers alike. Another excellent feature is the tables of agreement and disagreement. These are core to the ideology unit, so having them so plainly written is extremely helpful.'

– **Lucy Ryall**, Poole High School, Dorset

'An earlier edition of this book ignited my passion for A-Level Politics due to its ability to make complex political concepts interesting and digestible. This revised version is a perfect progression as it is tailored perfectly for the Pearson specification, but with enough challenge and detail for anyone interested in ideologies to develop their understanding of the ideas which shape our world.'

– **Ciara McCombe**, Convent of Jesus and Mary Language College, London

ESSENTIALS OF POLITICAL IDEAS

PEARSON *EDEXCEL* POLITICS A-LEVEL

Kathy Schindler and
Andrew Heywood

Second Edition

BLOOMSBURY ACADEMIC
LONDON • NEW YORK • OXFORD • NEW DELHI • SYDNEY

BLOOMSBURY ACADEMIC
Bloomsbury Publishing Plc
50 Bedford Square, London, WC1B 3DP, UK
1385 Broadway, New York, NY 10018, USA
29 Earlsfort Terrace, Dublin 2, Ireland

BLOOMSBURY, BLOOMSBURY ACADEMIC and the Diana logo
are trademarks of Bloomsbury Publishing Plc

First published in Great Britain 2018
This edition published 2024

Cover design: Eleanor Rose
Cover image © gmast3r / Getty Images

A catalogue record for this book is available from the British Library.

A catalog record for this book is available from the Library of Congress.

ISBN: HB: 978-1-3504-4141-5
          PB: 978-1-3503-8238-1
     ePDF: 978-1-3503-8239-8
   eBook: 978-1-3503-8236-7

Typeset by Integra Software Services Pvt. Ltd.

To find out more about our authors and books visit www.bloomsbury.com
and sign up for our newsletters.

Brief Contents

Contents

Illustrations

Figures

Photos

Maps

Tables

Worked Examples

About the Authors

KATHY SCHINDLER has been teaching Politics for over 30 years, working in a large comprehensive school in London for most of that time. Kathy is part of the Senior Examination Team for a large exam board and was involved in the development of the 2017 Politics specification. She leads many training sessions for the exam board around the country, helping teachers to get to grips with the demands of the new specification as well as supporting individual politics departments and holding student revision conferences in schools. In addition to this book, Kathy has also written textbooks published by Pearson. You can also find Kathy on Facebook (search for the page Politics_Tutor) and on Twitter/X as @politics_tutor.

ANDREW HEYWOOD is author of such best-selling textbooks as *Politics*, *Political Ideologies*, *Global Politics* and *Political Theory*, used by hundreds of thousands of students around the world and translated into over twenty languages. He was Vice Principal of Croydon College, having previously been Director of Studies at Orpington College and Head of Politics at The Sixth-Form College Farnborough. Andrew had many years' experience as an A-Level Chief Examiner for Government and Politics, and Principal Examiner for Political Ideologies and Global Politics. He currently works as a freelance author.

Tour of the Book

Specification Checklist

A useful checklist of the points from the Edexcel specification that will be covered in the chapter.

Key Questions

At the start of each chapter, there is a list of the key questions you will explore.

Tensions Within

Boxes that offer an overview of how different strands of the same ideology feel about important topics.

Exam Tips

Key advice on how to do well in specific aspects of your exam.

Specification Key Terms

A definition of the key terms named in the Pearson Edexcel specification. It is important to know what these are because they can be used in exam questions.

Summary Boxes

Bullet-pointed reminders of key concepts to allow you to refresh and consolidate your understanding as you read.

Definitions

A definition of other political terms that are essential to a good understanding of political ideas.

Key Thinker Profiles

Detailed coverage of the key thinkers you are required to learn for your exam.

Exam Focus Chapter

A whole chapter devoted to exam skills, with detailed instructions on how to structure your essays and meet key A-Level requirements.

STUDENT EXTRACT – 'To what extent is socialism more divided than united?' – looking at thinker-driven vs strand-driven answers

✗

Marx and Engels believe that society is dominated by ideas of the ruling class, known as bourgeois hegemony. These ideas work to divide the workers, therefore they need to be eradicated to create a classless society. On the other hand, more modern thinkers such as Crosland, believe in not eradicating class, but attempting to minimize the divide and close the gap between rich and poor.

✓

Revolutionary socialists believe that class control of society is a consequence of who owns the means of production. This control is exercised by the dominant class over the working class. Marx and Engels believe that society is dominated by ideas of the ruling class, this is known as bourgeois hegemony. These ideas work to divide the proletariat, therefore they need to be eradicated to create a classless society. On the other hand, social democrats, like Crosland, believe in not eradicating class, but attempting to minimize the divide and close the gap between rich and poor.

Chapter Summary

A bullet-pointed list of what was covered in the chapter, reminding you of what you have read.

Chapter Summary

- Conservatism is primarily an ideology which is concerned with conserving and protecting society.
- The three strands are traditional conservatives, One Nation conservatives and the New Right.
- The New Right is a marriage of two seemingly inconsistent strands – neoliberalism and neoconservatism.
- The New Right fundamentally reject almost all of the values of traditional and One Nation conservatism.

Exam Style Questions

1. To what extent do conservatives agree over the state?
2. To what extent do conservatives agree over human nature?
3. To what extent do conservatives disagree over the economy?
4. To what extent is there agreement within liberals over the economy?
5. To what extent is conservatism a coherent ideology?
6. To what extent are conservatives committed to tradition?
7. To what extent do conservatives support paternalism?

Further Resources

Adams, I. Political Ideology Today (2001). Chapter 3, Conservatism and the Right' is a straightforward read for A-Level students which explores the prevalence of conservative ideas.

Edwards, A. and Townshend, J. (2002). Interpreting Modern Philosophy from Machiavelli to Marx. Chapter 2, 'Hobbes', and Chapter 6, 'Burke' are useful for students looking for a deeper insight into these two key thinkers.

Leach, R. Political Ideology in Britain (2015). Chapter 3, 'Conservatism' is an excellent chapter which goes through the development of conservative ideas and values.

Fawcett, E. Conservatism: The Fight for a Tradition (2020). A comprehensive history of conservative thought from the nineteenth century to the present.

Kelly, P. et al. The Politics Book (2013). A clearly written, concise book which covers many of the thinkers discussed in this chapter.

Muller, J., ed. Conservatism: An Anthology of Social and Political Thought from David Hume to the Present (1997). The best general reader of traditional conservative political writings.

O'Sullivan, N. (1976) Conservatism. A very readable book which explores the many ideas of conservatism.

Scruton, R. Conservatism: An Invitation to the Great Tradition (2018). An erudite exploration of the development of conservative thought and an even-handed defence of traditional conservatism in the modern political discourse.

Sedgewick, M. Key Thinkers of the Radical Right: Behind the New Threat to Liberal Democracy (2019). A timely anthology exploring the intellectual foundations of far-right and alt-right conservative ideology that has gained increasing prominence in twenty-first-century politics.

Vincent, R. Modern Political Ideologies (1995). Chapter 3, 'Conservatism', can be used to stretch and extend a student's knowledge of the content covered in this chapter.

Visit our companion website at https://bloomsbury.pub/essentials-of-political-ideas-2e for more worked examples.

Further Resources

A list of books, articles, websites and films that will help you to explore further.

Exam Style Questions

These questions are in the same style as the ones you will respond to on your exams. You can use them to practise your question interpretation and planning skills, as well as to practise drafting full answers.

Worked Examples

This takes all the knowledge from the chapter and shows how to use them to plan exam questions.

Tensions within socialism over the role of the state

Worked example

Paragraph One – Agreement within socialism

✓ Evolutionary socialists like social democrats and the Third Way agree that the democratic, parliamentary process via the state, and not revolution, is the best way to help improve the conditions for the most vulnerable in society (Webb)
✓ Evolutionary socialists agree that a welfare state is a key tool in helping to create a fairer and more just society (Crosland)
✓ Both social democrats and the Third Way agree that the right kind of state can drive change and play a key role in ensuring that capitalism works in the interests of the most vulnerable

Paragraph Two – Disagreement within socialism

✗ Social democrats and third-way socialists disagree on the extent of the role of the state
✗ Social democrats (Crosland) support the nationalisation of the commanding heights', whereas the Third Way accepted the privatization agenda of neoliberalism (Giddens)
✗ Social democrats support increased taxation for the rich and a 'cradle to grave', welfare system, whereas the Third Way does not seek punitive tax bands and prefers a welfare system that encourages work

Paragraph Three – Disagreement within socialism

✓ Revolutionary socialists disagree with both social democrats and third-way socialists over the state, arguing that is a truly constrained society, the state will 'wither away'
✓ Revolutionary socialists (Marx and Engels) argue that the state is not neutral and is part of the superstructure, controlled by the economic base, rejecting Webb's 'inevitability of gradualness'
✓ Revolutionary socialists reject the idea that socialism can be achieved via the state in a top-down manner arguing that the working class must be involved in the process of creating a socialist society (Luxemburg)

Digital Resources

Accompanying this book is a suite of supportive online resources to help you get the most out of your learning.

Go online to the companion website at https://bloomsbury.pub/essentials-of-political-ideas-2e to access further learning materials to support each chapter.

Bonus worked examples – Access a range of additional essay plans to support your understanding of how to apply your knowledge to exam questions.

Further resources booklet – Delve into a range of engaging news articles, blog posts, reports, videos and political websites to explore chapter topics further.

Revision planner – Explore these tips from the authors on how to plan and organize your revision effectively.

Flashcards of key terminology – Check your knowledge and understanding of specification terms and other important political concepts.

Further sample student answers – Read examples of exam answers written by students. Guided author annotations will help you to pinpoint exactly what examiners are looking for.

How to Use This Book

Welcome to the latest edition of *Essentials of Political Ideas*, which has been fully revised and updated to cover every aspect of the 2017 Pearson Edexcel Specification. Between the two of us, we have decades of experience in teaching politics and extensive knowledge of the Pearson Edexcel specification. We wanted to outline for you the changes we have made to this edition of the book and why we think it's in a good position to help you do well in this subject.

All the chapters in the book relate directly to a part of the Pearson Edexcel specification for A-Level Politics. You will see in the Tour of the Book (pages xvi-xvii) that we have listed the relevant parts of the specification at the beginning of each chapter. This allows you to see clearly how the content of each chapter relates to the specification. In addition, the page design is also organized to help you identify content and features that are related to the specification, the exam and the skills needed. For example, you will notice that the specification key terms, the tips and the specification checklists are all presented in the same colour (light green) throughout the book. We have also gone beyond the content traditionally found in textbooks to help you understand the debates that will form the basis of the essay questions you will be set, and to help you understand how to bring the content together to answer essay questions.

A unique and exciting aspect of the book is that it offers an entire chapter to help you understand the skills needed to write good answers – answers that address the three Assessment Objectives on which you will be assessed. The Exam Focus chapter at the end of the book is packed full of helpful advice on how to write essays, use comparative language, develop your synoptic skills and ensure you're fully prepared for the A-Level Politics exams.

A final thing to note is that throughout the book you will find links to our companion website. You will find it packed with additional debates as well as downloadable templates and some useful revision tips. Most importantly, we will be regularly adding to the website and plan to provide further examples of annotated essay answers.

We really hope you find this book helpful. We have put all our experience and expertise together to make it the ideal guide for all students of A-Level Politics.

Andrew Heywood

Kathy Schindler

Acknowledgements

I would like to thank all those at Bloomsbury who we have worked with to make this new edition a reality.

I have been using Andy Heywood's Ideologies books since I first started teaching over thirty years ago, and every edition has been even better than the last. It has been an absolute honour to have worked on this edition to adapt his brilliant content to the demands of the new specification. I hope I have done it justice.

Of course I couldn't do the work I do without the support of my husband, Danny, who is always the most proud and the most excited about everything I do – thank you.

1 LIBERALISM

Historical overview

Liberalism resulted from the breakdown of feudalism in Europe, and the growth, in its place, of a capitalist society. Liberalism reflected the aspirations of the rising middle classes, whose interests conflicted with the established power of absolute monarchs and the landed aristocracy. At the time, liberal ideas were radical as they challenged the absolute power of the monarchy. In place of absolutism, they advocated constitutional and representative government. Liberals criticized the privileges of the aristocracy and the unfairness of a feudal system in which social position was determined by an 'accident of birth'.

The nineteenth century was in many ways the liberal century. As industrialization spread throughout Western countries, liberal ideas triumphed. Liberals advocated an industrialized and market economic order 'free' from government interference, in which businesses would pursue profit and states encouraged to trade freely with one another.

The character of liberalism changed as the rising middle classes succeeded in establishing their economic and political dominance, and industrialization led liberals to question, and then to revise, the ideas of early liberalism. Whereas classical liberalism had been defined by the desire to minimize government interference in the lives of its citizens, later modern liberalism came to be associated with welfare provision and economic management.

Key Questions

» How did liberalism originate?

» What are the main principles that are central to liberalism?

» What are the key strands of liberalism?

» What are the areas of similarity and difference within liberalism?

Specification Checklist

1. Liberalism: core ideas and principles:

» Individualism
» Freedom (liberty)
» The state
» Rationalism
» Equality (justice)
» Liberal democracy

2. Differing views and tensions within liberalism:

» Classical liberalism
» Modern liberalism

3. Liberal key thinkers and their ideas:

» John Locke (1632–1704)
» Mary Wollstonecraft (1759–97)
» John Stuart Mill (1806–73)
» John Rawls (1921–2002)
» Betty Friedan (1921–2006)

Alex Walker/Getty

Definition

Feudalism: A system of agrarian-based production that is characterized by fixed social hierarchies and a rigid pattern of obligations.

Absolutism: A form of government in which political power is concentrated in the hands of a single individual or small group, in particular, an absolute monarchy.

Introduction to liberalism and its strands

The central theme of liberal ideology is a commitment to the individual and the desire to construct a society in which people can be free. Liberals believe that humans are first and foremost rational individuals (see page 8). This implies that individuals should enjoy as much freedom as possible, as long as it is consistently applied to all. However, although individuals are entitled to equal legal and political rights, they should be rewarded in line with their talents and their willingness to work. Liberal societies are organized around the twin principles of constitutionalism and consent, designed to protect citizens from the danger of government tyranny. Nevertheless, there are significant differences between classical liberalism and modern liberalism.

Classical liberalism

Classical liberalism is the earliest liberal tradition whose ideas developed during the transition from feudalism to capitalism and reached their high point during the early industrialization of the nineteenth century. Classical liberalism is characterized by a belief in a 'minimal' state, whose function is limited to the maintenance of order and personal security. This is associated with their support for egoistical individualism and negative freedom (see page 14) based on the idea that people need to be left alone to maximize their freedom. For classical liberals individualism was seen as the best advancement for society as a whole.

Modern liberalism

Modern liberal ideas relate to the further development of industrialization and capitalism. Industrialization had brought about a massive expansion of wealth for some, but was also accompanied by the spread of slums, poverty, ignorance and disease. In these changing circumstances, liberals found it more difficult to maintain the belief that capitalism had brought prosperity and liberty for all. Consequently, many came to revise the early liberal view that the unrestrained pursuit of self-interest produced a free society. As a result, modern liberals rethought their attitude towards the state, freedom and individualism. Modern liberals were therefore prepared to advocate the development of an interventionist or enabling state.

1. Liberalism: core ideas and principles

Individualism

This can be included in a discussion of the liberal view of society, human nature and the economy.

In the modern world, the concept of the individual is so familiar that it may seem difficult to articulate. As feudal societies moved towards a capitalist one, people, perhaps for the first time, were encouraged to think for *themselves*, and to think of *themselves* in personal terms. As a result, society was increasingly understood from the viewpoint of the individual.

A belief in the primacy of the individual is the characteristic theme of liberalism, and has influenced it in different ways. Individualism is the belief in the supreme importance of the individual over any social group or collective body and suggests that the individual is central to any political theory. Individuals are private, separate and unique entities who have an identity distinct to others which must be respected. For liberals, society is established by individuals for the fulfilment of their own ends, not the other way round.

Individualism also implies that society should be constructed to benefit the individual, giving moral priority to individual rights, needs or interests. This is best summed up by liberal thinker **John Stuart Mill (1806–73)** when he suggested that '*Over himself, over his own body and mind, the individual is sovereign.*' For liberals, protecting the individual and the achievement of individual happiness are the supreme goals. Individuals were thought to possess personal and distinctive qualities; each was of special value. German Enlightenment philosopher Immanuel Kant (1724–1804) best expressed this when discussing the dignity and equal worth of human beings in his conception of individuals as 'ends in themselves' and not merely as means for the achievement of others.

Liberalism's commitment to the individual is inextricably linked to its belief in the rational capacities of the individual. It sees the individual as a rational human being responsible for their own behaviour, capable of making decisions for themselves. Moreover, each individual is thought to know their own best interests. This cannot be decided on their behalf by some paternal authority, such as the state. Equally, no one else can judge the quality of an individual's happiness. If each individual is the sole judge of what is in their own interest and gives them pleasure, then the individual alone can determine what is morally right for them. In other words, the individual should be at the heart of decisions about their economic, political and social life.

Individualism

Summary box

- Liberalism believes in the power and capacity of individuals to transform their own lives.
- It places the individual at the centre of decision making.
- The individual has higher claims than the group.
- It is often understood in the sense of personal autonomy.

Freedom (liberty)

This can be included in a discussion of the liberal view of society, human nature and the economy.

A belief in the supreme importance of the individual leads naturally to a commitment to individual freedom. Freedom can be defined as the ability to think or act as one wishes. Individual liberty (liberty and freedom being interchangeable) is for liberals the supreme political value and, in many ways, the unifying principle within liberalism. For early liberals, liberty was a natural right, an essential requirement for leading a truly human existence. It also gave individuals the opportunity to pursue their own interests by exercising choice: the choice of where to live, for whom to work, what to buy and so on.

John Locke (1632–1704), an early liberal thinker, focused on freedom under the law and economic freedom, seeing private property as the embodiment of individual liberty, i.e. the individual's right to own property and sell their labour. **Mill** expanded on this concept of freedom by introducing more human elements. For **Mill**, freedom wasn't just about individuals' economic rights over their property, but also about freedom of speech, thought and religion. It meant being able to develop as an autonomous individuals through education.

Mill's ideas have been described as the 'heart of liberalism'. This is because he provided a 'bridge' between classical and modern liberalism as his ideas look back to the early nineteenth century and forward to the twentieth century. The ideas developed in *On Liberty* (1859) best show **Mill's** contribution to liberal thought. This work contains some of the boldest statements in favour of individual liberty and negative freedom which **Mill** believed to be an important condition for liberty, but not in itself a sufficient one for all. He thought that liberty was a positive and constructive force. It gave individuals the ability to take control of their own lives, to gain autonomy or achieve self-realization.

Mill also believed passionately in individuality. The value of liberty is that it enables individuals to develop, to gain talents, skills and knowledge and to refine themselves. For **Mill**, there were 'higher' and 'lower' pleasures. **Mill** was concerned with promoting those higher pleasures that develop an individual's intellectual, moral or artistic feelings. He was not concerned with 'lower' pleasure-seeking, but with personal self-development. As such, he laid the foundations for developmental individualism that placed emphasis on human flourishing rather than the crude satisfaction of interests.

Definition

Natural rights: (God-given) rights that are fundamental to human beings and are therefore inalienable (they cannot be taken away).

Individuality: Self-fulfilment achieved through the realization of an individual's distinctive or unique identity or qualities; what distinguishes one person from all others.

Freedom (liberty)

Summary box

- The ability to think or act as one wishes.
- Closely linked to individualism.
- Liberals believe that the individual should be as free as possible.
- But that it must be constrained to some extent.
- Society must be based on individual freedom for individuals to flourish.

The state

This can be included in a discussion of the liberal view of the state, society and the economy.

Support for a state is a key feature of liberalism. However, although liberals support the existence of a state, they're deeply concerned about it too. In the words of Thomas Paine, they see the state as a 'necessary evil'; 'necessary' to create an ordered society where freedom can flourish, but 'evil' in its potential to undermine individual liberty.

Liberal thinking about the state is underpinned by the assumption that the liberty of one person is always in danger of becoming the ability to abuse another. Each person can be said to be both a threat to, and under threat from, every other member of society. Our liberty therefore requires that other members of society are restrained from encroaching on our freedom, and in turn, their liberty requires that they are safeguarded from us. This protection is provided by a sovereign state, capable of restraining all individuals and groups within society.

Spec key term

Social contract theory: The idea that the state is set up with agreement from the people to respect its laws which serve to protect them.

This is broadly what is known as social contract theory which was developed by theorists like **Locke**. He constructed a picture of what life had been like before government was formed, in what was called a 'state of nature'. Locke described it as a state of perfect freedom, a state of equality (foundational equality) and bound by a law of nature. It would 'be a state of liberty, yet it is not a state of licence … the state of nature has a law of nature to govern it, which obliges everyone'. **Locke** recognized, however, that there were problems with life in the state of nature. When natural laws were violated, there were no police, prosecutors or judges, the victims must enforce the law themselves. **Locke** suggested that people would realize that a state of nature is unsatisfactory and agree to transfer these rights to a government. **Locke** argued that it was reasonable for a community to surrender some of its liberty in favour of a government, which is better able to protect those rights than any one person could alone. This is the theory of the social contract; legitimate government is established by the explicit consent of those governed.

Definition

State of nature: A society characterized by unrestrained freedom and the absence of established authority.

According to **Locke**, citizens do not have an obligation to obey all laws, especially if they come from an arbitrary or unlimited government. Government is established in order to protect natural rights. When these are protected by the state, citizens should respect government and obey the law. However, if government violates the rights of its citizens, they in turn have the right of rebellion.

The social contract argument embodies some important liberal attitudes towards the state:

» First, it emphasizes that political authority comes 'from below', i.e. the consent of the people.

» It is created by citizens themselves, not by some higher unknown force.

» It exists to serve the needs and interests of the people.

» The individual is more important than society.

» Roles and people are interchangeable, i.e. individuals should be able to rise and fall according to merit.

» Society has no fixed social structures.

Spec key term

Mechanistic theory: The idea that the state was created by the people to serve them and act in their interests.

The state embodies the interests of all its citizens and acts as a neutral referee when individuals come into conflict with one another. This is known as mechanistic theory of the state.

For **Locke** the contract between state and citizen is a limited one: to protect a set of defined natural rights. As a result, **Locke** believed in limited government. The legitimate role of government is limited to the protection of '*life, liberty and property*'. Therefore, government should not extend beyond its three 'minimal' functions:

» Maintaining public order and protecting property

» Providing defence against external attack

» Ensuring that contracts are enforced

Other issues and responsibilities are the concern of private individuals. Thus, although liberals are convinced of the need for government and state, they are also acutely aware of the dangers that government embodies. In their view, all governments are potential tyrannies against the individual.

The state
Summary box

- All liberals believe that the state is necessary, although it has potential for evil.
- They believe it can serve a useful role in society.
- This is based on social contract theory.
- Also useful here is the harm principle.

Role of the state in the economy
This can be included in a discussion of the liberal view of the economy, the state and society.

As the feudal economic system was replaced by capitalism, liberals recognized a connection between their ideology and capitalism. As a consequence, liberals have largely been supportive of the capitalist system, recognizing the role it could play in upholding individual liberty and supporting meritocracy and also because of the wealth creating ability of a capitalist economic model.

Locke famously described individual's fundamental rights as, '*life, liberty and property*' highlighting the importance of ownership as fundamental to human existence. For **Locke**, the right to private property is key. He argues that all individuals' labour power belongs to them. Individuals can use their labour power to create goods (property) which belong to them. However, Locke makes four key stipulations:

1. Individuals can't take something if it involves harming someone else.

2. Individuals can't take possession of more than they can use.

3. Individuals must leave '*enough and as good*' for others.

4. Individuals can only acquire property by their own labour.

All liberals recognize the capitalist system as the clearest embodiment of individualism. For liberals, the free market encourages individuals to make rational choices about how they work, what they buy, sell, save or spend. The marketplace therefore upholds the key principle of free choice. They also accepted that capitalism would result in some inequality, which they argued would play an important role in incentivizing individuals. As Milton and Rose Friedman argued in *Free to Choose* (1979), '*the essential part of economic freedom is freedom to use the resources we possess in accordance with our own values – freedom to enter any occupation, engage in any business enterprise, buy from and sell to anyone else, so long as we do so on a strictly voluntary basis*'. The role of the state in these affairs was simply to ensure property was secure and contracts were honoured to allow free trade and market competition to flourish.

So, liberals broadly agree that the economy should be based on private property and private enterprise. This leads all liberals to support the economic system of capitalism that puts private property at the heart of all economic arrangements.

However, liberalism encompasses two contrasting economic traditions – classical liberals have viewed the market economy as a vast network of commercial relationships, in which both consumers and producers indicate their wishes through the price mechanism. Modern liberals, on the other hand, reject the idea of a self-regulating market economy, arguing instead that the economy should be regulated, or 'managed', by government.

The economy

Summary box

- All liberals support private property and capitalism.
- All liberals believe that the state plays a useful role in the economy.
- They believe the economy should enhance individualism and freedom.

Rationalism

This can be included in a discussion of the liberal view of human nature.

Rationalism is the idea of basing one's opinions and actions on reason and knowledge rather than on religious, emotional or superstitious notions. It is the belief that knowledge flows from reason rather than experience, and places heavy emphasis on the capacity of human beings to understand and explain their world, and to find solutions to problems.

Liberals are firmly of the belief that humans are guided by reason, capable of knowing their own mind and making decisions in their own best interests. In other words, they have the capacity to weigh things up and recognize the costs and benefits of one course of action over another. This is why liberals believe individuals are capable of benefiting from freedom. Further, liberals believe that individuals are capable of personal self-development and of bringing about wider social and political change. A faith in reason, moreover, leads liberals to believe that conflict can generally be resolved by debate, discussion and argument, greatly reducing the need for force and bloodshed.

For **Mary Wollstonecraft (1759–97)**, reason was at the heart of her philosophy for the equal treatment of men and women. She criticized male writers who considered '*females rather as women than human creatures*' and argued that both men and women should be treated equally, as they were both rational human beings. The rights of 'man' should therefore apply to both genders.

This commitment to rationalism shows how liberalism is very much part of the Enlightenment project. The central theme of the Enlightenment in the seventeenth and eighteenth centuries was the desire to release humans from their reliance on superstition, prejudice and ignorance. Before the Enlightenment, assumptions about society suggested that humans couldn't and shouldn't think for themselves and that instead they should rely on the knowledge and wisdom of those in positions of authority to tell them what to do, an outlook known as paternalism. The Enlightenment challenged this approach, and centred instead on the idea that reason is the primary source of authority and legitimacy. It advocated ideas like liberty, progress, tolerance and constitutional government and encouraged the idea that every human is a rational individual who is the best judge of their own interests and who exercises free will.

Rationalism

Summary box

- At the core of rationalism is the belief in reason and logic.
- All liberals believe that humans have rational capacities.
- They believe that humans are capable of making progress through rational thought.
- Hence they should be free to exercise their rationality.

The Enlightenment

1610	Galileo publishes *The Sidereal Messenger* which suggests that the earth revolves around the sun. It was considered one of the texts that started the Enlightenment movement.
1687	Isaac Newton sets out his main laws of motion and gravity in his book *Mathematical Principles of Natural Philosophy*.
1689	John Locke publishes *Two Treatises of Government* which outlines a passionate defence of natural rights and indicates the view that rulers need to serve the public: if they do not, they lack authority. This book will go on to be highly influential in the American and French Revolutions.
1721	In his book, *Persian Letters*, Montesquieu mocks King Louis XIV, Catholicism and satirises all social classes. This was unheard of at the time.
1734	In *Letters on England*, Voltaire criticises religious and political systems. This causes outrage and he is forced to flee Paris.
1751	The *French Encyclopédie* is first published which collates, for the first time, the principal works of the Enlightenment.
1762	*The Social Contract* is published by Jean-Jacques Rousseau. It rejects the idea that power and authority in society is passed down by the state and the Church, rather than through the general will of the people. He famously argues that "man is free yet everywhere he is in chains".
1776	The United States Declaration of Independence famously states that, "We hold these truths to be self-evident, that all men are created equal, that they are endowed by their Creator with certain unalienable Rights, that among these are Life, Liberty and the pursuit of Happiness." These ideas are the basis of the values of the Enlightenment.
1787	In an attempt to avoid bankruptcy due to his extravagance, King Louis XVI seeks to raise taxes in France. This causes a crisis leading to the beginning of the French Revolution.
1791	Thomas Paine publishes *The Rights of Man*, arguing that popular revolution is permissible when a government does not safeguard the natural rights of its people. This is seen as clear support of the French Revolution and republicanism in general.

The liberal theory of justice is based on a belief in equality of various kinds; however, it is important to note that for liberals, equality is understood in a fundamentally different way to socialists (see Chapter 3). Liberals recognize equality in three different ways.

Equality (justice)
This can be included in a discussion of the liberal view of society, the economy and human nature.

(i) Foundational equality

In the first place, individualism implies a commitment to foundational equality. Humans are 'born' equal in the sense that each individual is of equal moral worth, an idea embodied in the notion of natural or human rights. The key word to understand here is 'worth'. All humans are considered to be of equal value; in other words, one cannot grade humans in order of importance or significance on the basis of age, wisdom, birth, wealth or any other factor. All humans are valuable, all human life is deemed to be sacred, and all are endowed with what Thomas Jefferson referred to as inalienable rights because humans are entitled to them by virtue of being born: they cannot, in that sense, be taken away. To be born human is to have inalienable rights. It is also worth noting that the liberal view of tolerance is based on foundational equality.

Spec key term

Foundational equality: Rights that all humans have by virtue of being born which cannot be taken away.

Natural rights are now more commonly called human rights. For **Locke** and Jefferson, rights are 'natural' as they are invested in humans by nature (or God). Natural rights establish the essential conditions for leading a truly human existence. For **Locke**, it was '*life, liberty and property*'. Jefferson, in the American Declaration of Independence, described inalienable rights as those of '*life, liberty and the pursuit of happiness*'. It is interesting to note that by including 'the pursuit of happiness', Jefferson was giving a nod to individualism and acknowledging that each individual should decide for themselves what this meant.

(ii) Formal equality

Foundational equality implies a belief in formal equality, the idea that individuals should enjoy the same formal status within society, particularly with the distribution of rights. Consequently, liberals disapprove of social privileges that are enjoyed by some but denied to others on the basis of factors such as gender, race, colour, religion or social background. Formal equality should not be reserved for any particular class of person, such as men, white people, Christians or the wealthy, but given to all, universally. The most important forms of formal equality are legal equality and political equality.

» **Legal equality** emphasizes 'equality before the law' which is a fundamental principle of the *rule of law*, that the law should 'rule'. It is a core principle of liberal democracy, upholding limited government and preventing arbitrary government. The law should apply equally to all members of society, regardless of whether they are citizens or public officials. Its core features therefore include:

- The idea of equality before the law
- You can only be punished if you break the law
- If the law is broken there should be certainty of punishment
- No one is above the law

» **Political equality** is the idea of universal adult suffrage and underpins the liberal commitment to democracy. Other aspects of political equality include the right to protest, freedom of expression and also the rights to join a political party, run for office and participate freely in political rallies, events or protests.

Formal equality has provided fertile ground for the growth of liberal feminist beliefs. Liberal feminism (discussed more fully in Chapter 6) has been articulated by thinkers ranging from **Wollstonecraft** to **Betty Friedan (1921–2006)**. Liberalism was one of the earlier advocates of women's rights based on the ideas of foundational and formal equality. **Wollstonecraft** argued that women were human beings deserving of the same rights as men and rejected the view of many authoritative writers at the time, like Jean-Jacques Rousseau, who wanted to deny women a formal education, educating them only for the pleasure of men.

Equality of opportunity

Liberals also subscribe to a belief in equality of opportunity. This is the idea that every individual should have the same chance to rise or fall in society. Liberals believe social equality (as supported by socialists) to be undesirable because people are not born the same. They possess different talents and skills, and some are prepared to work much harder than others. Liberals believe that it is right to reward merit (defined as the ability and the willingness to work); indeed, they think it is essential to do so if people are to have an incentive to realize their potential and develop the talents with which they were born. Equality, for a liberal, means that individuals should have an equal opportunity to develop their unequal abilities.

This leads to a belief in meritocracy. A meritocratic society is one in which inequalities of wealth and social position solely reflect the unequal distribution of talent among humans. Such a society is supposedly based on justice because individuals are judged not by their gender, the colour of their skin or their religion, but according to their talents and willingness to work, or what Martin Luther King Jr called 'the content of their character'.

Betty Friedan wrote about the need for women to have the same opportunities as men in society. She wrote about the difficulties women faced by being restricted to the domestic sphere, and not having the same prospects as men, which she called 'the problem with no name'. **Friedan** described it in the opening of her book *The Feminine Mystique* (1963): '*as she made the beds, shopped for groceries … she was afraid to ask even of herself the silent question — "Is this all?"*'. **Wollstonecraft** had argued a century earlier that women were denied the crucial educational opportunities that support the development of rational intellect because they were considered significantly inferior to men.

Spec key term

Formal equality: The idea that all individuals have the same legal and political rights in society.

Definition

Human rights: Rights to which people are entitled by virtue of being human; human rights are universal, fundamental and absolute.

Inalienable rights: Certain rights are beyond the control of government, being naturally endowed to every individual at birth, and retained throughout their life.

Rule of law: The principle that all conduct and behaviour, of private citizens and government officials, should conform to a framework of law.

Spec key term

Equality of opportunity: The idea that all individuals should have equal chances in life to rise and fall.

Meritocracy: A society organized on the basis that success is based on ability and hard work.

Equality (justice)

Summary box

- Liberals believe that everyone is born equal, known as foundational equality.
- From this comes a belief in formal equality, i.e. legal and political rights.
- Liberals believe in a society which is based on equality of opportunity, so that all individuals can have equal access – this is meritocracy.

Liberal democracy

This can be included in a discussion of the liberal view of society.

The liberal form of democracy has a 'liberal' commitment to limited government blended with a 'democratic' belief in popular rule. Its key features are:

1. The right to rule is gained through success in regular and competitive elections based on universal adult suffrage.
2. Constraints on government imposed by a constitution, checks and balances and separation of powers.
3. Protections for individual rights, usually via a bill of rights.
4. Tolerance of differing views.

Toleration

A commitment to toleration is at the heart of liberalism. It is famously expressed by the French writer Voltaire (1694–1778) that, '*I detest what you say but will defend to the death your right to say it.*' In this way toleration does not mean that one accepts or agrees with these alternative views, but that they recognise the right of others to the same free speech that they have. Toleration, pluralism and free speech are essential parts of a liberal society as they establish guidance about how humans should behave towards one another. **Locke** argued that, since the proper function of government is to protect life, liberty and property, it has no right to meddle in '*the care of men's souls'.* Toleration should therefore be extended to all matters regarded as 'private', on the grounds that, like religion, they concern moral questions that should be left to the individual.

In On Liberty (1859), **Mill** developed a wider justification for toleration that highlighted its importance to society as well as the individual. From the individual's point of view, toleration is primarily a guarantee of personal autonomy; moreover, toleration is also necessary to ensure the vigour and health of society as a whole. Contest, debate and argument are the key to diversity, and are the motors of social progress. **Mill** (1859) was thus able to argue, '*If all mankind minus one, were of one opinion, and only one person was of the contrary opinion, mankind would be no more justified in silencing that one person, than he, if he had the power, would be justified in silencing mankind.*'

Liberal fear of power

Although liberals are convinced of the need for government, they are also acutely aware of the dangers that government embodies. In their view, all governments are potential tyrannies against the individual, based on the idea that government exercises sovereign power, and so pose a constant threat to individual liberty. On the other hand, it reflects a distinctively liberal fear of power. As humans are self-seeking creatures, if they have power, they will naturally use it for their own benefit and at the expense of others. Simply put, the liberal position is that ego plus power equals corruption. This was expressed in Lord Acton's famous warning '*Power tends to corrupt, and absolute power corrupts absolutely*', and in his conclusion that '*Great men are almost always bad men*' (1887). Liberals therefore fear arbitrary government and uphold the principle of limited government. Government can be limited through the establishment of constitutional constraints and by democracy.

Spec key term

Toleration: A willingness to accept views or actions with which one is in disagreement.

Definition

Pluralism: A belief in diversity or choice, or the theory that political power is or should be widely and evenly dispersed.

Spec key term

Limited government: The role of government is limited by checks and balances, and a separation of powers because of the corrupting nature of power.

Definition

Bill of rights: A constitutional document that specifies the rights and freedoms of the individual and so defines the relationship between the state and its citizens.

Checks and balances: The idea that a government must divide power between various branches to ensure that no one branch of government can become more dominant than the other.

Separation of powers: The principle that legislative, executive and judicial power should be separated through the construction of three independent branches of government.

How government power can be constrained

1. Constitutions

A constitution is a set of rules that seeks to allocate duties, powers and functions among the various institutions of government. It therefore establishes the rules that govern the government itself. It both defines the extent of government power and limits it. Support for constitutionalism can take two forms:

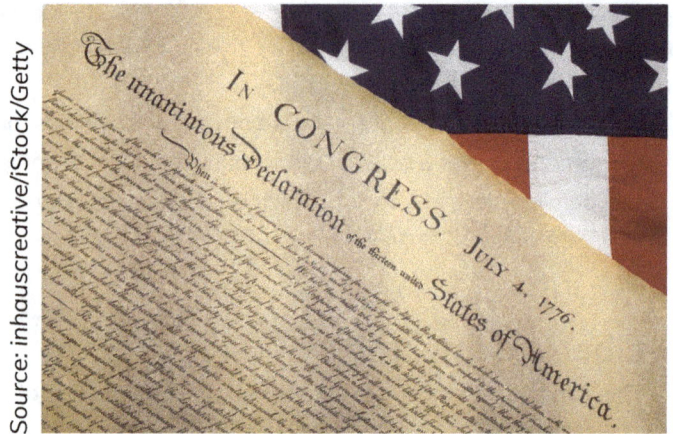

Photo 1.1 **The US Constitution, which defines and limits government power in the United States.**

a. Power can be limited by external, legal constraints. The most important of these is a codified constitution, which categorizes the major powers and responsibilities of government institutions within a single document. In many cases, bills of rights also exist, which entrench individual rights by providing a legal definition of the relationship between the individual and the state.

b. Power can also be constrained by the introduction of internal constraints which disperse power among a number of institutions and create a network of 'checks and balances'. As the French political philosopher Montesquieu (1689–1775) put it, '*power should be a check to power*'. All liberal political systems exhibit some measure of internal fragmentation. This is achieved by a separation of powers, proposed by Montesquieu. This seeks to prevent any individual or small group from gaining dictatorial power by controlling the legislative, executive and judicial functions of government. This can be seen in **Figure 1.1** where all aspects of the state are separated from each other, but at the same time, they have a constitutional responsibility to check on each other to ensure tyranny does not prevail.

2. Democratic rule

Democracy literally means rule by the people. Perhaps a more helpful starting point is Abraham Lincoln's Gettysburg Address, delivered in 1863, which extols the virtues of what he called government '*of the people, by the people, for the people*'. Government by the people emphasizes the need, at some level, for the participation of citizens in the government. Government for the people implies that the essence of democracy is ruling in the public interest. This is associated with the need for representatives to act on behalf of the people, with their right to rule deriving from success in a competitive election. This

Liberal Democracy

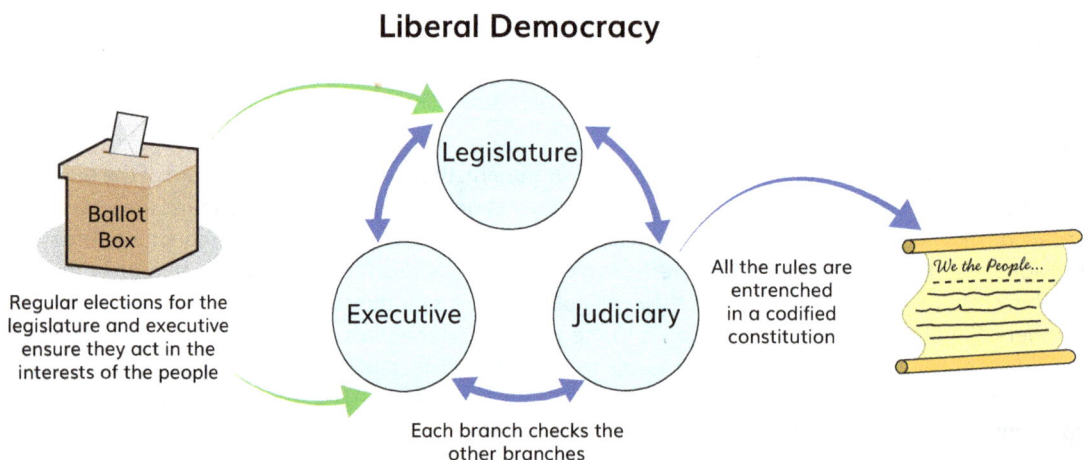

Figure 1.1 **Shows how liberty is protected in a liberal democracy with a separation of powers, checks and balances, codified constitutions and elections.**

model of democracy is usually called representative democracy, and its most common form is liberal democracy.

Liberal democracy

Summary box

- Liberal democracy embodies the principles of liberalism and the principle of democracy to produce a 'type' of democracy.
- The 'liberal' part of this principle is that all citizens are treated equally and their rights and liberties are protected, and importantly that government is limited and also subject to rules.
- The democratic element is that the majority earn the right to form a government and make law; however, the majority have to respect the rights of the minority.

Differences between liberals over democracy

Earlier liberals often saw democracy as threatening or dangerous and raised several concerns:

1. The central liberal concern was that democracy could become the enemy of individual liberty. This arises from the fact that 'the people' are not a single entity but rather a collection of individuals and groups, possessing different opinions and opposing interests. Liberals therefore fear that democracy will focus on the needs of the group, and that the wishes of individuals will be ignored.

2. The 'democratic solution' to conflict is the application of majority rule: the principle that the will of the majority should prevail over that of the minority. Democracy thus comes down to the rule of the 51 per cent, a prospect that the French politician Alexis de Tocqueville (1805–59) famously described as 'the tyranny of the majority'. Individual liberty and minority rights can thus be crushed in the name of 'the people'.

3. Liberals expressed reservations about democracy because of the composition of the majority in modern societies. For **Mill**, political wisdom was unequally distributed and largely related to education. The uneducated masses were more likely to act according to narrow class interests, whereas the educated were able to use their wisdom and experience for the good of others. He therefore insisted that elected politicians should speak for themselves rather than reflect the views of their electors, and he proposed a system of voting that would disenfranchise the illiterate and allocate one, two, three or four votes to people depending on their level of education or social position. Ortega y Gasset (1883–1955), the Spanish social thinker, expressed such fears more dramatically in *The Revolt of the Masses* (1930). Gasset warned that the arrival of mass democracy had led to the overthrow of civilized society and the moral order, paving the way for authoritarian rulers to come to power by appealing to populism.

However, by the twentieth century, liberals had come to see democracy as a virtue.

1. The earliest liberal justification for democracy was founded on consent, and the idea that citizens need a way to protect themselves from government. As early as the seventeenth century, **Locke** developed a theory of *protective democracy* by arguing that voting rights should be extended to the propertied, who could then defend their natural rights against government. If government, through taxation, possesses the power to take property, citizens are entitled to protect themselves by deciding the composition of the tax-making body – the legislature.

2. Another liberal endorsement of democracy is linked to the benefits of political participation through the writings of **Mill**. For **Mill**, the central virtue of democracy is that it promotes the '*highest and most harmonious*' development of human capacities. By participating in political life, citizens enhance their understanding and achieve a higher level of personal development. This form of *developmental democracy* sees democracy as, primarily, an educational experience. **John Rawls (1921–2006)** agreed with this, arguing that the debating, discussing and contemplating that occurs before an election, is what gave democracy value.

Exam Tip – It is important to note that this is **NOT** a disagreement between classical and modern liberals, but more a shift within the whole of liberal thought from an earlier notion against democracy, to a later one embracing it.

3. However, since the mid-twentieth century, liberal theories about democracy have tended to focus less on consent and participation and more on the need for consensus in society. The attraction of democracy is that it is the only system of rule capable of managing the competing groups within modern societies by tying them into the democratic process. Democracy gives competing groups a political voice, it binds them to the political system and the outcome of fairly run elections and so maintains political stability.

Tensions within liberalism over democracy	
AGREEMENT	**DISAGREEMENT**
✓ Liberals support democracy on the basis of 'protective democracy'	✗ Democracy can become the enemy of individual liberty
✓ Liberals also support democracy on the basis of *developmental* democracy, where they improve their knowledge to be involved in decision making	✗ Individual liberty and minority rights can be crushed in the name of the people – known as '*the tyranny of the majority*'
✓ Liberals recognize that democracy is the only system capable of giving competing groups a voice	✗ Liberals also feared that mass democracy could undermine civilized society, by allowing authoritarian rulers to come to power by appealing to the basest instincts of the masses

2. Differences between the two liberal strands

Classical liberalism

Having looked at the core principles of liberalism it is useful to look at how classical liberals have interpreted them. As discussed earlier, classical liberals were advocates of a small state and self-reliance, believing that individuals should be encouraged to look after themselves. When looking at their approach to the core principles we can see that idea reflected throughout.

Individualism

While all liberals recognize individualism as of primary importance for liberal society, the two strands differ in their understanding of what individualism means. Classical liberals subscribe to egoistical individualism, which places emphasis on self-interestedness and self-reliance. Egoistical individualism means to care about oneself and the satisfaction of one's own desires rather than others; humans are rational beings, who are naturally drawn to serving their own interests.

It has led classical liberals to view society as simply a collection of self-interested individuals, all seeking to satisfy their own needs and interests. Such a view has been equated with atomism; indeed, it can lead to the belief that 'society' itself does not exist but is merely a collection of self-sufficient individuals. The individual is understood as a single self-enclosed being, where the limits of the body are the limits of the individual.

Freedom

While liberals agree about the value of liberty, they have not always agreed about what it means for an individual to be 'free'. In his 'Two Concepts of Liberty' (1958), Isaiah Berlin distinguished between a 'negative' theory of liberty and a 'positive' one.

Classical liberals believe in negative freedom, that freedom consists of humans being left alone, free from interference and able to act in whatever way they choose. This understanding of freedom is 'negative' as it is based on the absence of external constraints on the individual; it leaves the

Spec key term

Egoistical individualism: The idea that individualism is associated with self-interest and self-reliance.

Definition

Atomism: A belief that society is made up of a collection of self-interested and largely self-sufficient individuals, or atoms, rather than social groups.

Spec key term

Negative freedom: The absence of external restrictions or constraints on the individual, allowing freedom of choice.

All liberals believe in...

INDIVIDUALISM

- Making decisions in your own interest
- Self sovereignty
- Individuals know what's best
- 'Over their mind and body the individual is sovereign' - John Stuart Mill

Classical Liberals

Egoistical individualism
- Self-reliant
- Self-restraint
- Self-sufficiency
- Atomism

Modern Liberals

Developmental individualism
- Flourish
- Develop potential
- Self-determined
- Live worthwhile lives

FREEDOM

- Society should allow the maximum freedom for all

Negative freedom
- Left alone
- Free from interference
- Unrestricted

Positive freedom
- Be who you were meant to be
- Help to be free

STATE

'Is a necessary evil' – Paine

Keep order   Potential to restrict liberty

- Social Contact Theory

Minimal state
- Nightwatchman state in the background
- Harm principle

Enabling state
- Enables people to be free
- Equality of opportunity
- Beveridge's 'Five Giants'

ECONOMY

- Private property
- Capitalism

Free-market
- Laissez-faire
- Limited government intervention

Keynesian economy
- Government intervention
- Welfare

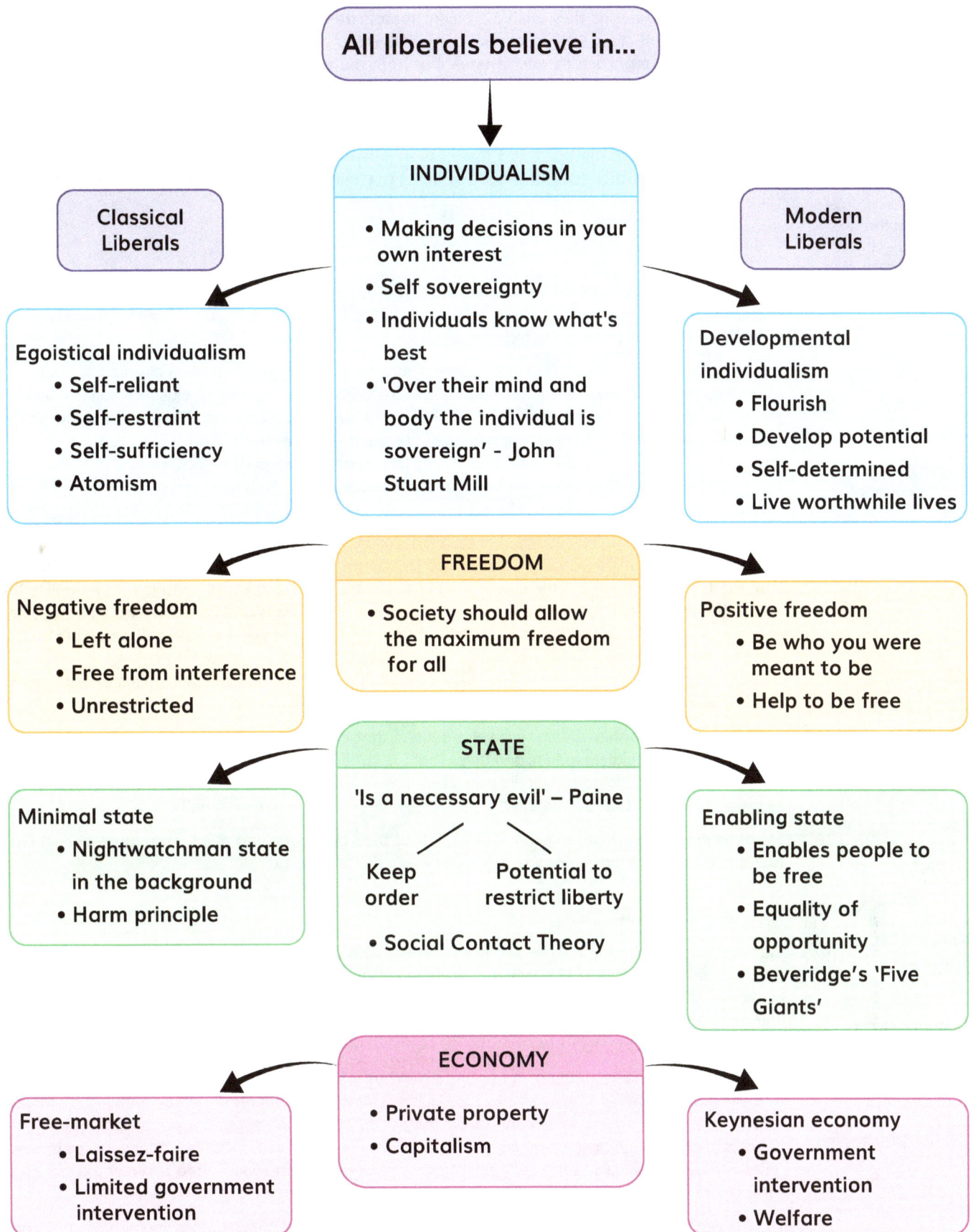

Figure 1.2 Agreement and tensions within Liberalism.

individual free to act as they wish. Classical liberals are very clear that individual liberty can be maximized only if clear limits are placed upon law and government. Poverty, disadvantage and disease may be regarded as misfortunes, but from the view of classical liberals, they cannot be said to limit freedom. Supporters of negative freedom portray it as a neutral concept; it simply allows individuals to go their own way, leaving the individual free to pursue their own view of a good life. **Mill** argued that a person should be left as free as possible to pursue their own interests as long as this does not harm the interests of others. Those who understand freedom in this negative sense are therefore inclined to support the 'minimal' state and sympathize with laissez-faire capitalism.

The state

The distinction between modern and classical liberals' views on individualism and freedom holds significant implications for their views on the role of the state. The key issue is how far the state can extend before it stops enhancing freedom and starts to infringe it.

The classical liberal view of the state focuses more on its potential for 'evil'. In classical liberalism's view, if liberty is unlimited it can become a 'licence' to abuse others. Hence classical liberals seek a minimal state which prevents harm to others but still allows liberty to flourish. They seek a state which guarantees order, defends borders and upholds contracts. This has been known as a 'nightwatchman' state. This phrase was coined to suggest a state that largely remains in the background as a warning to those who may wish to break the law that there would be consequences and punishments to such actions.

The rationale for this state can be found in classical liberalism's belief in egoistical individualism and its commitment to negative freedom. Taken together, these two concepts suggest that free and rational individuals need nothing but the smallest state to enable them to take advantage of their ability to rely on themselves and satisfy their own needs. In many ways, classical liberalism's view of the state can best be understood by looking to **Mill's** harm principle. In *On Liberty* (1859) **Mill** argued that *'the only purpose for which power can be rightfully exercised over any member of a civilized community, against his will, is to **prevent harm to others**'*. **Mill's** position accepts only the most minimal restrictions on individual freedom, and only then in order to prevent 'harm to others'.

Further, he distinguished clearly between actions that are 'self-regarding', over which individuals should exercise absolute freedom, and those that are 'other-regarding', which can restrict the freedom of others or do them damage. **Mill** did not accept any restrictions on the individual that were designed to prevent a person from damaging themselves, either physically or emotionally.

So, although the individual may be sovereign over their own body and mind, each must respect the fact that every other individual also enjoys an equal right to liberty.

The economy

Classical liberal thinking on the economy largely derives from the work of figures such as the philosopher Adam Smith (1723–90), and economist David Ricardo (1770–1823). Smith's *The Wealth of Nations* (1776) was in many respects the first economics textbook. His ideas drew heavily on liberal and rational assumptions about human nature and made a powerful contribution about the desirable role of government. Smith argued that the economy works best when it is left alone by government.

Smith thought of the economy as a market, indeed as a series of inter-related markets. He believed that the market operated according to the decisions of free individuals. Freedom within the market means freedom of choice: the ability of businesses to choose what goods to make, the ability of workers to choose an employer and the ability of consumers to choose what goods or services to buy. Relationships within such a market – between employers and employees, and between buyers and sellers – are thus voluntary and contractual, made by self-interested individuals.

The clear implication of this is that government is relieved of the need to regulate economic activity; it can be left to the market itself. Indeed, if government interferes in economic life, it runs the risk of upsetting the delicate balance of the market. In this view, so long as the economy operates as a free market, efficiency and prosperity are guaranteed by the tendency of the market to draw resources to their most profitable use. This is linked to the doctrine of laissez-faire which suggests that the state should

Spec key term

Minimal state: The idea that the role of the state must be restricted in order to preserve individual liberty.

Spec key term

Harm principle: The idea that individuals should be free to do anything except harm other individuals.

Definition

Self-regarding act: An act that affects only oneself.

Other-regarding act: An act that affects others.

Free market: The principle or policy of unfettered market competition, free from government interference.

Spec key term

Laissez-faire capitalism: Literally, 'leave to do'; the doctrine that economic activity should be free from government interference.

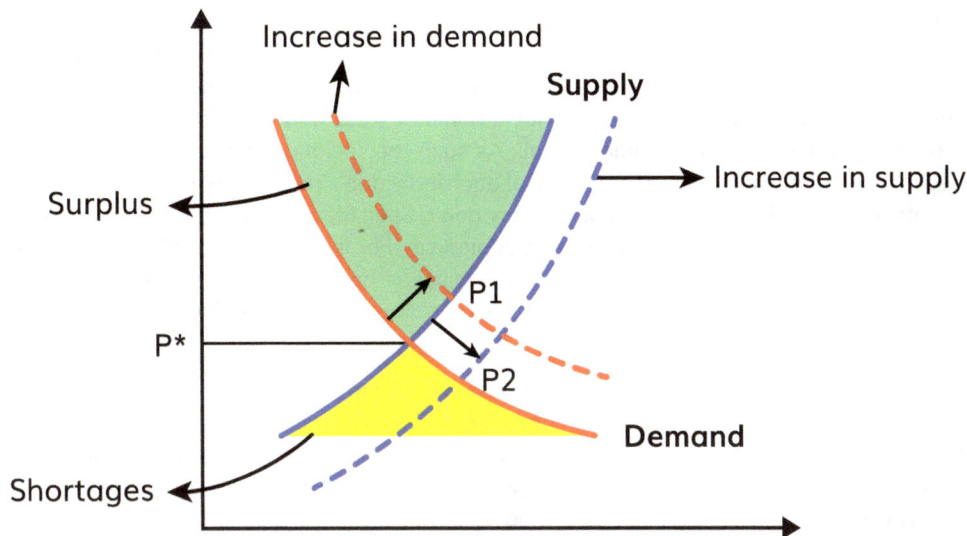

Figure 1.3 The 'invisible hand' of demand and supply shows how the free market allocates resources efficiently and determines their price.

leave the economy alone and allow entrepreneurs to act as they please. Such economic individualism is usually based on a belief that the unrestrained pursuit of profit will ultimately lead to general benefit.

The attraction of free-market economics to classical liberals was that the economy is thought to operate according to market forces that, they argue, tends to promote economic prosperity and well-being. For instance, no single producer can set the price of a commodity – prices are set by the market, by the number of goods offered for sale and the number of consumers who are willing to buy. These are the forces of supply and demand. The market is a self-regulating mechanism; it needs no guidance from outside. The market should be 'free' from government interference because it is managed by what Smith referred to as an 'invisible hand' as shown by Figure 1.3. This idea of a self-regulating market reflects the liberal belief in a naturally existing harmony among the conflicting interests within society. Smith (1776) expressed the economic version of this idea as '*It is not from the benevolence of the butcher, the brewer or the baker that we expect our dinner, but from their regard to their own interests.*' The 'invisible hand' of demand and supply indicates very clearly where the price of a product should be (p*). This is known as the equilibrium point. The more demand for a good, and prices will rise (p1), whereas an increase in supply will lead to prices falling (p2). As long as markets respond to changes in demand and supply, they will avoid surpluses or shortages.

Rationalism

While classical liberals understand human nature as being based in rationality, they also believe that individuals are self-seeking, self-reliant individuals who flourish most when left alone. They believe that humans need to be independent from the state and that individuals should be allowed to be in charge of their own destiny.

Classical liberalism would recognize an atomistic approach as the one in which humans thrive. This is the idea that society is simply a collection of self-interested individuals, each seeking to satisfy their own needs. The individual is understood as a self-sufficient being. They argue that humans are naturally drawn to serving their own interests and given that each individual is the best judge of their own interest, this role cannot be fulfilled by any other body. Furthermore, their view of human nature is based on the idea that the individual's skills and talents are theirs to own and control and that any goods that stem from them belong solely to them. The only good is individual good.

Equality of opportunity

While all liberals support foundational and formal equality, they have disagreed about how the principles of equality of opportunity should be applied in practice as they have very different interpretations of what they mean and how they are established.

For classical liberals, equality of opportunity is the right to rise or fall, grow rich or remain poor according to one's own actions. It is no surprise to see how easily this notion fits in with other ideas promoted by classical liberals, namely, egoistical individualism, negative freedom and a minimal, laissez-faire state. Classical liberals argue that a minimal state and laissez-faire economy provide all the conditions for equal opportunities for all. As such the social positions of individuals could be explained in terms of the talents and hard work of each individual. Those with ability and a willingness to work prosper, while the incompetent or the lazy don't. Such ideas of individual responsibility were widely employed by supporters of free-market capitalism. For instance, Richard Cobden advocated an improvement of the conditions of the working classes but argued that it should come about through '*their own efforts and self-reliance, rather than from law*'. He advised them to '*look not to Parliament, look only to yourselves*'.

Ideas of individual self-reliance reached their boldest expression in Herbert Spencer's *The Man versus the State* (1884). Spencer developed a vigorous defence of the doctrine of laissez-faire, drawing on the ideas of Charles Darwin. Spencer used the theory of natural selection to develop a social principle of 'the survival of the fittest', known as Social Darwinism. Individuals who are best suited to survive rise to the top, while the less fit fall to the bottom. Inequalities of wealth, social position and political power are therefore a consequence of one's own actions, and no attempt should be made by government to interfere with them. Spencer's US disciple, William Sumner (1840–1910), stated this principle boldly in 1884, when he asserted that '*the drunkard in the gutter is just where he ought to be*'.

Modern liberalism

Modern liberals have also interpreted the core principles in line with their values. Modern liberals came to the view that the ideas and values of classical liberals weren't providing the maximum freedom for all. As such, their interpretation tends to seek to support individuals in their quest for greater freedom.

Individualism

Spec key term

Developmental individualism: The idea that individual freedom is linked to human flourishing.

Modern liberals, in contrast to classical liberals, have advanced a form of developmental individualism that prioritizes humans development over merely satisfying their immediate needs. This is based on a more optimistic, but still rational, view of human nature. Modern liberals believe that individualism is moderated by a sense of social responsibility, especially a responsibility for those who are unable to look after themselves. Developmental individualism seeks to focus on individual potential. It is interested in the progress individuals can make and has been identified as leading to a fuller form of genuine citizenship that allows all citizens to live worthwhile lives.

One of the reasons why modern liberalism adopted a form of developmental individualism is that, in the face of the consequences of unrestrained capitalism, the classical liberal approach of atomism came to be regarded as morally naïve. For modern liberals like L.T. Hobhouse, J.A. Hobson and T.H. Green, mass poverty, unemployment and illness were social issues which could not be the concern of the single individual as they transcended individual capacities; the good of the individual was tied to the good of the whole. As Green said in Liberal Legislation and Freedom of Contract (1861) '*Our modern legislation ... with reference to labour, and education, and health ... is justified on the ground that it is the business of the state ... to maintain the conditions without which a free exercise of the human faculties is impossible.*'

Freedom

Spec key term

Positive freedom: The idea that freedom is about personal fulfilment, self-realization and the development of human capacities.

As time progressed and capitalist society developed, liberals began to have concerns about negative freedom. In the late nineteenth century, the work of the T.H. Green was highly influential. Green believed that the unrestrained pursuit of profit, as advocated by classical liberalism, had given rise to new forms of poverty and injustice. The economic liberty of the few had ruined the life chances of the many. The simple belief of positive freedom is that a person may appear free with many rights and liberties to their name, but if they are uneducated, live in poverty and are overworked for low wages, in what real sense are they free?

Green thus challenged the classical liberal notion of freedom. Negative freedom merely removes external constraints on the individual, giving the individual freedom of choice. In the case of businesses that wish to maximize profits, negative freedom justifies their ability to hire the cheapest labour possible, or to employ children rather than adults. Negative freedom can therefore lead to exploitation

Tensions within liberalism over society

AGREEMENT	DISAGREEMENT
✓ All liberals agree that society should be organized to promote individualism and freedom	✗ Modern and classical liberals disagree in their understanding of freedom and individualism in society
✓ All liberals agree that society should be organized to enhance the liberal notions of equality	✗ Liberals disagree over equality of opportunity in society
✓ All liberals recognize the role that democracy plays in a free society	✗ There have been disagreements over the benefits of democracy within liberalism

and undermining of other's freedom. **Rawls** echoed these views arguing that society needed to be organized along the principles of distributive justice.

Green therefore proposed that freedom should also be understood in positive terms. In this light, freedom is the ability of the individual to develop and achieve individuality; it involves humans being able to achieve their potential, gain skills and knowledge, and achieve fulfilment. Positive freedom recognizes that liberty may be threatened by social disadvantage and inequality. The state could not force people to be good; it could only provide the conditions in which they were able to make more responsible moral decisions. The central thrust of modern liberalism is therefore the desire to help individuals to help themselves. For Green, freedom was to be the best that one can be.

The state

The modern liberal defence of a larger, enabling state is based on a belief in promoting wider freedom in society. As with classical liberals, it is clear to see the modern liberal rationale for an enabling state when looking at their commitment to developmental individualism and belief in positive freedom. This view of freedom is associated with a more optimistic view of the state recognizing its role in enabling individuals to flourish and experience a free life.

As the twentieth century emerged, it was clear to many liberals that the original understanding of freedom (as promoted by classical liberals) had not led to a truly free society. Most people were unable to benefit from negative freedom and sought ways to enable more people to achieve the level of freedom enjoyed by the few. In the words of William Beveridge 'a starving man is not free'.

Tensions within liberalism over freedom

AGREEMENT	DISAGREEMENT
✓ Freedom is the defining political value for all liberals and of supreme importance for all liberals	✗ Liberals disagree over how to define freedom. Classical liberals define it in negative terms and modern liberals define it in positive terms
✓ All liberals recognize that freedom is linked to individualism; only when free can individuals make decisions for themselves	✗ Liberals disagree over how society can best be organized to accommodate the maximum freedom for all
✓ All liberals believe that freedom and individualism are based on a belief on human rationality	

Exam Tip – One area that is misunderstood is that modern liberals support negative freedom as well as positive freedom. Modern liberals would like to move towards a society where only negative freedom was necessary; however, they recognize that this is unlikely and so support it alongside positive freedom for those who need greater help to be free.

Spec key term

Enabling state: A larger state that helps individuals to achieve their potential and be free.

Modern liberals found themselves defending a larger role for the state on this basis. They would perhaps place more emphasis on the 'necessary' element of Paine's statement that the state is a 'necessary evil'. If the role of the state was to protect and enable freedom, then modern liberals felt justified in using the state to promote positive freedom.

For modern liberals, this took the form of governments providing welfare support for its citizens to overcome poverty, disease and ignorance. Hence modern liberals support welfare based on positive freedom and equality of opportunity. If some individuals are disadvantaged by their social circumstances, then the state possesses a social responsibility to reduce these disadvantages to create more equal life chances.

Rawls argued that social institutions at the heart of society – education, healthcare, welfare – were the key to distributive justice. **Rawls** believed that only a capitalist economy *with* strong social institutions could result in a fair and just society as capitalism on its own was not sufficient to ensure fairness.

In the UK, the expanded welfare state was based on the Beveridge Report (1942), which set out to attack the so-called 'five giants':

» Want (caused by poverty)

» Ignorance (caused by a lack of education)

» Squalor (caused by poor housing)

» Idleness (caused by the inability to gain employment)

» Disease (caused by inadequate health care provision)

It memorably promised to protect citizens 'from the cradle to the grave'.

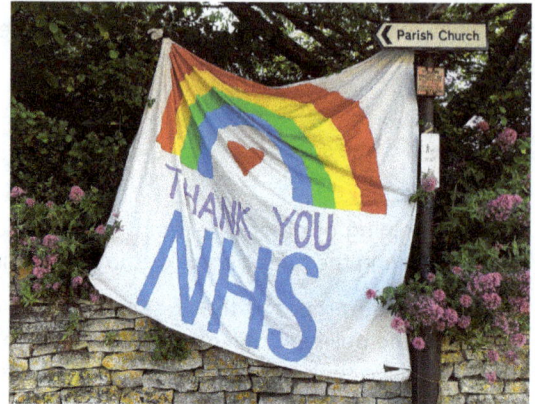

Photo 1.2 **The NHS is an important part of the British welfare state.**

Tensions within liberalism over the role of the state	
AGREEMENT	**DISAGREEMENT**
✓ All liberals agree that there must be a state in society	✗ Modern and classical liberals disagree over the extent of the role of the state
✓ All liberals agree that the state is a necessary evil	✗ Modern and classical liberals disagree on how the state protects individualism and freedom
✓ All liberals agree that the state is formed on the basis of social contract theory	✗ Modern and classical liberals disagree on the role of the state in the economy

The economy

Modern liberals reject the idea of a self-regulating market economy, arguing instead that the economy should be 'managed' by government. In this view, although it remains the ultimate source of economic dynamism, if left to its own devices, the market is flawed, tending towards inequality. This helps to explain the attraction of Keynesianism to many modern liberals.

Modern *liberals* found themselves, once again, rejecting classical liberal thinking, in particular its belief in a self-regulating free market. This movement away from laissez-faire came about because of the complexity of capitalist economies and their inability to guarantee general prosperity. The 1930s led to high levels of unemployment throughout the world which was the most dramatic demonstration of the failure of the free market. After the Second World War, virtually all Western states adopted policies of economic intervention to prevent a return to the pre-war levels of unemployment. To a large extent these interventionist policies were guided by the work of the UK economist John Maynard Keynes (1883–1946).

In *The General Theory of Employment, Interest and Money* (1936), Keynes challenged classical economic thinking and rejected its belief in a self-regulating market. Keynes argued that economic growth and employment levels are largely determined by the level of demand in the economy, and that government can encourage demand through economic and tax policy, to deliver full employment.

Keynes suggested that governments could 'manage' their economies by government spending which stimulates the economy, supporting job creation. Taxation, on the other hand, takes money out of the economy: it reduces demand and decreases economic activity. At times of high unemployment,

Keynes recommended that governments should 'stimulate' their economies by either increasing public spending or cutting taxes. Unemployment could therefore be solved, not by the 'invisible hand' of capitalism, but by government intervention.

Keynesian economic theory thus promised to give governments the ability to influence employment and to secure economic growth. As well as this, it also reinforced the modern liberal's ideas of developmental individualism and positive freedom, where individuals are supported to achieve their potential. As with the provision of welfare, modern liberals have seen economic management as being constructive in promoting prosperity and harmony in society.

Tensions within liberalism over the economy

AGREEMENT	DISAGREEMENT
✓ All liberals support private property	✗ Liberals disagree over the involvement of the state in the capitalist economy
✓ All liberals recognize the importance of market capitalism	✗ Liberals disagree over the role of welfare in the economy and how it enhances individual freedom
✓ All liberals support the idea that the economy should enhance individual freedom	

Rationalism

T.H. Green rejected the early liberal idea of humans as self-seeking utility maximizers and suggested a more optimistic view of human nature. While still agreeing that rationalism is the basis of human nature, this did not exclude an ability to care about the interests of others and how this effects the wider environment in which they all live. '*The idea of the end or unconditional good is that of the self as realised. And this self is social, i.e., its good includes that of others, who are also conceived as ends in themselves*' (*The Prolegomena to Ethics*, 1884). Individuals may care about what is happening to their neighbours in the hope that their neighbours might, in turn, care about what is happening to them. Rational individuals will intervene if they see a person in trouble, anticipating that the favour be returned. This leads to a society based on rationality but tempered with a sense of altruism. The individual possesses an interest in the wider society they inhabit and not merely their individual responsibilities. They are hence linked to other individuals through the society in which they all live. The good of the individual is tied to the good of the whole community.

Definition

Altruism: Concern for the interests and welfare of others, based on enlightened self-interest.

Tensions within liberalism over human nature

AGREEMENT	DISAGREEMENT
✓ All liberals believe humans are rational creatures and reject the view that humans are limited	✗ Liberals disagree on the nature of rationalism based on their view of individualism
✓ All liberals believe that humans are capable of deciding what's in their own best interests	✗ Liberals disagree on how humans are best able to flourish in society
✓ All liberals view humans as being of equal moral worth with foundational equality, not superior/inferior based on birth right	✗ Liberals disagree on how equality of opportunity enhances human nature

Equality of opportunity

As one may have come to expect, modern liberals found it difficult to reconcile themselves to the classical liberal understanding of equality of opportunity. It was patently obvious to them that their basic premise – that society was already providing equal opportunity for all – was fundamentally flawed. Individuals were born into profoundly differing circumstances, and many were not born with any of the advantages or abilities to 'help themselves'. Those born into poverty and lacking the means to educate themselves or even keep themselves from dying were clearly unable to rise in society. It was the aim of modern liberals therefore, to improve the life chances or equality of opportunity for all – to create a fair society. They recognized that only a minority were able to rise and fall in society according to their merit and that this opportunity needed to be extended to many more. Modern liberals wanted to break the clearly implied link within classical liberalism between poverty and laziness. For modern liberals, they argued that a just, meritocratic society could only exist when all were given equal chances to rise and fall.

Rawls, a modern liberal, wrote extensively on the principle of justice within liberalism. He focused on the notion of distributive justice, that is, how a fair society can be developed by the way resources are allocated. He argued that a just society can be established according to what he calls the '*difference principle*'. Here he asks us to place ourselves in '*the original position*' where we have no knowledge of our own status in society, rich or poor, educated or ignorant, healthy or sick. From this '*veil of ignorance*' we are asked to consider how society should be run. Will there be huge discrepancies between rich and poor, how will money be distributed, should taxes be high or low and what government support should there be? When faced with these choices, what decisions would self-interested people make without knowing how it would affect them? The answer, according to **Rawls**, seems to be a society where the least advantaged person would not be worse off than anyone would wish to be if it were them. Hence a broad consensus tends to appear, based around a society where there is inequality, in order to incentivize individuals to work and achieve, but not as stark as modern industrialized society. **Rawls** argued that people whose work benefited society could earn more, e.g. doctors and teachers, as society would suffer if there was no incentive to do these jobs. For **Rawls**, these ideas are entirely consistent with liberal notions of individualism, freedom and justice as they seek to create a genuinely meritocratic society.

Tensions within liberalism over equality	
AGREEMENT	**DISAGREEMENT**
✓ All liberals support foundational equality	✗ Liberals disagree over the extent of equality of opportunity in society
✓ All liberals support formal equality	✗ Liberals disagree over how society can best be organized to accommodate the maximum freedom for all
✓ All liberals support the idea of equality of opportunity in society	

Table 1.1 Tensions within liberalism over the core principles

	Classical liberalism	Modern liberalism
Individualism	• Egoistical individualism	• Developmental individualism
Freedom	• Negative freedom	• Positive freedom
State	• Fears the state acting in society • Welfare leads to dependency • Free market • More evil than necessary	• Accepts the state being active in society • Accepts welfare • Willing to accept a mixed economy • More necessary than evil
Rationalism	• Egoistical rationalism	• Altruistic rationalism
Equality	• Believe individuals are born into a society with equality of opportunity	• Believe the state should play are role in creating equality of opportunity
Liberal democracy	• Suspicious of growing democracy*	• Values the protective benefits of democracy*

*Note this does not denote the difference between classical and modern liberals, but between earlier and later liberals.

3. Liberalism key thinkers

Key thinkers are an important part of understanding each ideology. The exam board has specified five key thinkers per ideology and TWO must be included in an answer to avoid a cap (please check the Exam Focus chapter (Chapter 9) for lots more discussion of key thinkers). Although key thinkers (and other thinkers) have been discussed throughout the chapter, here we look at each one in detail.

John Locke (1632–1704)

Portrait of Locke.

Mikroman6/Getty

Locke was an early English liberal philosopher whose views developed against the backdrop of the English Revolution and are often seen as providing justification for the 'Glorious Revolution' of 1688, which ended absolutist rule in Britain, establishing a constitutional monarchy.

Rights

Locke placed particular emphasis on the idea of natural rights. This is a way of expressing the idea that there are certain moral rights that apply to all people. Today we would call these human rights. Locke defined these as the right to life, liberty and property. This means that while all have a right to these, others have a duty not to deprive people of their lives, liberty and possessions. He argued that one of the principal justifications for government was the protection of these rights and believed that the purpose of law was to preserve and enlarge freedom, 'where there is no law, there is no freedom'. Hence the law exists to restrain but also support freedom.

Locke's attitudes towards property rights are generally thought to be among his most important contributions in political thought. He believed that God gave the earth to all, but that the labour of our body and the work of our hands can convert property from common to private ownership. So, when one picks acorns or berries, they belong to the person who picked them up.

Social contract

Locke was a social contract theorist, he argued that society without a state, known as a 'state of nature' could be one of 'peace, goodwill, mutual assistance and preservation'. However, he also recognized that it had its weaknesses, especially if natural laws were violated.

Hence, Locke suggested that people would agree to transfer these rights to a government which makes the justice system the legitimate function of government. For Locke, legitimate government is established by the consent of the governed.

Limited and legitimate governments

Locke argued that no one can become subject to any law, except by their consent, arguing that government needed to be limited to protecting property, keeping the peace and protecting citizens from foreign attack to ensure people's freedom. An illegitimate government fails to protect the rights of its subjects, and in the worst cases, will violate the rights of its subjects. Locke is very clear that illegitimate government should be overthrown by the people: 'Revolt is the right of the people'.

Toleration

In Locke's Letter Concerning Toleration, he argued that government should not use force to try to convince people that a certain view is true, and this applied to all other groups in society too. True faith cannot be forced, and one has no more reason to think that they are right than anyone else. Hence for Locke, 'The care, therefore, of every man's soul belongs unto himself, and is to be left unto himself', i.e the government has no business interfering in people's views.

Mary Wollstonecraft (1759–97)

Hulton Archive/Stringer/Getty

Mary Wollstonecraft was a pioneer feminist thinker. Her A Vindication of the Rights of Woman (1792) stressed the equal rights of women, especially in education, based on the notion of 'personhood'.

Reason

Wollstonecraft's work drew on a belief in reason but developed a more complex analysis of women as the objects and subjects of desire. Throughout her work, Wollstonecraft maintained the view that women were deserving of the same fundamental rights, opportunities and education as men.

One of Wollstonecraft's main objectives was that women should be viewed as human first and foremost rather than as a separate and different species to men. She boldly declared '*I shall first consider women in the grand light of human creatures, who, in common with men, are placed on this earth to unfold their faculties*.' She argued that both men and women should be treated equally, based on the view that men and women are rational human beings.

Independence

The idea that reason must rule is a running theme of Wollstonecraft's works as is her insistence that girls and young women be made to acquire 'inner resources' so as to make them as psychologically independent as possible. '*I wish to show that elegance is inferior to virtue, that the first object of laudable ambition is to obtain a character as a human being, regardless of the distinction of sex.*'

She wanted to enable women to become rational and independent beings whose sense of worth came not from their appearance but from their inner perception of self-command and knowledge. Women were ill-prepared for their duties as social beings and imprisoned in a web of false expectations that would inevitably make them miserable. '*Taught from infancy that beauty is woman's sceptre, the mind shapes itself to the body, and roaming round its gilt cage, only seeks to adorn its prison.*'

Education

Wollstonecraft's most fundamental ideas were that women were seen as secondary in nature to men in society. They are '*rendered weak and wretched*' and this was predominantly the result of the discriminating system of education. Women are treated as subordinate beings, that are '*so much degraded*' that they are not even seen as human beings and are wholly unaware of their inferior conditions. '*I do not wish them [women] to have power over men; but over themselves.*'

Their total disadvantage and narrowness of mind was entirely down to society's false systems of education. As women were unable to gain a fair education, they were incapable of defending their basic rights and were doomed to a life of misery and dissatisfaction. She sought to transform this through increased access to education and basic female citizenship.

John Stuart Mill (1806–73)

traveler1116/Getty

A British philosopher, Mill's work straddles the divide between classical and modern forms of liberalism. Mill's major writings include *On Liberty* (1859), *Utilitarianism* (1861) and *Considerations on Representative Government* (1861).

Harm principle

Mill believed that individuals must be free to pursue their own notion of a good life. He defended the role of government according to the harm principle, and was very clear that restricting individuals for their own good was not sufficient reason, even if it is believed that the individual would be happier. '*These are good reasons for remonstrating with him, or reasoning with him, or persuading him, or entreating him, but not for compelling him or visiting him with any evil in case he do otherwise.*' For Mill, the harm principle is the sole legitimate basis for restricting individual liberties.

For Mill there were different threats to liberty. The old threat was from monarchy or aristocracy, but these were not the only ones, democracies contained their own threats to liberty. In *Considerations on Representative Government* Mill argued that a form of representative democracy is the best form of government for societies with sufficient resources, security, and culture of self-reliance. '*It is important that every one of the governed should have a voice in the government*' because it best satisfies two key criteria: 1) government promotes the common good, i.e. promoting the moral, intellectual, and active traits of its citizens; and 2) that government is good when it makes effective use of institutions and the resources of its citizens to promote the common good. However, he expressed concern over the notion of universal suffrage arguing that those with more knowledge should have more votes than those who were ignorant and uneducated. Mill's support for extra votes for the educated sounds deeply illiberal to modern ears.

Individuality

Mill believed that individuality was the foundation of a healthy society and was concerned about what de Tocqueville called the 'tyranny of the majority'. This referred to social tyranny, which he feared could lead to unthinking conformity and political tyranny which could limit the individual freedom. The unthinking following of customs should be discouraged in society as the key to a vibrant civil society was tolerance and pluralism. '*The despotism of custom is everywhere the standing hindrance to human advancement.*' Mill argued that without freedom of thought and expression, progress, knowledge and innovation would be restricted. Individuals needed to challenge their ideas against other rival ideas in order to assess their validity.

Mill distinguished between higher and lower pleasures. Lower pleasures were physical ones that all mammals enjoyed or needed such as food, drink, exercise, sexual relations and shelter. Higher pleasures were limited to humans who had intellectual, cultural, philosophical and spiritual capabilities, like art, music and poetry, socializing with and entertaining others. For Mill, 'higher' pleasures were far superior to 'lower' ones as once humans connected with their higher pleasures, they would never be happy to be without them. Individuals who employ higher faculties are often less content, because they have a deeper sense of the limitations of the world. Mill writes, '*It is better to be a human being dissatisfied than a pig satisfied; Socrates dissatisfied than a fool satisfied. And if the fool, or the pig, are of a different opinion, it is because they only know their side of the question.*'

John Rawls (1921–2002)

Frederic REGLAIN/Getty

A US political philosopher, John Rawls used a form of social contract theory to reconcile liberal individualism with the principles of redistribution and social justice. In his major work, *A Theory of Justice* (1970), he developed the notion of 'justice as fairness'.

Justice as fairness

'Justice as fairness' is Rawls's theory of justice for a liberal society; it recommends equal basic rights, equality of opportunity and promoting the interests of the least advantaged members of society. Justice meant society should be accessible to all. A society with fundamental inequality of opportunity at its heart could not be a just one. Rawls identified two guiding principles:

1. Each person is to have an equal right to the most extensive liberty compatible with a similar liberty for all.
2. Social and economic equalities are to be organized so they are both:
   a. to the greatest benefit of the least advantaged
   b. allow all positions and offices to be open to all under conditions of equality of opportunity.

The first principle has a clear commitment to liberty. The second principle is aiming towards what is known as distributive justice, i.e. that inequalities of wealth to incentivize people are acceptable as long as they raise the prosperity of the least well-off. However, Rawls was very clear that the first principle takes priority over the second; liberty for all is more important than the prosperity of society, i.e. if reducing liberty would result in greater economic growth and prosperity, the economic advantages are not worth the loss of liberty.

For Rawls, the way to do this was via the social institutions at the heart of society: education, healthcare, welfare. Rawls believed that a capitalist economy with strong social institutions would result in a fair and just society. Capitalism on its own was not sufficient to ensure fairness.

The original position, veil of ignorance and the difference principle

Rawls suggested a way of agreeing how society should organize itself where citizens are free and equal, and society fair. The 'original position' is Rawls' hypothetical scenario where people are set the task of reaching an agreement about how to create a just society. These decisions are made behind a 'veil of ignorance' where knowledge of one's gender, race, age, intelligence, wealth, skills, education and religion are unknown. Rawls argued that this was the best way to ensure no one considered their own vested interests.

He suggested that all rational individuals in these circumstances would advocate an unequal society, but one where the differences between individuals was not too great. This position is expressed in the 'difference principle', according to which, in a system of ignorance about one's status, one would strive to improve the position of the worst off, because he might find himself in that position.

Betty Friedan (1921–2006)

UPI/Bettman/Getty

Betty Friedan is seen as the founder of the women's liberation movement. It may seem surprising to see Betty Friedan as a key thinker in liberalism, but as a liberal feminist she has much to add to the debate about equality of opportunity as well as reforming society through legal, gradual means.

Liberal feminists like Friedan believe that women are insufficiently free in society. They argue that decisions are made for women that don't truly reflect their capabilities and their needs. This results in women being unable to develop and flourish in society. Liberal feminists understand freedom to mean personal autonomy, in other words, to be able to live the life of one's own choosing as well as political autonomy, which means being able to directly influence the conditions under which one lives.

Problem with no name

Friedan fell upon her most famous discovery while asking alumni during a college reunion to complete a survey on their experiences of the workplace since graduating. Their responses were so similar that Friedan realised she was on to something. This was described as the "problem with no name", outlined by Friedan in the beginning of *The Feminine Mystique* (1963): '*The problem lay buried, unspoken, for many years … a sense of dissatisfaction, a yearning that women suffered … Each suburban [house]wife struggled with it alone. As she made the beds, shopped for groceries … she was afraid to ask even of herself the silent question — "Is this all?"'*

This is linked to the notion of positive freedom, developmental individualism and equality of opportunity. Women were unable to thrive, grow or develop in society as their choices had been predetermined. Society had already decided that a life of domesticity (looking after a home, a husband and children) made women happy. It was so pervasive in society that women who felt stifled and unfulfilled wondered what was wrong with them. Why were they unhappy? They felt guilty for not feeling more fulfilled.

Friedan argued that women were as capable as men of any type of work or any career path, which, at the time, ran contrary to the wide perceptions in the media and wider society. Friedan revealed a pervasive paternalistic culture which sought to keep women in a lower position in society with the argument that this was their 'natural' role, where men knew what was best for women rather than the equal moral worth agenda espoused by so many liberals at the time. This was the same paternalism that liberalism had been seeking to eradicate in society. Friedan was simply asking that women were treated like humans too, as J.S. Mill had begun to do a century before. She was seeking to challenge attitudes that limited the freedom and individualism of half the population of the world.

4. How to apply knowledge to liberalism answers

In this section of the chapter, we are going to be looking at how to apply the knowledge learnt so far to areas of agreement and disagreement within liberalism. These areas will help you to understand how to answer 24-mark essays on liberalism. But please use this section in conjunction with the Exam Focus chapter (Chapter 9), which explores the different ways to approach answering 24-mark questions. These worked examples below identify possible ways to address questions. It is important to note that there are many approaches that can be taken and that the Exam board does not prescribe any fixed way of structuring answers. It is essential however, to hit all Assessment Objectives, which is what these suggestions are based on.

Tensions within Liberalism over the state

Worked example

Paragraph One – Agreement within liberalism

- ✓ All liberals agree that there must be a state in society
- ✓ All liberals agree that the state is a necessary evil
- ✓ All liberals agree that the state is formed on the basis of social contract theory **(Locke)**

Paragraph Two – Disagreement within liberalism

- ✗ Modern and classical liberals disagree over the extent of the role of the state
- ✗ Classical liberals believe in a minimal state and modern liberals believe in an enabling state
- ✗ These differences are due to their respective views on individualism and freedom, with classical liberals believing in egoistical individualism and negative freedom and modern liberals believing in developmental individualism and positive freedom

Paragraph Three – Disagreement within liberalism

- ✗ Modern and classical liberals disagree on the role of the state in the economy
- ✗ Classical liberals believe in a free market, laissez-faire economy with a minimal role for the state and modern liberals support a Keynesian approach, which means a larger role for the state in the economy
- ✗ They also disagree on the benefits of using the state for welfare. Classical liberals argue that welfare is a disincentive for self-reliance and self-improvement, whereas modern liberals believe that using the state for welfare is at the heart of a modern liberal approach towards a free society **(Rawls)**

Tensions within liberalism over society

Worked example

Thematic approach

Paragraph One – Theme – Role of individualism and freedom in society

- ✓ All liberals agree that freedom and individualism are of fundamental importance in society **(Mill)**
- ✗ However, there are fundamental differences between classical and modern liberalism over the role of individualism in society as classical liberals believe in egoistical individualism and modern liberals believe in developmental individualism

Continued...

× Also, there are fundamental differences between classical and modern liberalism over what freedom in society looks like as classical liberals believe in negative freedom and modern liberals believe in positive freedom

Paragraph Two – Theme – Role of state in society

✓ All liberals agree that it is essential to have a state in order to allow society to flourish, and that this state is founded on the basis of social contract theory

× However, modern and classical liberals disagree over the extent of the role of the state; classical liberals believe in a minimal state and modern liberals believing in an enabling state (**Rawls**). This has a significance impact of the type of society that emerges.

× Moreover, classical liberals believe the state should only 'prevent harm to others', whereas modern liberals believe its role should be extended beyond this

Paragraph Three – Theme – Role of equality in society

✓ All liberals agree that foundational equality is the most importance basis of society (**Wollstonecraft**)

✓ All liberals also agree that formal equality is enshrined in law as part of a liberal society

× However, modern and classical liberals disagree fundamentally in their understanding and recognition of equality of opportunity in society. Classical liberals argue that society already benefits widely from equality of opportunity and individuals need to look to themselves to rise. Modern liberals reject this, arguing that society needs support from the state to ensure a meritocratic society where each is able to rise according to merit (**Friedan**)

Tensions within liberalism over human nature

Worked example

Paragraph One – Agreement within liberalism

✓ All liberals believe humans are rational creatures

✓ All liberals believe that humans are capable of deciding what's in their own best interests

✓ All liberals view humans as being of equal moral worth, not superior/inferior based on birth right or gender (**Wollstonecraft**)

Paragraph Two – Disagreement within liberalism

× Modern and classical liberals disagree on the nature of rationalism based on their view of individualism

× Classical liberals' view of human nature is based on egoistical individualism, where individuals are self-reliant and self-seeking (a more selfish form of rationalism)

× Modern liberals' view of human nature is based on developmental individualism. While still agreeing that rationalism is the basis of human nature, this commitment to rationalism does not exclude an ability to care about the interests of others and how this effects the wider environment in which they all live

Paragraph Three – Disagreement within liberalism

× Modern and classical liberals disagree on how humans are best able to flourish in society

× Classical liberals believe that in order for humans to flourish, they should be left alone and be free from restrictions. This is the concept of negative freedom. Self-seeking, self-reliant individuals flourish most when left alone

× Modern liberals believe that in order to flourish, individuals need help to be free and become the people they were meant to be. This is associated with modern liberals' idea of positive freedom. They possess an interest in the wider society they inhabit and not merely their individual responsibilities (**Rawls**)

Tensions within liberalism over the economy

Worked example

Paragraph One – Agreement within liberalism

- ✓ All liberals support private property **(Locke)**
- ✓ All liberals recognize the importance of market capitalism
- ✓ All liberals support the idea that the economy should enhance individual freedom

Paragraph Two – Disagreement within liberalism

- ✗ Modern and classical liberals disagree over the extent of the role of the state in the economy
- ✗ Classical liberals believe in free-market laissez-faire capitalism, whereas modern liberals support a Keynesian approach to the economy
- ✗ These differences are due to their respective views on the role of the state with classical liberals believing in a minimal state and modern liberalism believing in an enabling state

Paragraph Three – Disagreement within liberalism

- ✗ Modern and classical liberals disagree on the role of welfare in the economy
- ✗ Classical liberals are clear that welfare is a disincentive for self-reliance and self-improvement, whereas modern liberals believe that using the state for welfare is at the heart of a modern liberal approach towards a free society
- ✗ These differing approaches to welfare reflect their different interpretations of freedom and individualism **(Rawls)**

Chapter Summary

- Liberalism is an ideology with the overriding concern of freedom and individualism.
- The two main strands are classical and modern liberalism.
- There is clear disagreement between these two strands on almost all of liberalisms' core principles.
- In the main, this is due to their differing interpretations of what it means to be free.

Exam Style Questions

1. To what extent do liberals agree over the state?
2. To what extent do liberals agree over society?
3. To what extent do modern and classical liberals disagree over the economy?
4. To what extent is there agreement within liberals over human nature?
5. To what extent are the views of modern liberalism consistent with the views of classical liberalism?
6. To what extent are different liberals committed to freedom?
7. To what extent do liberals support democracy?

Further Resources

Bellamy, R. *Liberalism and Modern Society: An Historical Argument* (1992). An analysis of the development of liberalism that focuses on the adaptations necessary to apply liberal values to new social realities.

Fawcett, E. *Liberalism: The Life of an Idea* (2015). A fluent and stimulating history of liberal thinking from the early nineteenth century to the present day.

Gray, J. *Liberalism*, 2nd edn (1995). A short and not uncritical introduction to liberalism as the political theory of modernity; contains a discussion of post-liberalism.

Kelly, P. *Liberalism* (2005). An engagingly written defence of liberalism as a political theory, which examines its link to equality.

Kelly, P. et al. *The Politics Book* (2013). A clearly written, concise book which covers many of the thinkers discussed in this chapter.

Vincent, R. *Modern Political Ideologies* (1995). Chapter 2, 'Liberalism' can be used to stretch and extend a student's knowledge of the content covered in this chapter.

Visit our companion website at https://bloomsbury.pub/essentials-of-political-ideas-2e for more worked examples.

2 CONSERVATISM

Historical overview

Although conservative ideas had been in existence since feudal times, they didn't form a coherent set of ideas until later. One of the earliest statements of conservative principles is contained in **Edmund Burke's** *Reflections on the Revolution in France* (1790), which deeply regretted the revolutionary challenge to the *ancien régime* (the French ruling system before the Revolution in 1789). It also outlined the key conservative value that change should occur slowly and naturally, and advocated a prudent willingness to 'change in order to conserve', rather than blind resistance. The Burkean approach dominated conservative thought until the nineteenth century, when the industrial revolution and the full force of free-market capitalism were felt, and conservative values were challenged by liberalism, socialism and nationalism.

By the end of the nineteenth century, conservative thought adapted to the changing industrialized world. Benjamin Disraeli (1804–81), conservative Prime Minister, accepted the Burkean notion of 'change in order to conserve' and understood that the biggest challenge to the status quo was a hugely divided society of 'rich and poor'. His aim was to create one nation and conservatism was able to reinvent itself and maintain its relevance. This One Nation approach was reinforced a century later by conservatives such as Prime Minister Harold Macmillan (1894–1986).

Modern conservatism underwent major changes in the 1970s, shaped by growing concerns about economic intervention and the welfare state. The Thatcher government in the UK (1979–90) practised a radical and ideological brand of conservatism known as the New Right. The New Right drew heavily on free-market economics and, in so doing, exposed deep divisions within conservatism, but they nevertheless remain part of conservative ideology as they have supported conservative social principles such as a belief in order, authority and discipline, known as neoconservatism.

Key Questions

» How did conservatism originate?
» What are the main principles that are central to conservatism?
» What are the key strands of conservatism?
» What are the areas of similarity and difference within conservatism?

Specification Checklist

1. Conservatism: core ideas and principles:

» Pragmatism
» Tradition
» Human imperfection
» Organicism
» Paternalism
» Libertarianism

2. Differing views and tensions within conservatism:

» Traditional conservatism
» One Nation conservatism
» New Right conservatism

3. Conservative key thinkers and their ideas:

» Thomas Hobbes (1588–1679)
» Edmund Burke (1729–97)
» Michael Oakeshott (1901–90)
» Ayn Rand (1905–82)
» Robert Nozick (1938–2002)

Andrea Pucci/Getty

Introduction to conservatism and its strands

As a political ideology, conservatism has been defined by the desire to conserve, reflected in a suspicion of change. However, while the desire to resist change is significant within conservatism, it is its commitment to pragmatism that sets it apart from other ideologies. Earlier conservatives sought to uphold the organic structure of society, value tradition and believe in human imperfection. Their overall thinking is guided by what works best in current circumstances. Conservatism nevertheless encompasses a range of tendencies. The chief distinction within conservatism is between Traditional and One Nation strands of conservatism and the more modern New Right.

Traditional conservatism

Traditional conservatives seek to defend established institutions and values on the ground that they safeguard the fragile 'fabric of society', giving security-seeking humans a sense of stability. They argue that society develops naturally to support the humans who exist within it and is more valuable than any single individual. They value the importance of tradition and hierarchy and believe that humans are imperfect, meaning they need to be supported and guided by those who know better.

One Nation conservatism

One Nation conservatism takes its name from the writings of Benjamin Disraeli. In the light of dramatic industrialization in the eighteenth and nineteenth centuries, Disraeli recognized that although laissez-faire capitalism brought huge riches to some, it also resulted in great poverty for others. Disraeli set about making gradual changes to the social and economic positions of the working class in order to improve their lives, in the interest of preserving society, and the ruling elite's position within it. His desire to unite the 'two nations' of the rich and the poor was given the label One Nation conservatism.

The New Right

The New Right emerged as a wholly unique strand of conservatism in the 1970s. It is characterized by belief in a strong but small state, combining both economic freedom (an updated version of classical liberalism) with social authoritarianism, as represented by the terms neoliberalism and neoconservatism, and is associated with the Thatcher government of the 1980s. The key to understanding the New Right is not just in understanding what it believes, but also 'how' it believes. It is highly ideological, and radical, rejecting the pragmatic, consensus-seeking of centuries of conservatism. This form of conservatism represented a dramatic shift from the past.

1. Conservatism: core ideas and principles

Pragmatism

This can be included in a discussion of the conservative view of society, the economy and the state.

Pragmatism is one of the most important principles to understand the values and outlook of conservatism. Pragmatism suggests a flexible approach to dealing with issues thrown up by society. Conservatives are sometimes misunderstood as people who reject change. However, it is better to understand conservatives as those who don't advocate change but nonetheless recognize that there are times when change is necessary. This is because the fundamental focus for conservatives is to preserve and protect the stability of society and social order. This can be best understood as 'change in order to conserve'.

One of the earliest, and perhaps the classic, statement of conservative principles is contained in **Edmund Burke's (1729–97)** *Reflections on the Revolution in France* (1790). In *Reflections*, **Burke** emphasized the dangers of mob rule, fearing that the Revolution destroyed French society. He appealed instead to the British virtues of continuity, tradition, hierarchy and property. The lesson **Burke** drew from the French Revolution was that change can be natural and inevitable, in which case it should not be resisted. '*A state without the means of some change*', he suggested, '*is without the means of its own conservation*.' The characteristic style of Burkean conservatism is cautious, modest and pragmatic; it reflects a suspicion of fixed principles.

Pragmatism

Summary box

- Rejects theory and ideology in favour of experience – empiricism.
- Doesn't tie down conservative thinking to a rigid set of beliefs.
- Humans lack the intellectual ability and powers of reasoning to fully comprehend the complex realities of the world.

Tradition

This can be included in a discussion of the conservative view of society, the state, society and human nature.

In its broadest sense, tradition encompasses anything that is passed down from the past to the present. Anything from long-standing customs, institutions or sets of beliefs can therefore be regarded as a tradition. This can include traditional institutions like the monarchy as well as traditional values such as marriage, family, religion and morality. For some conservatives, the emphasis on tradition reflects their religious faith. If the world is thought to have been created by God the Creator, traditional customs and practices in society will be regarded as 'God-given'. **Burke** thus believed that society was shaped by '*the law of our Creator*'. If humans tamper with the world, they are challenging the will of God, and as a result they are likely to make human affairs worse rather than better.

Source: MB Media/Contributor/Getty

Photo 2.1 Crowds showing their support and respect for the monarchy at the coronation of King Charles III and Queen Camilla in 2023.

Most conservatives, however, support tradition without needing to argue that it has divine origins. **Burke**, for example, described society as a '*partnership not only between those who are living, but between those who are living, those who are dead and those who are to be born*'. Tradition reflects the accumulated wisdom of the past. The institutions and practices of the past have been 'tested by time' and should be preserved for the generations to come. To stand the test of time means that generations have found the practices or institutions to be relevant; they have survived through different time periods and circumstances and maintained their usefulness. Such a notion reflects an almost Darwinian belief that they have demonstrated their fitness to survive. Tradition also incorporates into it the idea that any changes to society should be cautious, slow and organic in nature. Conservatives in the UK, for instance, argue that the institution of monarchy should be preserved because it embodies historical wisdom and experience. In particular, the monarchy has provided the UK with a focus of national loyalty and respect 'above' party politics.

Tradition

Summary box

- Ideas, practices, customs and ways of life which have survived because they are considered to be beneficial.
- Tradition provides stability and continuity, because humans are drawn to what is familiar. They feel reassured.
- Accumulated wisdom of the past, ideas and institutions that have 'stood the test of time'.
- Tradition also creates social cohesion by connecting people to the past, providing them with a collective identity.

Human imperfection

This can be included in a discussion of the conservative view of human nature.

Spec key term

Human imperfection: The belief that humans are flawed in a number of ways which makes them incapable of making good decisions for themselves.

In many ways, conservatism is a 'philosophy of human imperfection' (O'Sullivan, *Conservatism*, 1976). Other ideologies assume that humans are naturally 'good', or that they can be made 'good' if their social circumstances are improved. In their most extreme form, they envisage the perfectibility of humankind in an ideal society. Conservatives dismiss these ideas as, at best, idealistic, and argue instead that humans are both imperfect and imperfectible.

Human imperfection is understood in several ways:

» In the first place, humans are thought to be *psychologically* limited and dependent creatures. In the view of conservatives, people fear isolation and instability. They are drawn to the safe and the familiar, and, above all, seek the security of knowing 'their place'. Such a portrait of human nature is very different from the liberal idea of self-reliant, enterprising individuals.

» Humans' *intellectual* powers are also thought to be limited. Conservatives have traditionally believed that the world is simply too complicated for humans to fully grasp, as **Michael Oakeshott (1901–90)** (see page 57) put it, '*in political activity men sail a boundless and bottomless sea*'. He was suggesting that the world was too complex to fully understand and that this was compounded by human imperfection, as people do not have the ability to make sense of the complex, modern world. He argued that other ideologies tend to simplify problems and promote solutions using 'rational' ideas which he suggested leads to distortion and simplification.

Definition

Original sin: The sin of Adam and Eve, who disobeyed God as they were tempted to eat the forbidden fruit in the Garden of Eden.

» Whereas other political philosophies trace the origins of immoral or criminal behaviour to society, conservatives believe it is rooted in humans. Humans are thought to be *morally* imperfect. Conservatives hold a pessimistic, Hobbesian, view of human nature. Humankind is innately selfish and greedy, anything but perfectible; as **Thomas Hobbes (1588–1679)** put it, the desire for 'power after power' is the primary human urge. Some conservatives explain this by reference to the Old Testament doctrine of 'original sin'. Crime is therefore not a product of inequality or social disadvantage, as other ideologies believe; rather, it is a consequence of 'immoral' human instincts and appetites.

Intellectually Imperfect

Meaning that humans have limited rational capacity – this is why Conservatives:

- Reject ideological approaches and prefer tried and tested methods such as empiricism
- Support hierachy and authority in society, believing that as some are born to rule and others to be ruled.

Morally Imperfect

Meaning that humans are tainted by original sin and find it hard to resist temptation – this means they:

- Can't make good moral choices
- Need the threat of tough punishments to uphold law and order
- Need to be guided by a strict moral code which imperfect individuals will seek to break.

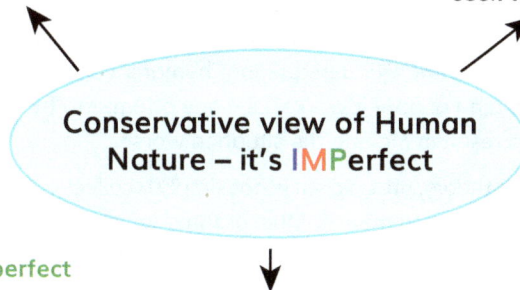

Conservative view of Human Nature – it's IMPerfect

Psychologically Imperfect

Meaning that humans need to feel safe and secure – this is why conservatives support:

- Tradition, so society remains familiar
- Organicism, as humans take comfort from knowing their place
- Reject multiculturalism, so the customs and values of society remain unchanged from generation to generation
- Nationhood/Patriotism because humans get a sense of security from the shared experience of being part of a nation.

Figure 2.1 The Conservative view of human imperfection.

Human imperfection

Summary box

- Humans are limited in many ways and are prone to make mistakes and unwise choices in life.
- They are intellectually imperfect and do not have the capacity to make sense of the world.
- They have limited capacity in psychological terms, seeking security and familiarity.
- In moral terms they are unable to distinguish right from wrong and will stray if not threatened with punishment.

Organicism

This can be included in a discussion of the conservative view of state, society and human nature.

Definition

Organicism: Sees society as a living entity with all its parts working together in harmony. Society is maintained by a delicate set of relationships. If this is disturbed, society will be undermined.

Conservatives believe that humans are dependent and security-seeking, who need to belong, to have 'roots' in, society. Humans need to be part of social groups that nurture them: family, friends, colleagues, local community and even the nation. These groups provide human life with security and meaning. As a result, conservatives are reluctant to support negative freedom, where individuals are left alone, which, they argue, would result in what the French sociologist Émile Durkheim (1856–1917) called anomie, resulting from the breakdown in society.

Conservatives instead believe that it is through membership of society that humans find the stability they crave. Society, according to **Burke**, is like a tree, growing from the accumulated wisdom of past generations. He argued we should be *cautious when venturing upon pulling down an edifice which has answered, to any tolerable degree, the common purpose of society*. Thus, Burke's attitude towards the state was that it should seek to maintain society through gentle pruning rather than radical change. The state should be used for reform, only when necessary while seeking to maintain society as much as possible.

Definition

Anomie: A weakening of values and rules, associated with feelings of isolation, loneliness and meaninglessness.

Such ideas are based on a view of state and society called organicism. Conservatives have traditionally thought of them as living things, organisms, whose parts work together just as the brain, heart, lungs and liver do within a human. For conservatives like **Burke**, society resembled a living organism like a plant that may be changed when necessary to preserve political stability and social harmony.

An organic society and state differ from a mechanistic one (see Liberalism chapter) in several important respects:

1. Primarily, organic societies and states develop naturally as needed. For example, the family has not been 'invented' by any political theorist but is a product of natural social impulses such as love and responsibility. In no sense do children in a family agree to a 'contract' on joining the family – they simply grow up within it and are nurtured and guided by it. As organic society has been shaped by natural forces beyond human understanding, humans cannot attempt to 'fix' society, as they have no real understanding of how it works. Like any attempt to fix something one has no working knowledge of, it would result in making the situation worse.

2. Also, unlike mechanistic theory, organicism is not simply a collection of individuals who can move up and down in society according to merit. Within organic society, the whole (society) is sustained by a fragile set of relationships between and among its parts. Everyone within it has a specific role, place and purpose, hence society and the state has a natural fixed social hierarchy, this is what **Burke** meant when he referred to '*loving the little platoons to which you belong*'.

3. Linked to this is the idea that authority comes from 'above'. Connected to the idea of human imperfection, conservatives believe that those 'born to rule' should occupy a higher position in the state and shoulder the burden of decision making. As such they must be listened to by those occupying lower positions.

4. Lastly, one of the key aspects of organicism is the idea that the whole (society) is more important than the individual parts (the people). The interests of the whole of society must come before the rights of individuals.

Two other concepts underpin the idea of organicism and help to understand how it functions.

> **Spec key term**
>
> **Hierarchy:** The belief that society is naturally organized in fixed tiers, where one's position is not based on individual ability.

Hierarchy

Conservatives have traditionally believed that society is naturally hierarchic, characterized by fixed social tiers. Social equality is therefore rejected as undesirable and unachievable; power, status and wealth are always unequally distributed. Conservatives such as **Burke** were able to embrace the idea of a 'natural aristocracy', arguing that we should respect '*institutions on the principle which nature teaches us to respect individual men: on account of their age, and on account of those from whom they are descended*'. Just as the brain, the heart and the liver all perform very different functions within the body, the various classes and groups that make up society also have their own specific roles. There must be leaders and there must be followers; there must be owners and there must be workers; for that matter, there must be those who go out to work and those who stay at home and bring up children. The belief in hierarchy is strengthened by the emphasis conservatives place on authority.

> **Spec key term**
>
> **Authority:** The idea that people in higher positions in society are best able to make decisions in the interests of the whole society; authority thus comes from above.

Authority

Conservatives believe that authority, like society, develops naturally from the need to ensure that people are cared for, kept away from danger and guided to make sensible decisions which benefit them and society. Authority also promotes social cohesion by giving people a clear sense of how they 'fit in' and what is expected of them. Consider the role of a parent: it is their job to ensure their children are safe, have a healthy diet, go to bed at sensible times and so on. Such authority can only be imposed 'from above', quite simply because children do not know what is good for them. It does not and cannot come 'from below': in no sense can children be said to have agreed to be governed. Authority is therefore rooted in the nature of society. Conservatives believe that authority is beneficial as people need the guidance, support and security that comes from knowing 'where they stand' and what is expected of them. **Hobbes** argued that there were '*laws of nature*', by which everyone was bound (what would now be called morality) which humans couldn't determine for themselves, they needed to be led and guided.

Organicism

Summary box

- Organicism sees society as a living entity with all its parts working together in harmony.
- People cannot exist separately from society and society provides individuals with a sense of security and purpose.
- Society is maintained by a delicate set of relationships. If this is disturbed, society will be undermined.
- Humans accept the duties, responsibilities and bonds that go with belonging to society.

Paternalism

This can be included in a discussion of the conservative view of, state, society and human nature.

Paternalism refers to power or authority being exercised over others with the intention of providing benefit or preventing harm. As a consequence, it involves limiting individual freedom in the interests of what benefits wider society. It is here we can see how intrinsically linked this idea is to the notion of organicism which identified the whole (society) being more important than the individual.

Paternalism comes from the Latin 'pater' meaning father, which reflected the hierarchy of society where the father was the authority figure, responsible for the welfare of his wife and children. In this model, 'father knows best'. He knows what's best for his wife and for his children. Hence the term paternalism reflects this hierarchy and extends it to wider society. Those in positions of authority are considered to know what was best for the rest of society. **Burke** claimed that his own social class should govern the country on the basis of paternalism and that there was a natural hierarchy within society, with each class accepting their place. **Burke's** paternalism comes from the view that wisdom and experience are unequally distributed in society; and those in authority 'know best'. It's based on the notion that those at the top of society have a duty to care for the lower social ranks, an idea inextricably linked to conservative's views of hierarchy, authority and organicism. In other words, it is the idea that others can make decisions about what's in your best interests.

Paternalism

Summary box

- Paternalism is the belief in a higher authority which knows best and acts in the best interests of all.
- For conservatives this is the state, acting as a wise and benevolent parent, guarding against wrong choices steering all to the right paths to take in life.
- Conservatives' belief in paternalism is inextricably linked to their views on hierarchy, authority and organicism.

Libertarianism

This can be included in a discussion of the New Right view of the economy, human nature, the state and society.

Libertarianism refers to a range of theories that give strict priority to liberty (understood in negative terms) over other values, such as authority, tradition and society. Libertarian thinking, as with neoliberalism within the New Right, seeks to maximize individual freedom, seeing the state as the principal threat to liberty.

Libertarians believe that individuals must not be coerced to serve the overall good of society. **Robert Nozick (1938–2002)**, a libertarian thinker, argued that individuals must have self-ownership and be left alone. Related to this, they uphold a strong distinction between the public and the private sphere of life believing that individuals are morally free and sovereign. For **Ayn Rand (1905–2002)**,

> **Exam Tip –**
> Unlike the other core principles above, libertarianism is a principle supported only by the New Right strand of conservatism.

a libertarian thinker, this was identified via her belief in 'objectivism' which argued that people were rationally self-interested creatures, and gave unashamed support to selfishness, criticizing altruism. Pure libertarians (which the New Right are not) also questions the moral boundaries imposed on individuals by the state and paternalistic values. The ideas of libertarian conservatives are explored in the New Right section of the chapter starting on page 46.

Libertarianism

Summary box

- Libertarianism is the belief in extending the most amount of freedom to the individual for them to make individual choices.
- Libertarianism emphasizes the rights of individuals to liberty, advocating only minimal state intervention in the lives of citizens. The primary role of the state is to protect individual rights.
- The libertarian strand in conservatism can be seen at times to be at odds with some of the other core principles.
- They believe that individuals prosper most when restrictions are minimal.

> **Exam Tip –** Although property is not on the Edexcel specification as a core principle, it is useful to help us understand conservative approaches to the economy.

> **Definition**
>
> **Property:** The ownership of physical goods or wealth, whether by private individuals, groups of people or the state.

The economy and property

This can be included in a discussion of the conservative view of the economy.

All conservatives support private property and the capitalist system it underpins. While traditional conservatives like **Burke** were advocates of early capitalism, this was also moderated by support for protectionism, where governments used tariffs and duties to protect home-grown products. One Nation conservatives felt compelled to moderate the extremes of capitalism in the nineteenth and twentieth centuries to preserve the stability of society and reduce the divide between the rich and poor. The New Right was a break with both earlier strands of conservatism, being ideologically committed to the free market, placing less emphasis of the cohesion of society.

Conservatives also consider property to have a range of psychological and social advantages. In an unpredictable world, property ownership gives people a sense of security, something to 'fall back on'. Property, whether the ownership of a house or business or savings in the bank, provides individuals with a source of protection. Property ownership also promotes a range of important social values. Those who possess and enjoy their own property are more likely to respect the property of others. They will also be aware that property must be safeguarded from disorder and lawlessness. Property owners therefore have a 'stake' in society; they have an interest, in particular, in maintaining law and order. In this sense, property ownership can promote what can be thought of as the 'conservative' values of respect for law, authority and social order.

2. Differences between the conservative strands

Traditional conservatism

In order to understand traditional conservatism, it is important to appreciate the circumstances into which these ideas were born. Traditional conservative ideas existed alongside a feudal, agricultural economy which was hierarchic and deferential. In the feudal economy, the landed aristocracy controlled society because they owned land, as the basis of their wealth. The agricultural economy relied upon raising cattle and growing produce so the more land someone owned, the richer they became.

Pragmatism

Traditional conservatism has drawn heavily on the ideas of **Burke**, who advocated a prudent willingness to 'change in order to conserve'. He argued that pragmatism would bring about change organically. Traditional conservatives seek to base their actions on experience (known as empiricism) and prefer not to be tied down to a rigid, ideological set of beliefs, as **Oakeshott** said, '*to be a conservative is to prefer the tried to the untried*'. This is because traditional conservatives believe that humans lack the intellectual ability and powers of reasoning to fully comprehend the complexities of the world. As a result, the outcome of human considerations (i.e. ideologies) is based on flawed reasoning and cannot ever really be relied upon. Pragmatic decisions are ones based on a workable consensus and practical solutions as opposed to ideological inflexibility.

This has led many to argue that conservatism is a disposition, an outlook, not an ideology. As **Oakeshott** said it is more '*psychology than ideology*'. As a result, conservative thought has been able to vary considerably as it adapted itself to existing traditions and national cultures and allowed it to be as flexible as **Burke** would have liked.

> **Spec key term**
>
> **Empiricism:** The idea that knowledge comes from real experience and not from abstract theories.

Tradition

Traditional conservatives are firm supporters of tradition, believing that one should always look to the past to inform the present and the future. G.K. Chesterton (1874–1936), the UK novelist and essayist, expressed this idea as '*Tradition means giving votes to the most obscure of all classes: our ancestors. It is a democracy of the dead. Tradition refuses to submit to the arrogant oligarchy of those who merely happen to be walking around.*'

Traditional conservatives support tradition because it generates a sense of identity. Established customs are ones that individuals can recognize; they are familiar and reassuring. '*The accumulated wisdom of the ages, as the heritage of society, is the best source of virtue and goodness,*' said **Burke**. Hence tradition provides stability and continuity, providing people with a feeling of 'rootedness' and belonging. It generates social cohesion by linking people to the past and providing them with a collective sense of who they are, as they are drawn to what is familiar and constant. Tradition makes people feel connected to something bigger, a sense of belonging. Change, on the other hand, is a journey into the unknown: it creates uncertainty and insecurity, and so endangers our happiness.

Human imperfection

Traditional conservatives support the idea of human imperfection arguing that humans are imperfect and imperfectible.

Psychologically imperfect

» The belief that humans seek security and belonging has led traditional conservatives to emphasize the importance of social order, and be suspicious of liberty. Order ensures that human life is stable and predictable; it provides security in an uncertain world. Liberty, on the other hand, presents individuals with choices and can generate change and uncertainty. **Hobbes** argued that humans should be prepared to sacrifice liberty in the cause of social order. He believed that war was a more natural state to humans than order, and that order was only possible when humans abandon their natural selfishness and delegate decisions to a higher sovereign authority. **Hobbes** described a society without a sovereign as a '*state of nature*' and argued it would be a '*war of every man against every man*' and live in '*continual fear, and danger of violent death*' where life would be '*solitary, poor, nasty, brutish and short*'.

Intellectually imperfect

» Traditional conservatives are suspicious of abstract ideas that claim to understand what is incomprehensible. They prefer to ground their decisions in tradition, experience and history, adopting a cautious, moderate and above all pragmatic approach, and avoiding doctrinaire beliefs. Radical reform and revolution, they warn, often lead to greater suffering rather than less, a conservative will always wish to ensure, in **Oakeshott's** words, that '*the cure is not worse than the disease*'.

Morally imperfect

» Humans can only be persuaded to behave appropriately if they are deterred from expressing their anti-social impulses. Hence for traditional conservatives, the only effective deterrent is strictly enforced law. This explains their preference for 'tough' criminal justice, based on long prison sentences. For conservatives, the role of law is not to protect liberty, but to preserve order. The concepts of 'law' and 'order' are so closely related in the conservative mind that they have become a single, fused concept.

Organicism

Traditional conservatives are enthusiastic advocates of an organic society and state. They argue that people cannot exist separately from society and society provides individuals with a sense of security and purpose, thus society emerged naturally (organically) as it was needed. Organic theory is based on the idea that the unity of society is more important that the rights of any individual and this is maintained by a delicate set of relationships, which, if disturbed, will undermine society, leading to its breakdown.

Authority

Traditional conservatives recognized the importance of authority in society. Within organic society, the needs of society come before anything else and guidance is needed 'from above'. So, emphasis is placed on a willing acceptance of social obligations and by 'doing one's duty'. When, for example, parents instruct children how to behave, they are not constraining their liberty, but providing guidance for their children's benefit. Traditional conservatives believe that a society in which individuals know only their rights, and do not undertake their duties, would be rootless and atomistic. Indeed, it is the bonds of duty and obligation that hold society together.

Traditional conservatives believe that authority should be exercised within limits and that these limits are imposed not by an artificial contract but by the natural responsibilities that authority entails. Parents should have authority over their children, but this does not imply the right to treat them in any way they choose. The authority of a parent is intrinsically linked to the obligation to nurture, guide and, if necessary, punish their children.

Hierarchy

Alongside a need for authority from above, traditional conservatives support the idea of a fixed social hierarchy. They believe there are natural inequalities between humans which lead to a hierarchical society where, as **Burke** said, '*the wiser, stronger and more opulent*' are at the top. Genuine social equality is therefore a myth; in reality, there is a natural inequality of wealth and social position, justified by a corresponding inequality of social responsibilities. The working class might not enjoy the same living standards and life chances as their employers, but they do not have the livelihoods of others resting on their shoulders. Hierarchy and organicism have thus led traditional conservatism towards paternalism.

Paternalism

For traditional conservatives, paternalism was justified with the idea that those in higher positions in societies had greater wisdom and knew what was best for the whole of society. It was therefore the duty of the rest of society to obey those 'above them', much in the same way as a child was expected to obey their father. The notion of paternalism was based on a society which was naturally unequal and was used to justify the imposition of laws on the lower classes.

Before we express our concern at this notion, it is important to view modern society and recognize that paternalism is still alive and well. Welfare and laws such as the compulsory wearing of seat belts in cars are examples of paternalism, as was the government's response to the coronavirus pandemic.

These are all examples of the state imposing rules on people who, perhaps, can't be trusted to know what they need to do to keep themselves and others safe.

The economy and property

Traditional conservatives understand the importance of property in promoting social cohesion. They view property ownership as an extension of one's personality. Possessions are not merely external objects, valued because they are useful, but also reflect something of the owner's personality and character. A home is the most personal of possessions, it is decorated and organized according to the tastes of its owner.

As well as that, traditional conservatives like **Burke** were strong defenders of private property and cautious of government economic intervention, **Burke** described Adam Smith's *The Wealth of Nations* as being '*perhaps the most important book ever written*'. He was concerned about ensuring stability and cautioned governments against the unintended consequences of state intervention which could make it harder for consumers and producers to '*mutually discover each other's wants*'. **Burke's** position highlighted the importance of caution, insisted that local communities should remain free to address local problems and stressed that governments should focus on their core functions and have the modesty to know their limits.

@john_cameron/Unsplash

Photo 2.2 A media screen in London, 2020, providing guidance to residents during the pandemic. The UK government's response to the coronavirus pandemic demonstrates paternalism in action.

Libertarianism

Traditional conservatives reject the ideas of libertarianism, supporting instead the idea of an organic state and society. Whereas libertarianism highlights the freedom of the individual as it key value, traditional conservatives value the stability and continuity of society.

One Nation conservatism

The UK's One Nation tradition is usually traced back to Benjamin Disraeli (1804–81), UK Prime Minister in 1868 and again 1874–80. Disraeli developed his political philosophy in two novels, *Coningsby* (1844) and *Sybil* (1845), which emphasized the principle of social obligation. Writing against a background of growing industrialization, poverty, inequality and, in Europe, revolutionary upheaval, he realized that as capitalism thrived and the ruling elite became more prosperous, the working classes suffering increased. He tried to draw attention to the danger of Britain being divided into two: the rich and the poor. Disraeli wrote that Britain was '*two nations; between whom there is no intercourse and no sympathy; who are as ignorant of each other's habits, thoughts and feelings, as if they were dwellers in different zones, or inhabitants of different planets*'.

Although Disraeli never used the term 'One Nation', his work as Prime Minister sought to bridge the divide through paternalistic policies that encouraged the wealthy to assist the less well-off. These ideas were based on the feudal principle of noblesse oblige, the obligation of the aristocracy to be honourable and generous. His ideas contributed to a reforming tradition that appealed to both the pragmatic instincts and sense of social duty of conservatism.

In his famous Crystal Palace speech of 1872, Disraeli said he had three objectives: to maintain the institutions of the country, to uphold the empire and to elevate the condition of the people. It is important to understand how One Nation conservatism sits in relation to traditional conservative values. In this section, we will attempt to assess this.

Spec key term

Noblesse oblige: The duty of the wealthy and privileged to look after those less fortunate.

Pragmatism

It is clear that One Nation conservatism adopts the pragmatic approach favoured by traditional conservatives. Disraeli understood that growing social inequality contained the seeds of revolution; a poor and oppressed working class, he feared, would not simply accept its misery. The revolutions that had broken out in Europe in 1830 and 1848 seemed to bear out this belief. Reform would therefore be sensible, because stemming the tide of revolution would ultimately be in the interests of the rich and privileged. Disraeli understood that a One Nation approach would enable conservatives to reach out to all sections of society. As he said in 1848: '*The palace is not safe when the cottage is not happy.*'

The pragmatic balance that One Nation conservatives like Disraeli were seeking was one which balanced the 'rights' of the individual and the collectivist desire of the emerging socialist traditions. Pragmatic conservatives support neither the individual nor the state in principle, but are prepared to support either, or, more frequently, recommend a balance between the two, depending on 'what works'.

As Ian Gilmour (1978) put it, '*the wise Conservative travels light*'. The values that conservatives hold most dear – tradition, order, authority, property and so on – will be safe only if policy is developed in the light of practical circumstances and experience. Such a position will rarely justify dramatic or radical change but accept a cautious willingness to 'change in order to conserve'. This commitment to pragmatism has served One Nation conservatives well; their ability to adapt and reinvent themselves has proven to be a highly effective way of winning elections.

One Nation conservatism in the 1950s and 1960s was based on the need for a non-ideological, 'middle way' between the extremes of laissez-faire liberalism and socialist state planning. It was therefore the way of moderation and sought to draw a balance between rampant individualism and overbearing collectivism.

> **Spec key term**
>
> **Laissez-faire:**
> A preference towards minimal government intervention in business and the state.

Tradition

One Nation conservatives also support tradition. Like traditional conservatives, One Nation conservatives sought to unify people by encouraging them to look to the past in considering the future. A key aim of One Nation conservatives was order and social harmony, which was threatened by the emergence of capitalism and the insecurity it created. Disraeli was concerned that society would fracture if capitalism was left to its own devices and understood that action was necessary. In considering their response, One Nation conservatives needed to balance the need for change and the desire to conserve society as it was. In seeking reform, Disraeli was thus careful to ensure that it came via the respected traditional institutions of the state rather than via rebellion. He sought to bring people from all walks of life closer together and thereby forge one cohesive nation. Consequently, his reforming agenda was successful in satisfying the working classes while maintaining the status quo for the ruling elite. As a result, he sought to preserve and respect the traditions of society and its key institutions, while establishing gradual, but necessary change.

Like traditional conservatives, One Nation conservatives understood that maintaining traditions and customs that had been around for generations helped to make people feel safe and secure in a changing world.

Organic society, authority and hierarchy

A belief in organic society is the idea that society is more important than the individual and that a cohesive, united society is important. It is clear then, that One Nation conservatives are supporters of organicism. Disraeli's concern about social division shows the commitment to creating unity.

One way this is evident is through the enaction of social reforms to improve the conditions of the working classes. Disraeli was concerned about the devastating effects of free-market capitalism on the cohesiveness of society and set about trying to reduce the divide between the rich and poor. He believed the problems created by capitalism were everyone's responsibility. Disraeli appealed to the moral values of the aristocracy. He suggested that wealth and privilege brought with them social obligations, in particular a responsibility for the less well-off, known as noblesse oblige. He believed that society was naturally hierarchic, but also that inequalities of wealth or privilege gave rise to an inequality of responsibilities. The wealthy and powerful must shoulder the burden of social responsibility, which, in effect, is the price of privilege.

Paternalism

The traditional conservative notion of paternalism was based on the authority of the 'father' who knew what was best for his 'children'. This form of paternalism was authoritarian, as traditional conservatives did not have to concern themselves with the 'will of the people'. One Nation conservatives in the nineteenth century were responding to very different circumstances. They wanted to hold on to their core values, but now needed to convince 'the people' of the relevance of their vision for One Nation. Consequently, they had to soften their approach; they needed to persuade people that their approach was beneficial to the upper and working classes alike. Paternalism thus moved away from a 'father knows best' approach, to a 'we can look after you; we can support and protect you' approach. Both can be considered paternalistic, but they are clearly different styles.

As previously discussed, Disraeli committed his governments to improving the conditions of the working classes as evidence of this form of paternalism.

Disraeli's reforms were very popular among the newly enfranchised working classes, and some would argue that it prevented the emergence of rebellion or revolution. Consequently, this form of paternalism has been adopted by many One Nation conservative governments subsequently as it has been able to portray a caring image to the working classes who do not naturally benefit from preserving society as it is.

Human imperfection

It is clear that there is a synergy between the views of traditional conservatives and One Nation conservatives over human imperfection. Earlier in the chapter we identified that traditional conservatives recognize three components of human imperfection: psychological, moral and intellectual. It is clear that all three are evident in One Nation conservatives thought.

In their appeal to patriotism and organicism, there is a link to **psychological imperfection**. Here One Nation conservatives recognize that humans need to feel safe and secure. Patriotism unites people of all classes under the common banner of 'the nation' and gives them a feeling of togetherness and belonging. An organic view of society also relates to psychological imperfection where everyone is safe and secure in 'their place' and life is stable with no fear of revolution.

In their commitment to pragmatism and paternalism, One Nation conservatives show their understanding of **intellectual imperfection**. This suggests that humans have limited rational capacities and to be fearful of doctrinaire ideas. In supporting a pragmatic approach, One Nation conservatives recognize that the world is too complex for humans to understand, and an approach based on 'what works' and experience is always best. Their paternalistic approach to reform also reinforces this view of human imperfection. By letting the ruling elite make decision for the betterment of the working classes, One Nation conservatives recognize the limited rational capacities of humans.

Lastly, their need for order in society is linked to their belief in **moral imperfection**. One Nation conservatives emphasis on order in society is evidence of their agreement with this aspect of human imperfection. While Disraeli wished to improve the working conditions of the working class, he believed that the working classes needed moral guidance from the ruling elite.

The economy and property

Disraeli was concerned that free-market capitalism was creating social division and so he adopted a pragmatic approach to the economy. He may be most famous for the 1867 extension of the franchise to some working-class men, but his government was also responsible for laws to improve housing, sanitation, labour relations and factory reforms to improve the working conditions of the working classes. This intervention to limit the exploitative nature of capitalism did not stem from a desire to create greater equality in society, he understood that, with the franchise set only to extend more widely to all working people, it was essential to ensure that they had no reason to look towards revolution or socialism. Disraeli wrote to a friend that these Acts '*will gain and retain for the Conservatives the lasting affection of the working classes*'.

Another high point of the One Nation tradition was reached a century after Disraeli in the 1950s and 1960s, when the Conservative Party embraced economic management and the goal of full employment, as well as supporting enlarged welfare provision. In the UK, this idea was most clearly expressed in Harold Macmillan's *The Middle Way* (1938). Macmillan, who was Prime Minister from

1957 to 1963, advocated '*a mixed system which combines state ownership, regulation or control of certain aspects of economic activity with the drive and initiative of private enterprise*'.

Such ideas resurfaced more recently in the UK under David Cameron, Prime Minister from 2010–16, with the notion of 'compassionate conservatism', even though it may, in practice, have served as little more than a rhetorical device. It is, nevertheless, important to remember that One Nation conservatism provides only a limited basis for social and economic intervention. The purpose of One Nation conservatism is to consolidate hierarchy rather than to remove it, the wish to improve the conditions of the less well-off being motivated to a significant degree by the desire to ensure that they don't pose a threat to the established order.

Libertarianism

As with traditional conservatism, One Nation conservatives reject the premise of atomistic individualism, and human rationality in favour of a pragmatic, organic, paternalist approach to society.

New Right conservatism

The New Right is a marriage between two seemingly contrasting ideological traditions:

» The first of these are free-market theories that were revived in the second half of the twentieth century as a critique of 'big' government and economic and social intervention. This is called neoliberalism. Neoliberalism is a twentieth-century version of classical liberalism (see Chapter 1).

» The second element of the New Right is a more traditional conservative social theory, especially its defence of order, authority and discipline. This is called neoconservatism.

The New Right seeks to support a strong but minimal state: although it seeks to 'roll back' the state in the economic sphere, it aims to strengthen it in the social sphere.

The New Right developed in the 1970s in the UK and the US in reaction to the wider role governments were playing in people's lives. In the UK, successive governments had supported a Keynesian approach to society to solve society's problems, even though it was clear by the 1970s that things weren't improving.

Keynesianism was one of the chief targets of neoliberal criticism, with free-market **laissez-faire** ideas gaining renewed credibility during the 1970s as governments experienced increasing difficulty in delivering economic stability and growth using Keynesian approaches. Doubts consequently developed about whether it was in the power of government to solve economic problems. After winning the 1979 UK election, Thatcher embarked on a radical agenda, abandoning the pragmatic, consensus approach of her predecessors who had supported a nationalized, Keynesian approach, whereas she had radical plans to break up the nationalised monopolies by privatising industries to create competition, lower taxes, reduce welfare and deregulate the economy.

Neoliberalism

Neoliberalism reasserts the case for minimal state. The state is coercive: restricting individual initiative and self-respect. Government, unintentionally, has a damaging effect on human affairs. Instead, faith is placed in the individual and the market. Individuals should be encouraged to be self-reliant and to make rational choices in their own interests. The market is respected as a mechanism through which the sum of individual choices will lead to progress and general benefit.

While unregulated market capitalism delivers efficiency, growth and widespread prosperity, the 'dead hand' of the state saps initiative and discourages enterprise. Key neoliberal policies include privatization, spending cuts, tax cuts and deregulation. Neoliberalism has absolute faith in the capacity of the market to solve all economic and social problems. **Nozick** (see page 59) argued that individuals should be at the heart of all decisions made; however, measures by governments to reduce inequality undermine individuals and reduce them to a 'means to an end', with successful individuals having to work for the state to support less successful ones. In his book *Anarchy, State & Utopia* (1974) **Nozick** argued that '*Individuals have rights, and there are things no person or group may do to them (without* *violating their rights).*' As such, neoliberalism has attempted to establish the dominance of libertarian, atomistic ideas over paternalistic ones within conservative ideology.

Economists Friedrich Hayek and Milton Friedman argued that the task of allocating resources in a complex, industrialized economy was simply too difficult for any state to achieve successfully. The virtue of the market, on the other hand, is that it acts as the central nervous system of the economy, reconciling the supply of goods and services with the demand for them. It allocates resources to their most profitable use and ensures that consumer needs are satisfied. In the light of the re-emergence of unemployment and inflation in the 1970s, Hayek and Friedman argued that government was invariably the cause of economic problems, rather than the cure. As Ronald Reagan (US President 1980–88) said in his inauguration speech in 1981, '*Government is not the solution to our problem, government is the problem.*'

Neoliberalism is also opposed to public ownership. Starting with Thatcher in the UK in the 1980s but later extending to many other Western states, the policy of privatization effectively dismantled the UK's mixed economy by transferring industries from public to private ownership. Nationalized industries were criticized for being inefficient, because, unlike private firms and industries, they were not disciplined by the profit motive. Neoliberalism's belief was that governments should promote growth by providing conditions that encourage producers to produce.

Neoconservatism

The neoconservatism element of the New Right can be seen as a reaction against the permissive, anything goes, values of the 1960s. Neoconservative thought focuses on the need for coherence in attitudes and morality in order to ensure order. In sharp contrast to neoliberalism, neoconservatism seeks to strengthen state authority in society.

Neoconservatism relates to both domestic and foreign policy. In domestic policy, neoconservatism is defined by support for a strong state where they have sought to restore public order, strengthen 'family' values and reinforce national identity. In foreign policy, neoconservatism's central aim was to reinforce the nation by encouraging patriotism and national unity. The principal concerns of neoconservatism have been:

(i) social order

(ii) public morality

(iii) national identity

Neoconservatives believe that social order is undermined by rising crime and anti-social behaviour because of a decline in authority since the 1960s. They have therefore called for a strengthening of social discipline and authority at every level and are anti-permissiveness. This can be seen in relation to the family. For neoconservatives, the nuclear family is an authority system: it is both naturally hierarchical – children should listen to, respect and obey their parents – and naturally patriarchal. The

> **Spec key term**
> **Atomism:** The idea that society is made up of self-interested and self-sufficient individuals (also known as egoistical individualism).

> **Spec key term**
> **Anti-permissiveness:** A rejection of permissiveness, which is the belief that people should make their own moral choices, suggesting there is no objective right and wrong.

Tensions within the New Right	
NEOLIBERALS	**NEOCONSERVATIVES**
• A primary focus on the economy	• A primary focus on society/morality
• Views economic decay to be the fault primarily of government involvement	• Views decay to be the loss of a moral and possibly spiritual compass
• Views collectivism with distaste	• Will accept state action to preserve order
• Atomistic	• Patriotic
• Libertarian	• Authoritarian
• Believes the market can deliver everything	• Thinks that the free market has limits

husband is the provider and the wife the homemaker. The family is the best way to socialize children into the way they are expected to behave in society, respecting those in authority.

(i) Neoconservatism is concerned with a desire to reassert the moral foundations of society. A particular target of neoconservative criticism has been the 'permissive 1960s'. In the face of this, Thatcher proclaimed her support for 'Victorian values', and a return to 'family' values.

As well as the commitment to the importance of the nuclear family, neoconservatives like Thatcher set themselves against the promotion of so-called 'alternative lifestyles'. Thatcher's infamous Section 28 stopped councils and schools 'promoting the teaching of the acceptability of homosexuality as a pretended family relationship'. The meant that teachers were prohibited from discussing same-sex relationships with students.

(ii) Neoconservatism also seeks to strengthen national identity in the face of threats from inside and out. The nation binds society together, giving it a common culture and shared identity which is all the stronger for being rooted in history and tradition. For neoconservatism, the most significant threat to the nation 'from within' is multiculturalism, which weakens the bonds of nationhood by undermining a shared culture. Hence immigration should be limited and any immigrants must accept and assimilate into the culture and identity of prevailing British society. The threats to the nation 'from without' are various. In the UK, the main perceived threat came from European integration, a process that commenced in the 1980s under Thatcher and culminated in withdrawal from the EU in 2020.

It is clear that the New Right have shifted quite significantly away from many of the core values of conservatism and are motivated by very different beliefs, most of which are in clear opposition to the core principles outlined earlier in the chapter.

Sandrocenni/Unsplash

Photo 2.3 Stop Brexit march in London, 2019. The withdrawal of the UK from the EU highlighted a neoconservative concern with preserving the nation and protecting it from perceived external threats.

Pragmatism

The New Right reject pragmatism in favour of an ideological outlook. To be ideological is to believe in a set of beliefs and values in a firm and fixed way. Ideological thinking is usually based on theories. Those who take on an ideological way of thinking are reliant on the view that humans are able to make sense of the world, explain it and outline ways to make it better. In other words, they believe humans are rational, not imperfect, and the world is knowable. This is clearly contrary to the views of traditional and One Nation conservatives who support a pragmatic approach to change, believing that humans lack the intellectual capacity to make sense of the world and, that the world is unknowable and shaped by organic features.

In the case of the New Right, their economic ideology is based on the theories of Adam Smith, Friedrich von Hayek and Milton Friedman (1912–2006), and **Rand**. For **Rand**, the creation of wealth was to be praised and supported, over and above the attempts by the state to redistribute that wealth, which limited humans. She argued that the state's monopoly of power was immoral as it could legally use force to make people pay taxes or regulate businesses. There must be *'a complete separation of state and economics, in the same way and for the same reasons as the separation of state and church'*. Laissez-faire capitalism was the only system capable of allowing rational individuals to live a free life as it emphasized individual rights and property rights and was the only system founded on protection of these rights. These ideological views fly in the face of the pragmatism of Traditional and One Nation conservatives.

Tensions within conservatism over pragmatism	
AGREEMENT	DISAGREEMENT
✓ Traditional and One Nation conservatives support a pragmatic approach to change	✗ The New Right promote a highly principled belief in economic liberty and an authoritarian state while traditional and One Nation conservatives seek to be flexible and responsive to change
✓ Traditional and One Nation conservatives are suspicious of abstract ideologies because they believe humans are intellectually limited.	✗ The New Right's ideological approach tended towards radical changes, whereas traditional and One Nation conservatives sought to make changes gradually, recognizing the importance of tradition.
✓ Traditional and One Nation conservatives prefer to base their ideas in tradition, experience and history	✗ The New Right's ideological approach is based on a belief in human rationality, whereas traditional and One Nation conservatives pragmatic approach is based on human imperfection
✓ Their support for pragmatism is based on the idea of 'change in order to conserve'	

Tradition

Where Traditional and One Nation conservatives supported connections between the past, present and future, seeking to make, slow, incremental change, the New Right were radical. The word radical means someone who seeks extreme change in society and the New Right sought 'root and branch' change to British society; not satisfied to make small adjustments, they wanted to change it fundamentally. These radical beliefs were based on their ideological support for free-market economics (neoliberalism) and social authoritarianism (neoconservatism). In her essays and popular novels, **Rand** advanced a moral justification for private enterprise, proclaiming herself to be a *'radical for capitalism'*. Once again this is contrary to the views of Traditional and One Nation conservatives who value and respect the past, ensuring that change happens gradually, learning from the past, keeping the best elements, and only changing that which is essential.

Spec key term

Radical: The idea of drastic political, economic and social change.

Tensions within conservatism over tradition	
AGREEMENT	**DISAGREEMENT**
✓ Traditional and One Nation conservatives support the role of tradition in society	✗ While traditional and One Nation conservatives emphasize the importance of tradition, the New Right support radical change in society
✓ Tradition represents the accumulated wisdom of past generations and creates a link between past and future generations	✗ The New Right's belief in radical change is linked to their support for ideological change, whereas for traditional and One Nation conservatives, their support for tradition is linked to their support for pragmatism
✓ Traditional and One Nation conservatives recognized that traditions that had been around for generations, helped to make people feel safe and secure, strengthened social cohesion, personal security and rootedness	✗ Traditional and One Nation conservatives believe in human imperfection, whereas the New Right believe in the rationality of humans

Organic society, authority and hierarchy

The New Right appears to have contradictory responses to the idea of an organic society. On the one hand, Thatcher famously proclaimed that '*there is no such thing as society, there are individuals and there are families*' while, at the same time, insisting on imposing a shared culture and morality on society. It is clear that the neoliberal and neoconservative elements within the New Right are inconsistent here.

For neoliberalism, atomistic individualism replaced the idea of organic society. The idea that the whole is more important than the individual is anathema to them. They reject the notion of binding society together, of looking after the less well-off in order to preserve stability, arguing instead that individuals need to stand on their own two feet and be self-sufficient. Neoliberalism argued that society is a product of the actions of self-seeking and largely self-reliant individuals. **Nozick** argued that '*There are only individual people, different individual people, with their own individual lives*.'

Neoliberalism criticizes the welfare state for having created a culture of dependency: it saps initiative and enterprise and robs people of dignity and self-respect. It also allowed families to abandon their childcare responsibilities to society in the form of the welfare state. Welfare is thus the *cause* of disadvantage, not its cure. A further neoliberal argument against welfare is based on a commitment to individual rights. **Nozick** advanced this most forcefully in condemning all policies of welfare and redistribution as a violation of property rights. In this view, so long as property has been acquired justly, to transfer it, via taxation, without consent, from one person to another amounts to '*legalised theft*'.

Also within the neoliberal element of the New Right, the liberal concept of meritocracy has replaced the idea of hierarchy and authority from above. Neoliberalism believes that one's place it society reflects merit, those who work hard and possess talent will, and should, acquire wealth and rise. Welfare and state intervention stops individuals from being able to achieve their potential and rise (or fall) in society. The interventionist, organic state, with its notions of top-down authority and fixed hierarchy undermines the individual's ability to look after themselves and subverts the natural rise and fall of society.

However, while neoliberal ideas within the New Right recoiled at the idea of state-imposed authority, the neoconservative element suggested it was vital. Neoconservative thought seeks to reassert the moral foundations of society, reconnect with a national identity, resulting in improved social order.

Neoconservatism emphasis on authority demonstrates that it has roots in Traditional conservatism. However, it differs markedly from One Nation conservatism, which also draws heavily on organic ideas. Whereas One Nation conservatives believe that community is best maintained by social reform and the reduction of poverty, neoconservatives look to strengthen community by restoring authority and imposing social discipline.

Tensions within conservatism over society

AGREEMENT	DISAGREEMENT
✓ Traditional and One Nation conservatism believe in an organic society to provide stability and security based on their view of human nature	✗ Traditional and One Nation conservatism have an organic view of society, whereas the New Right takes an atomistic view of society
✓ Traditional and One Nation conservatism argue that the delicate elements of an organic society should not be disturbed	✗ While traditional and One Nation conservatism support a hierarchic society, the New Right support meritocracy
✓ Traditional and One Nation conservatism acknowledge the importance of hierarchy and authority which reinforces organic society	✗ There are differences within the New Right over society. Neoconservatism believes in the cohesion of an organic society but neoliberalism believes in a society that allows free individuals to flourish

Paternalism

While we recognize Traditional and One Nation conservatives as being paternalistic, it might be more appropriate to think of the New Right (specifically, neoconservatism) as being more authoritarian. An authoritarian government is one in which authority is exercised over a population with or without its consent. While the New Right government of Thatcher was elected and hence had the consent of the people, in many ways, they governed in a manner that appeared unconcerned with the effects and consequences of their decisions on many millions of people they governed. Their authoritarian approach can be linked to their ideological approach; they were convinced of the correctness of their approach and were determined to enforce it, some would say impose it, on the population.

Neoconservatism argues that permissive values have undermined the importance of family values. They argued that one-parent families, divorce, abortion and easily available contraception encouraged a decline in morality and the nuclear family which, in turn, has undermined the cohesiveness of society. Instead of children being raised to understand how to behave and what is expected of them, the insecurity of childhood has led to a rise in anti-social behaviour, drug and alcohol abuse and addiction.

This social authoritarianism is matched by state authoritarianism, the desire for a strong and powerful state was reflected in a tough stance on law and order. Neoconservatism sought to be tough on crime and not interested in the social causes of crime. This led to a greater emphasis on longer prison

Tensions within conservatism over the role of the state

AGREEMENT	DISAGREEMENT
✓ All conservatives agree that there must be a state in society	✗ Traditional and One Nation conservatives are pragmatic over the role of the state, whereas the New Right are ideological
✓ Traditional, One Nation and Neoconservatism within the New Right agree that the state is a force for good helping to ensure order	✗ One Nation conservatives support the welfare state, whereas the New Right are opposed to the welfare state
✓ All conservatives agree that the state important to uphold law and order	✗ There is disagreement within the New Right over the extent of the role of the state, with neoliberals wanting a minimal state and neoconservatives wanting a strong authoritarian state
✓ Traditional, One Nation and Neoconservatism within the New Right agree that the state needs to defend traditional values, property and institutions	

sentences, reflecting the belief that 'prison works'. However, this authoritarianism is in sharp contrast to neoliberal views which argue that the collective power of government is the principal threat to the individual, and freedom can only be ensured by 'rolling back' the state.

Human nature

It is difficult to have a coherent understanding of the human nature that underpins New Right thinking. The two distinctive approaches have their foundation in two unrelated approaches to human nature.

» Neoliberalism is clearly founded in atomistic individualism, where rational individuals make decisions in their own best interests. Underpinning this view is the idea that people owe nothing to society and are, in turn, owed nothing by society. **Nozick** was a libertarian who advocated free-market capitalism on the basis of self-sovereignty. As he argued, 'the state may not use its coercive apparatus for the purpose of getting some citizens to aid others, or in order to prohibit activities to people for their own good or protection'. **Rand** was also a vigorous defender of the virtues of selfishness, seeing the central purpose of life as a quest for excellence, achieved by the exercise of rational self-interest. While selfishness allows people to exist to advance their life's project by striving to be outstanding (wealth being the key measure of success in this respect), selflessness represents failure, a squandering of one's chances of excellence.

» However, neoconservatism must be understood in the light of imperfect humans who are unable to know what to make of the world and need to be guided by an authority figure from above. Neoconservatism sees two dangers in leaving individuals to make decisions for themselves. In the first place, the freedom to choose one's own morals or lifestyle could lead to the choice of immoral views. The second danger is not so much that people may adopt the wrong morals or lifestyles but may simply choose different moral positions. For neoconservatism, moral pluralism is threatening because it undermines the cohesion of society. A permissive society lacks unifying moral standards. It is a 'pathless desert', which provides neither guidance nor support for individuals and their families.

Human nature appears hugely contradictory in New Right thinking, they seem to divide human nature into two: the rational consumer and the imperfect citizen.

Definition

Moral pluralism: The idea that there can be conflicting moral views that are each worthy of respect.

Tensions within conservatism over human nature	
AGREEMENT	DISAGREEMENT
✓ Traditional and One Nation conservatism both agree that the humans are intellectually, psychologically and morally imperfect	✗ While traditional and One Nation conservatism believes in human imperfection, the New Right embraces a rational understanding of human nature
✓ Consequently, traditional and One Nation conservatism believe in some form of paternalism, promote stability and security and a strong state to create order and stop crime	✗ For the New Right, society is a collection of self-interested individuals, whereas traditional and One Nation conservatism have an imperfect view of human nature which lends itself to an organic, paternalistic society an organic society
	✗ There are differences within the New Right over human nature. The neoliberal element of the New Right recognizes humans as rational creatures in contrast to neoconservatism who instead recognize humans as imperfect

Libertarianism

It is clear that within the New Right, neoliberalism is entirely libertarian in its approach. However, the New Right are not consistent libertarians. While economically they believe in economic individualism and 'getting government off the back of business', the neoconservative element are less prepared to extend this principle of individual liberty to other aspects of social life. Consistent libertarians like **Nozick** and **Rand** are coherent and extend this thinking to all aspects of social life as well as the economic sphere.

The economy and property

The New Right approach to property is consistent from both the neoliberal and the neoconservative aspects. They support private property and believe that property ownership is an important aspect of society. However, despite this consensus, neoliberalism advocated property as a reflection of effort, it is earned by hard work and they believe the ability to accumulate wealth is an important economic incentive. Neoconservatism supports property ownership for the values it creates; it gives people a stake in society, it encourages them to want to protect their property from harm and promotes order in society.

Tensions within conservatism over the economy and property

AGREEMENT	DISAGREEMENT
✓ All conservatives recognize the significance and importance of free enterprise and its capacity to build and create wealth	✗ One Nation conservatism take a pragmatic position over free-market economics and government intervention, which contrasts with the New Right's ideological approach
✓ Conservatives recognize the importance of property in providing individuals with a sense of security	✗ The New Right's commitment to free-market economics is based on a belief in atomistic individualism. This is in contrast to One Nation conservatism's approach, based on imperfection and the need for social cohesion
✓ Conservatives see property as giving individuals a stake in society which promotes important values like law and order	✗ There is disagreement within conservatism between the One Nation conservatism and the New Right over the role of welfare in the economy

Table 2.1 Tensions within Conservatism

	Traditional Conservatives	One Nation Conservatives	The New Right
Pragmatism	• Change in order to conserve • Pragmatic and flexible	• Pragmatic and flexible • Seeks to heal divisions in society	• Ideologically driven
Tradition	• Values institutions and customs which have stood the test of time	• Values institutions and customs which have stood the test of time	• Rejects tradition preferring radical change
Human Imperfection	• Believes humans are intellectually, morally and psychologically imperfect	• Believes humans are intellectually, morally and psychologically imperfect	• Believes in human rationality and hence individualism
Organic Society	• Society more important than individuals • Everyone should accept their place in a hierarchic society • Authority comes from above	• Society more important than individuals • Sees society as hierarchic and organic • Believes that authority comes from above	• Rejects organicism in favour of individualism
Paternalism	• The state knows what is best so the people must do what they are told	• An obligation on the wealthy to look after those who are unable to look after themselves	• Rejects paternalism, supporting individualism and freedom
Libertarianism	• Rejects libertarianism in favour of tradition and continuity	• Rejects libertarianism in favour of tradition and continuity	• Seeks to uphold liberty and choice, mainly in the economy

3. Conservatism key thinkers

Key thinkers are an important part of understanding each ideology. The exam board has specified five key thinkers per ideology and TWO must be included in an answer to avoid a cap (please check the Exam Focus chapter (Chapter 9) for lots more discussion of key thinkers). Although key thinkers (and other thinkers) have been discussed throughout the chapter, here we look at each one in detail.

Thomas Hobbes (1588–1679)

Universal History Archive/Getty

An English political philosopher, Hobbes, in his classic work *Leviathan* (1651), used social contract theory to defend absolute government as the only alternative to chaos and disorder.

Order

For Hobbes, social order demands a decisive and coercive role for the state. '*How could a state be governed, or protected ... if every individual remained free to obey or not to obey the law according to his private opinion?*' Unlike Locke, Hobbes' state of nature was a state of war, which he believed was the natural end point of uncontrolled human freedom.

He believed that peace should be the aim of any society. Without peace, he observed, humans live in '*continual fear, and danger of violent death*', and what life they have is '*solitary, poor, nasty, brutish, and short*'. Hence an authoritarian state was needed to prevent the collapse of social order.

According to Hobbes, freedom without order and authority would have disastrous consequences for society. No one could live in safety, as the overriding concern would be to do whatever was necessary to secure survival, there would be a war, '*and such a war as is of every man against every man*'. This could only be avoided if humans surrendered to a sovereign authority over them to ensure order.

Social contract

While Hobbes is a social contract theorist, he views it differently from liberal social contract theorists like Locke or Rousseau. He agreed that the relationship between rulers and ruled was contractual, but, once they decided to accept the sovereign power, they were giving their consent to be ruled in an authoritarian fashion. In Hobbes' social contract, the people traded liberty for safety.

People were bound by the social contract so long as the sovereign could protect their subjects. However, if the sovereign failed and the people felt their condition was no worse than the free-for-all outside the state, they had the right to disobey the sovereign authority. At this point people can deprive the sovereign of their power.

Human nature

Hobbes is widely accepted to have a pessimistic view of human nature. He argued that humans were not capable of restraint and even the most moderate would turn to violence to protect themselves and their belongings. In other words, all humans are naturally competitive and aggressive. They will compete violently for the necessities of life and to gain the reputation where others fear to challenge them. They are also easily led astray in their attempts to understand the world around them as their capacity for reason is fragile. As a result, they think more highly of themselves than others and place too much emphasis on their own short-term interests and needs.

As a result, Hobbes believed that war comes more naturally to humans than order. According to Hobbes, humans are in '*a perpetual and restless desire for power after power that ceases only in death*'. To live in order requires humans to supress their natural instincts and allow a sovereign power to rule over them. The best people can hope for is a peaceful life under a sovereign authority to guarantee order and security.

Edmund Burke (1729–97)

Mikroman6/Getty

A Dublin-born British statesman and political theorist, Burke was the father of the British conservative political tradition. His major work, *Reflections on the Revolution in France* (1790), opposed the French Revolution commitment to abstract principles such as 'the universal rights of man', arguing that wisdom resides largely in experience, tradition and history.

Change

Burke argued that political change should be undertaken with caution and should be organic and not on the basis of abstract speculation. Instead, change begins by accepting that society is too complex to be fully understood and the consequences of radical change cannot be predicted. As he argued, '*Very plausible schemes, with very pleasing commencements, have often shameful and lamentable conclusions*', This did not mean never seeking change, rather, that one should adapt to changing circumstances carefully and prudently.

His criticism of the French Revolution was that high-sounding phrases like '*liberté, fraternité, equalité*' were without any concrete understanding of how to create a new society. Burke rejected the idea that humans were capable of replacing one set of social rules with another; he believed humans lacked the capacity to fully understand the world into which they were born.

Tradition

Burke was fully committed to the idea of tradition. Using the language of his contemporaries, he argued that '*Society is indeed a contract*', but the partners of this contract are '*those who are living, those who are dead, and those who are yet to be born*'. The present generation do not know better than previous ones. Burke believed that rights could only be understood in the context of historical tradition and were passed down from generation to generation.

According to Burke, continuing respect for tradition promotes continuity and stability. It also establishes an obligation or duty for each generation to protect and hand on the accumulated wisdom of tradition to their successors.

Organicism, hierarchy and paternalism

Burke was committed to the idea of organic society, believing there was a natural hierarchy within society, and each component must play their role as part of a living organism. He argued that humans need to be connected to other people to feel safe and to flourish, and he identified the family, church and local community as the key groups that ground humans and help them live a virtuous life. He argued we should '*learn to love the little platoons in society to which we belong*'.

His belief in paternalism was also evident, arguing that only the aristocracy, who were 'born to rule', had the wisdom to govern, as other classes could not help but put their own narrow interests first. This was expressed during his time as an MP of Bristol, '*your representative owes you, not his industry only, but his judgment; and he betrays, instead of serving you, if he sacrifices it to your opinion*'.

Michael Oakeshott (1901–90)

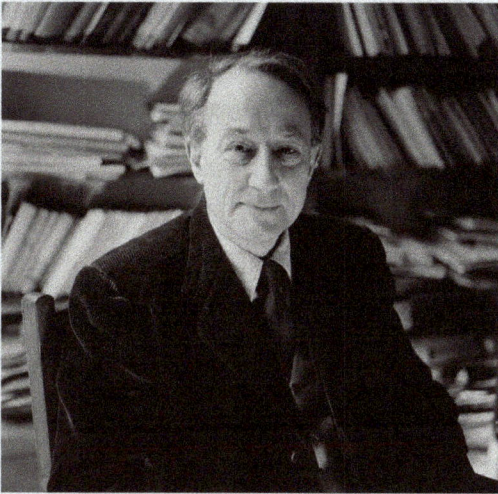

Evening Standard/Stringer/Getty

A British political philosopher, Oakeshott advanced a powerful defence of a non-ideological style of politics that supported a cautious approach to change. Oakeshott's best-known works include *Rationalism in Politics* (1962) and *On Human Conduct* (1975).

Human imperfection

For Oakeshott, the realm of political ideas is beyond the limited understanding of humans, he suggested that '*In political activity ... men sail a boundless and bottomless sea; there is neither harbour for shelter nor floor for anchorage, neither starting-place nor appointed destination.*' He is suggesting that the world is unknowable and unpredictable and hence beyond the grasp of humans.

He argued that instead of trying to create a new society, with radical untested ideas, political leaders should instead attempt to '*keep afloat on an even keel*'. To continue the sailing metaphor, Oakeshott argued that the sea is unpredictable and that the only option is to keep the ship afloat. Attempts to radically steer the ship in a different direction will inevitably lead to its capsizing.

In his essay 'On Being Conservative' (1956) Oakeshott explained what he regarded as the conservative disposition: '*To be conservative ... is to prefer the familiar to the unknown, to prefer the tried to the untried, fact to mystery, the actual to the possible, the limited to the unbounded, the near to the distant, the sufficient to the superabundant, the convenient to the perfect, present laughter to utopian bliss.*' This shows a clear understanding of the conservative belief in psychologically, intellectually and morally imperfect humans.

Anti-rational

Oakeshott suggested that 'rationalism' was the belief, that there are 'correct' answers to political questions and that this was fundamentally wrong. It was an error to think that correct decisions can be made simply by applying rules or by calculating consequences. Politics, he suggested, should be '*a conversation, not an argument*'. Decisions should be based upon consensus and practical solutions based on experience, not ideology.

Oakeshott argued that the world is complicated, and one should be suspicious of leaders who claim that they can 'pilot' the ship to a specific destination, as this is unlikely. The British Parliament had not developed on the basis of rationalism or ideology, instead it had developed over centuries in response to the circumstances, i.e. to limit political power and protect against tyranny of early monarchs.

His views on rationalism are inevitably linked to his view of human nature. He distrusted rational arguments, preferring traditional values and established customs based on the conservative disposition outlined above. Oakeshott maintained that politics can only be successfully conducted if it accommodates existing traditions, and practices.

Ayn Rand (1905–82)

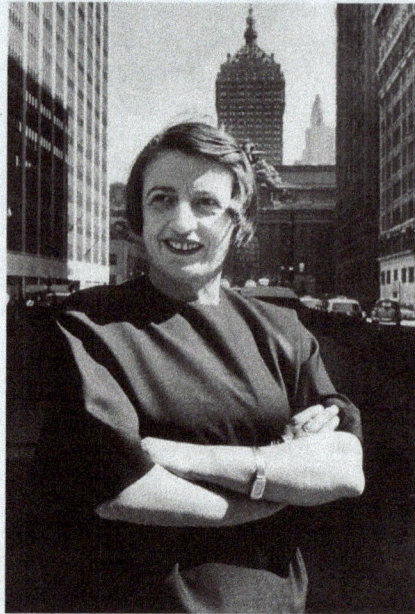

A Russian-born writer and philosopher who emigrated to the USA when she was twenty-one, Rand's (born Alice Rosenbaum) most influential works were her best-selling novels, *The Fountainhead* (1943) and *Atlas Shrugged* (1957), the latter a portrait of a dystopian USA.

Objectivism

Rand is associated with the philosophical position of 'objectivism', a philosophy of rational individualism, where there is no greater moral goal than achieving one's happiness. She described it as '*the concept of man as a heroic being, with his own happiness as the moral purpose of his life, with productive achievement as his noblest activity, and reason as his only absolute*'. She called it a practical '*philosophy for living on earth*'. Arguing that reason and rationality are the only things one can be sure of.

In *Atlas Shrugged*, published in 1957, which was considered her masterpiece, Rand showed that without the efforts of rational and productive people, the economy would collapse, and society would fall apart.

New York Times Co./Getty

Rand described the theme of the novel as '*the role of the mind in man's existence – and … the demonstration of a new moral philosophy: the morality of rational self-interest*'. Rand's beliefs were a form of rational egoism which she believed were the only guiding moral principle. She said the individual should '*exist for his own sake, neither sacrificing himself to others nor sacrificing others to himself*'. For her, egoism was '*the virtue of selfishness*' and she condemned altruism as incompatible with human happiness.

She also argued that conforming to the norms of society hindered humans ability to be free, '*that a man has rights which neither god nor king nor other men can take away from him, no matter what their number, for his is the right of man, and there is no right on earth above this right*'. Here Rand is arguing that each society broke out of one form of conformity straight into another, each one enslaving humans in different ways. The only way to be truly free was to break away from conformity and live as each one sees fit.

She considered reason to be the single most significant aspect of her philosophy, stating: '*I am not primarily an advocate of egoism, but of reason. If one recognises the supremacy of reason and applies it consistently, all the rest follows.*'

Freedom

Rand defended laissez-faire capitalism on the grounds that it guarantees freedom and provides for the emergence of the elites needed to govern society. Objectivism favours a political and economic system consistent with both individualism and laissez-faire capitalism.

Her novel *Atlas Shrugged* showed state intervention paralysing business. The heroes of her book are the entrepreneurs and industrialists; those whose productivity underpins society. '*Man – every man – is an end in himself, not the means to the ends of others.*' She believed that any attempt to control the actions of others undermined individuals' ability to work freely and productively.

Robert Nozick (1938–2002)

A US political philosopher, Nozick developed a form of rights-based libertarianism in response to the ideas of John Rawls. His major work, *Anarchy, State, and Utopia* (1974), rejects welfare and redistribution, and advances the case for minimum government and minimal taxation.

Libertarianism

Nozick's work was a revival of libertarian ideas. He argued that any state apart from the most minimal was incompatible with individual rights. The main argument in *Anarchy, State, and Utopia* is that only a minimal state is morally justified. By minimal state, Nozick meant one which ensured '*protection against force, theft, fraud, enforcement of contracts and so on*', in other words, a nightwatchman state.

Nozick echoes Locke's theory of property ownership, suggesting that everyone has the right to claim as property the products of one's labour and the right to dispose of one's property as one sees fit, provided that doing so does not violate the rights of anyone else. Everyone also has the right to punish those who violate or attempt to violate one's own natural rights.

Taxation and entitlement theory

One of the most famous conclusions of his book *Anarchy, State, and Utopia* was that taxation was morally indefensible. Nozick saw taxation as '*legalised slavery*', where a person was forced to work for free towards another person's gain. He argued that any compulsory taxes that were used to benefit others were unjust, because it amounts to 'forced labour' by those who must pay the tax. Following in the footsteps of Kant, he argued that individuals own their bodies, talents, abilities and labour and are therefore an 'end in themselves'. Humans are therefore entitled to dispose of their property as they wish.

Nozick hence introduced the idea of 'entitlement theory' to challenge Rawls' idea of distributive justice. According to Nozick, anyone who acquired property through just means was morally entitled to it. Nozick recognized three legitimate ways to justly acquire property (something he called 'holdings'):

» If something is unowned, where the acquisition would not disadvantage others

» The voluntary transfer of ownership to someone else

» The transfer of ownership to rectify past injustices

For Nozick, '*a distribution is just if everyone is entitled to the holdings they possess under the distribution*'; however, as not everyone follows these rules '*some people steal from others, or defraud them, or enslave them, seizing their product and preventing them from living as they choose, or forcibly exclude others from competing in exchanges*'. The third principle is needed to rectify this.

4. How to apply knowledge to conservatism answers

In this section of the chapter, we are going to be looking at how to apply the knowledge learnt so far to areas of agreement and disagreement within conservativism. These areas will help you to understand how to answer 24-mark essays on conservatism. But please use this section in conjunction with the Exam Focus chapter (Chapter 9), which explores the different ways to approach answering 24-mark questions.

Tensions within conservatism over the role of the state

Worked example

Paragraph One – Agreement within conservatism

✓ All conservatives agree that there must be a state in society

✓ Traditional, One Nation conservative and neoconservatism agree that the state needs to provide order in society **(Hobbes)**

✓ Traditional, One Nation conservative and neoconservatism agree that the state needs to defend traditional values and give clear moral guidance. This is based on an organic view where authority comes from above

✓ Traditional and One Nation conservatives agree that it is the role of the state to protect and safeguard institutions which have stood the test of time **(Burke)**

Paragraph Two – Disagreement within conservatism

✗ Traditional and One Nation conservatism's approach to the state is based on pragmatism **(Oakeshott)**, whereas the New Right instead hold a highly ideological stance, believing in a small, but strong state

✗ One Nation conservatives have been prepared to use the state to provide welfare when necessary, whereas the New Right reject the state providing extensive welfare **(Nozick, Rand)**

Paragraph Three – Disagreement within conservatism

✗ There are differences within the New Right over the state; as neoconservatism and neoliberalism sets itself up as a web of internal contradictions

✗ Neoliberalism supports a minimal state to provide order, whereas neoconservatism believes in a stronger state, with a reach beyond this

✗ Neoliberals believe a minimal state leads to dynamic markets **(Rand, Nozick)**, neoconservatives by contrast believe that a strong state is necessary to preserve order **(Hobbes)** and uphold traditional values and institutions

Tensions within conservatism over society

Worked example

Paragraph One – Agreement within conservatism

✓ Traditional and One Nation conservatism believe in an organic society and see a strong society as providing stability and security

✓ Traditional and One Nation conservatism argue that the delicate elements of an organic society should not be disturbed **(Oakeshott)**

Continued...

✓ Traditional and One Nation conservatism acknowledge the importance of hierarchy and authority which reinforces organic society **(Burke)**

Paragraph Two – Disagreement within conservatism

✗ Traditional and One Nation conservatism have an organic view of society where the individual cannot be separated from society, whereas the New Right takes an atomistic view where humans are self-reliant individuals and society is merely a collection of individuals **(Rand)**

✗ While Traditional and One Nation conservatism support a hierarchic society with authority coming from above **(Burke)**, the New Right support meritocracy in society believing that individuals should rise and fall in society based on merit

Paragraph Three – Disagreement within conservatism

✗ There are differences within the New Right over society. Neoconservatism believes that the cohesion of an organic society is safeguarded by strong leadership and government authority, however, neoliberalism rejects the idea of organic society believing instead that society works best by allowing free individuals to flourish **(Nozick)**

✗ While neoliberalism seems to trust individuals in society to make decisions for themselves, neoconservatism supports imposing a strict moral code on individuals in society

Tensions within conservatism over human nature

Worked example

Paragraph One – Agreement within conservatism

✓ Traditional and One Nation conservatism agree that humans are intellectually imperfect. They see the world as too complicated for humans to grasp **(Oakeshott)**. Consequently, Traditional and One Nation conservatism believe in some form of paternalism

✓ Traditional and One Nation conservatism agree that humans are psychologically imperfect, they are dependent creatures, craving order, familiarly and the security of knowing their place

✓ Traditional and One Nation conservatism see humans as morally imperfect, unable to resist temptations to act immorally. This is why they believe you need a strong state to create order and stop crime **(Hobbes)**

Paragraph Two – Disagreement within conservatism

✗ Whilst Traditional and One Nation conservatism believes in human imperfection, the New Right, particularly neoliberalism, embraces a rational understanding of human nature based on atomistic individualism **(Rand)**

✗ Their differing beliefs on human nature results in differing approaches to society. For the New Right, society is merely a collection of self-interested individuals **(Nozick)** which completely contrasts with Traditional and One Nation conservatism's view of imperfect humans who support an organic society

Paragraph Three – Disagreement within conservatism

✗ There are differences within the New Right over human nature. The neoliberal element of the New Right commits to a rational approach based on a belief in atomistic individualism **(Rand, Nozick)**. This is in contrast to neoconservatism who reject human rationality, and instead believe in human imperfection **(Oakeshott, Hobbes)**

✗ By emphasizing the restoration of authority, reinforcing law and order and bringing back traditional morality, neoconservatism recognizes a belief in human imperfection. However, within the New Right, neoliberalism's commitment to a minimal state, free-market economics, reduced welfare and freedom of the individual shows they believe human nature is one of rationality and not imperfection

Tensions within conservatism over economy

Worked example

Paragraph One – Agreement within conservatism

✓ All conservatives recognize the significance and importance of free enterprise and its capacity to build and create wealth **(Burke)** as they believe that humans are motivated by material gain

✓ Conservatives also recognize the importance of property in providing individuals with a sense of security, which humans crave **(Hobbes)**

✓ Conservative also see property as giving individuals a stake in society which promotes important values like law and order

Paragraph Two – Disagreement within conservatism

✗ One Nation conservatives take a pragmatic position over the economy, prioritizing social cohesion and stability. This approach contrasts the New Right, whose commitment to capitalism is distinctly ideological **(Nozick)** and rejects any form of increased state intervention in the economy **(Rand)**

✗ The New Right commitment to free-market economics is based on a belief in atomistic individualism **(Rand, Nozick)**. This is in contrast to One Nation conservatism's pragmatic approach which is based on a belief in human imperfection and the need for social cohesion **(Oakeshott, Hobbes)**

Paragraph Three – Disagreement within conservatism

✗ Another key area of disagreement is between the One Nation conservatism and the New Right over welfare. One Nation conservatives recognize the need for welfare in order to reduce instability in society. The New Right reject this arguing that welfare creates a dependency culture and restricts individuals from achieving their potential **(Rand)**

✗ One Nation conservatives are willing to use welfare schemes in order to maintain the cohesiveness of society. This is based on the pragmatic approach One Nation conservatism takes to the role of the state in the economy, whereas the New Right's approach reflects their ideological commitment to the individual over the cohesiveness of society

Chapter Summary

- Conservatism is primarily an ideology which is concerned with conserving and protecting society.
- The three strands are traditional conservatives, One Nation conservatives and the New Right.
- The New Right is a marriage of two seemingly inconsistent strands – neoliberalism and neoconservatism.
- The New Right fundamentally reject almost all of the values of traditional and One Nation conservatism.

Exam Style Questions

1. To what extent do conservatives agree over the state?
2. To what extent do conservatives agree over human nature?
3. To what extent do conservatives disagree over the economy?
4. To what extent is there agreement within liberals over the economy?
5. To what extent is conservatism a coherent ideology?
6. To what extent are conservatives committed to tradition?
7. To what extent do conservatives support paternalism?

Further Resources

Adams, I. *Political Ideology Today* (2001). Chapter 3, 'Conservatism and the Right' is a straightforward read for A-Level students which explores the prevalence of conservative ideas.

Edwards, A. and Townshend, J. (2002). *Interpreting Modern Philosophy from Machiavelli to Marx*. Chapter 2, 'Hobbes', and Chapter 6, 'Burke', are useful for students looking for a deeper insight into these two key thinkers.

Leach, R. *Political Ideology in Britain* (2015). Chapter 3, 'Conservatism' is an excellent chapter which goes through the development of conservative ideas and values.

Fawcett, E. *Conservatism: The Fight for a Tradition* (2020). A comprehensive history of conservative thought from the nineteenth century to the present.

Kelly, P. et al. *The Politics Book* (2013). A clearly written, concise book which covers many of the thinkers discussed in this chapter.

Muller, J., ed. *Conservatism: An Anthology of Social and Political Thought from David Hume to the Present* (1997). The best general reader of traditional conservative political writings.

O'Sullivan, N. (1976) *Conservatism*. A very readable book which explores the history and ideas of conservatism.

Scruton, R. *Conservatism: An Invitation to the Great Tradition* (2018). An erudite exploration of the development of conservative thought and an even-handed defence of traditional conservatism in the modern political discourse.

Sedgewick, M. *Key Thinkers of the Radical Right: Behind the New Threat to Liberal Democracy* (2019). A timely anthology exploring the intellectual foundations of far-right and alt-right conservative ideology that has gained increasing prominence in twenty-first-century politics.

Vincent, R. *Modern Political Ideologies* (1995). Chapter 3, 'Conservatism', can be used to stretch and extend a student's knowledge of the content covered in this chapter.

Visit our companion website at https://bloomsbury.pub/essentials-of-political-ideas-2e for more worked examples.

3 SOCIALISM

Historical overview

Socialism arose as a reaction against the social and economic conditions generated by the growth of capitalism, and its ideas were linked to the development of a growing class of industrial workers, who suffered poverty and degradation. Socialism is thus a critique of capitalism and defined by its attempt to offer an alternative to it.

The character of early socialism was influenced by the harsh and often inhuman conditions in which the working class lived and worked. Wages were low, child labour was commonplace, the working day was long and the threat of unemployment ever present. As a result, early socialists often sought a radical, even revolutionary alternative. Early socialists like Charles Fourier (1772–1837) and Robert Owen (1771–1858) experimented with communities based on sharing and cooperation. The Germans **Karl Marx (1818–83) and Friedrich Engels (1820–95)** developed more complex and systematic theories.

Towards the end of the nineteenth century, socialism was transformed by a gradual improvement in working-class living conditions and the advance of democracy. The growth of trade unions and working-class political parties meant it became difficult to see the working class as a revolutionary force. Socialist parties adopted legal and parliamentary tactics, encouraged by the gradual extension of the vote to working-class men.

By the First World War (1914–1918), the socialist world was divided between those who had sought power through the ballot box and those who proclaimed a continuing need for revolution. The Russian Revolution of 1917 created a split between revolutionary and evolutionary socialists. For example, revolutionary socialists like **Rosa Luxemburg (1871–1919)** sought to abolish capitalism via a revolution, whereas evolutionary socialists like the social democrats and the Third Way embraced the gradualism of **Beatrice Webb (1858–1943)** and aimed to reform capitalism via evolutionary, parliamentary means.

Key Questions

» How did socialism originate?
» What are the main principles that are central to socialism?
» What are the key strands of socialism?
» What are the areas of similarity and difference within socialism?

Specification Checklist

1. Socialism: core ideas and principles:

» Collectivism
» Common humanity
» Social class
» Equality
» Workers' control

2. Differing views and tensions within socialism:

» Revolutionary socialism
» Social democracy
» Third Way

3. Socialist key thinkers and their ideas:

» Karl Marx (1818–83) and Friedrich Engels (1820–95)
» Beatrice Webb (1858–1943)
» Rosa Luxemburg (1871–1919)
» Anthony Crosland (1918–77)
» Anthony Giddens (1938–)

Luis Alvarez/Getty

Introduction to socialism and its strands

Socialism, as an ideology, has traditionally been defined by its opposition to capitalism and the attempt to provide a more humane and socially worthwhile alternative. At the core of socialism is a vision of humans as sociable, united by their common humanity. Socialists therefore prefer cooperation to competition and the defining value of socialism is equality. Socialism, however, contains a variety of divisions and rival traditions. These divisions have been about both 'means' (how socialism should be achieved) and 'ends' (the nature of the future socialist society). This chapter looks at the three strands of socialism named in the specification.

Revolutionary socialists

Revolutionary socialists seek to create a socialist society via a revolution and consider it impossible to achieve it any other way. They reject the evolutionary socialist approach as they argue that power in a capitalist society is not held by the state or with the people, therefore attempts at reform via the state will always be unsuccessful. They seek to completely abolish capitalism and replace it with socialism. They envisage a communist society, developed after the revolution, which will be stateless and classless. They therefore have revolutionary 'means' and fundamentalist 'ends'.

Table 3.1 Ways to categorise socialism.

Strand	Revolutionary socialism	Social democracy	Third Way
Means	Revolutionary	Evolutionary	
	Seeks change via revolution	Seeks gradual change via democratic, parliamentary route	
Ends	Fundamentalist	Revisionist	
	Believes in the abolition of capitalism and its replacement with socialism	Believes that capitalism should not be abolished, but adapted to support the most vulnerable	

Social democrats

Social democrats are evolutionary socialists which means they intend to use the state to change society. They also seek to tame capitalism rather than replace it, which makes them revisionist as their 'ends' are more limited than fundamentalist socialists. For example, instead of committing to a fully equal society, they seek just to reduce inequality. They seek to achieve a 'more socialist' society, specifically by nationalizing key industries and using a progressive tax system to fund a welfare state. They support Keynesian economics and government intervention in the economy. They therefore have evolutionary 'means' and revisionist 'ends'.

Third Way

The Third Way is also an evolutionary form of socialism which means they seek to use the state to change society. They are also known as neo-revisionism as they goes beyond the revisionism of social democracy. They seek to connect socialist aims to a market economy. In so doing, they have redefined many socialist ideas, moving towards equality as inclusion, or equality of opportunity. They also value the power of the community, rather than focusing on class, but argue community involves reciprocal rights and responsibilities. They therefore have evolutionary 'means' and revisionist 'ends'.

1. Socialism: core ideas and principles

Collectivism

This can be included in a discussion of the socialist view of the state, society, human nature and the economy.

Collectivism is the view that the group is more significant that the individual. Collectivist societies are organized so that communities are prioritized over individuals. It also means that power is in the hands of the people as a whole, not in the hands of a few powerful individuals. In a collectivist society, decisions benefit all people, not the elite few. Collectivism is based on the belief that collective human endeavour is of greater practical and moral value than individual self-striving. It thus reflects the idea that human nature is sociable and implies that social groups are meaningful political units.

At its heart, socialism is a collectivist ideology and offers a vision of humans as social animals, capable of overcoming social and economic problems by drawing on the power of the community rather than individuals. This is collectivist because it stresses the capacity of human beings for collective action, their willingness and ability to pursue goals by working together.

For socialism, collectivism is based on the idea that when working together, humans can achieve much more than they can when working alone. At the heart of this collectivist vision of society is the belief that humans will support and nurture each other, hence close, positive relationships between people are at the heart of the collectivist vision. Most socialists would be prepared to echo the words of the English poet John Donne (1571–1631):

No man is an Island entire of itself;
every man is a piece of the Continent, a part of the main …
any man's death diminishes me, because I am involved in mankind; and therefore never send to
know for whom the bell tolls;
it tolls for thee.

It is clear to socialists that humans are not self-reliant individuals, but are part of an indivisible community. Human beings are therefore 'comrades', 'brothers' or 'sisters', tied to one another by the bonds of a common humanity. This is expressed in the principle of fraternity. Socialists argue that humans best understand themselves and are happiest when identifying as part of something bigger and more powerful. They might point to large crowds at live sporting and music events as indication that humans crave being part of something bigger; part of a crowd singing along to a favourite song or cheering together when their team scores.

Spec key term

Fraternity: This refers to the bonds of sympathy and solidarity between and among human beings.

Jimmy Conover/Unsplash

Photo 3.1 Fans in a sports stadium cheering on their team together is an example of social unity.

Collectivism

Summary box

- At the heart of socialism is the primacy of the group.
- Socialists believe that society is made up of groups.
- Collective human effort is both of greater practical value to the economy and moral value to society than the effort of individuals.

Common humanity

This can be included in a discussion of the socialist view of society, human nature and the economy.

The socialist commitment to collectivism is very closely tied to their view of human nature. Socialists see human nature as elastic, shaped by the experiences and circumstances of life. In the debate about whether 'nurture' or 'nature' determines humans, socialists side resolutely with nurture. Socialists consider the idea of a separate or atomized 'individual' absurd. They believe that the individual is inseparable from society and can only be understood, and understand themselves, through the communities and groups to which they belong. The behaviour of humans therefore tells socialists more about the society in which they have been brought up, than it does about human nature. Socialists have an optimistic, positive belief in human nature, interested not just in what people are, but in what they have the capacity to become. This has led socialists to develop a progressive vision of a better society, in which humans can achieve genuine liberation and fulfilment as part of a community. Their understanding of human nature is of a people bound together with a common humanity, based on their view that the natural relationship between them is one of cooperation rather than competition.

Socialists argue that human nature can revert to its natural state by the removal or reform of capitalism, which encourages cooperation. According to this theory, cooperation and collaboration make more economic sense than competition, which often replicates and wastes resources. Moreover, humans who work together rather than against each other develop bonds of sympathy and affection – a common humanity. Working towards a common aim, for a common purpose, reinforces humans' connections with each other. Furthermore, the energies of the community rather than those of the single individual can be harnessed.

Socialists also believe that human beings can be motivated by moral incentives, and not merely by economic incentives. In theory, capitalism rewards individuals for the work they do: the harder they work, the greater their rewards will be. For socialists, however, the moral incentive to work hard is the desire to contribute to the common good, which develops out of a empathy, or sense of responsibility, for fellow human beings, especially those in need.

Spec key term

Cooperation: Working collectively to achieve mutual benefits.

Common humanity

Summary box

- Socialists believe that humans are naturally bound in groups.
- Humans are social creatures with a tendency to cooperation.
- Socialist believe that all humans are born good but that their life experiences determines their nature.
- Human behaviour is socially determined.
- Humans cannot be understood without reference to society.

Social class

This can be included in a discussion of the socialist view of the economy and society.

Socialists have traditionally viewed social class as the most politically significant division in a capitalist society. They argue that in capitalism, humans have been divided into different social groups based on the way they work. The working class has developed because of similarities in the way its members work and live, resulting in the development of a working-class culture.

As a result, socialist attitudes towards class have been expressed in two ways:

» First, socialists use class as a way of understanding and analysing society. Socialists suggest that in early history, humans tended to think and act together with others with whom they shared a common economic position or interest, i.e. as a class, and that each class acting in its own interests caused divisions in society. In other words, social classes, not individuals, are the principal players in history and therefore provide the key to understanding social and political change. This is demonstrated most clearly by **Karl Marx's (1818–83) and Friedrich Engels's (1820–95)** belief that historical change comes out of class conflict.

» Secondly, socialism focuses specifically on the working class, which they view as the biggest in any society and the one that suffers the most. Socialists view them as the class that can change society, and are most concerned with working-class political struggle and liberation. Socialism has been viewed as the ideology of the working class, and the working class are seen as the vehicle through which socialism will be achieved.

Nevertheless, socialists don't accept social class as a permanent feature of society. Often it is quite the opposite: socialists either want a classless society or one in which class inequalities are substantially reduced.

Social class

Summary box

- Socialists believe that society is stratified according to economic class.
- Economic inequality reinforces and continues this pattern of class divide.
- Marxists believe that society is in conflict and that class struggle is at the core of this conflict.

Equality
This can be included in a discussion of the socialist view of the state, society, human nature and the economy.

A commitment to equality is, in many respects, the defining feature of socialism, being the value that most clearly distinguishes socialism from its rivals. Socialist egalitarianism is usually characterized by a belief in equality of outcome.

The socialist approach to equality should not be confused with the liberal approach. While socialists believe that foundational, formal equality and equality of opportunity are all fundamental requirements for an equal society, they are not a sufficient measure. For most socialists, equality must be measured by outcome; in other words, by how people experience society, and describes a situation in which people have similar wealth and income, or in which the general economic conditions of everyone's lives are alike. The aim of equality of outcome is to eliminate economic inequalities.

Connected to equality of outcome is the idea of social equality, this means being treated equally by society. Fundamentalist socialists, like **Marx and Engels**, would argue that genuine social equality is impossible in a capitalist society as it is an inherently unequal system which encourages inequality. Socialists are not satisfied to simply allow individuals an equal opportunity to develop their unequal skills, but rather demand social equality. They argue that social inequality is not only unjust, but encourages rivalry, resentment and social divisions. Socialists value equality as it enables humans to work together cooperatively and harmoniously, ensuring social cohesion and fraternity.

Socialists have advanced several arguments in favour of this form of equality:

» First, equality upholds social justice. Socialists reject the explanation that inequality of wealth reflects innate differences of ability among individuals. Instead, socialists argue that capitalism encourages competitive and selfish behaviour and human inequality reflects the unequal structure

Definition

Social class: A social class is a group of people who share a similar socio-economic position.

Egalitarianism: A theory or practice based on the desire to promote equality.

Equality of outcome: The idea that equality should be measured by the way people live in society, focusing on tangible outcomes rather than equal opportunities.

Formal equality: Equal rights and equality in the eyes of the law

Social equality: When all individuals are treated equally within society, usually resulting in the absence of social classes.

Fundamentalist socialism: A form of socialism that seeks to abolish capitalism and replace it with a significantly different kind of society. This can be achieved by revolutionary OR evolutionary ways.

Spec key term
Social justice: A distribution of wealth that is morally justifiable and implies a desire to limit inequality.

of society. They argue that the differences in humans' abilities are relatively small and that the differences in wealth are much larger, due to this flawed system.

» Second, Social equality demands that people are treated equally by society in terms of their rewards and economic circumstances. Socialists view formal equality as inadequate because it disregards the structural inequalities of capitalism. To them, equality of opportunity legitimizes inequality by maintaining the myth of the inherent inequality of humans.

» Third, equality underpins community and cooperation. If people live in equal social circumstances, they will be more likely to identify with one another and work together for common benefit. In this view, equal outcomes strengthen community. Inequality, by the same token, leads to conflict and instability.

» Lastly, socialists support equality as they believe that it is the only genuine way to ensure human needs are met. Basic needs, such as the need for food, water, shelter, healthcare and education, are fundamental to the human condition. Since all people have broadly similar needs, distributing wealth on the basis of need-satisfaction is the only just way to organize society.

Equality

Summary box

- A defining principle of socialism is the belief in equality.
- Socialists seek to move beyond equality of opportunity to radically redistribute and provide equality of outcome.
- Marx would say equality must be based on the principle 'From each according to his ability, to each according to his need.'

Workers' control

This can be included in a discussion of the socialist view of the state, society and the economy.

Socialists have often traced the origins of competition and inequality to private property, by which they usually mean 'capital', i.e. businesses and factories, rather than personal belongings such as clothes, furniture or homes. This attitude to property sets socialism apart from liberalism and conservatism, which both regard private property as natural and proper. Socialists criticize private property for several reasons:

» Private property is *unjust*: wealth is produced by the collective effort of human labour and should therefore be owned by the community, not by private individuals.

» Private property encourages people to be materialistic, to believe that human happiness or fulfilment can be gained through the pursuit of wealth. Those who own property wish to accumulate more, while those who have little or no wealth long to acquire it.

» It is *divisive*. It promotes conflict in society, for example, between owners and workers, employers and employees or the rich and the poor.

Socialists have therefore proposed that private property either be abolished and replaced by some form of common ownership of productive wealth, or, at the least, that the right to property be balanced against the interests of the community.

Beatrice Webb and her husband Sidney were involved in writing the famous Clause IV of the 1918 Labour Party's Constitution (see Figure 3.1) which committed the Labour Party to a form of evolutionary and fundamentalist socialism that sought to replace capitalism with socialism, as the '*common ownership of the means of production distribution and exchange*' left no room for the profit motive and competition required by capitalism.

Workers' control is linked to the idea of **common ownership** as it seeks an equal distribution of resources as well as power. According to this idea, decisions on how resources are used should be made by, and benefit, the whole community, not the elite few. Additionally, the aim of workers' control is to enable class distinctions to be eliminated. By removing the separation between owners and workers, socialists aspire to eliminate class distinctions and create a more equal society. Workers'

Spec key term

Common ownership: Common ownership of industry refers to the idea that industries should not be owned by private individuals and shareholders, but by all so everyone is able to benefit from the wealth of society.

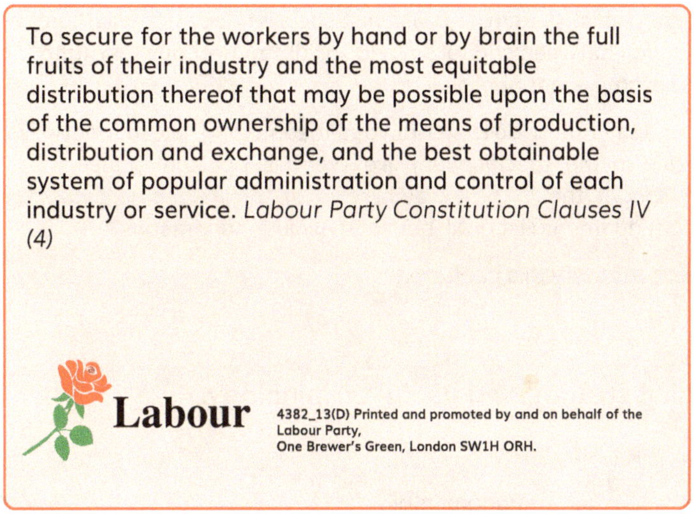

> To secure for the workers by hand or by brain the full fruits of their industry and the most equitable distribution thereof that may be possible upon the basis of the common ownership of the means of production, distribution and exchange, and the best obtainable system of popular administration and control of each industry or service. *Labour Party Constitution Clauses IV (4)*

Labour 4382_13(D) Printed and promoted by and on behalf of the Labour Party,
One Brewer's Green, London SW1H ORH.

Figure 3.1 **Labour Membership Card showing Beatrice and Sidney Webb's original Clause Four (1918).**

control can mean workers owning a business, or part of it. The modern socialists' preference is often workers' control via the democratically elected state, i.e. nationalization.

The aim of workers' control is to create a society based on the values of collectivism and equality where all people in the chain of production have an equal say.

Workers' control

Summary box

- This is the notion of the extent the working class taking ownership of the goods and services which they produce.
- Socialists have a variety of interpretations of workers control.
- Revolutionary socialists seek to remove control of industry from the bourgeoisie, whereas evolutionary forms of socialism look towards state ownership.

2. Differences between the socialist strands

The socialism specification requires knowledge of three strands of socialism:

» Revolutionary socialism

» Social democracy

» Third way

However, **Beatrice Webb**, a socialist key thinker, is associated with a different strand, democratic socialism, which is not a named strand on the specification. Consequently, this chapter will not focus on democratic socialism, but has referenced **Webb** wherever relevant and useful.

There are many ways of categorizing socialist strands and one that is useful is to distinguish between their 'means' – the way they wish to achieve their goals – and their 'ends' – their goals. It is important not to confuse these terms.

The terms revolutionary and evolutionary are terms that describe socialist 'means'. Revolutionary socialists believe the only way to achieve their aims is via a revolution, whereas evolutionary socialists believe that it is possible to achieve their goals via, peaceful, democratic, gradual means.

When it comes to 'ends' we use two different terms, fundamentalist and revisionist – these terms are often misunderstood. A fundamentalist socialist is one who seeks to abolish capitalism completely

Spec key term

Communism: The communal organization of social existence based on the common ownership of wealth.

Marxism: An ideological system within socialism that drew on the writings of Marx and Engels and has at its core a philosophy of history that explains why it is inevitable that capitalism will be replaced by communism.

Definition

Means of production: The components needed to produce goods and services: land, labour and capital, i.e. industry.

and replace it with a socialist system. A revisionist socialist does not wish to abolish capitalism, but seeks an accommodation between capitalism and socialism; **Anthony Crosland (1918–77)** wanted to 'tame' capitalism for example, not abolish it.

However, to be a fundamentalist does not always mean being revolutionary. Democratic socialists (NOT a named strand in the specification) like **Webb** supported Clause IV of the Labour Party Constitution which sought the '*common ownership of the means of production, distribution and exchange*' – clearly a fundamentalist goal, but, with evolutionary means.

The table below seeks to clarify this confusion.

Table 3.2 Socialist strands and useful terminology.

Means	Revolutionary		Evolutionary	
Ends	Fundamentalist		Revisionist	
Strand name	Revolutionary socialism	(Democratic socialism)	Social democracy	Third way
Key thinkers	Marx and Engels Luxemburg	Beatrice Webb	Anthony Crosland	Anthony Giddens

However, while at times it may be useful to categorize the different socialist strands in this way, it should never be done at the expense of their strand name.

Revolutionary socialism

The revolutionary socialist tradition is defined by the need for the revolutionary overthrow of capitalism, a rejection of private property and a clear preference for common ownership. Its most significant association has undoubtedly been with **Marx and Engels.** For them, communism is a society characterized by classlessness as wealth is owned in common, and statelessness, as the state 'withers away'. At the core of Marxism is a study of history which suggests that capitalism is doomed, and communism is destined to replace it.

Social class

Marxism set out a critique of capitalism in the latter nineteenth century, and the following section outlines the Revolutionary Socialist view of class as well as their critique of capitalism.

Marx and Engels argued that in a capitalist society there were two main classes, the bourgeoisie and the proletariat.

» Bourgeoisie: those who own the means of production – industry

» Proletariat: non-owners of the means of production – those who only own their labour

Marx was clear that the ownership of industry by the bourgeoisie was the cause of all exploitation and of class conflict. He explained this through the idea of surplus value. According to this theory, profit can only be achieved by paying the proletariat less than the value their labour generates. Marx adapted the 'labour theory of value' from classical liberal economist Adam Smith (1729–37). This theory stated that labour is the source of value, and therefore the value of anything depends upon the amount of labour which went into its production. For example, a hand-carved chair is worth more than a factory produced one because the hand-carved one took a skilled carpenter longer to create.

Marx and Engels believed that exploitation is the defining characteristic of the relationship between the two main classes, and hence of capitalism itself. This exploitation is a necessary feature of capitalism, as the bourgeoisie *have* to exploit their workers to make a profit and stay in business. **Marx** argued that profit being kept from the worker is the basis of exploitation by the bourgeoisie to the proletariat.

The aim of profit maximization is central to capitalism, and so requires the bourgeoisie to constantly squeeze more and more surplus value from the proletariat if they wish to survive and thrive. There is thus an inherent and irreconcilable conflict of interest between the two main classes in capitalism. According to **Marx**, reforming the capitalist system (as revisionists like Social Democracy and the Third Way wish to) can alleviate, but cannot eliminate the relationship of exploitation and conflict, which defines capitalism.

Historical materialism

What made **Marx's** analysis different from other socialists was that he believed that economics (materialism) was the driving force in history, historical materialism. **Marx and Engels** believed that someone's economic circumstances determine their social development. '*It is a simple fact of life that mankind must first of all eat, drink and have shelter and clothing; therefore must work, before it can pursue politics, science, art and religion.*'

Marx uses the terms 'base' and 'superstructure' to refer to the two aspects of society:

» The 'base' refers to the economy.

» The 'superstructure' refers to all the other institutions that exists in society and the state, i.e. the political system, the legal system, the military and all other institutions of the state. Also included are the family, the media, art and culture, the education system and religion.

» The key values and beliefs that society holds (its culture) also form part of the superstructure and these ideas exist to justify the system's economic base, this process is known as false consciousness.

In *A Contribution to the Critique of Political Economy*, written in 1859, **Marx** argues that the economic base determines (controls) the superstructure. In other words, real power comes from ownership of industry not from Parliament or the people.

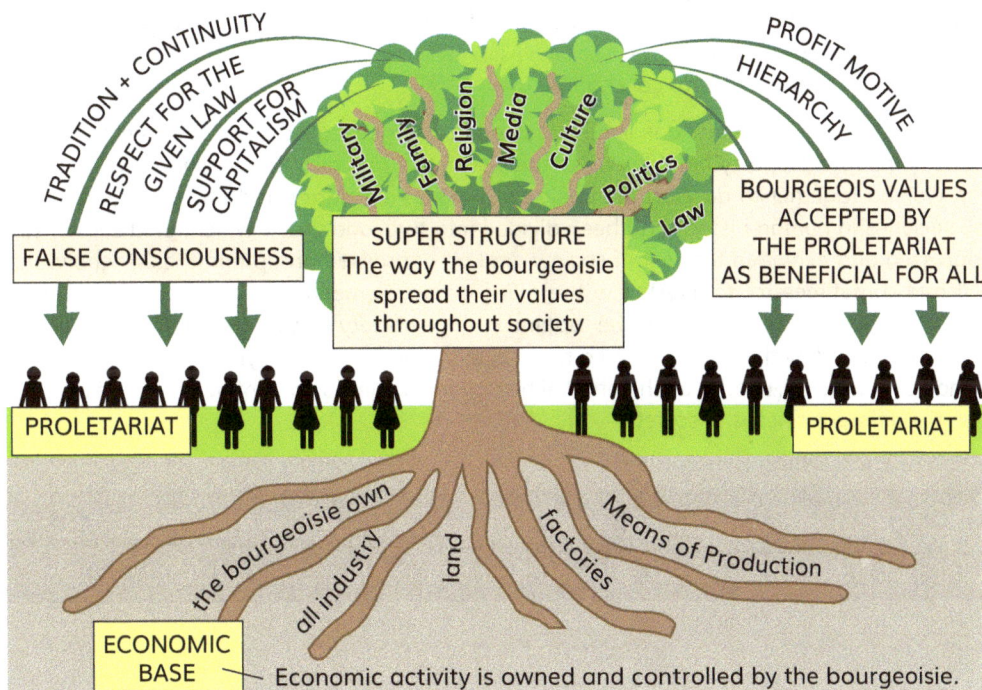

Figure 3.2 **Base and superstructure.**

Marx argued that in capitalist societies, the ruling class imposes its own set of ideas and values, which uphold and protect their position, spreading them through society via the superstructure. As Marx said, '*the ideas of the ruling class are, in every age, the ruling ideas*'.

Exam Tip – Marx referred to his 'brand' of socialism as communism, and it is often also called Marxism; however, it is vital to understand that Marx's communism cannot be understood by looking to the historical practices that called themselves communism, i.e. in Russia and China. While they may, at some point, have attempted to carry out the communism of Marx and Engels, their actions have not always aligned with these ideas. The specification **does not require any analysis of these regimes** as part of an understanding of Revolutionary Socialism.

Definition

Surplus value: A Marxist term suggesting that profit made by the bourgeoisie is in fact money owed to the proletariat as their labour has created the commodity.

False consciousness: According to Marxism, this is the delusion that prevents the proletariat from recognizing their own exploitation.

As the bourgeoisie owns and controls the economy (the base), this allows them to control the culture and ideas of the whole of society, through control of the superstructure. These values will sound familiar, they consist of a belief in the importance of private property, free-market capitalism, competition, individualism, authority and hierarchy, patriotism, tradition and continuity, respect for the given law and order. **Marx** argued that these values in fact only benefit the elite few – the bourgeoisie – but are shown as ideas that benefit all. The superstructure is used to spread this false information which creates a 'false' consciousness, as the proletariat is duped/brainwashed by the bourgeoisie. This is what led **Marx and Engels** to declare that '*religion is the opiate of the masses*' which implies that religion was used to suppress the proletariat into accepting their status in society as if it were the will of God.

These values, which uphold and support the ruling class's dominance, becomes the dominant values throughout society, which is known as **bourgeois hegemony**, which favours keeping society as it is. False consciousness can only be eliminated with the abolition of all classes and class rule via a revolution, i.e. with the establishment of a communist, classless society.

It is important to understand that **Marx and Engels** are revolutionary because of their view that base determines superstructure. They argue that it is impossible to create a socialist society via the state, as the state is part of the superstructure and therefore controlled by the bourgeoisie. The only way to create a communist society is to seize control of the economic base from the all-powerful bourgeoisie using the only power the proletariat have, force and strength in numbers.

Dialectical materialism

An additional and somewhat complex aspect of Marxist analysis of society is the notion of the **dialectic**. **Marx** believed that historical change results from class conflict in society. This is known as **dialectical materialism**. According to **Marx and Engels**, this is how history moves forward, via conflict between a dominant force (thesis) and its opposing force (antithesis) producing a new historical stage (a synthesis) which in turn becomes the new dominant force (thesis). This is shown in Figure 3.3.

Human history is thus a struggle between the exploited and the exploiter. Throughout history, classes have been irreconcilably in conflict with each other. In the words of *The Communist Manifesto* (1848), '*The history of all hitherto existing societies is the history of class struggle*'. Classes, rather than individuals, are the agents of historical change.

In the early stages of history humans lived in a condition **Engels** called 'primitive communism'. Here, there was no private property but simply primitive societies in which people shared what little they had and worked together to develop the basic skills of survival. **Marx and Engels** argued that after that, all societies in human history had been divided into two, one group which ruled society (thesis) and oppressed and exploited the rest of society, and an oppressed group (antithesis) who would try to resist and sometimes try to overthrow the ruling group. Sometimes the oppressed group at the bottom would overthrow the group at the top and change society and at other times the two groups would both be ruined by the struggle and a new society would emerge (synthesis). They argued that the method of production used in each period of history had an important influence on the relationship between the different classes in society.

> For a more detailed explanation on how the dialectical stages of history evolved, please see the online case study.

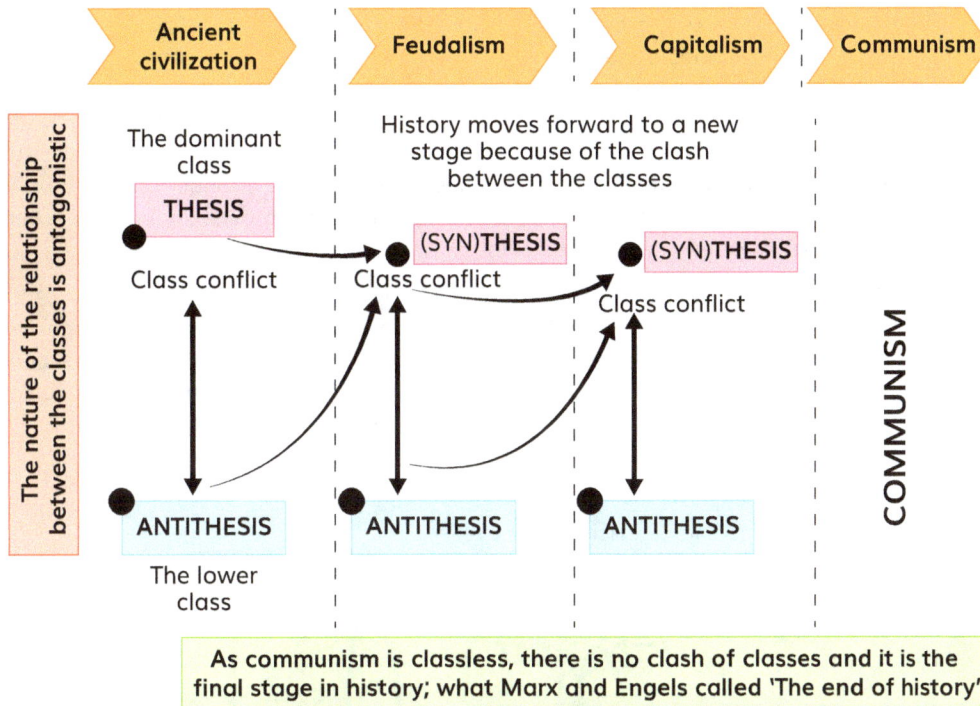

Figure 3.3 **Marxist theory of history as class conflict.**

Crisis of capitalism

Marx and Engels believed that capitalism was inherently unstable. In a capitalist economy, the workers produce all the wealth yet remain poor, while the bourgeoisie's wealth grows. However, to stay in business, capitalists must constantly better their rivals by producing more goods at lower costs. There is constant pressure on the capitalist to exploit their workers more and more.

Marx drew attention to capitalism's cyclical tendency, experiencing booms and then slumps. He saw overproduction as one of the most fundamental contradictions of capitalism. On the one hand, he argued, there was ever-greater production of goods based on ever-greater exploitation of workers, while on the other hand, that same exploitation reduced the workers' ability to buy the goods produced. Because workers couldn't afford the goods they were producing, production would outstrip demand, as Marx said, '*Production without regard to the limits of the market lies in the nature of capitalist production*.' When this happens, goods

STORYPLUS/Getty

Photo 3.2 **Waste material from a clothes factory is dumped in a canal in this image from Dhaka, Bangladesh. Overproduction is a common problem in the fast fashion industry.**

go unsold, profits plunge, workers are made redundant and factories close. This reduces demand still further and so more factories close, and this continues until the whole economy collapses into recession resulting in widespread unemployment. Eventually workers become desperate to work at any price. This provides an opportunity to any bourgeoisie still in business, who may find it profitable to start production again. Demand eventually increases, and the economy begins to recover. But the slump will have driven some capitalists out of business, and only the stronger ones will be left to take advantage of the recovery. With each slump the capitalist class grows smaller and richer, and competition reduces, as the working class grows larger and suffers more.

Marx believed that each successive boom and slump would be deeper and more catastrophic than the last. Eventually the slumps would be so great that the disparity of wealth between the bourgeoisie and proletariat would be too obvious for even false consciousness to hide. Hence, as Marx said, '*Capitalism contains within itself the seeds of its own destruction.*' The extreme poverty of the proletariat forces it to see its own situation clearly, undistorted by false consciousness, at the point of **polarisation**.

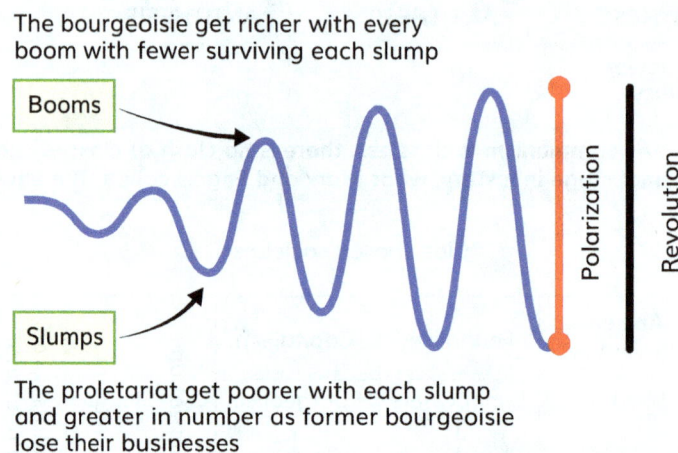

Figure 3.4 **The cyclical nature of capitalism.**

Marx argued that this is when the proletariat finally understand the role they must play in leading the revolution, arriving at **class consciousness**, they become a **'class for itself'** from a **'class in itself'**. **Luxemburg** was clear that this could not be done *for* the working class, but must be done *by* them:

'*the proletariat requires a high degree of political education, of class-consciousness and organization. All these conditions cannot be fulfilled by pamphlets and leaflets, but only by the living political school, by the fight and in the fight, in the continuous course of the revolution.*'

However, **Marx** recognized that there could be no immediate and automatic switch from capitalism to communism. He thought that a transitional stage would exist which would last as long as class antagonisms persisted. He called this the **dictatorship of the proletariat**. The purpose of this temporary period was to prevent counter-revolution by the dispossessed bourgeoisie. As class antagonisms faded, with the emergence of full communism, the state would lose its purpose as an agent of false consciousness and the state would as **Engels** states, '*wither away*'.

Collectivism

Revolutionary Socialists like **Marx and Engels** were clear that communism was a collectivist ideology, placing the community at the heart of all decision making. They argued that communist society should be organized on a communal basis, and that all goods and property should be owned in common. What would this ensuing communist society look like? **Marx and Engels** were frustratingly vague on this topic. However, they did establish some clear characteristics of a communist society:

» No state

» No classes

» Common ownership

» Absolute equality

» Production according to human need

Famously, distribution under communism would be organized according to the principle, 'from each according to ability, to each according to need', meaning that everyone would work towards the common good of the community to the best of their ability, and everyone would be able to access what they needed. They argued that capitalism had unlocked the secrets of production and so in a communist society, this could be put towards the benefit of the whole of society, not the pursuit of profit to the small minority.

Common humanity

Revolutionary Socialists believe that although human nature is naturally sociable, it can be moulded by circumstances, so, in a capitalist society, human nature takes on the attitudes needed to survive. **Marx and Engels** argued that humans were socialized from birth via the capitalist system into a set of ideas which benefited the capitalist elite and not the working class, known as 'false consciousness'. They argued that capitalism sets humans against each other, seeing others as rivals in a highly competitive world. This competition encourages humans to ignore their common humanity and social nature rather than embrace it. According to **Marx**, competition between people develops only a limited range of social characteristics and promotes selfishness and aggression.

Equality

Revolutionary socialists like **Marx and Engels** believe in absolute equality, brought about by the abolition of private property and common ownership of productive wealth. This is the most radical form of equality, which suggests that equality is at the heart of the way society is designed.

For **Marx and Engels**, equality was based on society being classless, and on how goods are produced not how they are distributed. Marx was clear that work would be life affirming as, even when engaged in more mundane tasks, the satisfaction of contributing towards the common good made the task enjoyable. As he said in The German Ideology (1845), 'society regulates the general production and thus makes it possible for me to do one thing today and another tomorrow, to hunt in the morning, fish in the afternoon, rear cattle in the evening, criticise after dinner ... without ever becoming hunter, fisherman, shepherd or critic'.

Workers' control

As discussed earlier, **Marx and Engels** referred to the unfair distribution of profit as 'surplus value'. Workers' control, is justified because workers are a significant part of any business. For **Marx and Engels,** giving workers control of production is the only way of avoiding alienation. **Marx and Engels** envisaged the abolition of private property, and the creation of a classless, communist society in place of capitalism, with property owned collectively and used for the benefit of all.

For Polish revolutionary **Rosa Luxemburg (1871–1919)**, it was essential that workers were involved in the creation and development of a truly socialist society. A socialist society was one where the workers, not bureaucrats made decisions about how society developed, as she said, 'The whole mass of the people must take part of it ... Otherwise, socialism will be decreed from behind a few official desks, by a dozen intellectuals.'

Evolutionary socialism

As the nineteenth century progressed, enthusiasm for revolution diminished. Capitalism had matured, wages and living standards started to rise and the working class had a range of institutions that protected their interests. Furthermore, there had been a gradual advance of the franchise to the working classes. The effect of these factors was to shift the attention of socialists away from revolution and persuade them that there was an alternative evolutionary, democratic, parliamentary road to socialism.

> ### Definition
>
> **Absolute equality:** Based on the communal production of wealth and abolition of class, in which all individuals would receive what they needed and would work to the best of their ability.
>
> **Alienation:** To be separated from one's essential nature; used by Marxists to describe the process whereby, under capitalism, labour is reduced to being a mere commodity.

!

Exam Tip –
Remember the term evolutionary socialism is not a strand but an umbrella term that describes the 'means' of the two socialist stands of Social Democracy and Third Way. It also includes **Webb** and her important idea of 'inevitability of gradualness'.

However, it is important to note that this was never accepted by revolutionary socialists. As **Luxemburg** argued, '*Those who declare themselves in favour of the method of legislative reform in place of and in contradiction to the conquest of political power and social revolution, do not choose a more tranquil, calmer and slower road to the same goal, but a different goal.*' In other words revolutionary socialists believe the evolutionary approach can never result in true socialism. For them, changing the path changed the goal.

The Fabian Society, formed in 1884, took up the cause of parliamentary socialism in the UK. Such ideas were developed more thoroughly by the German thinker Eduard Bernstein, whose *Evolutionary Socialism* (1898) developed ideas that paralleled the Fabian belief in gradualism. Bernstein believed that the establishment of a democratic state made the call for revolution redundant. He argued that the working class could use the ballot box to introduce socialism, which would therefore develop as an evolutionary outgrowth of capitalism.

Definition

Gradualism:
Progress brought about by gradual, piecemeal improvements, rather than dramatic upheaval; change through legal and peaceful reform.

Tensions within socialism over the role of the state	
AGREEMENT	**DISAGREEMENT**
✓ Evolutionary socialists like social democrats and the Third Way agree that the democratic, parliamentary process via the state, and not revolution, is the best way to help improve the conditions for the most vulnerable in society	✗ By far the biggest disagreement exists between Evolutionary socialists and Revolutionary Socialists over the role of the state
✓ Evolutionary socialists like social democrats and the Third Way agree that a welfare state is a key tool in helping to create a fairer and more just society	✗ Revolutionary socialists believe the state upholds and promotes capitalism whereas evolutionary socialists believe the state can be used to support socialist aims
✓ Evolutionary socialists like social democrats and the Third Way agree that the state can play a key role in ensuring that capitalism works in the interests of the most vulnerable	✗ Evolutionary socialists like social democrats and the Third Way disagree over the extent of the role of the state in ownership of industry. They also disagree over the extent of the welfare state

While there are many forms of evolutionary socialism, this chapter will focus, as the specification requires, on Social Democracy and the Third Way.

Social democracy

Spec key term

Revisionism:
Accepting that capitalism doesn't need to be abolished and that it can be tamed or humanized by socialist governments.

Social democracy took shape around the mid-twentieth century, as socialist parties adopted parliamentary strategies and revised their goals. In particular, they abandoned the goal of abolishing capitalism and sought instead to reform or 'humanize' it, known as revisionism. Social democracy supports a broad balance between market capitalism, on the one hand, and state intervention on the other, favouring a gradual approach to change. Being based on a compromise between the market and the state, social democracy is inherently vague. It is nevertheless associated with the following ideas:

1. Capitalism is the only reliable means of *generating* wealth, but it is morally defective at *distributing* wealth because of its tendency towards poverty and inequality.

2. The defects of the capitalist system can be rectified through economic and social intervention, the state being the defender of the public interest.

3. Social change can and should be brought about peacefully and constitutionally.

Collectivism

Social Democrats moved considerably away from the collectivist goals outlined by Revolutionary Socialists. **Crosland** argued that capitalism was no longer a system of class exploitation, and that a wholly collectivist society was no longer necessary to protect the interests of the working class. He argued that modern capitalism bore little resemblance to the nineteenth-century model that **Marx** had experienced. **Crosland** suggested that a new class of managers, experts and technocrats had replaced the old capitalist class and come to dominate all advanced industrial societies. The ownership of wealth had therefore become separated from its control. Whereas shareholders, who own businesses, were principally concerned with profit, the managers, who make the day-to-day business decisions, had a broader range of goals, including keeping their employees happy and upholding the public image of the company.

According to **Crosland**, the means of production need not be owned collectively, because wealth could be redistributed through a welfare state, financed by progressive taxation. It is worth noting that nationalized industries and a welfare state funded by progressive taxes are based on the notion of collectivism as they rely on the idea of a community where the wealthiest in society support the less wealthy.

Such developments implied that the fundamentalist goal of replacing capitalism with socialism had become irrelevant: if capitalism was no longer a system of class exploitation, the notion of replacing capitalism with socialism was outdated. **Crosland** thus reinterpreted socialism with the aim of social justice, rather than the politics of ownership. Wealth could be redistributed through a welfare state financed by progressive taxation. However, social democrats like **Crosland** recognized that economic growth played a crucial role in the achievement of socialist goals. A growing economy was essential to generate the tax revenues needed to finance generous social spending, and the wealthy would only be prepared to finance the needy if their own living standards were secured by economic growth

This rejection of a centralized planning model towards significant nationalization left social democracy with three more modest collectivist objectives:

> The *mixed economy*, a blend of public and private ownership. Nationalization is reserved for the 'commanding heights' of the economy.

> *Economic management*, seeing the need for capitalism to be regulated to deliver sustainable growth. After 1945, most social democratic parties were converted to Keynesianism as a way of controlling the economy and delivering full employment.

> The *welfare state*, viewing it as the principal means of reforming or humanizing capitalism. Its attraction is that it acts as a redistributive mechanism that helps to promote social justice and eradicate poverty.

Based on these goals, capitalism no longer needed to be abolished, only modified.

Common humanity

Social democrats have an optimistic view of human nature and agree that human nature is positive. Human fulfilment is linked to being part of a community and that humans are bound together with other humans in a spirit of cooperation.

As revisionists, they recognize the corrupting influence of capitalism on human nature; however, they argue it is not as extreme as Revolutionary Socialism suggests. Nonetheless, they agreed that inequality and class distinctions in society create inferiority and resentment which limits humans' ability to advance, restricting the development of their true humanity. Greater social equality encourages cooperation and a sense of community.

Equality

Social democrats, as revisionist socialists, believe that a more equal society can be created alongside the capitalist system. Consequently, their commitment to equality was limited in recognition of this. Social democrats like **Crosland** believe in *relative* social equality, which means reducing inequality rather than striving for an equal society. They seek to use the state to reduce inequality via the redistribution of wealth through the welfare state and a system of progressive taxation. The social democratic desire to tame capitalism rather than abolish it reflects an acceptance of a continuing role for economic incentives, and their aims are largely confined to the eradication of poverty, not the endorsement of equality of outcome.

Spec key term

Keynesian economics: The idea that government intervention can stabilize the economy and deliver full employment and price stability.

Spec key term

Revisionist: A form of socialism that can work alongside capitalism to improve society for the most vulnerable, rather than seek its abolition.

Definition

Progressive taxation: A system of taxation in which the rich pay a higher proportion of their income in tax than the poor.

Tensions within socialism over human nature	
AGREEMENT	**DISAGREEMENT**
✓ Socialists agree that human nature is malleable, shaped by the experiences and circumstances of life	✗ Revolutionary socialists and social democrats argue that competition develops only a limited range of social characteristics, whereas the Third Way argues that competition is inevitable in the modern, globalized world and humans should be as prepared as possible to compete
✓ Socialists have an optimistic, positive belief in what human nature can become with the right social relations	✗ Revolutionary socialists believe that humans are motivated by moral incentives, whereas the Third Way believes that humans are motivated by material and moral incentives
✓ Socialists understanding of human nature is of a people bound together with a common humanity	✗ Revolutionary socialists and social democrats believe that there is a common humanity amongst all people which motivates humans to support others, so all can live a decent life. However, the Third Way, through its belief in communitarianism, believes that humans should take greater responsibility for themselves
✓ Socialists believe the natural relationship between humans is one of cooperation rather than competition	
✓ Socialists believe that the individual is inseparable from society	

Class

Social democrats have tended to define social class in terms of income and status differences between the middle and working class. **Crosland** suggested that the Marxist notion of classes defined by ownership was out of date, as share ownership had widened, meaning that many different types of people had shares in companies. From this perspective, their concern is associated with the narrowing of divisions between the middle and working class, brought about through economic and social intervention. Social democrats therefore believed in social improvement and class harmony rather than social polarization and class war.

Workers' control

Social democrats have been prepared to accept levels of private property alongside some form of workers' control. Like many evolutionary socialists, they have been attracted to the state as an instrument of workers control, through which wealth can be collectively owned via the nationalization of key industries as part of a mixed economy. In the UK, for example, Clement Attlee, Prime Minister of the 1945–51 Labour government, nationalized the 'commanding heights' of the economy: major industries such as Electricity, coal, iron, steel, and transport. Through these industries, the government hoped to regulate the capitalist economy in the interest of the whole of society. Nonetheless, social democrats like **Crosland** have gradually distanced themselves from the 'politics of ownership', arguing that the ownership of wealth had become separated from its control, preferring instead to focus on the pursuit of a reducing inequality in society rather than extending workers' control or public ownership of industry.

Social democracy is based on an unstable compromise shown by a conflict between its commitment to economic efficiency and a more equal society. On the one hand, there was a pragmatic acceptance of capitalism, as the only reliable means of generating wealth – this meant that socialism became just an attempt to reform, not replace, capitalism. On the other hand, there is the idea that poverty and inequality should be reduced through the redistribution of wealth from rich to poor, while seeking to minimize class divisions. However, recession in the 1970s meant that it struggled to retain its relevance with the advance of neoliberalism and changing economic and social circumstances. The UK Labour Party lost four successive general elections between 1979 and 1992, trying to maintain a social democratic agenda in an ever-increasing individualist society.

Spec key term

Evolutionary socialism: A parliamentary route, which would deliver a long-term transformation in a gradual, piecemeal way through legal and peaceful means, via the state.

Definition

Nationalization: The extension of state or public ownership over private assets or industries, either individual enterprises or the entire economy.

Mixed economy: An economy in which there is a mixture of publicly owned and privately owned industries.

Tensions within socialism over society*

AGREEMENT	DISAGREEMENT
✓ All socialists believe that equality enables humans to work together cooperatively and harmoniously, encouraging social cohesion and fraternity	✗ Socialists disagree over the meaning of the word equality, with varying types of equality being promoted by different socialists
✓ Socialists believe in the importance of community. They believe people are defined by the social groups they belong to, so membership of a community or society offers fulfilment	✗ While all socialists recognize the importance of community, the variation is so great that it is almost impossible to see them in the same way
✓ All socialists agree that capitalism doesn't have the interests of the most vulnerable at heart	✗ Revolutionary socialists are fundamentalists, so they completely reject capitalism, whereas the Third Way and social democrats are revisionists and believe capitalism has some useful purpose

*There are many areas you can include in this answer, for example the role of class in society and the way society shapes human nature.

Third Way

Since the late 1980s, reformist socialist parties undertook a further bout of revisionism, sometimes termed 'neo-revisionism'. In so doing, they distanced themselves from the principles of Social Democracy. The ideological stance has been described in various ways, including the Third Way. **Anthony Giddens (1938–)** suggested that the Third Way was a rational response to a new political social and economic environment.

In the UK, it has been associated with Tony Blair, who was elected in 1997 as a New Labour, Third Way Prime Minister. The central theme of the Third Way is as an alternative to both capitalism and socialism. In its modern form, the Third Way represents an alternative to old-style social democracy and neoliberalism. As Blair explained '*It moves decisively beyond an old left preoccupied by state control, high taxation and producer interests, and a new right treating public investment, and often the very notions of 'society' and collective endeavour, as evils to be undone*.' Although the Third Way is perhaps inherently vague and subject to competing interpretations, certain characteristic themes can nevertheless be identified.

One of Blair's first acts after winning the leadership election in 1994 was to rewrite Clause 4 of the Labour Party constitution, originally written by **Webb** and the Fabians, which committed the Labour Party to the '*common ownership of the means of production, distribution and exchange*'. For the final new version of Clause Four, please see Figure 3.5.

This revised Clause 4 very much reflects the principles of community, rights and responsibilities, equality of opportunity and realization of potential, which at times reads as much about modern liberalism as it does socialism.

> **Definition**
>
> **Third Way:** The Third Way is a centrist position that broadly adopts – and attempts to reconcile – centre-left social policy and centre-right economic policy.

> **The Labour Party** is a democratic socialist party. It believes that by the strength of our common endeavour we achieve more than we achieve alone, so as to create for each of us the means to realise our true potential and for all of us a community in which power, wealth and opportunity are in the hands of the many not the few, where the rights we enjoy reflect the duties we owe, and where we live together, freely, in a spirit of solidarity, tolerance and respect.
>
> 🌹 **Labour**
>
> 4382_13(D) Printed and promoted by and on behalf of the Labour Party, One Brewer's Green, London SW1H ORH.

Figure 3.5 **The Labour Party's revised Clause 4, 1994.**

Workers' control

The Third Way moved away from the evolutionary socialist tradition of nationalization, arguing instead that capitalism had many positive traits, and it was better to concentrate on supporting the most vulnerable in society from the wealth capitalism creates, rather than stifling its ability to create economic growth. **Giddens** argued for a '*new mixed economy*' with an acceptance of the need for private partnerships with public services, and of consumer-friendly, efficient public services. This indicated that socialism, at least in the form of top-down state intervention, was dead. Instead there was a general acceptance that decisions were made by the market over the state, and the adoption of a pro-business and pro-enterprise stance, meant that the Third Way built on, rather than reversed, the neoliberal revolution of the 1980s and 1990s. It emphasized the need for British industry to be able to compete in a globalized world, and that business had a responsibility towards society.

Collectivism

Definition

Communitarianism: The belief that a person is formed through their community, and thus owes them respect and consideration. It is grounded in an acknowledgement of reciprocal rights and responsibilities.

The Third Way put the idea of 'community' at the heart of their values, recognizing that humans are sociable. However, the Third Way's understanding of community suggests that people have an obligation to each other and the communities they live in, but unlike other strands of socialism, this is not connected to the idea of equality. The Third Way's definition of community is that people, not the state, have a responsibility to create a fair and decent community. They argued that people's rights and responsibilities in society are bound together and must be balanced against each other; this was known as **communitarianism**.

The cornerstone of communitarianism is that rights and responsibilities are intrinsically bound together: all rights must be balanced against responsibilities, and vice versa. This incorporated the idea of all people as stakeholders in their society. Hence, there is a responsibility on businesses, workers, institutions and government to rejuvenate society. The Third Way seeks to end the influence of individualism in society and emphasize that everyone must contribute. This highlights the Third Way's emphasis on community as a moral responsibility. Thus even though the Third Way accepts many of the economic theories of neoliberalism, it firmly rejects the philosophical basis of individualism.

Tensions within socialism over the economy

AGREEMENT	DISAGREEMENT
✓ All socialists believe that the economy should work in the interests of all in society and that equality enables humans to work together cooperatively and harmoniously, encouraging social cohesion and fraternity	✗ Revolutionary socialists believe that capitalism is fundamentally flawed and seeks its abolition. Social democrats also think it is flawed. Only the Third Way sees capitalism as positive
✓ Revisionist socialists Social Democrats and the Third Way accept that capitalism can do some good for society and therefore agree over capitalism as a stable economic system	✗ Revolutionary socialists disagree with social democrats and the Third Way over the welfare state, arguing that this helps to reinforce the idea that capitalism can help the working class, which revolutionary socialists reject
✓ Evolutionary socialists agree that the welfare state is essential in a capitalist economy	✗ Socialists disagree over the meaning of the word equality, with varying types of equality being promoted by different socialists

Class

The Third Way tends to adopt a consensus view of society, it rejects the idea that society is composed of two classes that are in conflict. This is evident in their tendency to highlight ties that bind all members of society together, and thus to ignore class differences.

Hence the Third Way rejects class-based analysis completely, preferring to focus on supporting the most vulnerable in society and refusing to recognize capitalism as a system of class exploitation. **Giddens** preferred a consensual, community model of society, working on the ties that bind people together rather than seeing it as consisting of two opposing classes in conflict. A faith in consensus and social harmony is also reflected in the values of the Third Way, which argue that you shouldn't have to choose between an efficient economy and a fair one. The Third Way thus endorses enterprise and fairness, opportunity and security, self-reliance and interdependence. While this may demonstrate that the Third Way goes 'beyond left and right', as **Giddens** argued, it also leaves it open to the criticism that it is at best ambiguous and at worst simply incoherent.

Tensions within socialism over class	
AGREEMENT	**DISAGREEMENT**
✓ Socialism uses class as a way to understand and analyse society	✗ Socialists disagree over the significance of class in a modern capitalist society
✓ Most socialists have traditionally viewed social class as the deepest and most politically significant division in a capitalist society	✗ Revolutionary socialists believe class is based on ownership and non-ownership of industry, whereas other socialists take a more nuanced approach to defining class
✓ Most socialists focus on the working class and are concerned with its political struggle and liberation	✗ Revolutionary socialism and social democrats still recognize the significance of class in society, whereas the Third Way has moved away from class-based analysis

Equality

The Third Way shifted the boundaries on what equality means, moving away the greater social equality endorsed by Social Democrats to social justice and equality of opportunity, with a focus on social inclusion. This is the idea that all institutions must make sure that even the poorest and traditionally 'excluded' members of society are encouraged to participate. Equality of outcome was less important than equality of opportunity, which enables individuals to realize their potential.

The Third Way has been more supportive of capitalism and rejected the Social Democratic model of wealth redistribution via the state. Instead they support encouraging individual's to support themselves by increasing their skills and capacities, rather than relying on the state. Third-way proposals for welfare reform also typically reject both the neoliberal emphasis on 'standing on your own two feet' and the social-democratic belief in 'cradle to grave' welfare. Instead, welfare should be targeted at the socially excluded and should help people to help themselves, 'genuinely providing people with a hand up not a hand out', as Blair famously described his vision of a welfare state. This aimed to widen access to work, school and university, for example, supporting the belief that this the best way out of poverty. **Giddens** redefined 'equality as inclusion' and with it a far greater emphasis on providing opportunities for citizens to improve themselves with education rather than welfare, as it promotes employability and opportunities.

> **Definition**
>
> **Social inclusion:** The idea that opportunities must be available to all in society, particularly those who have traditionally felt excluded from certain aspects of society.

Tensions within socialism over equality	
AGREEMENT	**DISAGREEMENT**
✓ All socialists believe that equality enables humans to work together cooperatively and harmoniously, encouraging social cohesion and fraternity	✗ Socialists disagree over the meaning of the word equality, with varying types of equality being promoted by different socialists
✓ Socialists tend to measure equality by outcome seeking a more equal society	✗ Revolutionary socialists believe in absolute equality which can only be achieved in a classless, stateless society, whereas evolutionary socialists believe in equality within a capitalist economy
✓ Socialists recognize that equality underpins community and cooperation and that equal outcomes strengthen community	✗ Also, there is disagreement between social democrats who believe in reducing inequality in society and the Third Way who has redefined its commitment to equality as tackling poverty

Common humanity

For third-way socialists like **Giddens**, humans share a common responsibility towards humanity by reinforcing the importance of community and acknowledge a sense of responsibility towards others. They recognize that humans can be motivated by both material and moral incentives and argue for a balance of some kind between them. The individual can be empowered by the opportunities presented by the free market. Equally, third-way socialists are passionate advocates of community, believing that humans are not unconnected atoms, but part of a community with responsibility towards each other.

Table 3.3 Tensions within socialism

	Revolutionary socialism	Social democracy	Third way
Collectivism	'From each according to ability to each according to need'	Nationalize the 'commanding heights' of the economy	Socialism can be adapted and delivered via the current capitalist system
Common humanity	Humans are naturally sociable, identifying themselves as part of a group but their behaviour is socially determined	Human nature has a predisposition for a fair and just society	Humans balance their wish for a fair and just society against individual need
Equality	Absolute equality	Greater social and economic equality	Social justice/equality of opportunity
Social class	Class conflict is at the core of society	Break down the barriers between classes to minimize distinctions	Class is no longer relevant in modern society
Workers' control	Means of production are placed in the hands of the workers	More important to focus on control and regulation of capitalism than ownership	Ownership should remain as it is. State should not seek to own

3. Socialism key thinkers

Key thinkers are an important part of understanding each ideology. The exam board has specified five key thinkers per ideology and TWO must be included in an answer to avoid a cap (please check Exam Focus chapter (Chapter 9) for lots more discussion of key thinkers). Although key thinkers (and other thinkers) have been discussed throughout the chapter, here we look at each one in detail.

Karl Marx (1818–83) and Friedrich Engels (1820–95)

Karl Marx was a German philosopher, economist and life-long revolutionary. Alongside Friedrich Engels, they wrote an extensive critique of capitalism that highlighted systemic inequality and fundamental instability. Their vast works include *The Communist Manifesto* (1848) and the three-volume *Das Kapital* (1867, 1885 and 1894)

Nastasic/Getty

Historical materialism

Marx believes that economic factors are the driving force behind human history, which is known as historical materialism. According to this view, producing enough to survive is the first priority, and is at the heart of all human activity. Marx argued that the development of human society, through a series of historical stages, culminating in communism, is a necessary and inevitable process.

Historical determinism

Marxism is also deterministic and seeks to explain the 'laws of development of human history'. Marx argued that human progress towards a classless communist society is inevitable. This is known as historical determinism. Almost all the stages prior to communism have classes, and class conflict provides the central driving force for change and progress, hence the first sentence of *The Communist Manifesto*: '*the history of all hitherto (previous) existing societies is the history of the class struggle*'.

ZU_09/Getty

Human nature is socially determined

Marx, like many socialists, believed that human nature was not fixed, but the product of specific economic and social systems. '*It is not the consciousness of men that determines their existence, but on the contrary, it is their social existence which determines their consciousness.*' Therefore, in a capitalist society, individuals become competitive, acquisitive and aggressive, but they are equally capable of being unselfish and cooperative in an appropriate social system. Thus, for Marx the values associated with a capitalist society are a biased and distorted set of ideas which support the interests of the ruling class.

Alienation

Marx used the term 'alienation' to describe the situation of the worker in capitalist society who is not producing for himself but for someone else under conditions of exploitation. The worker is therefore alienated from and dissatisfied with their work as they lack control over the processes, and gain no satisfaction from it. Marx suggested that in the process of production the worker is exploited by their employer, and is in constant competition with other workers. They are therefore also alienated from their fellow workers, and from society.

Revolution

Marx supported a revolution because he believed that it was impossible to reform capitalism via the state. Marx argued that the bourgeoise state works hard to ensure that everyone in society, including the proletariat, buys in to the values that capitalism requires, even though these values are not in the interest of the working classes. He argued that 'false consciousness' will stop the working class from understanding that the values of socialism are in their interests, and capitalist ones are not.

Beatrice Webb (1858–1943)

Hulton Archive/Stringer/Getty

The Fabian Society, formed in 1884, took up the cause of parliamentary socialism in the UK. The Fabians, led by Beatrice Webb and Sidney Webb (1859–1947), included noted intellectuals such as George Bernard Shaw and H.G. Wells. In their view, socialism would develop naturally and peacefully out of liberal capitalism.

Webb understood that political action required the formation of a socialist party, which would compete for power against established parliamentary parties and they were actively involved in the formation of the UK Labour Party and helped to write its 1918 constitution. Webb employed the tactic of 'permeation', which was the idea of converting people of power and influence, irrespective of their political affiliations, to the policies of socialism.

The arrival of democracy in the late nineteenth and early twentieth centuries caused a wave of optimism to spread throughout the socialist movement, reflected in the Fabian notion of 'the inevitability of gradualness'. Evolutionary socialists like Webb highlighted the logic of the democratic process itself. Their optimism was founded on a number of assumptions:

1. The progressive extension of the franchise would eventually lead to the establishment of universal adult suffrage, and therefore of political equality.

2. Political equality would work in the interests of the majority; that is, those who decide the outcome of elections. Socialists thus believed that political democracy would invest power in the working class.

3. Socialism was thought to be the natural 'home' of the working class. The electoral success of socialist parties would therefore be guaranteed by the numerical strength of the working class.

4. Once in power, socialist parties would be able to carry out a fundamental transformation of society through social reform. In this way, political democracy not only opened up the possibility of achieving socialism peacefully, it made this process inevitable.

The expansion of the state to deliver socialism

Webb was a strong critic of the Poor Law system in Britain

She produced a report in 1909 which disagreed with the Royal Commission report on both the facts of and the solution to poverty and outlined the need for a coordinated provision of welfare, including education, healthcare, pensions and work. She argued that in order to 'secure a national minimum of civilised life open to all alike, of both sexes and all classes' they needed 'sufficient nourishment and training when young, a living wage when able-bodied, treatment when sick, and modest but secure livelihood when disabled or aged'. A young William Beveridge famously produced his own report along similar lines in 1942, which formed the basis of the Attlee reforms of 1945.

Rosa Luxemburg (1871–1919)

A Polish-born socialist and exponent of revolutionary Marxism, Luxemburg advanced the first Marxist critique of the Bolshevik revolution. She condemned Lenin's conception of a tightly centralized vanguard party as an attempt to exert political control over the working class. Luxemburg was arrested and murdered during the Spartacist uprising in Berlin.

Mass strike

For Luxemburg, the mass strike was a revolutionary idea and the most important tool in the struggle for a worker's revolt. In *Dialectic of Spontaneity and Organisation* (1904), she argued that political organization would develop naturally from within, as workers found their voice and power by participating in strikes. She argued that there would be many strikes, of varying success, until a final mass strike which would bring down capitalism. She argued, '*Tomorrow the revolution will rise up again, clashing its weapons, and to your horror it will proclaim with trumpets blazing: I was, I am, I shall be!*' Luxemburg argued that the mass strike would radicalize workers and drive the revolution forward and that revolution was an inevitable result of the realities of the capitalist economic model.

Universal History Archive/Contributor/Getty

In contrast to Lenin, she rejected the need for a tight party structure, believing that organization would emerge naturally from the struggle. Where Lenin argued that the Bolshevik Party must spearhead the revolution on behalf of the workers, she believed that leaders should only represent the consciousness of workers ambitions and not direct or agitate them to act. She argued, '*The modern proletarian class does not carry out its struggle according to a plan set out in some book or theory; the modern workers' struggle is a part of history, a part of social progress ... we learn how we must fight.*' She correctly foresaw that in giving the role of the 'vanguard' to the Bolshevik party, Lenin was creating the recipe for dictatorship and '*brutalisation of public life*'.

Evolutionary socialism and revisionism

Luxemburg rejected Eduard Bernstein's revisionism and in *Reform or Revolution* (1899), she defended Marxism and the necessity of revolution, arguing that Parliament was nothing more than a bourgeois sham. While Luxemburg was an advocate of a socialist democracy, this is not to be confused with the revisionism of Bernstein or other Evolutionary socialists. She explained, '*Socialist democracy begins simultaneously with the beginnings of the destruction of class rule and of the construction of socialism*', meaning that in her vision of democracy, society should be organized by all the people, not a ruling elite.

Luxemburg was concerned, very early on, with the undemocratic nature of the ruling Bolshevik Party. She was clear that a democratic society was essential as part of the creation of a socialist society, arguing that this society should enable real freedoms for all.

Anthony Crosland (1918–77)

A British Labour politician and social theorist, Crosland was a leading exponent of revisionist Social Democracy. In *The Future of Socialism* (1956), he dismissed Marxism on the grounds that capitalism had fundamentally reformed. This became a seminal work for the moderate British left. Crosland was an intellectual but also a Cabinet minister who believed that the Labour Party had to apply its values to a changing world to win elections and be capable of serving in government.

Dennis Oulds/Stringer/Getty

Revisionism

Labour revisionism was a powerful ideological tendency within the party in the 1950s and 1960s. Crosland's rejection of Marxism was based on his belief that the Marxist analysis of ownership in capitalism was redundant. Ownership of industry was spread more widely now with the creation of companies who had many shareholders. As such, Crosland argued that capitalism could be humanized, and the goal was to redevelop socialist principles and bring the Labour Party's policies up to date.

He also argued that socialism should also concern itself with the quality of people's lives, beyond their material circumstances, helping and encouraging people to find self-fulfilment. However, he wanted to shed Labour of its image of 'the state knows best' approach. Crosland believed that Labour couldn't win as a narrow 'class-based, socialist party' but needed the support of the centre, non-partisan voters who may switch their vote from Labour to Conservative and vice versa. Representing the constituency of Grimsby, Crosland believed that Labour had to accept that the world had moved on and to stop mourning a working class which no longer existed in the same way. He thought that Labour should recognize that the party's liberal social values were out of sync with working-class communities who were comfortable with the sense of belonging and solidarity and pride in their country.

Humanized capitalism

Crosland's revisionism rejected the view that socialism should be identified with the ownership of industry. Continuous nationalization was not his central aim. Instead, Crosland supported a diverse and radical set of means to advance socialist goals. These included a strengthened welfare state, Keynesian economics, the wider use of progressive taxation and expanded social ownership. However, he was frustrated by the dominance of the Webbs ideas within the Labour Party, and challenged their centralizing, 'top-down', bureaucratic socialism. He sought to replace it with a more modern vision of an ideal society.

Crosland defined socialism in terms of ethical goals, notably equality, personal liberty, social welfare and social justice, rather than class antagonism and common ownership. According to Crosland, rhetoric of destroying or overthrowing the rich elite should be downplayed in favour of policies of progressive taxation, more widespread educational opportunity and expanded social services, alongside the need for a market-based mixed economy with a central role for capitalism and entrepreneurship. He argued that the welfare state should equip people with the skills they needed to flourish.

Anthony Giddens (1938–)

A British academic and social theorist, Giddens had a strong impact on the development of a new social democratic agenda in the UK and elsewhere and was sometimes referred to as 'Tony Blair's guru'. In works such as *Beyond Left and Right* (1994) and *The Third Way* (1998), he examined the traditional forms of both socialism and conservatism in terms of the emergence of globalization and market economics.

Third Way and the radical centre

Giddens argued that there was a Third Way between traditional left and right politics and that it was possible to be radical from the centre of politics. Giddens discarded the possibility of a single, comprehensive, all-embracing ideology. Instead, he advocated smaller programmes where people could feel the impact of them in their home, workplace or local community. According to Giddens: '*The overall aim of Third Way politics should be to help citizens pilot their way through the major revolutions of our time: globalisation, transformations in personal life and our relationship to nature.*'

Placing a particular emphasis on the impact of globalization, Giddens argued that modern societies had become so complex that they must be organized substantially through the market and global networks, rather than by the state. He insisted that such developments opened new opportunities for progressive politics.

New mixed economy

A key part of Giddens' Third Way was an emphasis on a new mixed economy and an acceptance of the need for public-private partnerships, and consumer-friendly public services. He did not see this as succumbing to neoliberalism (as his critics suggested), but as going beyond both the free-market attitudes of neoliberalism and the top-down statism of social democracy. Globalization meant it was impossible for economic decisions in one country to be made without due regard to the rest of the world, making it possible, even necessary, to spread progressive ideas beyond the UK. Giddens argued that '*the regulation of financial markets is the single most pressing issue in the world economy*' and that the '*global commitment to free trade depends upon effective regulation rather than dispenses with the need for it*'.

Communitarianism and inclusion

Giddens also redefined equality as the 'equality as inclusion' putting greater emphasis on providing opportunities for citizens to improve themselves by the government's investment in them via education and training rather than the pursuit of equality of outcome. He believed it was important to commit to the use of public resources to build the national stock of **human capital** which would increase competitiveness in the economy and improve economic performance.

Related to this is the idea that rights come with responsibilities to society, otherwise known as communitarianism. Giddens argued that '*the theme of community is fundamental to the new politics*', emphasizing the need for a more active and engaged community which would take greater responsibility for itself. This is the idea of 'stakeholding' where everyone is invested in their community and society.

> **Definition**
>
> **Human capital:** This consists of the knowledge and skills that people invest in and accumulate throughout their lives, enabling them to realize their potential as productive members of society.

4. How to apply knowledge to socialism answers

In this section of the chapter, we are going to be looking at how to apply the information and ideas of the book so far to areas of agreement and disagreement within socialism. These areas will help you to understand how to answer 24-mark essays on socialism.

Tensions within socialism over the role of the state

Worked example

Paragraph One – Agreement within socialism

- ✓ Evolutionary socialists like social democrats and the Third Way agree that the democratic, parliamentary process via the state, and not revolution, is the best way to help improve the conditions for the most vulnerable in society **(Webb)**
- ✓ Evolutionary socialists agree that a welfare state is a key tool in helping to create a fairer and more just society **(Crosland)**
- ✓ Both social democrats and the Third Way agree that the right kind of state can drive change and play a key role in ensuring that capitalism works in the interests of the most vulnerable

Paragraph Two – Disagreement within socialism

- ✗ Social democrats and third-way socialists disagree on the extent of the role of the state
- ✗ Social democrats **(Crosland)** support the nationalization of the 'commanding heights', whereas the Third Way accepted the privatization agenda of neoliberalism **(Giddens)**
- ✗ Social democrats support increased taxation for the rich and a 'cradle to grave', welfare system, whereas the Third Way does not seek punitive tax bands and prefers a welfare system that encourages work

Paragraph Three – Disagreement within socialism

- ✓ Revolutionary socialists disagree with both social democrats and third-way socialists over the state, arguing that in a truly communist society, the state will 'wither away'
- ✓ Revolutionary socialists **(Marx and Engels)** argue that the state is not neutral and is part of the superstructure, controlled by the economic base, rejecting Webb's 'inevitability of gradualness'
- ✓ Revolutionary socialists reject the idea that socialism can be achieved via the state in a top-down manner arguing that the working class must be involved in the process of creating a socialist society **(Luxemburg)**

Tensions within socialism over society

Worked example

Thematic approach

Paragraph One – Theme – Equality

- ✓ All socialists believe that an equal society enables humans to work together cooperatively and harmoniously, encouraging social cohesion and fraternity
- ✗ However, socialists disagree over what an equal society looks like, with varying types of equality being promoted by different socialists
- ✗ While revolutionary socialists believe in absolute equality **(Marx and Engels)**, social democrats believe in reducing inequality in society and the Third Way have redefined their commitment to equality in terms of opportunity or inclusion

Continued...

Paragraph Two – Theme – Community

✓ All socialists recognize the importance of community in society, believing people are defined by the social groups they belong to

✗ However, while all socialists recognize the importance of community, the variation is so great that it is almost impossible to see them in the same way

✗ Revolutionary socialists believe that society needs to be fully organized to facilitate communal living and collectivism, whereas social democrats **(Crosland)** seek to support community via redistributive taxes, the welfare state and nationalized industries. The Third Way have focused on communitarianism in society suggesting that rights come with responsibilities **(Giddens)**

Paragraph Three – Theme – Capitalism

✓ All socialists agree that a capitalist society doesn't have the interests of the most vulnerable at heart

✗ However, the range of views towards capitalism is too great to be seen as an area of agreement.

✗ Revolutionary socialists are fundamentalists, so completely reject a capitalist society **(Luxemburg)**, whereas the Third Way and social democrats are revisionists and believe capitalism serves some useful purposes in society

Tensions within socialism over human nature

Worked example

Paragraph One – Agreement within socialism

✓ Socialists have an optimistic, positive belief in human nature, and believe that humans have huge capacities to progress

✓ They all argue that the natural relationship between humans is one of cooperation rather than competition

✓ Socialists also recognize that human nature is malleable, shaped by the experiences and circumstances of life **(Marx and Engels)**

Paragraph Two – Agreement within socialism

✓ Socialist understanding of human nature is of people bound together with a common humanity

✓ Most socialists believe that the individual is inseparable from society

✓ Human beings can only be understood, and understand themselves, through the social groups to which they belong

Paragraph Three – Disagreement within socialism

✗ Revolutionary socialists and social democrats argue that competition develops only a limited range of social characteristics, whereas the Third Way argue that competition is inevitable in the modern, globalized world and humans should be able to compete

✗ Revolutionary socialists believe that human beings are motivated by moral incentives, whereas the Third Way believes that humans are motivated by economic and moral incentives **(Giddens)**

✗ Revolutionary socialists and Social Democrats believe that there is a common humanity amongst all people which motivates humans to support each other. However, the Third Way's belief in communitarianism, indicates that humans should take greater responsibility for themselves **(Giddens)**

Tensions within socialism over the economy

Worked example

Thematic approach

Paragraph One – Theme – Attitude towards capitalism

✓ All socialists believe that the economy should work in the interests of all in society and revisionist socialists like Third Way and social democrats accept that capitalism can do some good for society

✗ However, revisionist socialists disagree on how positive capitalism is. Social democracy sees it as flawed, likely to produce poverty and inequality so must be humanized **(Crosland)** The Third Way sees capitalism as a tool to set the individual free and build a competitive state to deliver social inclusion **(Giddens)**

✗ Fundamentalist socialists, like Marx and Engels, totally disagree with revisionist socialists and believe that capitalism is fundamentally flawed and seek its abolition **(Marx and Engels)**

Paragraph Two – Theme – Role of the state in the economy

✓ Evolutionary socialists like Third Way and social democrats believe that the welfare state is essential in a capitalist economy **(Webb)**

✗ However, there is disagreement between social democrats and the Third Way about the type of welfare they want. Social democrats have been committed to 'cradle to grave' welfare, whereas the Third Way supports 'welfare to work' which is targeted rather than universal welfare

✗ However, revolutionary socialists reject the idea of a state. They argue that the state is a tool of the bourgeoisie and cannot be used to support or improve the lives of the working classes **(Luxemburg)**

Paragraph Three – Theme – Equality

✓ All socialists believe that equality can be improved through the economy

✗ However, socialists disagree over what equality looks like, with varying types of equality being promoted by different socialists, hence a variety of different economic structures are recommended

✗ While revolutionary socialists believe in absolute equality, social democrats believe in reducing inequality and the Third Way has redefined its commitment to equality in terms of opportunity or inclusion

Visit our companion website at https://bloomsbury.pub/essentials-of-political-ideas-2e for more worked examples.

Chapter Summary

- Socialism is a diverse ideology with many different views within it.
- Despite this there are a number of principles and values which they share in common.
- There is a fundamental conflict between revolutionary and evolutionary socialism over means and fundamentalist and revisionist socialists over ends.
- There are also significant areas of disagreement between social democrats and the Third Way, despite both being evolutionary and revisionist.

Exam Style Questions

1. To what extent do socialists agree over the state?
2. To what extent do socialists agree over society?
3. To what extent do socialists have conflicting views over how the economy should operate?
4. To what extent is there agreement within socialism over human nature?
5. To what extent is socialism a coherent ideology?
6. To what extent are different socialists committed to equality?
7. To what extent do all socialists support common ownership?

Further Resources

Adams, I. *Political Ideology Today* (2001). Chapter 5, 'Varieties of Socialism' and Chapter 7, 'Marxism' are a straightforward read for A-Level students and explore socialist ideas.

Edwards, A. and Townshend, J. *Interpreting Modern Philosophy from Machiavelli to Marx* (2002). Chapter 10, 'Marx' is useful for students looking for a deeper insight into this key thinker.

Honneth, A. *The Idea of Socialism: Towards a Renewal* (2016). An ambitious but important work that attempts to reconcile socialist thought with modern post-industrial societies.

Kelly, P. et al. *The Politics Book* (2013). A clearly written, student-friendly book which covers many of the thinkers discussed in this chapter.

Lamb, P. *Socialism* (2019). A clear and concise introduction to socialism, both as a philosophical and as an ideological and political platform.

Leach, R. *Political Ideology in Britain* (2015). Chapter 4, 'Socialism, Social Democracy and Labour' is excellent and goes through the development of socialist ideas and values.

McLellan, D. *Marxism after Marx* (2007). An authoritative and comprehensive account of twentieth-century Marxism and more recent developments that also contains useful biographical information.

Moschonas, G. *In the Name of Social Democracy – The Great Transformation: 1945 to the Present* (2002). An impressive and thorough account of the nature, history and impact of social democracy that focuses on the emergence of 'new social democracy'.

Socialist Appeal, www.socialist.net. A long-running British Marxist newspaper that has an extensive archive (and YouTube channel) of videos, writing and guides designed to explain all aspects of socialist and Marxist theory.

Vincent, R. *Modern Political Ideologies* (1995). Chapter 4, 'Socialism' can be used to stretch and extend a student's knowledge of the content covered in this chapter.

What is the Third Way? http://news.bbc.co.uk/1/hi/458626.stm. An in-depth analysis of Third Way ideas and policies.

4 ANARCHISM

Historical overview

The word anarchy means 'without rule' and has been in use since the French Revolution, employed in a negative sense to imply a breakdown of civilized order. The first classic statement of anarchist principles was produced by English journalist William Godwin in *Enquiry Concerning Political Justice* (1793), although Godwin never described himself as an anarchist. It was not until the French politician **Pierre-Joseph Proudhon (1809–65)** proudly declared 'I am an anarchist' in his book *What Is Property?* (1840), that the word was clearly associated with a systematic set of political ideas. At this time, anarchists sought mass support among the landless peasants of Russia and southern Europe and, more successfully, through anarcho-syndicalism among the industrial working class.

Syndicalism helped to make anarchism a mass movement in the early twentieth century, with powerful unions in France, Spain and Latin America being dominated by anarchists. Syndicalist ideas also influenced the Mexican Revolution led by Emiliano Zapata.

An anarchist revival came with the emergence of the New Left in the 1960s and the New Right in the 1970s. The New Left endorsed an activist style of politics based on popular protest and direct action and the New Right revived interest in libertarian ideas, expressed most radically through anarcho-capitalism. Anarchism gained prominence during the upsurge in anti-capitalist protests in the UK and Europe from the late 1990s onwards. This was through May Day anti-capitalist protests after the global financial crisis, including those organized by the Occupy movement and Reclaim the Streets.

Key Questions

- » How did anarchism originate?
- » What are the main principles that are central to anarchism?
- » What are the key strands of anarchism?
- » What are the areas of similarity and difference within anarchism?

Specification Checklist

1. Anarchism: core ideas and principles:

- » Rejection of the state
- » Liberty
- » Anarchy is order
- » Economic freedom
- » Utopian

2. Differing views and tensions within anarchism:

- » Collectivist anarchism
  - » Anarcho-communism
  - » Mutualism
  - » Anarcho-syndicalism
- » Individualist anarchism
  - » Egoism
  - » Anarcho-capitalism

3. Anarchism thinkers and their ideas:

- » Max Stirner (1806–56)
- » Pierre-Joseph Proudhon (1809–65)
- » Mikhail Bakunin (1814–76)
- » Peter Kropotkin (1842–1921)
- » Emma Goldman (1869–1940)

Introduction to anarchism and its strands

Anarchist ideology is defined by the central belief that political authority in all its forms, especially the form of the state, is evil and unnecessary. Anarchists see the state as evil because it is a sovereign, compulsory and coercive authority and goes against the principles of freedom and equality. Anarchists also believe that modern democracy is a sham, which seeks to promote the idea that the people are in control when, in fact, the choice is very limited. As Emma Goldman argued, "if voting could change anything they would make it illegal". Central to anarchism is the belief that people can manage their affairs without the need for hierarchies or systems of rewards and punishments.

Anarchism draws from two different ideological traditions resulting in rival individualist and collectivist forms. While both accept the goal of statelessness, they advance very different models of the future anarchist society.

Collectivist anarchism

Collectivist anarchism argues for a stateless society, where common ownership nurtures the rational, sociable and cooperative elements of human nature. Russian anarchist **Peter Kropotkin (1842–1921)** explains that the existing system of private ownership, for the sake of profits, works against the principles of justice and usefulness.

Under the banner of collectivist anarchism we consider:

» Anarcho-communism – The view that pure stateless communism is the the best way to realize the anarchist principles of liberty, economic freedom and natural order. As part of this, anarcho-communism advocates the abolition of private property.

» Mutualism – Mutualism appears to bridge the gap between collectivist and individualist anarchism, primarily because it does not reject all forms of private property, and supports the maintenance of 'possessions', which it distinguishes from private property.

» Anarcho-syndicalism – A form of revolutionary trade unionism which draws on the concept of class war, building on Bakunin's strategy of propaganda by the deed. In this strand, the trade-union movement is the revolutionary agent of change.

Individualist anarchism

Individualist anarchism sees society as a collection of separate individuals whose autonomy must not be restricted in any way. The state, with its coercive powers of taxation, conscription and law, is totally incompatible with this.

Under the banner of individualist anarchism we consider:

» Egoism: this advocates that the individual should act in any way they choose, and that there should be no restriction on individuality, and that there is no such thing as morality.

» Anarcho-capitalism: this is a pure, stateless, form of free-market capitalism which argues that current capitalism has mutated into a highly exploitative economic system because of the interference of government.

1. Anarchism: core ideas and principles

Rejection of the state

This can be included when discussing the anarchist view of the state, society, the economy and human nature.

The defining feature of anarchism is its opposition to hierarchy or domination, with the state being seen as the embodiment of this. Anarchists seek a stateless society in which free individuals manage their affairs by voluntary agreement, without force.

In *Encyclopédie anarchiste* (published between 1925 and 1934), French anarchist Sébastien Faure defined anarchism as '*the negation of the principle of Authority*'. The anarchist case against authority is simple: authority is an offence against the principle of liberty. Authority, based on the alleged right of one person to influence the behaviour of others, enslaves, oppresses and limits human life. It damages and corrupts both those who are *subject* to authority and those who are *in* authority. Since humans are free, to be subject to authority means to have one's essential nature suppressed and to become dependent on those above. To be in a position of authority is to acquire an appetite for prestige, control and domination where, according to the US anarchist and social critic Paul Goodman (1911–72), '*many are ruthless and most live in fear*' (1977). Russian anarchist **Emma Goldman (1869–1940)** is well known for her critique of the state as a '*cold monster*' which relies on the threat of violence to control people. She defined anarchism as '*the theory that all forms of government rest on violence, and are therefore wrong and harmful, as well as unnecessary*'.

In practice, anarchism's criticism of authority focuses on *political* authority, especially when it is backed up by the power of the modern state. Anarchism is defined by its radical rejection of state power. The essence of this anarchist critique of law and government is conveyed by **Pierre-Joseph Proudhon's** famous denunciation in 1851: '*To be governed is to be watched over, inspected, spied on, directed, legislated, regimented, closed in, indoctrinated, preached at, controlled, assessed, evaluated, censored, commanded; all by creatures that have neither the right, nor the wisdom, nor the virtue.*'

According to **Proudhon**, the state fulfils four criteria, with a fifth added later by US anarchist Randolph Bourne (1886–1918):

1. It is a **sovereign** body that exercises supreme authority over all individuals living within a defined geographical area. Anarchists emphasize that the state authority is absolute: law can restrict public behaviour, limit political activity, regulate economic life, interfere with private morality and so on.

2. The authority of the state is also **compulsory**. Anarchists reject the liberal notion that the state arises from voluntary agreement, through a 'social contract', and argue instead that individuals are subject to state authority by being born into it.

3. Furthermore, the state is a **coercive** body, whose laws must be obeyed because they are backed up by the threat of punishment. For **Goldman**, state was symbolized by '*the club, the gun, the handcuff, or the prison*' and can deprive people of their property, their liberty and, ultimately, their lives.

4. The state is also **exploitative**, in that it robs individuals of their property through taxation, once again backed up by law and the threat of punishment. Anarchists often argue that the state acts in alliance with the wealthy and privileged to oppress the poor and weak.

5. Finally, the state is **destructive**. This criteria was added by US anarchist Randolph Bourne, who suggested that '*War is the health of the state*' (1977). Individuals are required to fight, kill and die in wars that are triggered by the pursuit of territory, for national glory.

Although the state has been anarchist's main concern, the same criticisms apply to any other form of compulsory authority, especially the church in the nineteenth century. For anarchists, religion is problematic as it has often been seen as the ultimate source of authority. God represents the notion of a 'supreme being' who commands ultimate and unquestionable authority. For anarchists such as **Proudhon** and Russian anarcho-syndicalist **Mikhail Bakunin (1814–76)**, anarchist political philosophy had to reject Christianity, because only then could humans be regarded as free. Moreover, anarchists have suspected that religious and political authority usually work hand in hand. **Bakunin** proclaimed that '*the abolition of the Church and the State must be the first and indispensable condition of the true liberation of society*'. Anarchists see religion as spreading obedience and submission to spiritual leaders and earthly rulers. Earthly rulers have often looked to religion to legitimize their power, most obviously in the doctrine of the divine right of kings.

Moreover, religion seeks to impose a set of moral principles on the individual, and to establish a code of acceptable behaviour, something that anarchists like German anarchist **Max Stirner (1806–56)**, found particularly objectionable. Religion requires conformity to standards of 'good' and 'evil', which are defined and controlled by religious authorities.

Spec key term

Authority: From the anarchist perspective, authority is the right of one person or institution to influence the behaviour of others and is seen as commanding, controlling and corrupting.

Power: From the anarchist viewpoint, power is the means by which the state and other social institutions secure their authority.

Government: From an anarchist perspective, government is a system of rule, from monarchism to dictatorship to liberal democracy, based on deceit and violence.

Rejection of the state

Summary box

- Rejection of the state is the defining feature of anarchism.
- The state is immoral as it rules by coercion and deceit.
- It is unjust in its defence of economic inequality.

Tensions within anarchism over the role of the state

AGREEMENT	DISAGREEMENT
✓ All anarchists are defined by the belief in the rejection of the state	✗ Anarchists disagree over the reasons and way in which the state should be rejected
✓ All anarchists believe state authority is an offence against the principle of liberty	✗ Individualist anarchists believe the state supresses individual liberty
✓ All anarchists believe that all forms of established, institutionalized, coercive relationships must be abolished	✗ Collectivist anarchists believe the state upholds capitalism and oppresses the workers

Liberty

This can be included when discussing the anarchist view of the state, society, the economy and human nature.

For all anarchists, liberty means being genuinely free to pursue and explore one's choices to the full. It is also freedom from the state as liberty cannot be achieved within a state which is coercive and compels individuals to act against their wishes. Liberty also, therefore, includes freedom from the church, or imposed hierarchical relationships imposed by the state, like class or gender or ethnicity. As **Stirner** argued, '*I am free in no state*'. Further, all anarchists agree that humans can govern themselves and need liberty to be able to do this. Anarchists also argue that liberty is restricted by the state which corrupts human nature and stops humans being able to exercise their liberty. Finally, anarchists argue that genuine liberty is essential for social order to emerge as it allows natural order to develop.

However, as different anarchists see human nature in slightly different ways, they also understand liberty differently.

» Individualist anarchists see humans as rational, but self-reliant, recognizing the individualist nature of humans. Consequently, liberty means the ability to be free to make decisions for oneself and to explore one's individuality to the full; not be coerced by the state to conform. Because the state is coercive and compulsory, individuals are not free to act; they lack liberty and become a slave to the state and wider society. '*I am my own*', **Stirner** writes, '*only when I am master of myself, instead of being mastered ... by anything else.*' Moreover, in a future individualist anarchist society, liberty means the free association of individuals, described by **Stirner** as a Union of Egoists. Lastly, for anarcho-capitalists, liberty means a totally free market, unencumbered by any state, as the best way for individuals to achieve absolute liberty.

» Collectivist anarchists see human nature as rational, but also sociable, cooperative and based on altruism. For collectivist anarchism, one of the key ways the state undermines liberty is by its total support for capitalism. They argue that there can be no liberty under capitalism, as workers are forced to work in an exploitative relationship, where they have no choice. To refuse to work in a capitalist system, backed by a state, is to choose to starve. For collectivist anarchists, liberty cannot exist under capitalism, or any economic system imposed by a compulsory state. Liberty can only exist when the individual is free to achieve their genuine potential and where power in society is shared equally. For all collectivist anarchists this means that liberty cannot co-exist within

Definition

Union of Egoists: The informal association between individuals who themselves remain independent and self-determining.

Spec key term

Altruism: Concern for the interest and welfare of others based on rational self-interest or a belief that humans are social beings with a capacity for social solidarity.

a capitalist economic system. Collectivist anarchists like **Bakunin** argue that liberty can only be achieved by working as part of a community, whereas **Proudhon** argued that free individuals who choose to work together are more than a sum of their parts.

Liberty

Summary box

- Liberty means being free from the compulsory state to pursue and explore one's choices.
- Individuals only achieve liberty when they can pursue their individuality or where power is shared equally in society.
- Liberty is incompatible with any form of political authority.

Tensions within anarchism over society

AGREEMENT	DISAGREEMENT
✓ All anarchists are defined by a belief in the rejection of the state	✗ Anarchists have significantly different conceptions about the nature of an anarchist society, with collectivist anarchists believing in a more communal society and individualist anarchists believing in an atomistic one
✓ All anarchists agree that in anarchist society any economic system backed up by the state must be abolished	✗ Anarchists disagree over the economic basis of a future anarchist society
✓ All anarchists believe that humans are capable of living together peacefully without the need for imposed order	✗ Collectivist anarchists see order emerging in a future society as based on altruism; individualist anarchists see it as based on egoism

Anarchy is order

This can be included when discussing the anarchist view of the state, society the economy and human nature.

Anarchists regard the state as evil, and unnecessary. William Godwin sought to demonstrate this by turning social contract theory on its head. The social contract argument of Hobbes suggests that a stateless society amounts to a civil war of each against all, making orderly and stable life impossible. He argued that the source of such strife lies in human nature, which, is essentially selfish, greedy and potentially aggressive. Only a sovereign state can restrain such impulses and guarantee social order. According to Hobbes, order is impossible without law. Godwin, in contrast, suggested that humans are essentially rational creatures, with a tendency to live in accordance with universal moral laws. He believed that humans have a natural inclination to organize their own lives in a harmonious and peaceful fashion. He argued that it is the corrupting influence of the state, rather than human nature, that creates injustice, greed and aggression. Government is not the solution to the problem of order, but its cause. As **Proudhon** argued, '*Liberty is the mother, not the daughter, of order*.'

Anarchists believe that humans are capable of living together peacefully without the need for imposed order. It has thus sought to explain how social order can occur and be maintained without a state. This has been done in two ways.

The first way in which anarchists have upheld the idea of natural order is by considering human potential. For example, collectivist anarchists have highlighted the human capacity for sociable and cooperative behaviour, while individualist anarchists have drawn attention to the importance of enlightened human reason. Rather than seeing human nature as fixed, most anarchists believe that humans are products of their environment, while also being capable of changing it through positive interaction with others.

Some anarchists believe human nature, as part of the wider nature, is biased in favour of natural order. They have therefore been drawn to the notion of ecology, particularly the 'social ecology' of thinkers such as Murray Bookchin (eco-anarchism is discussed more fully in Chapter x).

The second way in which anarchists have supported the idea of natural order is by focusing on social institutions that promote positive human potential. In this view, human nature is 'plastic', shaped by social, political and economic circumstances. Collectivist anarchists thus endorse common ownership or mutualist institutions, while individualist anarchists have supported the market mechanism. Just as law, government and the state breed domination and control, these other social 'institutions' nurture respect, cooperation and harmony.

The belief in a stable and peaceful stateless, society has often been viewed as the weakest and most contentious aspect of anarchist theory. However, anarchists would argue that the ruling elite need the state to maintain their power; as such, any suggestion that it is not needed would be heavily criticized, as their power relies on humans believing that the state is essential.

» Collectivist anarchists believe that human nature is undermined by the competitive and divisive nature of capitalism, which seeks to intensify selfish acquisitiveness. They argue that community-based organizations, where all have a say in how society is run, will promote natural order, as **Bakunin** argued, '*Man becomes conscious of himself and his humanity only in society and only by the collective action of the whole society.*'

» Individualist anarchists like **Stirner** argue that humans' free spirits are hindered by laws which require them to act according to a 'moral' code which simply seeks to control them. Instead, humans should be free to decide for themselves, rationally, what is in their own best interests, as this will promote natural order. Anarcho-capitalists believe that a free market will create order, naturally, by allowing rational, self-interested individuals to organize their life for themselves.

Nonetheless, anarchism argues that, at their core, humans are cooperative and open-minded, and would understand the benefits of self-regulation which would be of wider benefit to all. They argue that humans are encouraged to portray the very worst aspects of human nature by a corrupt, immoral world, which values greed and injustice. In this world, behaving righteously and for the common good leaves you at a disadvantage. As such, it is unsurprising that human nature shifts towards a selfish, competitive and anti-social outlook because humans are unable to understand their actual capacity for decency and self-regulation.

Anarchists envisage a society where the voluntary cooperation of free individuals make decisions to live in a society that best fits their needs, where conflict will be resolved by reason, not violence or coercion, whether that be the collectivist anarchism of some or the individualist approach taken by others. In a society of one's own choosing and making, order will be natural, peaceful and stable. As Alexander Berkman argues in ABC of Anarchism (1929), '*maybe I can show you that we can be decent and live as decent folk even without growing wings*'.

Anarchists argue that when the state is removed, there will inevitability be a period of instability and disorder, but the enlightened, rational, self-preservation within all humans will come to see this as unsustainable and will seek to develop a stable, peaceful ordered society. This is when human nature will start to reach its potential and people will come together to create an ordered society without a state.

Anarchy is order

Summary box

- Contrary to the widely held view that anarchy means chaos, anarchists argue that anarchy represents order.
- The state encourages humans to be selfish aggressive and greedy.
- Only without a state can humans create a society based on natural order.

Tensions within anarchism over natural order	
AGREEMENT	**DISAGREEMENT**
✔ All anarchists believe that humans are capable of living together peacefully without the need for imposed order	✘ Collectivist anarchists have highlighted the human capacity for sociable and cooperative behaviour, while individualist anarchists have drawn attention to the importance of enlightened human reason
✔ They believe that a society without coercive institutions is feasible	✘ Collectivist anarchists see order in future society as based on altruism; individualist anarchists see it as based on egoism
✔ They believe that it is state and government which has a corrupting influence on humans, not the other way round	✘ Egoism is based on the belief that order will emerge from 'ownness', whereas anarcho-communism believes that order will arise from humans working together in a spirit of cooperation

Economic freedom

This can be included when discussing the anarchist view of the state, society, the economy and human nature.

Anarchists challenge the existence of a state as well as the other structures of social and economic life. They argue that the state entrenches a corrupt economic system that embeds advantage and privilege. All anarchists prefer an economy in which free individuals manage their own affairs without the need for a state. Within both collectivist and individualist anarchism, there is no clear agreement on an economic model. Instead, anarchism in general prefers that humans choose and construct, for themselves, an economic model which works according to their principles. The key for anarchism is that there is no compulsion, i.e. one should not feel compelled to participate in an economic model that doesn't work for them. This has allowed them to accept (although not necessarily agree with) a range of quite different economic systems, from anarcho-communism to anarcho-capitalism.

Nineteenth-century anarchists identified themselves with the poor and oppressed and sought to carry out a revolution in the name of the exploited masses in which both capitalism and the state would be swept away. **Bakunin** argued that '*political power and wealth are inseparable*'. Traditionally, anarchists subscribed to a broadly socialist philosophy. Capitalism was understood in class terms: a 'ruling class' exploited and oppressed 'the masses'. However, this 'ruling class' was not interpreted in narrow economic terms, but was seen to include all those who had wealth, power or privilege. It therefore included kings and princes, politicians and state officials, judges and police officers, bishops and priests, as well as industrialists and bankers. **Kropotkin** argued that although capitalism was an obstacle to progress, it was primarily the state which allowed capitalism to proliferate.

Bakunin argued that, in every developed society, three social groups can be identified:

1. A vast majority who are exploited.
2. A minority who are exploited but also exploit others in equal measure.
3. '*The supreme governing estate*', a small minority of '*exploiters and oppressors pure and simple*'.

Proudhon famously argued that '*property is theft*'. By this, he meant that private property was owned and accumulated by some and used to exploit others. He argued that private property allowed those privileged enough to have it, the ability to earn an income by this ownership, not their own effort. The state aligned itself with this privileged elite, entrenching their advantage.

However, it is in the economy that tensions are most keenly exposed within anarchism. While many acknowledge a connection with socialism, based on a common distaste for private property and inequality, others have defended property rights and even revered capitalism. This highlights the distinction between the two anarchist traditions, one of which is collectivist and the other individualist. Most collectivist anarchists advocate an economy based on cooperation and collective ownership, while anarcho-capitalists support the market and private property.

Despite such fundamental differences, anarchists nevertheless agree about their distaste for the economic systems backed by a state.

» Collectivist anarchists argue that state intervention like welfare merely props up a system of class exploitation, giving capitalism a human face. It supports and entrenches private property which causes inequality.

» Anarcho-capitalism suggests that intervention by the state distorts the competitive market and creates economies dominated by both public and private monopolies. They argue that the state must not be involved in the market at all, as the market is the best allocator of scarce resources, allowing individual to make choices in their own best interests.

» Egoists like **Stirner**, however, are not advocates of capitalism. He argued that the capitalism system is '*labour that amounts to the same thing as slavery*'. Capitalism uses the individual for its own benefit, exploiting and alienating individuals. Instead, work should be fulfilling where individuals can enjoy the fruits of their labour.

Economic freedom

Summary box

- The economy should be a space where free individuals can manage their own affairs without state ownership or regulation.
- Collectivist anarchists criticize the state for upholding an exploitative system.
- Anarcho-capitalists criticize the state for perverting the true nature of the market.

Tensions within anarchism over the economy	
AGREEMENT	DISAGREEMENT
✓ All anarchists believe that economic freedom is central to the freedom of the individual	✗ Anarchists fundamentally disagree over the type of economy they believe best serves humans
✓ All anarchists oppose the private ownership of industry propped up by the coercive state as it creates an exploitative relationship between the people	✗ Individualist and collectivist anarchists disagree over whether property should be owned in common or by free individuals
✓ All anarchists advocate economic freedom so that people can conduct economic affairs autonomously without state ownership, regulation or intervention	✗ Within individualist anarchists, there is disagreement over the role of capitalism

Utopian

This can be included when discussing the anarchist view of the state, society, the economy and human nature.

A utopia is usually taken to mean a perfect, or at least significantly better, society. Though utopias of various kinds can be imagined, most are characterized by the abolition of want, the absence of conflict and the lack of oppression and violence. It was used by Thomas Moore in its Latin format meaning 'no place' as though it was a heaven on earth and not achievable or practical. Utopianism also seeks to develop a critique of the existing order by constructing an ideal alternative, usually based on assumptions about the unlimited possibilities of humanity. It is also a comprehensive rejection of the status quo. Utopian thought highlights the potential for human self-development, suggesting that the achievement of total personal fulfilment is possible when freed from the existing society.

At the heart of anarchism lies unashamed utopianism, a belief in the potential natural goodness, of humankind. From this perspective, social order arises naturally and spontaneously; it does not require the machinery of law and order. This is why anarchist conclusions have only been reached by those with optimistic views of human nature. For example, collectivist anarchists stress the human capacity for sociable and cooperative behaviour, while individualist anarchists highlight the importance of enlightened human reason.

Even though anarchists emphasize that humans have significant, even unlimited potential, they are also highly critical about the corrupting influence of their surroundings. Humans can be either 'good' or 'evil' depending on their political and social circumstances. People who would naturally be cooperative, sympathetic and sociable become oppressive tyrants when raised up above others by power, privilege or wealth.

They also argue that the state dehumanizes society by seeking to discourage people from relating to each other as fellow humans. Humans are encouraged to follow rules, processes and procedures that, we are told, are necessary for mass decision making, and don't allow for individual considerations. In this modern world, decisions are made by algorithms rather than people, by faceless bureaucrats, rather than compassionate individuals. Humans are taught to be 'professional', dispassionate, to remove themselves and their feelings from a situation, to do their job more effectively. Anarchists argue that this is the way human nature is corrupted by the state. Consequently, society becomes less and less personal and people feel remote and disconnected from each other. Thus the state, as a source of sovereign, compulsory and coercive authority, is nothing less than a concentrated form of evil. For anarchists, it is not fanciful to consider human nature, undisturbed by the state, as having unlimited, positive potential.

However, the term utopianism also has a negative meaning, suggesting deluded thinking, a belief in an unrealistic and unachievable goal. A utopian idea, in this sense, is one which has a vision of a perfect society but does not describe in any real detail how it is to be achieved. Thus the belief in a stable and peaceful yet stateless society has usually been viewed as the weakest aspect of anarchist theory. Opponents of anarchism have argued that, however socially enlightened institutions may be, selfish or negative impulses are basic to human nature, not merely evidence of corruption, hence the prospect of natural order is utopian and unrealistic.

But as **Goldman** argued, '*Every daring attempt to make a great change in existing conditions, every lofty vision of new possibilities for the human race, has been labelled Utopian.*' In other words, any radical movement away from the status quo can be brushed aside with the claim of 'utopianism'. Anarchists like **Kropotkin** have used the scientific theory of evolution to show how species who work together survive, hence the need to cooperate and work together is natural not utopian. Moreover, one may suggest that the liberal principle of equality of opportunity is impossible in a capitalist society, but liberals are not criticized for being utopian. Anarchist ideas have been influential during the Spanish civil war in the 1930s, and the Zapatistas in Mexico are still going strong after twenty years.

Moreover, it can be argued that anarchists like **Kropotkin** were not utopian and instead, based their writing on analysis of tendencies that were already at work. In the introduction to a 2006 publication of Kropotkin's *The Conquest of Bread*, Charles Weigl argued that, as a scientist, Kropotkin '*knew the difference between theory and certainty*'. He went on to argue that *The Conquest of Bread* based itself on a thorough and detailed analysis of the historical development of human society.

Utopian

Summary box

- To consider the benefits of an idealized society in order to develop a critique of existing society.
- A belief in the unlimited potential and natural goodness, of humankind.
- To consider the criticisms levelled against anarchism as unachievable and unrealistic.

Tensions within anarchism over human nature	
AGREEMENT	**DISAGREEMENT**
✓ All anarchists agree that human nature is corrupted by the state and is moulded by the environment	✗ Individualist anarchists believe human nature is egoistical, whereas collectivist anarchists believe it is social and cooperative
✓ All anarchists agree that human nature or at the very least the potential of human nature should be seen optimistically	✗ Individualist anarchists seek the end of the state so individuals can be free to express their true nature, whereas collectivist anarchists seek freedom from the state so humans natural cooperative core can flourish
✓ All anarchists agree that social order can arise naturally from human nature and does not require the presence of the state or other coercive institutions	✗ Anarcho-capitalists believe that the market provides the mechanism for the full expression of human nature, whereas collectivist anarchists believe that human nature can only be truly expressed once capitalism is abolished

2. Differences between the anarchist strands

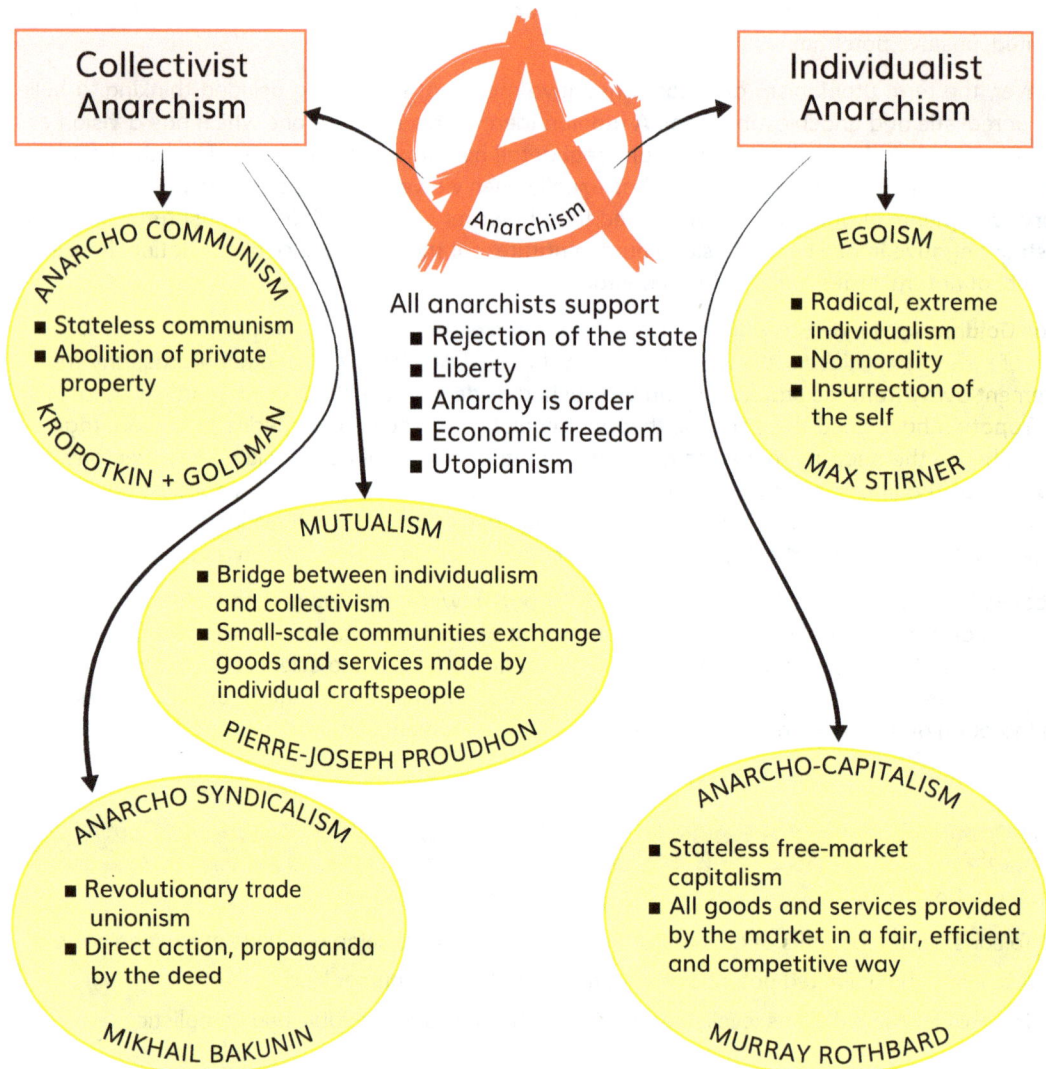

Figure 4.1 **Differences between the anarchist strands.**

Collectivist anarchism

The philosophical roots of collectivist anarchism lie in socialism. Collectivism is, in essence, the belief that humans are social animals, better suited to working together for the common good than striving for individual self-interest. Collectivist anarchism stresses the human capacity for social solidarity, or what **Kropotkin** termed 'mutual aid'. This does not amount to a naive belief in 'natural goodness', but rather highlights the potential for goodness that resides within all humans. Humans are, at heart, sociable, outgoing and cooperative creatures. In this light, the natural and proper relationship between humans is one of sympathy, affection and harmony. When people are linked together by the recognition of a common humanity, they have no need to be regulated or controlled by government: as **Bakunin** proclaimed, '*Social solidarity is the first human law; freedom is the second law*'. Not only is government unnecessary but, in replacing freedom with oppression, it also makes social solidarity impossible.

Overlaps between collectivist anarchism and Marxism are evident in several ways. They both:

» fundamentally reject capitalism

» endorse revolution

» prefer collective ownership of wealth and a communal society

» believe that a fully communist society would have no state

Nevertheless, collectivist anarchism and socialism disagree because:

» Anarchists dismiss parliamentary socialism as a contradiction in terms.

» The bitterest disagreement between collectivist anarchists and Marxists centres on Marx's 'dictatorship of the proletariat' as anarchists reject the state in any guise, even when it is purportedly there to do good.

Collectivist anarchism has taken a variety of forms. The most significant of these are:

» anarcho-communism

» mutualism

» anarcho-syndicalism

Anarcho-communism

Anarcho-communism is one of the strongest components of anarchist thought and advocates the abolition of private property. This is because, typically, a belief in social solidarity leads in the direction of collectivization and communism. Sociable and outgoing humans should lead a shared and communal existence. For example, labour is a social experience, people work in common with other humans and the wealth they produce should therefore be owned in common by the community, rather than by any single individual. In this sense, *all* forms of private property are theft: as they represent the exploitation of workers, who alone create wealth, by employers who merely own it. In *The Conquest of Bread* (1892) **Kropotkin** was clear that anarcho-communism meant that '*not a single man shall be forced to sell the strength of his right arm to obtain a bare subsistence for himself and his babes*'.

Property should be owned by the people and the economy should be coordinated through a network of voluntary associations where goods are distributed according to the needs of the individual, rather than according to labour. However, **Kropotkin** retained respect for personal property, arguing that a '*peasant who is in possession of just the amount of land he can cultivate*' and '*a family inhabiting a house which affords them just enough space ... considered necessary for that number of people*' and the artisan '*working with their own tools or handloom*' would not be interfered with.

Private property, however, can encourage selfishness and promote conflict and social disharmony. Inequality in the ownership of wealth encourages greed, envy and resentment, and therefore breeds crime and disorder. As such anarcho-communists support the removal of private property back into the common good to ensure that everyone would have access to what they needed. In *The Conquest of Bread*, **Kropotkin** wrote '*We do not want to rob any one of his coat, but we wish to give to the workers all those things the lack of which makes them fall an easy prey to the exploiter.*'

Government, according to **Kropotkin**, was destructive and divided people against each other, whether that be individuals, classes or countries. It was, the '*personification of injustice, oppression*

Spec key term

Solidarity: From an anarchist perspective, a relationship of sympathy, cooperation and harmony between people, which means that they have no need to be regulated by the state and any regulation makes solidarity impossible.

Collectivization: The abolition of private property and its replacement by a system of common ownership.

and monopoly' and must be eliminated and replaced by an anarchist society based on the principles of communism. From the anarcho-communist perspective, the communal organization of life has four key advantages:

1. As communities are based on the principles of sharing and collective endeavour, they strengthen the bonds of compassion and solidarity, and help to keep greed and selfishness at bay.

2. Within communities, decisions are made through a process of direct democracy, which guarantees a high level of participation and political equality. Self-government is the only form of government that would be acceptable to anarchists.

3. Small-scale communities allow people to manage their own affairs through face-to-face interaction.

4. Individuals would be part of these communities based on voluntary agreements, and communities would be connected as voluntary federations.

Anarcho-communism stresses the human potential for cooperation, expressed most famously by **Kropotkin's** theory of mutual aid. **Kropotkin** attempted to provide a biological foundation for social solidarity by re-examining Darwin's theory of evolution. Whereas theorists such as the UK social thinker Herbert Spencer (1820–1903) had used Darwinism to support the idea that humankind is naturally competitive and aggressive, **Kropotkin** argued that species are successful precisely because they manage to harness collective energies through cooperation. The process of evolution thus strengthens sociability and favours cooperation over competition. Successful species, such as humans, must have a strong propensity for mutual aid. Providing many examples, he showed that sociability is a dominant feature at every level of the animal world. Among humans, too, he found that mutual aid has been the rule rather than the exception, from the primitive tribe, peasant village and medieval commune to modern associations like trade unions, and organizations like the Red Cross which have continued to practise mutual support despite the rise of the coercive state. This tendency towards cooperation has been undermined by competitive capitalism, threatening the further evolution of humans.

Anarcho-communists such as **Kropotkin** and Errico Malatesta (1853–1932) have argued that true communism requires the abolition of the state and admired small, self-managing communities. **Kropotkin** envisaged that an anarchic society would consist of a collection of largely self-sufficient communities, each owning its wealth in common. In *The Conquest of Bread* **Kropotkin** described an anarcho-communist society:

> *Imagine a society ... engaged in ... a great variety of industries ... Suppose that in this society all children learn to work with their hands as well as with their brains ... that all adults ... work 5 hours a day from the age of twenty ... to fifty, and that they follow occupations ... considered necessary. Such a society could in return guarantee well-being to all its members; that is to say, a more substantial well-being than that enjoyed today by the middle classes.*

Mutualism

The anarchist belief in social solidarity has been used to justify various forms of cooperative behaviour. At one extreme, it has led to a belief in pure communism, but it has also generated the more modest ideas of mutualism, associated with **Proudhon**. In a sense, **Proudhon** stood between the individualist and collectivist traditions of anarchism, his ideas sharing much in common with those of US individualists such as Josiah Warren (1798–1874). In *What Is Property?* (1840), **Proudhon** came up with the famous statement that '*property is theft*' and condemned a system of economic exploitation based on the accumulation of capital.

Nevertheless, **Proudhon** was not opposed to all forms of private ownership, distinguishing between property and what he called 'possessions'. In particular, he admired the independence and initiative of small communities of peasants, craftsmen and artisans, especially the watchmakers of Switzerland, who had traditionally managed their affairs based on mutual cooperation.

Proudhon hence distinguished between what he considered to be two distinct forms of property. Although he claimed that '*property is theft*', he also argued that, sometimes, '*property is liberty*'. Property is theft when one person exploits the labour of another '*when it is related to a landowner or capitalist whose ownership is derived from conquest or exploitation and is only maintained through the state, property laws, police, and an army*'. However, property is liberty when ownership and exploitation are removed. It is freedom for '*the peasant or artisan family who have a natural right to a home, land they may cultivate ... to tools of a trade*'; in other words, when property is the product

Spec key term

Direct democracy: Citizens making law and policy decisions in person rather than through elected representatives in a form of popular, self-government.

Mutual aid: The most successful species are those that employ solidarity and cooperation rather than individualistic competition.

Exam Tip – Don't confuse Kropotkin's mutual aid with the mutualism of Proudhon.

Spec key term

Mutualism: A system of fair and equitable exchange, in which individuals or groups bargain with one another, trading goods and services without profiteering or exploitation.

of labour, based on occupancy and used to create liberty; as **Proudhon** said, it creates a society of '*possessors without masters*'.

Proudhon therefore sought, through mutualism, to establish a system of property ownership that would avoid exploitation and promote social harmony, what he referred to as '*the synthesis of the notions of private property and collective ownership*'. Interaction would be voluntary, mutually beneficial and harmonious, requiring no regulation or interference by government. **Proudhon's** followers tried to put these ideas into practice by setting up mutual credit banks in France and Switzerland, which provided cheap loans for investors and charged a rate of interest only high enough to cover the cost of running the bank, but not so high that it made a profit.

Anarcho-syndicalism

Although mutualism and anarcho-communism exerted significant influence, anarchism only developed into a mass movement in the form of anarcho-syndicalism. **Syndicalism** is a form of revolutionary trade unionism, drawing its name from the French word *syndicat*, meaning union. Syndicalism emerged first in France and was embraced by the powerful CGT union in the period before 1914. Syndicalist ideas spread to Italy, Latin America, the USA and, most significantly, Spain, where the country's largest union, the CNT, supported them.

Anarcho-syndicalism advances a theory of class war. Workers and peasants are an oppressed class, and industrialists, landlords, politicians, judges and the police are seen as their exploiters. Like most collectivist anarchists, they see the primary purpose of the state as a defence of private property and therefore of economic, social and political privilege. Workers should therefore defend themselves by organizing syndicates, based on particular crafts, industries or professions. In the short term, these syndicates act as conventional trade unions, raising wages, shortening hours and improving working conditions. However, anarcho-syndicalists are also revolutionaries,

Photo 4.1 **Flag of anarcho-syndicalists.**

who look to overthrow capitalism and promote the seizure of power by the workers.

Anarcho-syndicalism is based on three principles:

» Workers' solidarity – all workers are in the same situation and in order to have power they must stick together, in the same way that bosses in a capitalist system work together to protect their interests. Workers must support each other to be liberated.

» Direct action – direct action against the capitalist state is the only thing that will bring it down. By concentrating directly on a specific goal, whether that be boycotting products, sabotaging machinery or strike action, direct action can ultimately destabilize and then destroy the capitalist state.

» Workers' self-management/direct democracy – fundamental to all anarchist organization is the belief in non-hierarchic self-management. Anarcho-syndicalists believe that all syndicates should consist of workers making decisions for themselves. Rudolf Rocker in his pamphlet *Anarchism and Anarcho-Syndicalism (1938)* argued that anarcho-syndicalism had a dual purpose:

1. to enforce the demands of workers to raise living standards

2. to make workers familiar with the management of production so that they were equipped to take over this role for themselves. To create the foundations of a new anarchist society '*within the shell of the old*'.

For anarcho-syndicalism, unions combine a vehicle for revolution with a model for future society based on anarchist principles.

In *Reflections on Violence* (1908), Georges Sorel (1847–1922), the influential French syndicalist theorist, argued that such a revolution would come about through a general strike, what he poetically called a '*revolution of empty hands*'. Sorel believed that the general strike was a symbol of working-class power, capable of inspiring popular revolt. This is linked to the syndicalist idea of propaganda by the deed.

Definition

Propaganda by the deed: A politically motivated provocative act of violence (the deed), meant to broadcast an ideological message (the propaganda), to incite a response from authorities and serve as a catalyst to ignite a spirit of anarchy.

This is the idea that specific acts of violence aimed at the ruling class could ignite the 'spirit of revolt' in the people by demonstrating the state was not all-powerful and by offering hope to the downtrodden. It was also thought that this would expand support for the anarchist movement as the state grew more repressive in its response. **Bakunin** in *Letters to a Frenchman on the Present Crisis (1870)* argued that '*we must spread our principles, not with words but with deeds, for this is the most popular, the most potent, and the most irresistible form of propaganda*'. Examples of this were rioting, strikes and bank robberies, dubbed 'revolutionary expropriations' as they used the money to fund the cause,

Syndicalist theory exerted a strong attraction for anarchists who wished to spread their ideas among the masses. As anarchists entered the syndicalist movement, they developed the distinctive ideas of anarcho-syndicalism. Two features of syndicalism inspired anarchist enthusiasm:

» First, syndicalists rejected conventional politics as corrupting and pointless. Working-class power, they believed, should be exerted through direct action, boycotts, sabotage and strikes, and ultimately a general strike – where all workers strike together causing maximum upheaval.

» Second, anarchists saw the syndicate as a model for the decentralized, non-hierarchic society of the future. Syndicates typically exhibited a high degree of grassroots democracy and formed federations with other syndicates, either in the same area or in the same industry.

Although anarcho-syndicalism enjoyed genuine mass support, at least until the Spanish Civil War when it was crushed by Franco, it failed to achieve its revolutionary objectives. Beyond the idea of the general strike, anarcho-syndicalism did not develop a clear political strategy or a theory of revolution. Other anarchists have criticized syndicalism for concentrating too narrowly on short-term trade union goals, and therefore for leading anarchism away from revolution.

Individualist anarchism

The philosophical basis of individualist anarchism lies in the liberal idea of the sovereign individual. For example, William Godwin, considered the first modern proponent of anarchism, argued in *An Enquiry Concerning Political Justice (1793)* that government was a corrupting force on the individual, but one that will be rendered increasingly unnecessary by the gradual spread of knowledge and human understanding. He argued that individual personal morality would replace political rule.

For individualist anarchists, individual sovereignty implies the idea that absolute and unlimited authority resides within each human being. From this perspective, any constraint on the individual is evil; but when this constraint is imposed by the state, a sovereign, compulsory and coercive body, it amounts to an absolute evil. Quite simply, the individual cannot be sovereign in a society ruled by law and government. Individualism and the state are thus irreconcilable principles. As Robert Wolff, in *In Defence of Anarchism (1970)* put it, '*The autonomous man, insofar as he is autonomous, is not subject to the will of another.*'

Although these arguments may be liberal in inspiration, significant differences exist between liberalism and individualist anarchism:

» Anarchists believe that individuals can conduct themselves peacefully, harmoniously and prosperously without the need for government to 'police' society and protect them from their fellow humans.

» Anarchists differ from liberals because they believe that free individuals can live and work together constructively because they are rational and moral creatures. Reason and morality dictate that where conflict exists it should be resolved by arbitration or debate, and not by violence.

» Anarchists also dismiss the idea of limited, constitutional or representative government. All laws infringe individual liberty, whether the government that enacts them is constitutional or arbitrary, democratic or dictatorial. In other words, all states are an offence against individual liberty.

Anarcho-individualism has taken a number of forms. The most important of these are:

» egoism

» anarcho-capitalism

Egoism

The boldest statement of anarchism built on the idea of the sovereign individual is found in **Max Stirner's** *The Ego and His Own* (1845). **Stirner's** theories represent an extreme form of individualism and are arguably the most thought-provoking form of individualism.

The term 'egoism' can have different meanings. It can suggest that individuals are essentially concerned about their ego or 'self', that they are self-interested or self-seeking. In **Stirner's** view, however, egoism is a philosophy that places the individual self at the centre of their moral universe. For **Stirner**, the 'ego' meant one's self-awareness, an understanding of one's own genuine wishes and desires, removed from society's expectations. He argued that all people are capable of the self-awareness which would make them 'egoists', or true individuals. The individual, from this perspective, should therefore simply act as they choose, without any consideration for laws, social conventions, religious or moral principles. This is a position that clearly points in the direction of an extreme form of individualist anarchism.

Egoism, according to **Stirner**, is a form of autonomy where it is not possible to suspend one's own judgement for the benefit of the greater good. '*I am my own only when I am master of myself, instead of being mastered ... by anything else*.' For **Stirner**, to achieve 'ownness' one must avoid allowing oneself to be put in a subordinate position by others but equally one should also avoid being mindlessly dragged along by one's own appetites and develop a detachment from one's desires.

Stirner rejected the idea that egoism is necessarily anti-social, seeing the possibility of a Union of Egoists, based on the mutual consent of all members, who would come together through voluntary agreements. This would not involve any giving away of individual liberty. He argued that an egoist society is '*a full participation in whatever arouses interest, to the exclusion of whatever does not*'. **Stirner** argued that this is not the same as a modern society which requires all to submit their will to its higher rule.

For **Stirner**, egoism was the most advanced human state, which embodied a higher capacity to reason than modern society. He turns social contract theory on its head by arguing that society with a state is the more primitive form of organization, which humans evolve out of towards a stateless, egoist society. He equates this to the development from child to adult, at first needing support and protection, but then outgrowing it in adulthood to stand as a free individual. **Stirner** draws the lesson that the individual must rejecting the morality imposed by their parents and society. He referred to this process as insurrection, whereby individuals rise above the decaying establishment, leaving it to rot and die.

Stirner fervently attacked the 'modern' world. Religion, in particular, he saw as oppressive, seeking to force individuals to conform to strict social rules and 'so called' morality. **Stirner** was opposed to all religious as well as atheist doctrines, on the basis that they also seek to impose a 'correct' way of living. Instead, Stirner chose an open-minded engagement with the world, without any need for faith. As he wrote himself, he was '*not against love, but against sacred love, not against thought, but against sacred thought, not against socialists, but against sacred socialists*'.

Anarcho-capitalism

The revival of interest in free-market economics in the late twentieth century led to increasingly radical political conclusions, thinkers like Murray Rothbard (1978) and David Friedman (1973) pushed free-market ideas to their limit and developed a form of anarcho-capitalism. They argued that government should be abolished and be replaced by unregulated market competition.

Anarcho-capitalism begins from the concept of individual freedom and sees genuine free-market capitalism as the basis for a free society. Rothbard defined this as '*peaceful voluntary exchange*', in contrast to 'state capitalism' which he defined as a collusion between business and government, reliant on coercion. Anarcho-capitalists are keen to point out that the predatory capitalism of today bears little resemblance to their ideal vision of an anarcho-capitalist system, where natural market incentives and disincentives are skewed and undermined by state intervention. They argue that state intervention in the otherwise free market threatens economic freedom, efficiency and competition.

Spec key term

Autonomy: A form of self-government in which the individual is not subject to the will of the state or any other person.

Spec key term

Insurrection: Insurrection is not synonymous with revolution but is rather egoistic, not a political or social act, that allows individuals to elevate themselves above the established institutions, leaving the establishment to decay and die.

Additionally, the state limits individual sovereignty as it seizes money through compulsory taxation and gives people no real say in how it is spent. This violates the private property of the individual. As Rothbard says, '*if every man has the right to own his own body and if he must use and transform material natural objects in order to survive, then he has the right to own the product that he has made*'. Property should be owned by sovereign individuals, who may choose, if they wish, to enter into voluntary contracts with others. The individual thus remains free and the market, beyond the control of any individual, regulates all social interaction. Anarcho-capitalists diverge from the typical anarchist view of human nature, arguing that humans are autonomous, competitive and acquisitive individuals who, as Rothbard said, own themselves.

Anarcho-capitalists go well beyond the ideas of free-market liberalism. Arguing that 'public goods' such as the maintenance of order, the enforcement of contracts and protection against external attack, can be satisfied by the market, which can satisfy all human wants. For example, Rothbard recognized that in an anarchist society individuals will seek protection from one another but argued that such protection can be delivered competitively by privately owned 'protection associations' and 'private courts', without the need for a police force or a state court system. This free market will promote competition which will keep prices low by forcing suppliers to be efficient and respond to consumer demand, as only the 'invisible hand' of demand and supply can do.

According to anarcho-capitalists, profit-making protection agencies would offer a better service than the present police force because competition would provide consumers with a choice, ensuring that agencies are cheap, efficient and responsive to consumer needs. Similarly, private courts would be forced to develop a reputation for fairness to attract custom from individuals wishing to resolve a conflict. Most importantly, unlike the authority of public bodies, the contracts made with private agencies would be entirely voluntary, regulated only by impersonal market forces.

Many anarchists find it difficult to recognize anarcho-capitalism as falling under the anarchist umbrella, believing that free-market capitalism creates an unequal form of liberty, reliant on the exploitation of the many by the few, and so is incompatible with anarchist values.

Table 4.1 Tensions within anarchism over the core principles

	Anarcho-communism	Mutualism	Anarcho-syndicalism	Anarcho-capitalism	Egoism
Rejects the state	Rejects the state. True freedom can only exist without the corruptive power of the state				
Liberty	There can be no liberty under capitalism. Liberty is only possible if there is equality	Liberty can only exist when the individual is free to achieve their genuine potential and where power in society is shared equally	Liberty should be absolute; achieved through work and the collective. Liberty comes from communities	Liberty is a competitive free market creating choice, making suppliers efficient, cost effective and reflective of consumers' needs	Liberty is the freedom to be an individual without the states coercive powers of taxation, conscription, law and morality
Anarchy is order	Anarchy is order. Common ownership encourages altruism and co-operation, which will create and maintain natural order	A society based on mutual benefit will be an ordered one. Individuals and small associations would exchange their produce, to ensure access to necessities, ensuring social order	Trade unions will prepare the way for the mass strike to trigger a revolution. Afterwards, they will provide the basis for the future ordered, stateless society	The free market will allow rational, autonomous, competitive and self-interested individuals to make judgements in their own best interests, creating natural order	Union of Egoists means individuals have self-ownership and liberty; they enter into voluntary contracts to meet their own interests which is the best guarantee of social order
Economic freedom	Abolition of the state, capitalism and private property. Land and means of production are held in common to create equality and liberty	Supports possession, the right to use land, tools, etc., to ensure independence. 'property is theft', but 'property is liberty' if the individual can own the product of their own labour	Trade unions are the revolutionary agent of change who build non-hierarchic economic institutions. Self-sufficiency and equality in small communities will develop	The state must be replaced by the market, even with the provision of roads, education or health care. The market is always more effective than the state	Rejects capitalism, as working for someone is exploitative. Work should be purposeful and useful, and individuals should retain the fruits of their labour
Utopian	For collectivist anarchists, altruism will be nurtured by common ownership. Evidence of this is found in nature – mutual aid	An optimistic view of the potential of human nature will be a society of harmony, unrestricted liberty and order	No state allows humans to pursue a good moral society. Trade unions are the key associations that will bring down the state through the mass strike and form the basis of the new society	Autonomy and rationalism will flourish with the absence of the state, allowing a free society to develop spontaneously	Ego is everything, part of the essence of a human. Individuals should be true to themselves in all decisions

3. Anarchist key thinkers

Key thinkers are an important part of understanding each ideology. The exam board has specified five key thinkers per ideology and TWO must be included in an answer to avoid a cap (please check the Exam Focus chapter (Chapter 9) for lots more discussion of key thinkers). Although key thinkers (and other thinkers) have been discussed throughout the chapter, here we look at each one in detail.

Max Stirner (1806–56)

Max Stirner was a German philosopher, whose most important political work was *The Ego and His Own* (1845). Stirner developed an extreme form of individualism, based on egoism, which condemned all checks on personal autonomy. In contrast to other anarchists' stress on moral principles such as justice, reason and community, Stirner emphasized the 'ownness' of the human individual, thereby placing the individual self at the centre of the moral universe.

For Stirner, egoism meant each individual achieving self-realization: to be free is to truly be oneself. He described this as 'ownness' or as being one's own creature and own creator. In order to do this, one had to rise beyond societal expectations, which meant going against everything one had been brought up to do, but that this was the only way to escape domination. He argued that this was something all humans needed to work hard to strive towards and that egoism was the embodiment of a more advanced civilization.

Stirner argued that all social institutions were illusions in that the only thing that was real were individuals, all societal institutions were therefore 'ghosts'. As such he wanted to abolish not only the state but also society as an institution.

Stirner advocated a Union of Egoists, where individuals may choose to come together voluntarily and rationally if it serves their own interests. They may make agreements with other 'egos' if it is mutually beneficial, but equally, there is no compulsion to conform to anyone else's will. As he claimed, '*we two, the State and I, are enemies. I, the egoist, have not at heart the welfare of this "human society" I sacrifice nothing to it, I only utilise it; but to be able to utilise it completely I transform it rather into my property and my creature; I annihilate it, and form in its place the Union of Egoist.*'

Despite being an individualist anarchist, Stirner is no friend of capitalism. He argues that capitalism, like any other system of society, undermines the notion of egoism by expecting individuals to confirm to the capitalist ideology. The individual is as much a slave to capitalism as it is to the state. Stirner argued that work should be fulfilling and purposeful to each individual.

Stirner advocated insurrection rather than revolution. By insurrection he meant the ability to rise above government and morality by taking control of oneself and life. Hence insurrection was a personal journey, but one with 'revolutionary' consequences. Stirner argued that a typical revolution required individuals to overthrow the existing order but, without any changes to themselves, the new order may be plagued with similar problems to the previous one. For Stirner, the journey of change had to begin with oneself.

Pierre-Joseph Proudhon (1809–65)

adoc-photos/Contributor/Getty

Vera Orlova/iStock

A French social theorist, political activist and largely self-educated printer, Proudhon's writings influenced many nineteenth-century anarchists, socialists and communists. His best-known work, *What Is Property?* (1840), attacked both traditional property rights and collective ownership, and argued instead for mutualism, a cooperative productive system geared towards need rather than profit and organized within self-governing communities. Proudhon is considered by many to be the father of anarchism.

Proudhon may be most famous for saying 'property is theft', but what is much less well known is that he also said 'property is impossible', 'property is despotism', and, appearing to contradict all of that, 'property is freedom'. The first three pronouncements referred to the property of the landowner or capitalist, who he believed stole profits from labourers or workers. He described the employee of a capitalist as 'subordinated, exploited: his permanent condition is one of obedience'. Private property is illegitimate because it gives one person power over another, it is also the reason for state power, which exists to defend property rights.

With 'property is freedom', however, he was referring to the product of an individual's labour, as well as their home and tools, and the income received by selling their goods. For Proudhon, the only legitimate source of property was one's own labour. Proudhon called this 'possessions'.

Proudhon opposed both capitalism and state ownership of property, arguing instead for small-scale property ownership associated with peasants and artisans, a system he called mutualism, which involved workers controlling their own industries. In his scheme, artisans, peasants and cooperatives would trade their products on the market, and larger workplaces and factories would be run by their own workers according to the principles of direct democracy.

Producers would exchange goods and services in a way that was of mutual benefit. He also supported the idea of non-profit-making credit unions to help people start up their own business. He believed that once workers were organized in this way and property was replaced by possession, exploitation would disappear along with the state.

Interestingly, Proudhon did not support violent revolution, believing instead that society could be transformed peacefully from within. He argued that the reforms of production would bring about a reorganization of society along new lines, and the mutualist system of production would make the state redundant. Also, Proudhon's concept of revolution was about a moral transformation in humanity. In *The Confessions of a Revolutionary*, Proudhon asserted that 'Anarchy is order without power', the phrase which is said to later inspire the anarchist symbol.

Mikhail Bakunin (1814–76)

Heritage Images/Contributor/Getty

Mikhail Bakunin was a Russian political agitator and revolutionary and one of the key proponents of collectivist anarchism and a leading figure within the nineteenth-century anarchist movement.

Bakunin argued that political power was intrinsically oppressive and placed his faith in human sociability; his anarchism stems from the notion that all authority must be rejected, as submission to the state enslaves people. Liberty can only be achieved by the rejection of the state. Bakunin argued that humans were naturally social creatures, shaped by society, and could only achieve liberty through the society they live in. They could not exist outside society. He also argued that collective work was a way to be liberated, as social solidarity is key to human nature. Bakunin proposed that freedom could only be achieved through 'collectivism', by which he meant self-governing communities based on voluntary cooperation, the abolition of private property and its replacement with collective ownership, as liberty without equality is just privilege and injustice.

Bakunin was also ferociously anti-organized religion, believing that it was a tool of oppression to keep the people in a subservient position and help the powerful to maintain their position. Liberty therefore required the abolition of God. Religion encouraged people to follow an artificial code of conduct with pseudo-morality which demanded that people behave in certain ways. It stops people thinking for themselves and encouraged them to do as they are told. Bakunin believed the state and church worked hand in hand in order to control society. In *God and the State* 1882, he argued that '*the idea of God implies the abdication of human reason and justice; it is the most decisive negation of human liberty, and necessarily ends in the enslavement of mankind, in theory and practice*'.

Bakunin was well known for his commitment to extreme direct action, extolling the '*sacred instinct of revolt*'. Known as 'propaganda by the deed', like mass strikes, the refusal of conscription, non-payment of taxes, rents, debts and so on. Bakunin had a mystical faith in violent revolution to cleanse and transform. The aim of these actions was to empower the masses to free themselves as he believed that humans become truly fulfilled by exercising their ability to think and by rebelling against authority. He argued that '*the passion for destruction is also a creative passion*'. It also acts to strike fear into the heart of the state and act as a spark for spontaneous revolution from below.

Bakunin was also well known for his criticism of Marxism, specifically, the dictatorship of the proletariat. He argued that anyone raised up to a position of power would become corrupt. Even good people acting as guardians of society will become corrupt. They abandon truth and seek to protect their own power. In other words, privilege kills the heart and mind, '*If you took the most ardent revolutionary, vested him in absolute power, within a year he would be worse than the Tsar himself.*'

Peter Kropotkin (1842–1921)

Hulton Archive/Stringer/Getty

Peter Kropotkin was a Russian geographer and anarchist theorist. Kropotkin's work was imbued with a scientific spirit, based on a theory of evolution that he proposed as an alternative to Darwin's. He is a key influence on the anarcho-communist strand. Kropotkin's major works include *Mutual Aid* (1902), *The Conquest of Bread* (1892) and *Fields, Factories and Workshops* (1898).

In *Mutual Aid* (1902), Kropotkin sought to provide communist anarchism with a scientific basis. This involved taking issue with social Darwinism on the grounds that the quest for survival and human progress is more effectively served by cooperation than it is by competition. He argued that cooperation was the principal means of human and animal development and sought to provide an empirical basis for this. '... *if we resort to an indirect test and ask Nature: "Who are the fittest: those who are continually at war with each other, or those who support one another?" we at once see that those animals which acquire habits of mutual aid are undoubtedly the fittest*.' Kropotkin continued to develop these ideas, describing forms of mutual aid observed in the animal world and various types of social collaboration throughout history. Kropotkin wished to correct the individualistic, narrow interpretation, which saw only competition, and not the far more important factor of mutual aid, as the instrument of survival.

In 1892, Kropotkin published *Conquest of Bread* which was the clearest statement of his anarchist views. He argued that the wage system should be abolished in favour of equal rewards for all, where private property and inequality would be replaced by the free distribution of goods. Kropotkin argued that in an anarchist society no one would be compelled to work as work is '*a psychological necessity ... a necessity which is health and life itself*'. In other words, much like Marx, he argued that working was the essence of humanity. Kropotkin's anarchism focused on removing barriers to the development of mutual aid, notably the capitalist class system and government, and authoritarian relationships generally. Life would be communal and based on direct democracy with federations of linked communities. For Kropotkin, the promotion of equal relations happened through the creation of alternative institutions which led to changes in behaviour, and this was the essence of revolution.

Kropotkin was a fervent critic of the education system arguing that '*We are so perverted by an education which from infancy seeks to kill in us the spirit of revolt, and to develop that of submission to authority*.' He argued that education had indoctrinated us to reject even the possibility of anything other than state-led rule. However, he also rejected Bakunin's revolutionary party, insisting that freedom must be attained by libertarian rather than dictatorial means. He believed that it was important for intellectuals to promote the grounds for revolutionary action by the masses, but not to direct it in an authoritarian way. '*I am an anarchist and am trying to work out the ideal society, which I believe will be communistic in economics, but will leave full and free scope for the development of the individual*.'

Emma Goldman (1869–1940)

Bettman/Contributor/Getty

A Russian-born propagandist, political agitator and revolutionary, Goldman was a prominent figure in US anarchist circles between 1890 and her deportation to the Soviet Union in 1919.

Despite being associated with collectivist anarchism, Goldman developed an anarchist vision that drew from both the communist anarchism of Kropotkin and the individualism of Stirner. In her book *Anarchism and Other Essays* (1910) she wrote, '*Anarchism ... stands for the liberation of the human mind from the dominion of religion; the liberation of the human body from the dominion of property; liberation from the shackles and restraint of government.*'

Her critique of the state focused on three areas:

» First, it constrains human liberty, restricting social harmony. Humans should be able to organize themselves as free individuals, to work for themselves and for each other, without any contradiction.

» Secondly, she argued that it uses its legal system and the threat of force to protect the interests of the working class. The vast majority in society are expected to conform to the rules of society that do not benefit them. She rejected private property, advocating instead a loose federation of cooperative groups.

» Lastly, the state uses patriotism to ensure support for its military activities even though they go against the interests of the majority and only benefit the ruling elite. Patriotism stirs up divisions between countries and forces the people to be patriotically behind 'their' country and against fellow humans.

Goldman believed it was necessary for anarchist thinkers to live their beliefs, demonstrating their convictions with every action and word. As such, she was against the growing authoritarianism of the Bolsheviks, arguing, '*Our position as regards power and dictatorship has been strengthened by the events in Russia.*' She argued that once the Bolsheviks rose to power, they were as brutal as their opponents in destroying any rivals, indicating, like others before her, that power corrupts and undermines the human spirit of liberty.

Goldman's rejection of parliamentary politics is well known, and she has been credited with saying that '*If voting changed anything, they'd make it illegal.*' She used the example of the women's suffrage movement to indicate how the parliamentary process is corrupting. She suggested that once women were given the vote they would become part of the process that oppresses other women, in the same way that working-class men who became engaged in the parliamentary process had done.

For Goldman, freedom does not come from the ballot box, it comes from removing the state. In her book *Anarchism and Other Essays* (1910) she wrote, '*Anarchism stands for a social order based on the free grouping of individuals for the purpose of producing real social wealth.*'

4. How to apply knowledge to anarchism answers

Tensions within anarchism over the role of the state

Worked example

Paragraph One – Agreement within anarchism

- ✓ All anarchists believe the state is immoral as it restricts liberty and is coercive
- ✓ They believe individuals are sovereign, not the state
- ✓ They believe that democratic government is based on deceit and is supported by threat of violence **(Proudhon)**

Paragraph Two – Agreement within anarchism

- ✓ All anarchists agree with the view that any other form of organized authority must be abolished, for example the church
- ✓ Both individualist **(Stirner)** and collectivist **(Bakunin)** anarchists agree that the church suppresses liberty
- ✓ Anarchists agree that any economic system, backed up by the state, must be abolished

Paragraph Three – Disagreement within anarchism

- ✗ However, anarchists disagree over other reasons why the state should be rejected
- ✗ Collectivist anarchists like anarcho-syndicalists and anarcho-communists believe that capitalism and the state are oppressive systems that must be destroyed **(Kropotkin)**
- ✗ Anarcho-capitalists believe that state intervention in the economy threatens economic freedom, and that state taxation is institutionalized theft

Tensions within anarchism over society

Worked example

Thematic approach

Theme 1 – State

- ✓ All anarchists agree that a future anarchist society will have no state **(Proudhon)** and individuals will be free. Although they do not lay down blueprints for the free society, any society which does not include coercive institutions will meet the anarchist objective
- ✗ Collectivist anarchists and individualist anarchists have significantly different conceptions about the nature of an anarchist society
- ✗ Collectivists emphasize the importance of social solidarity and mutual bonds in a future society; individualist anarchists see society made up of individuals exercising their free will

Theme 2 – Economy

- ✓ All anarchists agree that in an anarchist society any economic system backed up by the state must be abolished **(Goldman)**
- ✗ Anarchists disagree over the economic basis of a future anarchist society
- ✗ Collectivist anarchists support a future society based on collective ownership **(Bakunin)**; anarcho-capitalists support a future society based on private ownership

Theme 3 – Order

- ✓ All anarchists believe that humans are capable of living together peacefully without the need for imposed order. They believe that a society without coercive institutions is feasible, and within the range of natural, imperfect, human behaviour
- ✗ Collectivist anarchists see order in future society as based on altruism; individualist anarchists see it as based on egoism
- ✗ Egoism is based on the belief that order will emerge from 'ownness' **(Stirner)**, whereas anarcho-communism believes that order will arise from humans working together in a spirit of cooperation **(Kropotkin)**

Tensions within anarchism over human nature

Worked example

Paragraph One – Agreement within anarchism

- ✓ All anarchists agree that human nature is corrupted by the state and is moulded by the environment **(Kropotkin)**
- ✓ Human nature, or at the very least the potential of human nature, should be seen optimistically
- ✓ Social order can arise naturally from human nature and does not require the presence of the state or other coercive institutions **(Goldman)**

Paragraph Two – Disagreement within anarchism

- ✗ Individualist anarchists believe human nature is egoistical, whereas collectivist anarchists believe it is social and cooperative
- ✗ Mutualism and egoism both show disagreements in their stances on human nature.
- ✗ **Proudhon** believes that humans are naturally altruistic and cooperative, whereas **Stirner** believes that humans are self-interested egoists, who are unique

Paragraph Three – Disagreement within anarchism

- ✗ Individualist anarchists seek the end of the state so individuals can be free to express their true nature, whereas collectivist anarchists seek freedom from the state so humans' natural cooperative core can flourish
- ✗ Anarcho-capitalists believe that the market provides the mechanism for the full expression of human nature, whereas communist anarchists believe that human nature can only be truly expressed once capitalism is abolished

Tensions within anarchism over the economy

Worked example

Paragraph One – Agreement within anarchism

- ✓ All anarchists believe that economic freedom is central to the freedom of the individual **(Bakunin)**
- ✓ All anarchists oppose the private ownership of industry propped up by the coercive state as it creates an exploitative relationship between the people
- ✓ All anarchists advocate economic freedom so that people can conduct economic affairs autonomously without state ownership, regulation or intervention

Paragraph Two – Disagreement within anarchism

- ✗ Individualist and collectivist anarchists disagree over whether property should be owned in common or by free individuals
- ✗ Anarcho-communists believe in common ownership in a stateless society **(Bakunin),** whereas anarcho-capitalists believe in free-market, stateless capitalism
- ✗ Mutualists reject private and common ownership, supporting ownership of possessions only **(Proudhon)**

Paragraph Three – Disagreement within anarchism

- ✗ Within individualist anarchists, there is disagreement over the role of capitalism
- ✗ Anarcho-capitalists argue that the state should be removed from the market so free competition becomes the mechanism to create freedom and social order. Egoists see private property and capitalism limiting autonomy and believe they should be destroyed **(Stirner)**
- ✗ Anarcho-capitalists advocate unregulated capitalism in its purest form to stimulate enhanced personal liberty, whereas egoism rejects capitalism as this exploits and alienates individuals restricting their liberty

Chapter Summary

- All anarchists are fundamentally opposed to the state, believing it to be coercive and oppressive.

- They are also opposed to any coercive institutions and relationships.

- There are two broad wings of anarchism: collectivist anarchist and individualist anarchism.

- Within these broader wings there are a number of different strands.

- Within collectivist anarchism, the strands are communist anarchism, mutualism and anarcho-syndicalism.

- Within individualist anarchism, the two main strands are egoism and anarcho-capitalism.

- There are significant differences between the two broader wings as well as clear differences between the strands within these wings.

Exam Style Questions

1. To what extent do anarchists agree over the role of the state?

2. To what extent is anarchism more divided than united?

3. To what extent do anarchists disagree about the nature of the society they wish to create?

4. To what extent do anarchists agree about the nature of the economy?

5. To what extent do individualist and collectivist anarchists agree about human nature?

6. To what extent do anarchists agree about natural order?

7. To what extent do anarchists agree about liberty?

Further Resources

An Anarchist FAQ https://theanarchistlibrary.org/library/the-anarchist-faq-editorial-collective-an-anarchist-faq. Collectively produced and freely licensed since 1995, An Anarchist FAQ is an enormous wealth of information on various anarchist branches, movements and history across the world, continuously updated.

Berkman, A. *The ABC of Anarchism* (1929). This book presents the case for communist anarchism clearly and intelligently. It is regarded as a classic statement of anarchists goals and methods.

Goodwin, B. *Using Political Ideas* (1997). Chapter 6, 'Anarchism', is an excellent, if high-level, chapter which can be used to extend and challenge students' understanding of anarchism.

Huemer, M. *The Problem of Political Authority* (2013). A thoroughly argued volume on anarchist philosophy and politics, and specifically anarcho-capitalism, which is less covered elsewhere.

Kelly, P. et al. *The Politics Book* (2013). A clearly written, student-friendly book which covers many of the thinkers discussed in this chapter.

Kinna, R., ed. *The Bloomsbury Companion to Anarchism* (2014). The most comprehensive handbook on anarchist scholarship and research, particularly from non-Western perspectives.

Kinna, R. *The Government of No One: The Theory and Practice of Anarchism* (2020). A sympathetic general introduction to anarchism, providing a general overview of its key principles, traditions and practices.

Marshall, P. *Demanding the Impossible: A History of Anarchism* (2009). A very comprehensive, authoritative and enthusiastic account of the full range of anarchist theories and beliefs.

Miller, D. *Anarchism* (1984). A well-researched book looking at the theory and history of anarchism in depth providing a fair and balanced assessment of the ideology.

Vincent, R. *Modern Political Ideologies* (1995). Chapter 5, 'Anarchism' can be used to stretch and extend a student's knowledge of the content covered in this chapter.

5 ECOLOGISM

Historical overview

Although modern environmental politics did not emerge until the 1960s, ecological ideas can be traced back to much earlier times. Many have suggested that the principles of contemporary ecologism owe much to ancient and eastern religions such as Hinduism, Buddhism and Daoism. However, ecologism was, and remains, a reaction against the process of industrialization. The growth of ecologism since the 1960s had been provoked by the further and more intense advance of industrialization and urbanization. Environmental concern has become more acute because of the fear that economic growth is endangering the survival of the human race and the planet it lives on.

A new generation of activist pressure groups also developed around the 1970s – Greenpeace and Friends of the Earth – to Extinction Rebellion and Just Stop Oil in the 2020s. Animal liberation activists and 'eco-warrior' groups also sprang up – campaigning on issues such as air, river and sea pollution, deforestation, animal experimentation and climate change and its associated challenges. Together with established and much larger groups, such as the Worldwide Fund for Nature, this led to the emergence of a high profile and increasingly influential green movement. From the 1980s onwards, environmental questions have been kept high on the political agenda by green parties, which now exist in most industrialized countries.

Since the turn of the twenty-first century, greater urgency has been injected into the quest for environmental protection by the recognition that the ecological crisis is getting more severe. This is particularly the case in relation to climate change. Although attempts have been made to promote a coordinated international response, notably by the 1997 Kyoto Protocol and the 2015 Paris climate accord, the initial opportunity to tackle climate change has been blown by decades of denial. Indeed, as emerging economies such as China and India have dramatically increased their greenhouse gas emission without a willingness on the part of developed states, especially the USA, to curtail theirs, the period since the mid-1990s has become the Golden Age of the carbon economy.

Key Questions

- » How did ecologism originate?
- » What are the main principles that are central to ecologism?
- » What are the key strands of ecologism?
- » What are the areas of similarity and difference within ecologism?

Specification Checklist

1. Ecologism: core ideas and principles:

- » Ecology
- » Holism
- » Sustainability
- » Environmental ethics
- » Environmental consciousness
- » Post-materialism and anti-consumerism

2. Differing views and tensions within ecologism:

- » Shallow green ecology
- » Social ecology
  - » Eco-socialism
  - » Eco-anarchism
  - » Eco-feminism
- » Deep green ecology

3. Ecologism key thinkers and their ideas:

- » Aldo Leopold (1887–1948)
- » Rachel Carson (1907–64)
- » Ernst Friedrich ('Fritz') Schumacher (1911–77)
- » Murray Bookchin (1921–2006)
- » Carolyn Merchant (1936–)

Introduction to ecologism and its strands

The term 'ecology' was coined by the German zoologist Ernst Haeckel in 1866. Derived from the Greek *oikos*, meaning habitat, he used it to refer to 'the investigations of the total relations of the animal both to its organic and its inorganic environment'. As an ideology, ecologism is based on the belief that nature is an interconnected whole, embracing humans and non-humans, as well as the inanimate world. This encouraged ecological thinkers to question (but not necessarily reject) the anthropocentric, or human-centred, assumptions of conventional ideologies, allowing them to come up with new ideas about, among other things, economics, morality and social organization.

Nevertheless, there are different strains and tendencies within ecologism depending on whether they see nature as there to serve humans or seeing nature as equal to humans who must learn to live in harmony with it.

Shallow green ecology

Some ecologists are committed to 'shallow' ecology, which attempts to harness the lessons of ecology to human ends and needs. This provides the basis for a reformist approach to ecologism, sometimes dubbed environmentalism or enlightened anthropocentrism. However, shallow ecologism is dismissed by deep ecology as part of the problem not the solution.

Social ecology

Social ecology is a range of ecological theories that acknowledge that the relationship between humankind and nature has an important social dimension. They argue that nearly all our present ecological problems arise from deep-seated social problems. These include eco-socialism, eco-anarchism and eco-feminist thinkers.

Deep green ecology

Deep ecologists, on the other hand, completely reject any lingering belief that the human species is in some way superior to, or more important than, any other species. Nature does not exist to sustain human life but rather nature has intrinsic value – this is called ecocentrism.

1. Ecologism: core ideas and principles

> Definition
>
> **Ecology:** The study of the relationship between living organisms and the environment; stressing the network of relationships that sustains all forms of life.
>
> **Ecosystems:** An area where plants, animals and other organisms as well as the weather and landscape work together sustaining each other.

» Ecology

» Holism

» Sustainability

» Environmental ethics

» Environmental consciousness

» Post-materialist and anti-consumerism of the Liberal view of society

Ecology

This can be included in a discussion of ecologism view of human nature, the state, society and the economy.

The central principle of all forms of green thought is ecology. Ecology developed as a distinct branch of biology: the study of animals and plant systems in relation to their environment, through a growing recognition that plants and animals are sustained by self-regulating natural systems – ecosystems – composed of both living and non-living elements. Examples of an ecosystem are a field, a forest or a pond, as shown in Figure 5.1. The simple lesson of ecology is an understanding of the interdependence of all life forms within an ecosystem, as well as an appreciation of the natural harmony and balance that exists and must not be disturbed. As US conservationist **Rachel Carson (1907–64)** said, '*in nature, nothing exists alone*'.

All ecosystems tend towards a state of harmony through a system of self-regulation. This is homeostasis. Food and other resources are recycled, and the population size of animals, insects and plants adjusts naturally to the available food supply. However, such ecosystems are not 'closed' or entirely self-sustaining – each interacts with other ecosystems. A lake may constitute an ecosystem, but it also needs to be fed with fresh water from tributaries and receive warmth and energy from the sun. In turn, the lake provides water and food for species living along its shores, including human communities. The natural world is therefore made up of a complex web of ecosystems, the largest of which is the global ecosystem, commonly called the ecosphere or biosphere.

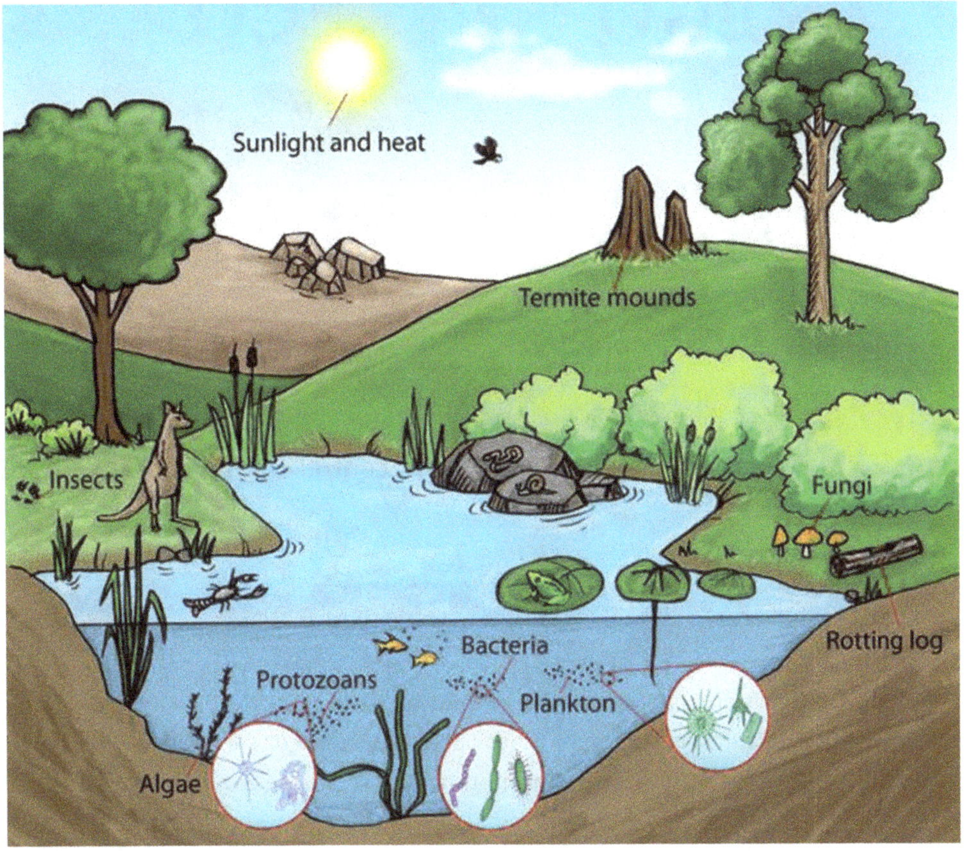

Figure 5.1 An example of an ecosystem.

Source: *Tsilia yotova*

Ecology radically challenged the conventional understanding of the natural world and of the place of humans within it. It challenged the view that humanity is nature's master, and instead suggests that a delicate network of interrelationships sustains every human community. **Carson** argued that humanity should not seek to dominate nature using science in the name of progress. She argued that, '*Man's attitude toward nature is today critically important simply because we have now acquired a fateful power to alter and destroy nature. But man is a part of nature, and his war against nature is inevitably a war against himself*'.

Green thinkers argue that humankind currently faces the prospect of environmental disaster precisely because, in its passionate but blinkered pursuit of material wealth, it has upset the 'balance of nature' and endangered the very ecosystems that make human life possible. American naturist **Aldo Leopold (1887–1948)** argued that humans needed to reconnect with nature which would lead to a greater understanding of our interdependence with it. All strands of ecologism reject the anthropocentrism associated with the belief that humans are above and outside nature, and that nature is purely a commodity for humanity to exploit. Ecologism thus favours ecocentrism and either rejects anthropocentrism altogether or seeks to recast it in line with the principle of ecology. This draws

---

Definition

Homeostasis: The tendency of a system to maintain its internal equilibrium.

Ecosphere/ biosphere: The regions of the universe, especially on the earth, that are capable of supporting life.

Spec key term

Anthropocentrism: A belief that human needs and interests are of overriding moral and philosophical importance; the opposite of ecocentrism.

Ecocentrism: A nature-centred rather than a human-centred system of values that gives priority to ecological balance.

attention to the most important distinction within the green movement; that is, the divide between what Norwegian ecologist Arne Naess termed shallow ecology and deep ecology.

The 'shallow' perspective accepts the lessons of ecology but uses them essentially to further human needs and ends. It argues that if we conserve and cherish the natural world, it will continue to sustain human life. This amounts to a form of 'enlightened' anthropocentrism, reflected in concerns such as cutting back on the use of non-renewable resources and reducing pollution. The 'deep' perspective, however, advances a form of 'strong' ecologism that dismisses any lingering belief that the human species is in some way superior to, or more important than, any other species, or indeed nature itself. It is based on the more challenging idea that the purpose of human life is to help sustain nature, and not the other way around. This is shown in Figure 5.2.

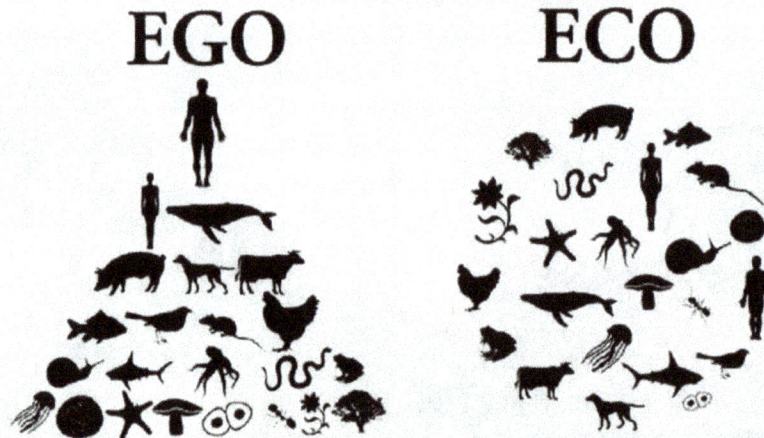

Figure 5.2 **The difference between an anthropocentric and an ecocentric outlook.**
Source: S. Lehmann, 2010

Ecology

Summary box

- The study of animals and plant systems in relation to their environment.
- An understanding of the network of relationships that sustains all life.
- The extent to which the relationship between living beings and the environment has implications for society.

Tensions within ecologism over humans' relationship with nature

AGREEMENT	DISAGREEMENT
✓ Ecologists reject the anthropocentric view that humans are above nature	✗ While shallow ecologists support enlightened anthropocentrism, this is rejected by deep greens and social ecologists
✓ Ecologists reject the view that nature is simply a commodity that humanity can exploit	✗ Deep greens see nature as having value in its own right, while shallow greens see nature as having instrumental value
✓ Ecologists stress a need to work towards a sustainable natural world	✗ Ecologists disagree over the type of sustainability they support

Holism

This can be included in a discussion of ecologism view of human nature, the state, society and the economy.

Traditional political ideologies have assumed that humans are the masters of the natural world and regarded nature as little more than an economic resource, available to satisfy human ends. Ecologists like Fritjof Capra and **Carolyn Merchant (1963–)** argued that this way of viewing nature was formalized during the Enlightenment, which radically changed scientific and philosophical thinking. Capra traced the origin of such thinking to the ideas of the French philosopher René Descartes (1596–1650) and the British scientist Isaac Newton (1642–1727). Instead of seeing the world as organic and something beyond human understanding and control, Descartes and Newton saw it as something that could be repaired, improved on or even replaced. During this time, science enabled remarkable advances to be made in human knowledge and provided the basis for the development of modern industry and technology. So impressive were the results of science, that intellectual inquiry in the modern world became dominated by scientism. However, green theorists argue that these benefits came at a high cost. By encouraging humans to think of themselves not as part of the natural world but as its master, the mechanistic world-view that lay at the heart of the 'Cartesian-Newtonian paradigm' fundamentally destabilized the relationship between humankind and nature. **Carson** argued, for example, that the use of harmful pesticides, in the interest of ever-greater production, had resulted in untold destruction to nature and damaged the earth's fragile ecosystem.

This led to a search for a new paradigm (or model), which drew green thinking into the spheres of science ancient myths and religions. One attempt to do this was made through the notion of holism. The term 'holism' was coined in 1926 by Jan Smuts, who used it to describe the idea that the natural world could only be understood as a whole and not through its individual parts. Smuts believed that science commits the sin of reductionism: it reduces everything it studies to separate parts and tries to understand each part in itself. In contrast, holism suggests that each part only has meaning in relation to other parts, and ultimately in relation to the whole. For example, a holistic approach to medicine would consider not just physical ailments but would see these as a manifestation of imbalances within the patient as a whole, taking account of psychological, emotional, social and environmental factors.

Although many green thinkers were concerned with the impact science brought to our world view, others have suggested that modern science may offer a new paradigm for human thought. During the twentieth century, physics moved a long way beyond the mechanistic and reductionist ideas of Newton. The breakthrough came in the early twentieth century when the German-born physicist Albert Einstein (1879–1955) advanced the theory of relativity. Einstein's theory of special relativity fundamentally challenged the traditional concepts of time and space. He suggested that the observations that one person makes about space and time differ somewhat from the observations of other people, who are moving at different speeds. Significantly, what Einstein's theory meant was that everything we experience is not necessarily how it actually is. For example, we might see lightening and hear thunder at different times due to the different speeds at which light and sound travel, but they happened at the same time, it is only the subjective experience which differs.

An alternative basis was found in religion and ancient mythology. For example, many in the green movement have been attracted to Eastern mysticism, seeing in it both a philosophy that gives expression to ecological wisdom and a way of life that encourages compassion for fellow humans, other species and the natural world. Particular attention in this respect has focused on Hinduism, Daoism and Buddhism as they

Definition

Scientism: The belief that scientific method is the only value-free and objective means of establishing truth and is applicable to all fields of learning.

Holism: A belief that the whole is more important than its parts; holism implies that understanding is gained by studying relationships among the parts.

Reductionism: Simplifying an issue by breaking it down into small parts that don't reflect how complex it actually is.

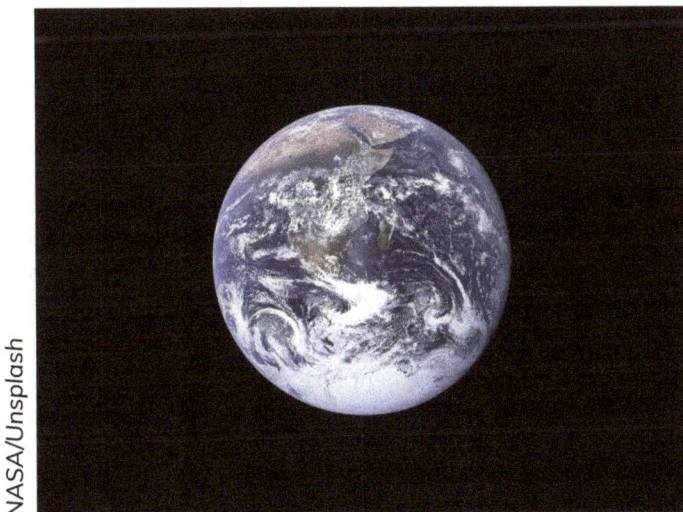

NASA/Unsplash

Photo 5.1 The first images of Earth from space sparked awareness of planetary boundaries.

Definition

Gaia hypothesis:
The hypothesis that the Earth is best understood as a living entity, which acts, above all, to maintain its own existence.

stress the unity or oneness of all things. German economist **Ernst Friedrich Schumacher's (1911–77)** thinking draws inspiration from Buddhist principles and he applied the principle that the impact of economics on both society and the biosphere must be 'light'.

Gaia

Such thinking has been most influential when it has been advanced through what James Lovelock termed the Gaia hypothesis. Gaia is the name of the Greek goddess of the earth. The Gaia hypothesis is the idea that the earth is best understood as a living entity that acts to maintain its own existence and that the Earth's biosphere, atmosphere, oceans and soil have the same self-regulating behaviour that characterizes other forms of life. Gaia has maintained homeostasis – a state of balance – despite the major changes that have taken place in the solar system. Gaia theory suggests that the earth and its natural cycles can be thought of like a living organism; when one natural cycle starts to break down, other cycles work to bring it back, continually optimizing the conditions for life on earth. The most dramatic evidence of this is the fact that although the sun has warmed up by more than 25 per cent since life began, the temperature on earth and the composition of its atmosphere have remained virtually unchanged. Another example is the way oceans are kept in balance; rivers dissolve salt from rocks and carry it to the ocean, yet the oceans' salt levels remain about the same, as it appears that the salt is removed again when water is recycled through cracks on the ocean floor. This process keeps the oceans' salt levels in balance and at a level that most lifeforms can tolerate.

Gaia theory implies that Earth's natural cycles work together to keep the earth healthy and support life. The idea of Gaia conveys the powerful message that humans must respect the health of the planet, and act to conserve its beauty and resources, the well-being of the planet being more important than that of any single species living on it at present. Lovelock suggested that those species that have prospered have been ones that have helped Gaia to regulate its own existence, while species that pose a threat to the delicate balance of Gaia are likely to be extinguished. Lovelock argued that humans have pushed Gaia to her limit. They filled the atmosphere with carbon dioxide, slashed away the 'lungs' (the rainforests) and driven many species to extinction. Eventually, he hinted, Gaia will pull things back into check, but it may be too late for the human race.

Holism

Summary box

- The belief that the whole – the ecosystem - is more significant than its individual parts.
- Opposition to the mechanistic, reductionist world view of post-enlightenment science that dominates society in its view of the non-human world.
- Includes the Gaia hypothesis – that Earth's natural cycles work together to keep the earth healthy and support life.

Sustainability

This can be included in a discussion of ecologism view of state, society and the economy.

Spec key term

Industrialism:
Based on large-scale production, a faith in science and technology, and the accumulation of capital and continuous growth to satisfy material needs.

Definition

Entropy: A tendency towards decay or disintegration, exhibited by all 'closed' systems.

One area of agreement between all ecologists is the need for the modern world to adapt to a sustainable future so that the health of the earth can be maintained. They agree that the current rates of growth and misuse of the earth's limited resources must stop, and a sustainable future must be considered. However, ecologists disagree about what this looks like. Green thinkers argue that the ingrained assumption of conventional politics, articulated by virtually all mainstream political parties (so-called 'grey' parties), is that human life has unlimited possibilities for material growth and prosperity. Indeed, green thinkers commonly lump capitalism and socialism together, and portray them both as examples of industrialism.

A particularly influential metaphor for the environmental movement has been the idea of 'spaceship Earth', as shown in Photo 5.1, because this emphasizes the notion of limited and exhaustible wealth. The idea that Earth should be thought of as a 'spaceship' was first suggested by Kenneth Boulding (1966). Boulding argued that humans have traditionally acted as though they live in a 'cowboy economy', an economy with unlimited opportunities, like the American West during the frontier period. He suggested that this encourages, *reckless, exploitative, and violent behaviour*'. However, the earth is a finite commodity, it is a 'closed' system. 'Open' systems receive energy or inputs from outside; for example, all ecosystems on earth – ponds, forests, lakes and seas – are sustained by the sun. However, 'closed' systems, as the earth itself becomes when it is thought of as a spaceship, show evidence of entropy or decay. All 'closed' systems tend to decay or disintegrate because they are not sustained by external sources. Ultimately, however wisely and carefully humans behave, the earth, the sun, and indeed all planets will be exhausted and die.

No issue reflects the law of entropy more clearly than the 'energy crisis'. Industrialization and mass affluence have been made possible by the exploitation of coal, gas and oil reserves, providing fuel for power stations, factories, motor cars, aeroplanes and so on. These 'fossil fuels' are non-renewable: once used up they cannot be replaced. In *Small is Beautiful* (1973), **Schumacher** argued that humans have made the mistake of regarding energy as an 'income', something that is being constantly topped-up, rather than as 'natural capital', i.e. something that is fixed and decreases every time it is used. This mistake has allowed energy demands to soar, at a time when finite fuel resources are, ecologists warn, close to depletion and unlikely to last to the end of the present century.

Green thinkers have argued that humans have been unwisely careless in plundering its resources through economic activity. Garrett Hardin (1968) developed a particularly influential model to explain why the over-exploitation of environmental resources has occurred, in the form of the tragedy of the commons. The concept of the tragedy of the commons draws parallels between global environmental degradation and the fate of common land. Common land or common fishing stocks encourage individuals to act in rationally self-interested ways, each exploiting the resources available to satisfy their needs and the needs of their families and communities. However, the collective impact of such behaviour can be devastating, as the vital resources on which all depend become depleted, Thus, as Hardin put it, 'Freedom in a commons brings ruin to all', an outcome that, in his view, could only be prevented by either stronger governance or population control.

Nevertheless, green economics is not only about warnings; it is also about solutions. Green thinkers argue that humans will only survive and prosper if they recognize that they are merely one element of a complex biosphere, and that only a healthy, balanced biosphere will sustain human life. Policies and actions must therefore be judged by the principle of sustainability. Sustainability sets clear limits on humans' material (economic) ambitions because it requires that production does as little damage as possible to the fragile global ecosystem. This can be ensured not merely through the implementation of government controls or taxes to discourage the over-exploitation of natural resources, but, at a deeper level, by the adoption of an alternative approach to economic activity. This is what **Schumacher** sought to offer in his idea of Buddhist economics. For **Schumacher**, this would involve humankind abandoning its obsession with wealth creation, and focusing instead on '*right livelihood*', a transformation created by a shift to smaller-scale living and working arrangements.

There is nevertheless considerable debate about what sustainability implies in practice.

» Shallow ecologists support 'weak' sustainability, which tries to reconcile ecology with economic growth through getting richer but at a slower pace. This is often conveyed by the notion of limits to growth which is the idea that economic growth should be limited to ensure that earth is secure for future generations, known as intergenerational equity. This would mean using non-renewable resources as well as investing in renewable resources to ensure that sustainable economic growth can be maintained. This is also known as sustainable development, meeting the needs of the present without compromising the ability of future generations to meet their own needs. Shallow ecologists also support the idea of green capitalism, which is the idea that as consumers become more ecologically minded, they will seek green solutions, which the market will then find and invest in. They would point to the growth in the availability of electric cars as an example of this. Others suggest that this can be supported by government regulation to tackle environmental problems as well as incentives for environmental practices like carbon reduction targets, banning of single use plastic and taxes on unecological activity.

» Radical ecologists, who include both social ecologists and deep ecologists, reject this notion of weak sustainability. US eco-anarchist **Murray Bookchin (1921–2006)** was highly critical of the 'limits to growth' approach, arguing that there was no way any ideology based on industrialism and exponential growth could ever remain within the ecological limits required. He argued that it prioritized human need over the wider need of earth to protect and preserve its resources. Instead, radical ecologists support (to different degrees) 'strong' sustainability, which places far greater

Definition

Tragedy of the commons: A parable that shows that economic resources will be ruined unless access to them is strictly constrained.

Spec key term

Sustainability: The capacity of the ecological system to maintain its health over time, one of the most contested ideas in ecologism.

Buddhist economics: This is economics as if people mattered based on the principle of meeting all human needs with no more consumption than is necessary.

Limits to growth: The finite earth, with the scarcity it implies, places limits on industrial growth.

Definition

Non-renewable resources: Non-renewable resources comes from sources that will eventually run out, such as oil and coal.

Renewable resources: An energy source that cannot be depleted and is able to supply a continuous source of clean energy, such as wind power.

stress on preserving 'natural capital' and are opposed to economic growth. They argue that any view which focuses on economic growth is incompatible with genuine ecological principles as it can only be achieved by further abuses of the earth's resources. All economic growth suggests increases in production and consumption, which places pressure of the earth and is simply unsustainable. Instead, ecologists have been arguing for degrowth and for steady-state economies. Degrowth implies the downscaling of production and consumption as societies use fewer natural resources by being organized differently or a steady-state economy, where the aim of economic growth is removed, focusing instead on ecological integrity, environmental protection and economic sustainability.

» As the origin of the ecological crisis lies in economics, consumerism and a fixation with economic growth, the solution would appear to lie in 'zero growth'. This would mean the construction of a 'post-industrial age' in which people live in small communities and rely on craft skills; a life that is simple in means, but rich in ends. For **Schumacher** it was about work that was creative and spiritually fulfilling rather than working solely for a pay packet in the forlorn hope of enjoying any leisure time. This could mean a fundamental and comprehensive rejection of industry and modern technology – literally a 'return to nature', what **Schumacher** referred to as his '*small is beautiful*' theory.

Sustainability

Summary box

- The capacity of the ecological system to maintain its health over time.
- To consider the ways to adapt to a sustainable future so that the health of the earth can be maintained.
- Different ecologists have different views on what constitutes sustainability.

Tensions within ecologism over sustainability

AGREEMENT	DISAGREEMENT
✓ All ecologists accept the concept of sustainability	✗ Shallow greens favour weak sustainability, whilst deep greens and social ecologists favours strong sustainability
✓ All ecologists take the view that current economic models are unsustainable	✗ Shallow greens' view of sustainability leads to a reformist approach, whilst for deep greens and social ecologists it leads to a radical approach
✓ All ecologists accept that the future economic model should recognize the principle of sustainability and work within these limits	✗ The shallow green view of sustainability places great faith in technology, which is rejected by deep greens and social ecologists

Environmental ethics

This can be included in a discussion of ecologism's view of human nature and society.

Ecologism is concerned with developing moral thinking in a number of different directions. This is because traditional ethical systems are clearly anthropocentric, based on the pleasure, needs and interests of humans. In such philosophies, the non-human world only has value if it satisfies human ends.

1. One ethical issue that even shallow ecologists grapple with is our moral obligations towards future generations. It is in the nature of environmental matters that many of the consequences of our actions will not be felt until decades or even centuries to come. For instance, why worry about the

accumulation of nuclear waste if the generations that will have to deal with it have yet to be born? Clearly, a concern with our own interests and perhaps those of our immediate family and friends only stretches a little way into the future. Ecologists are therefore forced to extend the notion of human interests to encompass the entire human species, making no distinction between the present generation and all future generations.

Such intergenerational equity may be justified in different ways. Care for and obligations toward future generations has sometimes been seen as a natural duty, an extension of a moral concern for our children by extension, their children and so on. A concern for future generations has also been linked to the idea of ecological stewardship. An example of this can be found in the debate, raised by the 'Fridays for Future' organization, encouraging students to strike on Fridays (see Photo 5.2) over whether young people's views on climate change should receive special consideration.

However, the notion of cross-generational justice has also been criticized. Traditional moral thinkers have sometimes argued that, as all rights depend on reciprocity, it is absurd to give people who have yet to be born, rights that impose duties on people currently alive. The present generation may, therefore, either be making sacrifices for the benefit of future generations who may prove to be much better off than themselves, or their sacrifices may be entirely inadequate to meet future needs.

Photo 5.2 **Fridays for Future march.**

2. An alternative approach to environmental ethics involves applying moral standards and values developed in relation to humans to other species and organisms. This can be seen in the growth of ethical veganism, which is a moral viewpoint that affects every aspect of a person's life and goes far beyond the adoption of a plant-based diet. They will try to exclude all forms of animal exploitation as far as possible. However, the most familiar attempt to extend moral standards to other species comes in the form of animal rights. In an argument that has had considerable impact on the animal liberation movement, Peter Singer claimed that an altruistic concern for the well-being of other species derives from the fact that, as sentient beings, they are capable of suffering. In *Animal Liberation* (1975), he pointed out that animals, like humans, have an interest in avoiding physical pain. Tom Regan in *The Case for Animal Rights* (1983) argued that animals were of value, with a life of their own, and that what happens to them mattered to them, so they should have rights. They both condemned any attempt to place the interests of humans above those of animals as speciesism.

3. However, the moral ethics of deep ecology go much further, in particular by suggesting that nature has intrinsic value in its own right, what **Leopold** describes as a '*land ethic*'. From this perspective, the value of nature has nothing to do with human usefulness and cannot be articulated through the extension of human values to the non-human world. Robert Goodin (1992), for instance, attempted to develop a 'green theory of value', which holds that resources should be valued precisely because they result from natural processes rather than human activity. **Leopold** went even further, arguing that an action is right if it preserves '*the integrity, stability and beauty*' of the biosphere and wrong if it did not. Additionally, **Leopold** argued that moral obligations must extend to a much broader community, for example, '*soils, waters, plants and animals, or collectively: the land*'.

Environmental ethics

Summary box

- Developing new moral standards and values for human relations with each other and the non-human world.
- These include moral obligations to future generations, other living entities and a respect for land as having value in itself – known as the land ethic.

Definition

Intergenerational equity: A concern about the future, implying that actions in the present should be judged by their impact on future generations.

Ecological stewardship: The notion that each generation has a duty to protect and conserve the natural environment for the benefit of generations to come.

Ethical veganism: The philosophical belief that cruelty and suffering to animals be avoided at all practical costs.

Animal rights: Moral entitlements that are based on the belief that as animals are non-human 'persons' they deserve the same consideration (at least in certain areas) as human beings.

Speciesism: A belief in the superiority of one species over other species, through the denial of their moral significance.

Tensions within ecologism over ethics

AGREEMENT	DISAGREEMENT
✓ Most ecologists view existing traditional ethics as anthropocentric	✗ Shallow greens' ethics are still anthropocentric while deep greens are based on the intrinsic value of nature
✓ Most ecologists have developed an ecological consciousness regarding the actions of humans	✗ Deep greens ethics seek human transformation from anthropocentric consciousness to an environmental consciousness, well beyond those of shallow greens
✓ Most ecologists agree on the need to move ethics beyond traditional ethical thinking and communities to protect the environment	✗ Deep greens ethics are based on biocentric equality/land ethic, whereas shallow greens arguing that intrinsic value is unrealistic and social ecologists think it is eco-la-la

Environmental consciousness

This can be included in a discussion of ecologism's view of human nature.

In their search for an alternative model of human understanding, some green theorists have emphasized the importance of 'quality of life' issues and concerns, separating happiness from material acquisition. In line with German psychoanalyst and social philosopher Erich Fromm (1979), they have placed 'being' above 'having'. The key feature of 'being' is that it seeks to rise above the individual, and recognize that each person is intrinsically linked to all other living things, and, indeed, to the universe itself.

Many deep greens have argued that to be truly ecocentric requires a transformation of the mind towards a new paradigm – an environmental consciousness. In order to achieve this, human nature needs to undergo a fundamental overhaul, even revolution, towards a sense of self within the context of nature, from EGO to ECO, and to take one's place alongside nature, not as its master (see Figure 5.2). This environmental consciousness would mean that for the first time, humans will seek to protect nature as an essential aspect of being human, seeing no distinction between ourselves and the natural world we are surrounded by.

For Arne Naess, self-realization is attained through a broader and deeper identification with others, he saw it as an identification so deep that one's own self is no longer defined by personal ego. Such ideas have often been shaped by Eastern religions, most profoundly by Buddhism. One of the core features of Buddhism is the doctrine of 'no self', the notion that the individual ego is a myth or delusion, and that enlightenment involves transcending the self and recognizing the oneness of life.

Environmental consciousness

Summary box

- A state of being where one's sense of self is fully realized by a deep identification with the non-human world.
- To consider a radical change in human nature towards nature, where personal ego is reduced or even removed.

Post-materialism and anti-consumerism

This can be included in a discussion of ecologism view of human nature, society and the economy.

Ecologism seeks not only to revise conventional moral thinking, but also to reshape our understanding of happiness and human well-being. In particular, green thinkers have advanced a critique of materialism and consumerism.

Materialism seeks to place possessions at the peak of achievement in society, whereby a person's value can be determined by the number of possessions they own, rather than on the content of their moral or spiritually being. Consumerism is linked to materialism as it indicates a person's happiness is equated with the consumption of material possessions, the inclination to seek fulfilment in acquisition and control. To ecologists, this is deficient in at least two respects.

1. It tends to undermine, rather than enhance, psychological and emotional well-being. As modern advertising and marketing techniques create ever-greater desires, they leave consumers in a constant state of dissatisfaction, because however much they acquire and consume they always want more. As such, consumers constantly have to work harder and longer in jobs they don't enjoy to earn more, to buy more – destroying their quality of life in the process. Consumerism thus works not through the satisfaction of desires, but through the generation of new desires, keeping people in an unending state of neediness, want and aspiration.

2. Materialism and consumerism provide the basis for environmental degradation, as consumption is seen as both good for the individual and good for society. This occurs as the 'consumer society' encourages people to place short-term economic considerations ahead of longer-term ecological concerns, in which case nature is nothing other than a commodity. In this light, ecologism can be seen to be associated with the ideas of post-materialism and anti-consumerism.

Shallow ecologists seek to respect consumerism and materialism, but within the confines of a wider ecological understanding, using humans' deeper sense of environmental concern to bring forward a new form of ecologically aware consumerism; to do more with less. Deep and social ecologists consider this nonsense, arguing that consumerism and materialism can never be reconciled to the broader aims of ecologism. As **Schumacher** argued, there needs to be a clean break with the idea that consuming equals happiness. One's well-being is best served, he argued, by moving towards a '*right livelihood*', which is spiritually fulfilling and creative work. The mind numbing and soul crushing work of gigantic capitalism leads humanity to have a '*greater concern with goods than with people*' and to an '*evil lack of compassion*'.

Deep and social ecologists therefore argue that we must enter a post-material world, understanding that true human satisfaction cannot be achieved by 'retail therapy' when it leads to the destruction of the source of all human and non-human life. They also argue that, deep down, humans understand that short-term retail fixes are not the key to human happiness. Instead, a deeper connection with nature and with fellow humans is the key to human happiness as well as ecological survival.

> ### Definition
>
> **Materialism:** That the acquisition of material goods is the ultimate aim in society and the equating of high status based on possession, not character.

> ### Spec key term
>
> **Consumerism:** Psychological and cultural view that focuses on consuming goods and services as a means to feel good about ourselves and drive economic growth.

Post-materialism and consumerism

Summary box

- Reshape our understanding of happiness and human well-being via a critique of materialism and consumerism and how to move beyond them.
- Seek a post-material outlook where happiness is not associated with the acquisition of greater and greater possessions.

Tensions within ecologism over society

AGREEMENT	DISAGREEMENT
✓ Ecologists put concern for the environment at the centre of their vision of society	✗ Ecologists disagree over anthropocentrism and ecocentrism
✓ Ecologists stress a more holistic and sustainable society	✗ Ecologists disagree over the type of sustainability they support
✓ Ecologists want societies that are less materialistic and consumerist	✗ Ecologists disagree over economic growth

2. Differences between the ecologist strands

» Shallow green

» Social ecology
   » Eco-socialism
   » Eco-anarchism
   » Eco-feminism

» Deep green

Shallow green ecology

Shallow green ecology refers to the form of ecologism that is practised by most environmental pressure groups and by a growing range of mainstream political parties. It is reformist in that it seeks to advance ecological principles and promote environmentally sound practices, but without rejecting the central features of capitalist society; in other words, seeking to balance ecologism with anthropocentrism. This form of enlightened anthropocentrism seeks to ensure that humans live in harmony with nature.

There are three key features of shallow ecology:

» The first is the recognition that there are environmental limits to growth, in the sense that pollution, increased CO_2 emissions, the exhaustion of non-renewable energy sources and other forms of environmental degradation ultimately threaten prosperity and economic performance. As the Limits to Growth Report (1972), which used a computer model to simulate the consequence of interactions between the earth and humans, concluded, '*If the present growth trends in world population, industrialisation, pollution, food production, and resource depletion continue unchanged, the limits to growth on this planet will be reached sometime within the next one hundred years.*'

» Linked to this is their commitment to environmentally sustainable capitalism, which means 'getting richer more slowly', shallow green ecology has therefore modest aims. Indeed, it is often condemned by more radical ecologists as hopelessly compromised: part of the problem rather than the solution.

» Lastly, shallow greens are committed to the idea of intergenerational equity by arguing that current generations have a responsibility to protect nature for the generations to come.

The two main ideological influences on shallow green ecology are liberalism and conservatism:

» Liberalism has, at best, an ambivalent relationship with ecologism. On the one hand, radical ecologists criticize individualism as a stark example of anthropocentrism, on the grounds that it equates happiness with material consumption. On the other hand, the stress on self-realization and developmental individualism found within modern liberalism can be said to sustain a form of 'enlightened' anthropocentrism, which encourages people to consider long-term, and not merely short-term, interests, and to favour 'higher' pleasures (including an appreciation of the natural world) over 'lower' pleasures (such as material consumption). This can be seen, for example, in J.S. Mill's condemnation of rampant industrialization and his defence of both a stationary population and a steady-state economy, grounded in the belief that the contemplation of nature is an indispensable aspect of human fulfilment.

» Conservatives, for their part, have showed sympathy for environmental issues and have drawn on a romantic and nostalgic attachment to a rural way of life threatened by the growth of towns and cities. It is clearly a reaction against industrialization and the idea of 'progress'. Such environmental considerations typically focus on the issue of conservation and on attempts to protect the natural heritage – woodlands, forests and so on – as well as the architectural and social heritage. The conservation of nature is therefore linked to a defence of traditional values and institutions.

Shallow green ecologism has advocated a range of policy solutions:

» First, they have advocated market-based solutions to environmental problems, espousing the idea of green capitalism, based on the assumption that the market mechanism can and will respond to pressure from more ecologically aware consumers by forcing firms to produce 'environmentally sound' goods and adopt 'green' technologies. Such thinking relies on the idea of consumer sovereignty and acknowledges the impact of the trend towards so-called 'responsible consumption'.

» Second, they have argued that national and supranational institutions need to work together, setting international environmental targets, to limit the human impact on the environment. They point to the Paris Climate Accord which, since 2015, has resulted in 196 countries and the EU backing the agreement to limit global warming to between 1.5°C and 2°C by 2050. Additionally, it requires individual states to impose restrictions and incentives to promote and encourage environmentally positive behaviour by its citizens and businesses, interfering with the market mechanism. These include carbon taxes, which a 2019 International Monetary Fund report said was 'the single most powerful and efficient tool to reduce domestic fossil fuel CO_2 emissions'.

» Lastly, they put their faith in technology and science to tackle environmental challenges. For example enabling scientists to use computer simulations of the planet's complex climate system to run different scenarios to see what works best and how to improve them. For example, the EU's Destination Earth initiative monitors climate developments and performs high-precision simulations to support policy making. This includes the strategic planning of solar farms and food management, for example. Additionally, carbon capture is one of the latest ways that technology is seeking to reduce emissions and stop global warming. Scientists argue that such schemes are vital weapons in the battle against global heating. They argue that carbon capture and storage is the only effective way to prevent industry from continuing to pour emissions into the atmosphere.

Definition

Consumer sovereignty: The notion, based on the theory of competitive capitalism, that consumer choice is the ultimately determining factor within a market economy.

Tensions within ecologism over state

AGREEMENT	DISAGREEMENT
✓ Some ecologists agree that the state has an important role in protecting the environment	✗ Eco-anarchists see the state as part of the problem and support decentralized communities, whereas shallow greens propose state solutions to environmental issues
✓ Some ecologists view the state as able to promote sustainability	✗ Deep greens reject the view that the state has an important role in protecting the environment as part of an anthropocentric perspective
✓ Many ecologists view the state as having a key role internationally, through signing global treaties	✗ Shallow greens propose market-based solutions to environmental issues, supported and directed by government targets and incentives

Social ecology

Social ecology refers to a range of ideas, each of which recognizes that environmental degradation is linked to existing social structures. **Bookchin** argues that nearly all present ecological problems arise from deep-seated social problems and systems. The advance of ecological principles therefore requires a process of revolutionary social change to overthrow existing societies and replace them with societies which are more consistent with ecological thinking. Social ecologists like **Bookchin** rejects ecocentrism as eco-la-la, by which he meant half-baked New Age gobbledygook masquerading as philosophy. Ecocentrism also denies the uniqueness of human beings, and the potentiality of this extraordinary species. Equally, it rejects anthropocentrism as domination that gives the privileged few the right to plunder the world. Instead, social ecology embraces complementarity which is the idea that by removing all power relationships between humans, humans will develop a relationship with nature based on mutuality.

Definition

Complementarity: The relationship between nature and humans based on an understanding of their mutual dependence.

Social ecology encompasses three distinct traditions:

» eco-socialism

» eco-anarchism

» eco-feminism

Eco-socialism

Eco-socialism has drawn from the pastoral socialism of thinkers such as William Morris, who extolled the virtues of small-scale craft communities, living close to nature as well as also being associated with Marxism. For example, Rudolph Bahro (1982) argued that the root cause of the environmental crisis is capitalism with its constant need to maximize profit. They argue that:

» The natural world has been ruined by industrialization, which is merely a consequence of capitalism's relentless search for profit.

» Capitalism's commitment to private property encourages the belief that humans are dominant over nature.

» The market economy 'commodifies' nature, in the sense that it turns it into something that has exchange-value and so can be bought and sold.

» The capitalist system breeds materialism and consumerism, and so leads to relentless growth.

» The concept of 'green capitalism' is a contradiction in terms; capitalism can never be used towards ecological aims as it is based on pursuing economic growth and industrialization. **Bookchin** argued that '*Capitalism can no more be "persuaded" to limit growth than a human being can be 'persuaded' to stop breathing*.'

» The only solution is to abolish the capitalist economic structure and replace it with a socialist model. This model will seek to regulate humanity's relationship with nature.

The core theme of eco-socialism is the idea that capitalism is the enemy of the environment, while socialism is its friend. Eco-socialists advocate a society without class divisions that lives in harmony with nature, based on the social use, not ownership of nature. Eco-socialists have supported the idea of 'system change, not climate change' that there are deep, structural, fundamental problems with the current economic system which is not just destroying our lives, but destroying the entire planet on which we ultimately depend. US climate journalist Eric Holthaus argues that the technology exists to switch to a carbon free energy world, but it won't happen because it doesn't benefit those already at the top of society. Studies show just a hundred companies are responsible for 71 per cent of the world's greenhouse gas emissions. John Bellamy Foster, a US professor, argued that an eco-socialist society would be based on '*a new triad*' of quality of life, human solidarity and ecological sensibility.

On the other hand, deep ecologists argue that eco-socialism can also been seen as another 'pro-production' political doctrine; it still promotes exploiting the wealth of the planet, albeit for the good of humanity rather than just the capitalist class which is still fundamentally anthropocentric.

Eco-anarchism

For more info on anarchism please see chapter 4

Some months before the publication of **Rachel Carson's** *The Silent Spring*, **Murray Bookchin** brought out *Our Synthetic Environment* (1962). **Bookchin** argued that anthropocentric ideas of humans' dominance over nature are linked to the idea that some humans must dominate others, and that society is hierarchical. Anarchism rejects the concept of a hierarchical society and so eco-anarchism extends that to the rejection of humanity's dominance over nature. **Bookchin** suggested that there is a clear link between the ideas of anarchism and the principles of ecology, particularly the anarchism of Kropotkin. This is based on the belief that ecological balance is the surest foundation for social stability. Just as an anarchist society is balanced by natural order and harmony between humans, eco-anarchists argue that humans are part of the natural balance of nature. Humans, however, need to recognize and understand that balance, and play their part in ensuring that it isn't disturbed.

There is, according to eco-anarchists, a natural affinity between the two ideologies. Anarchists believe in a stateless society, where harmony develops out of mutual respect and solidarity among humans founded on variety and diversity. Green thinkers also believe that harmony develops spontaneously within nature, in the form of ecosystems, and that these, like anarchist communities, require no external authority or control. The anarchist rejection of government within human society thus parallels the green thinkers' warnings about human 'rule' within the natural world. **Bookchin** therefore likened an anarchist community to an ecosystem and suggested that both are distinguished by respect for the principles of diversity, balance, complementarity and harmony.

It is clear to eco-anarchists like **Bookchin** that the solution to the ecological crisis lies in radical social change. This means nothing less that the overthrow of the state and all related hierarchic structure, for **Bookchin**, radical social change would include the removal of capitalism, as a system of domination, hierarchy and oppression, and its replacement with one based on mutual respect and social solidarity.

As such, eco-anarchists have advocated the construction of decentralized societies organized as a collection of communities; a social vision to which many deep ecologists are also attracted. Life in such communities would be lived close to nature, each community attempting to achieve a high degree of self-sufficiency. Such communities would be economically diverse; producing food and a wide range of goods and services, and therefore contain agriculture, craftwork and small-scale industry. For **Bookchin**, in an ecological society composed of a 'commune of communes', property would belong, ultimately, neither to private producers nor to a nation-state. Self-sufficiency would make each community dependent on its natural environment, generating an understanding of organic relationships and ecology. In **Bookchin**'s view, decentralization would lead to 'a more intelligent and more loving use of the environment'.

Although such thinking has been eagerly embraced by the radical wing of the green movement, it marks a clear divide between anarchism and mainstream ecologism, which sees government and state agencies as the principal means through which environmental issues should be addressed.

> **Spec key term**
>
> **Decentralization:** Decentralized societies based around communes, villages or bioregions that can achieve sustainability through a high level of self-sufficiency, making them dependent on their natural environment.

Tensions within ecologism over radical aims	
AGREEMENT	**DISAGREEMENT**
✓ All ecologists seek to put concern for the environment at the centre of their thinking	✗ Ecologists differ in radicalism over ecocentrism
✓ All ecologists seek a more sustainable society	✗ Ecologists differ over how radical a form of sustainability they support and a holistic approach
✓ All ecologists want societies which are less materialistic and consumerist	✗ Ecologists differ over materialism and consumerism

Eco-feminism

Eco-feminism has developed into one of the major philosophical schools of environmentalist thought, its key theorists including Karen Warren, Vandana Shiva and **Carolyn Merchant**. The basic theme of eco-feminism is that nature is a feminist issue as there are key links between the domination of women and the domination of nature. Ecological destruction thus has its origins in patriarchy: nature is under threat not from humankind but from men and the institutions of male power.

Merchant highlights links between the domination of nature and the domination of women, arguing that men learnt and applied methods to control them both for their own ends. For example, she argues that just as nature had been turned into an economic resource to be exploited for humanity, so women were pressurized to breed more workers in the name of economic profit. **Merchant** argued that 'the way out of this dilemma for me has been to re-think Nature, not as a mother, virgin, or witch, but as a partner ... Men and women can work with each other as partners, not as dominant or subordinate over each other and over Nature.' Equality eco-feminists – feminists who adopt an androgynous view of human nature – argue that patriarchy has distorted the instincts and sensibilities of men by divorcing them from the domestic world of nurturing, home-making and personal relationships. The sexual division of labour thus inclines men to subordinate both women and nature, seeing themselves as 'masters' of both. A society rid of patriarchy will see both men and women engaged in all aspects of society and as men throw off the notions of toxic masculinity promoted by patriarchy, they will become more in tune with the reciprocal relationship between humans and nature. **Merchant** referred to this as a 'partnership ethic'.

See Chapter 6 on the differences in feminism for more information on eco-feminism.

However, many eco-feminists subscribe to essentialism, the belief that there are fundamental and ineradicable differences between women and men. Such a position is adopted by Mary Daly in *Gyn/Ecology* (1979). Daly argued that women could liberate themselves from patriarchal culture if they aligned themselves with 'female nature'. The notion of an intrinsic link between women and nature is not a new one – primitive cultures often portrayed the earth or natural forces as a goddess, an idea resurrected in the Gaia hypothesis. Modern essentialist eco-feminists, however, highlight the biological basis for women's closeness to nature, in particular menstruation, pregnancy and lactation. The fact that women cannot live separately from nature's rhythms identifies them as part of the natural world. Essentialist eco-feminists argue that traditional 'female' values include reciprocity, cooperation and nurturing, values that have an ecological character. The idea that nature is a resource to be exploited or a force to be subdued is more abhorrent to women than men, because they recognize that nature operates in and through them, and intuitively sense that personal fulfilment stems from acting with nature rather than against it. The overthrow of patriarchy therefore promises to bring with it an entirely new relationship between human society and the natural world.

Spec key term

Biocentric equality: The principle that all organisms and entities in the biosphere are of equal moral worth, each being an expression of the goodness of nature.

Biodiversity: The range of species within a biotic community, often thought to be linked to its health and stability.

Environmental consciousness: A state of being where your sense of self is fully realized by a deep identification with the non-human world; this is the basis for a new form of ethics and social organization.

Mechanistic world-view: Post-enlightenment science sees nature exist for the convenience of humankind and nature as a machine where the parts can be understood, fixed or replaced in isolation from the whole.

| Tensions within ecologism over the economy ||
AGREEMENT	DISAGREEMENT
✓ Most ecologists reject materialism and consumerism	✗ Some ecologists support a green form of consumerism
✓ Most ecologists believe that economic growth presents a problem to the natural world	✗ Deep greens argue for an economy based on zero growth, whereas shallow greens advocate limits to growth
✓ Deep greens and social ecology reject capitalism	✗ Shallow greens argue that capitalism can be used to promote green aims

Deep green ecology

The term 'deep ecology' was coined in 1973 by Norwegian philosopher Arne Naess. For Naess, deep ecology is 'deep' because it persists in asking deeper questions and is concerned with fundamental philosophical questions about the impact of the human species on the biosphere. The key belief of deep ecology is that ecology and anthropocentrism (in all its forms, including 'enlightened' anthropocentrism) are simply irreconcilable; indeed, anthropocentrism is an offence against the principle of ecology. As such, deep ecology requires a total change in the way the world is seen, a fundamental shift in human consciousness.

This rejection of anthropocentrism has profound implications. Deep ecologists have viewed nature as the source of moral goodness. Nature has intrinsic value, not just value deriving from the benefits it brings to humans. A classic statement of the ethical framework of deep ecology is articulated in **Leopold's** *Sand County Almanac* (1948) in the form of the 'land ethic': *A thing is right when it tends to preserve the integrity, stability and beauty of the biotic community. It is wrong when it tends otherwise.* Such a moral stance implies biocentric equality. Naess expressed this in the idea that all species have an *equal right to live and bloom*, reflecting the benefits of biodiversity.

Such ecocentric thinking has been accompanied by a deeper and more challenging philosophical approach that amounts to nothing less than a new way of thinking about and understanding the world. Deep ecology calls for the adoption of an environmental consciousness. At the heart of this is a model of 'selfhood' that collapses the distinction between humankind and nature. **Schumacher** supported the idea of *good work* in small-scale organizations, using local resources to produce high-quality products as the basis for sustainability in nature and human happiness.

Deep ecology is also associated with a distinctive analysis of environmental degradation and how it should be tackled. Instead of linking the environmental crisis to particular policies or a specific political, social or economic system, deep ecologists argue that it has more profound cultural and intellectual roots which lies in the mechanistic world-view that has dominated the thinking of Western societies since the seventeenth century, around the globe. Above all, this dominant paradigm understands the world in terms of opposites (self/other, humankind/nature, individual/society, mind/matter, reason/emotion and so on) and thus allows nature to be thought of as passive and valueless in itself, a resource for satisfying human ends. In this light, nothing less than a paradigm change – a change in how we approach and think about the world – will properly address the challenge of environmental degradation.

In addition to its moral and philosophical outlook, deep ecology has been associated with a wider set of goals and concerns. These include:

» *Wilderness preservation.* Deep ecologists seek to preserve nature 'wild and free', based on the belief that the natural world, unspoilt by human intervention, is a source of wisdom and morality. Preservationism is nevertheless different from conservationism, in that the latter is usually protecting nature to satisfy long-term human ends. The 'wilderness ethic' of deep ecology is often linked to the ideas of Henry David Thoreau, whose quest for spiritual truth and self-reliance led him to flee from civilized life and live for two years in virtual solitude, close to nature, an experience described in *Walden* (1854). **Leopold**, whose work predates ideological ecologism, promoted wilderness preservation, arguing that all species in the wilderness must be left alone, irrespective of human concerns.

» *Population control.* Although greens from many traditions have shown a concern about the exponential rise in the human population, deep ecologists have placed a particular emphasis on this issue, often arguing that a substantial decrease in the human population is the only way of ensuring the flourishing of non-human life, as was argued by Paul Ehrlich in *The Population Bomb* (1968). However, more recently, deep ecology moved away from this, arguing instead that it is the greed of the wealthy, not population growth itself, that is destroying the planet.

» *Simple living.* Deep ecologists believe that humans have no right to reduce the richness and diversity of nature except, as Naess put it, to satisfy vital needs. As such, economies need to be organized locally, with local resources and knowledge wherever possible, rooted in the principles of strong sustainability, supporting and protecting local ecosystems. This is a philosophy of 'walking lighter on the earth'. It certainly implies an emphasis on promoting quality of life over quantity of possessions and is linked to a post-material model of self-realization, commonly understood as self-actualization.

» *Bioregionalism.* This is the idea that human society should be reconfigured in line with naturally defined regions, each 'bioregion', in effect, being an ecosystem. Bioregionalism is clearly at odds with established territorial divisions, based on national or state borders. Although deep ecologists seldom look to prescribe how humans should organize themselves within such bioregions, there is general support for self-reliant, self-supporting, autonomous communities.

Definition

Preservationism: The disposition to protect natural systems, often implying keeping things 'just as they are' and restricting the impact of humans on the environment.

Self-actualization: An 'inner', even quasi-spiritual, fulfilment that is achieved by transcending egoism and materialism.

Bioregionalism: The belief that the territorial organization of economic, social and political life should take into account the ecological integrity of bioregions.

Table 5.1 Types of ecologism

Anthropocentrism		Complementarity		Ecocentrism
Shallow ecology	Social Ecology			Deep ecology
	Eco-socialism	Eco-anarchism	Eco-feminism	
Key themes	• Enlightened anthropocentrism • Limits to growth • Weak sustainability • Future generations	• End of commodification • Collectivize wealth • Production for use	• Decentralization • Self-management • Critique of communism	• Essential difference between women and men • Women linked to nature • Men linked to culture	• Radical holism • Value in nature • Biocentric equality • Strong sustainability
Core goal	• Balance between ecology and capitalism modernity	• Social revolution: replace capitalism with socialism	• Dismantle structures of political authority	• Overthrow patriarchy	• Paradigm shift: cast off mechanistic/atomistic world view

3. Ecologism key thinkers

Key thinkers are an important part of understanding each ideology. The exam board has specified five key thinkers per ideology and TWO must be included in an answer to avoid a cap (please check the Exam Focus chapter (Chapter 9) for lots more discussion of key thinkers). Although key thinkers (and other thinkers) have been discussed throughout the chapter, here we look at each one in detail.

Aldo Leopold (1887–1948)

Library of Congress/Contributor/Getty

American-born naturalist Aldo Leopold is considered the father of wildlife ecology and the United States' wilderness system. Leopold developed an interest in the natural world, spending hours observing, journaling and sketching his surroundings. Leopold's work predates the rise of ecologism but has become an inspiration particularly for deep green thinking. His best-known work is *A Sand Country Almanac* (1937), part of which outlines his seminal principle of a Land Ethic. This calls for an ethical, caring relationship between people and nature. In 1922, he was instrumental in developing the proposal to manage the United States' first official wilderness area in 1924 and create a model for all wilderness preservation in the future.

The basic principle of a land ethic is the very simple idea of developing the relationship between humans and the land in the hope this will result in greater understanding and protection of the land. '*When we see land as a community to which we belong, we may begin to use it with love and respect.*' Leopold's concept of a land ethic expands the notion of 'community' to include not only humans, but soils, waters, plants and animals.

For Leopold the key to developing a land ethic was to promote the idea that nature and humans cannot be separated from each other; and particularly that humans cannot remove themselves from their duty to care for and protect the land. Leopold wrote that '*we can only be ethical in relation to something we can see, understand, feel, love, or otherwise have faith in*'. He believed that direct contact with the land and nature was the best way to instil a land ethic in humans, encouraging us to extend our ethics beyond our own self-interest. Within this community, humans are not conquerors but just members, who should respect fellow members and the community as a whole. '*In short, a land ethic changes the role of Homo sapiens from conqueror of the land-community to plain member and citizen of it. It implies respect for his fellow-members, and also respect for the community as such.*'

Leopold is also well known for his views on wilderness conservation. He argued that traditional conservation had failed as it was still focused on the anthropocentric idea of nature as an economic model. This would always fail as economics doesn't understand how to value the wilderness or its beauty, except from a selfish, human perspective. For him, '*conservation is a state of harmony between men and land*'. In the 1920s Leopold concluded that preservation of the wilderness needed to be embraced in American National Forests. He argued that wild species needed to be protected, including wolves and mountain lions, to ensure a healthy biotic community. In 1935, he helped found the Wilderness Society, dedicated to expanding and protecting the nation's wilderness areas.

Rachel Carson (1907–64)

A US marine biologist and conservationist, Rachel Carson did much through her writings to stimulate interest in scientific and environmental topics, contributing to the growth of the green movement. In her best-selling book, *The Silent Spring* (1962), she brought to public attention the issues around pollution while highlighting the science of ecology. Carson's writings are filled by a sense of wonder at the integrity, stability and beauty of nature, especially as found in the sea. She viewed life as a 'miracle beyond comprehension', insisting that all forms of life deserve respect.

In *The Silent Spring*, Carson highlighted the harmful consequences to humans, birds, fish and plant life of the widespread use of chemical pesticides, within US agriculture, reflecting the extent to which agri-business and state sponsorship threaten ecological balance and therefore sustainability. She showed that everything was connected to everything else.

Stock Montage/Contributor/Getty

We poison the gnats in a lake and the poison travels from link to link of the food chain and soon the birds of the lake margins become its victims. We spray our elms and the following springs are silent of robin song, not because we sprayed the robins directly but because the poison travelled, step by step, through the now familiar elm-leaf-earthworm cycle. These are matters of record, observable, part of the visible world around us. They reflect the web of life – or death – that scientists know as ecology.

She showed that insecticides such as DDT were poisoning food chains from insects upwards and even influenced President John F. Kennedy, who instructed his science advisory committee to investigate her claims. Its report vindicated Carson. Widespread use of pesticides was allowing poisons to build up in the food chain, posing a real risk to humans. She argued that 'the gods of profit and production' were responsible for this travesty against nature. Ten years and two presidents later, the production of DDT and its use in agriculture was banned in the US.

Silent Spring remains one of the most effective denunciations of industrial negligence ever written and is widely credited with triggering ecological awareness in the US and Europe, provoking the passage of a plethora of laws and creation of regulatory agencies.

The book was not just an ecological alarm call. It was an attack on post-war science, and American chemical conglomerates. She denounced the links between science and industry. 'When a scientific organisation speaks, whose voice do we hear – that of science or of the sustaining industry?' The question remains as relevant today as it did in 1962.

Ernst Friedrich ('Fritz') Schumacher (1911–77)

David Montgomery/Contributor/Getty

A German-born UK economist, statistician and environmental thinker, Schumacher championed the cause of human-scale production, intermediate technology and 'Buddhist economics'. This was a critique of economics and globalization.

Schumacher's seminal work, *Small Is Beautiful* (1973), was instilled with a deep spiritual vision and reflected a rejection of Western materialism and economic exploitation. In it, he advanced a critique of traditional economics' obsession with growth for growth's sake and condemned the value system on which it is based, particularly the fact that it is divorced from nature.

For Schumacher, size was a critical question. His championing of the small reflected deep reservations about the value of the traditional theory of economies of scale (or what he called 'rationalism by giantism'). He opposed the gigantism of big cities, mass production factories and industrialized agriculture – the idea that bigger is better. Instead, he believed that small-scale organizations promote compassion, morality and a sense of common purpose. He argued that '*any intelligent fool can make things bigger, more complex, and more violent. It takes a touch of genius – and a lot of courage to move in the opposite direction*'.

In 1955 Schumacher travelled to Burma as an economic consultant. While there, he developed the principles of what he went on to call 'Buddhist economics'. Buddhist economics was defined as '*economics as if people mattered*' arguing that '*the substance of man cannot be measured by Gross National Product*' and stressed the importance of '*right livelihood*' based on the belief that good work was essential for proper human development and that '*production from local resources for local needs is the most rational way of economic life*'.

Schumacher provided a critique of modern industrial practices, arguing that work has been dehumanized as transnational corporations seek the cheapest and quickest route to mass production via mechanization. Nature is seen purely as a resource to be used to garner ever-greater profits, and ecological damage is never factored into any costs. Schumacher wrote about the spiritual underpinnings of his approach and central to these was his notion of 'good work'. He believed that work had a threefold purpose:

» To provide people with useful goods and services.

» To provide people with the chance to use and perfect their gifts.

» To provide people with the chance to collaborate with others in order to liberate themselves from inbuilt egocentricity.

Crucial to his work was the belief that an infinite growth of material consumption is impossible in a finite world. As the world's resources of non-renewable fuels – coal, oil, and natural gas – are exceedingly unevenly distributed over the globe and undoubtedly limited in quantity, their exploitation at an ever-increasing rate is an act of violence against nature which must almost inevitably lead to violence between men.

Murray Bookchin (1921–2006)

Debbie Bookchin/Wikimedia Commons

A US social philosopher and environmentalist, Bookchin was drawn to the anti-authoritarian ideas of Kropotkin and other anarchists when he became disillusioned with Marxist socialism. Bookchin coined the phrase 'social ecology' and was a pioneer of the ecologist movement that was anti-capitalist and in favour of decentralization. His major works include *The Ecology of Freedom* (1982) and *Re-enchanting Humanity* (1995).

Bookchin was a leading proponent of the idea of 'social ecology', which he defined as being '*based on the conviction that nearly all of our present ecological problems originate in deep-seated social problems. It follows that these ecological problems cannot be understood, let alone solved, without a careful understanding of our existing society and the irrationalities that dominate it.*' He was arguing therefore that ecological destruction was a consequence of the way human society was organized based on domination and hierarchy. In *The Ecology of Freedom* (1982) he argued that '*The domination of nature by man stems from the very real domination of human by human.*' He believed that only by doing away with all hierarchies – man over woman, old over young, white over Black, rich over poor – could humanity avert ecological and economic collapse.

Bookchin held capitalism responsible for all destructive elements within society. He argued that capitalism had commodified humans, seeing them only as a resource and ignoring their humanity and it did the same with nature, seeing it as a resource to be used for profit and economic growth to maximize profit instead of enriching human lives. He suggested that '*The plundering of the human spirit by the market place is paralleled by the plundering of the earth by capital.*'

Bookchin emphasized the potential for non-hierarchic cooperation. He proposed a system of 'libertarian municipalism' to describe a form of communal, face-to-face, direct democracy. These would be decentralized communities without any hierarchy or dominance from above, replacing capitalism with human-centred forms of production. '*The long-term solution to the ecological crises is a fundamental shift in how we organise society, a new politics based on face-to-face democracy, neighbourhood assemblies and 'the dissolution of hierarchy.'*'

Carolyn Merchant (1936–)

David Iltis/Wikimedia Commons

A US eco-feminist philosopher and historian of science, Merchant highlighted the links between gender oppression and the 'death of nature'. Merchant's chief works include *The Death of Nature* (1983), *Radical Ecology* (1992) and *Autonomous Nature* (2015).

In *The Death of Nature* Merchant demonstrated how scientific progress curtailed the advancement of women. Merchant developed a feminist critique of the way in which the scientific revolution, beginning in the seventeenth century Enlightenment, had challenged the maternal image of the natural world. She questioned the idea that advances in science created progress for all. In fact, she argued, it had brought about the destruction of nature and the repression of women.

Merchant began by identifying the idea which projected a dual image of both nature and women. Prior to the Enlightenment, nature was considered the generous, if sometimes unpredictable, giver of life. The earth was a 'nurturing mother' who provided humanity with resources. This was also the image of women who maintained the household. Equally, both nature and woman could be seen as unpredictable, and chaotic, having the ability to grow and nourish but also to destroy. Some even went as far to present women, whose power they feared, as witches. Hence the Enlightenment brought about the 'triumph' of science, and along with it, the desire and ability for scientists, to understand and control nature and to dominate women.

Merchant's argues that the female gender attributed to Mother Nature is no accident and underlies superior attitudes towards women as well as nature. Hence when (male) scientists spoke about controlling an untamed and unruly nature, they revealed their attitudes towards women too. Merchant used the examples of Francis Bacon's book *The Masculine Birth of Time* (1603) to highlight this: '*she is either free ... or she is put in constraint, moulded and made as it were new by art and the hand of man; as in things artificial ... nature takes orders from man and works under his authority*'. In other words, both nature and women must comply to the will of men. For Merchant, nature had been turned into a useful resource for humanity in the same way that women were utilized for the benefit of male society. They were both victims of patriarchal, capitalist, male-dominated society. She argued that all systems of dominance and hierarchy must be overthrown for nature and women to be free from subordination. This is the only way to protect Planet Earth and gender relations.

For Merchant, the 'death of nature' was not only seeing meadows turned into fields and forests to timber, but the collapse of nature as a complex ecosystem built on interdependence and equilibrium. Instead, nature became an economic resource, stripped from its core values and turned into a machine in the service of men.

4. How to apply knowledge to ecologism answers

Tensions within ecologism over society

Worked example

Thematic approach

Theme 1 – Anthropocentrism vs ecocentrism

✓ All ecologists put environmental concerns at the core of their vision for society **(Carson)**

✗ Deep ecologists are ecocentric and want to create a society in which the needs of nature are on a par with the needs of humanity **(Leopold)** They disagree with shallow ecologism which they view as still anthropocentric

✗ Some forms of social ecology, like eco-socialism, are considered to value human needs above the environment, by deep ecologists

Theme 2 – Sustainability

✓ All ecologists emphasize a desire for a sustainable society

✗ Shallow ecologists support weak sustainability, whereas deep ecologists support strong sustainability

✗ Some forms of social ecology, like eco-socialism, do not appear to accept strong sustainability, whereas others, like eco-anarchism does **(Bookchin)**

Theme 3 – Capitalism/economic growth

✓ All ecologists want societies that are less materialistic and consumerist

✗ Shallow ecologists support limits to growth, whereas deep ecologists seek a society without economic growth

✗ Shallow ecologists support 'green capitalism', whereas all other forms of ecologism see capitalism as the problem **(Schumacher)**

Tensions within ecologism over humans' relationship with nature

Worked example

Paragraph One – Agreement within ecologism

✓ Ecologists reject the anthropocentric view that humans are above and outside nature **(Carson)**

✓ All ecologists reject the view that nature is simply a commodity that humanity can exploit

✓ Ecologists stress a need to work towards a sustainable natural world

Paragraph Two – Disagreement within ecologism

✗ While shallow ecologists support enlightened anthropocentrism, this is rejected by social ecologists who reject all forms of anthropocentrism and ecocentrism

✗ Deep greens are ecocentric and see nature as having value in its own right **(Leopold)**, while shallow greens see nature as having instrumental value

✗ Ecologists disagree over materialism and consumerism. Shallow greens suggest it can help to create a more pro-nature conscious world. Deep greens reject this as not radical enough, arguing that only a post-materialist, post-consumerist world can protect nature

Paragraph Three – Disagreement within ecologism

✗ Ecologists disagree over the type of sustainability they support

✗ Shallow greens support weak sustainability but deep greens reject this as not radical enough, supporting strong sustainability instead **(Schumacher)**

✗ Social ecologists also reject shallow green attitudes as not radical enough arguing that only radical social change can create a sustainable society **(Bookchin)**

Tensions within ecologism over the economy

Thematic approach

Theme 1 – Materialism and consumerism

- ✓ Most ecologists reject materialism and consumerism, and reject the linking of consumerism and materialism to happiness **(Schumacher)**
- ✗ Shallow greens believe that 'green' consumerism holds the key to a sustainable economy, whereas deep greens reject traditional economics **(Schumacher)** believing in the transformation of society and the economy
- ✗ Social ecology rejects materialism and consumerism as a root cause of uncontrolled growth. They believe consumerism is driven by producers not consumers

Theme 2 – Economic growth

- ✓ Most ecologists believe economic growth presents a problem to the natural world
- ✗ Deep greens reject economic growth whilst shallow greens want smarter but slower growth/ limits to growth
- ✗ Social ecologist disagree over growth, eco-anarchists argue that unless growth is traced to its source the demand for controlling growth is unattainable **(Bookchin)**, whereas eco-socialists disagree

Theme 3 – Capitalism

- ✓ Deep greens and social ecology reject capitalism, seeking an economy based on small scale, local production **(Bookchin) (Schumacher)**
- ✗ There is disagreement between shallow greens who favour 'green' capitalism and deep greens who reject capitalism favouring a post-industrial world of small-scale, decentralized and self-sufficient communes
- ✗ There is disagreement within social ecology over what social system should replace capitalism

Tensions within ecologism over the state

Worked example

Paragraph One – Agreement within ecologism

- ✓ Shallow ecologists believe the state plays an important role in protecting the environment through regulation and legislation
- ✓ The state can establish green taxes and emissions targets to promote sustainability
- ✓ Ecologists have successfully argued for international cooperation and agreements between states showing the importance of state action in protecting the environment

Paragraph Two – Disagreement within ecologism

- ✗ Shallow ecologists support the state to create sustainability, which is rejected by deep greens and social ecologists
- ✗ Deep greens want to replace the state and the systems it upholds, they are ecocentric and argue for a paradigm shift in our relationship with nature, rejecting the proposition that states can protect the environment **(Schumacher)**
- ✗ Some shallow ecologists support forms of green capitalism, whereas deep greens and eco-socialists reject capitalism as inherently anthropocentric and against green principles **(Leopold)**

Paragraph Three – Disagreement within ecologism

- ✗ Shallow ecologists support the role of the state to work globally to create a more sustainable world
- ✗ Eco-anarchists reject the notion that the state can ever play a positive role in improving ecological conditions **(Bookchin)**
- ✗ All social ecologists reject the role of the current state arguing that it is committed to upholding values which do not put the environment first

Chapter Summary

- Ecologism is a relatively new ideology which developed in the 1960s.
- It is a diverse ideology which has evolved and developed in many different directions.
- Shallow ecology is the approach that is most widely known and practised throughout the world.
- However, many of the core principles are based around the values of deep ecology.
- There are irreconcilable differences between shallow and deep ecology.
- There are also significant differences within social ecology.

Exam Style Questions

1. To what extent do ecologists agree over the role of the economy?
2. To what extent is ecologism more divided than united?
3. To what extent do ecologists agree over environmental ethics?
4. To what extent do ecologists disagree about the type of society they wish to create?
5. To what extent do ecologists agree about the role of the state in protecting the environment?
6. To what extent do ecologists argue that radical change in society is necessary?
7. To what extent is ecologism a clear rejection of anthropocentrism?
8. To what extent does ecologism reject existing social structures?

Further Resources

Bookchin, M. *Social Ecology versus Deep Ecology* (1987). Bookchin's biting rejection of deep ecology. http://dwardmac.pitzer.edu/Anarchist_Archives/bookchin/socecovdeepeco.html.

Dobson, A. *Green Political Thought* (2007). An accessible and useful account of the ideas behind green politics; a classic text on the subject.

Dyzek, J. and Schlosberg, D. *Debating the Earth: The Environmental Politics Reader*, 2nd edn (2005). A broad collection of readings highlighting key issues, debates and perspectives within environmental political discourse.

Gabrielson, T. et al. *The Oxford Handbook of Environmental Political Theory* (2016). The most authoritative text compiling the latest scholarship and research on green ideology, and its interactions with other ideologies.

Solutions Journal www.thesolutionsjournal.com. This open access peer-reviewed journal profiles environmental policy solutions as well as commentary and ideas on contemporary issues from a green standpoint.

The Aldo Leopold Foundation https://www.aldoleopold.org. An excellent website outlining the principles and values of Leopold.

Visit our companion website at https://bloomsbury.pub/essentials-of-political-ideas-2e for more worked examples.

6 FEMINISM

Historical overview

The first text of feminism is usually taken to be Mary Wollstonecraft's *A Vindication of the Rights of Woman* (1792). Liberal feminists like Wollstonecraft, were associated with 'first wave' feminism which campaigned for female suffrage and the same legal and political rights as men. The first wave ended with the achievement of female suffrage which many naively believed meant that women had achieved full emancipation. It was not until the 1960s that the women's movement was regenerated, with the emergence of feminism's 'second wave'.

The publication in 1963 of Betty Friedan's *The Feminine Mystique* did much to relaunch feminist thought. 'Second-wave' feminism recognized that the achievement of political and legal rights had not removed the exploitation of women, and their ideas became increasingly radical. Books such as Kate Millett's *Sexual Politics* (1970) and Germaine Greer's *The Female Eunuch* (1970) pushed the boundaries of what had previously been seen as 'political' by focusing attention on the personal and sexual aspects of female oppression.

'Third-wave' feminism, from around the 1990s, suggested that second-wave feminists had only been talking about the experiences of white, middle-class women, omitting the experiences of a wide range of other women's experiences. Third-wave feminism is therefore closely connected to intersectionality.

'Fourth-wave' feminism has been emerging since 2010s. It can be characterized by online campaigns, protests and movements like #MeToo, advancing from the fringes of society into the headlines of our everyday news. It has been described as focusing on sexual harassment, violence against women, workplace discrimination, body shaming, online misogyny and sexist imagery via social media activism, which has made it easier to connect and campaign globally. Laura Bates' 'Everyday Sexism' project is a good example of this newest wave.

Key Questions

- » How did feminism originate?
- » What are the main principles that are central to feminism?
- » What are the key strands of feminism?
- » What are the areas of similarity and difference within feminism?

Specification Checklist

1. Feminism: core ideas and principles:

- » Sex and gender
- » Patriarchy
- » Personal is political
- » Equality and difference feminism
- » Intersectionality

2. Differing views and tensions within feminism:

- » Liberal feminism
- » Socialist feminism
- » Radical feminism
- » Postmodern feminism

3. Feminist thinkers and their ideas:

- » Charlotte Perkins Gilman (1860–1935)
- » Simone de Beauvoir (1908–86)
- » Kate Millett (1934–2017)
- » Sheila Rowbotham (1943–)
- » bell hooks (1952–2021)

Denis Doyle/Getty

Spec key term

Waves of feminism: Feminism has been described as going through waves where a particular form of misogyny is confronted. This is 'resolved' until another form of misogyny appears and so on.

Introduction to feminism and its strands

Feminism is the belief in advancing the role of women by reducing gender inequality and has traditionally been defined by two basic beliefs: that women are disadvantaged because of their gender and that this disadvantage can and should be overthrown. Despite these common goals, feminism is difficult to pin down as a coherent ideology because it is made up of many different competing and sometimes even conflicting views.

The history of feminism is usually identified in waves. Since the eighteenth century, women have sought to remove barriers to their equality. Once successful, feminist ideas tended to retreat, like the tide, assuming that equality would arrive. Over time, however it became apparent that the original reforms were insufficient and so new feminist analysis grew around the new forms of female oppression, resulting in another wave, and so on. As society evolves, the way it discriminates against women changes and so feminism evolves to respond to it.

Definition

Foundational equality: Rights that all humans have by virtue of being born which cannot be taken away.

Formal equality: The idea that all individuals have the same legal and political rights in society.

Liberal feminism

Liberal feminism has its roots in the first wave of feminism and focuses primarily on legal and political rights, especially the right to vote. Liberal feminists concern themselves with women's foundational and formal equality as well as equality of opportunity, believing that a liberal society is one where women can flourish.

Socialist feminism

Traditionally, socialist feminists identified capitalism as the main cause of patriarchy, as it needed women to be in a subservient position to serve its ends. Socialist feminism more recently has focused on an interplay between capitalism and patriarchy, accepting them as independent but interlocking forces of exploitation of women.

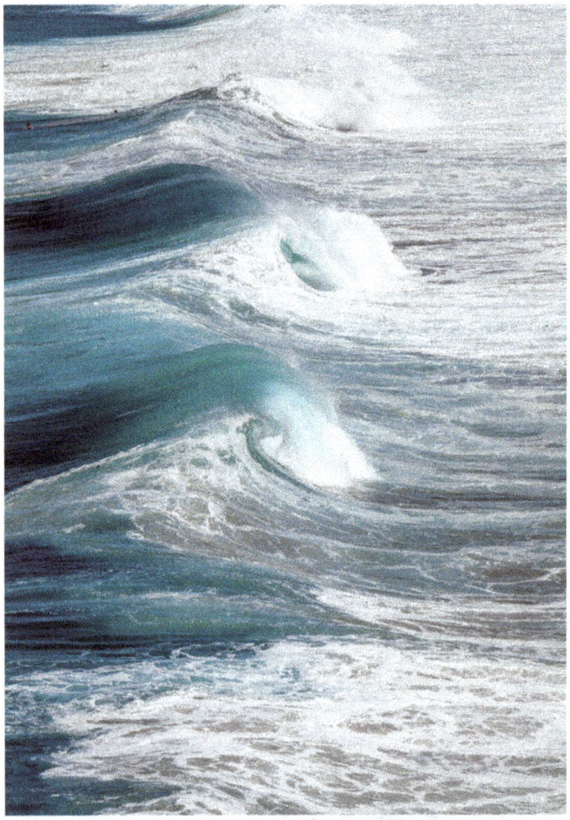

Photoholgic/Unsplash

Photo 6.1 The development of different types of feminism through history is often referred to as the movement's 'waves'.

Radical feminism

Radical feminists were the first feminists to identify patriarchy as the sole source of women's oppression. Radical feminism is not a single coherent belief system. Instead, it is a plethora of different voices, all seeking to explain the pervasive and systematic way that patriarchy oppresses women. Radical feminism has developed into a distinctive and established ideology, whose ideas and values challenge the most basic assumptions of conventional political thought.

Postmodern feminism

Postmodern feminism emerged as a critique of the radical feminism of the 1960s, which only focused on the experiences of white, middle-class women. This left women of colour, and those of different classes and religions, without a voice. Postmodern feminism sought to give those women a voice. It is also associated with a form of feminism that was much more fluid in its interpretation, encouraging women to define their oppression and their feminism for themselves.

1. Feminism: core ideas and principles

Sex and gender

This can be included in a discussion of the feminist view of human nature.

The most common of all misogynist arguments is that the gender divisions that run through society are 'natural': women and men merely fulfil the social roles for which nature designed them. That childbearing is unique to the female sex is seen as evidence that women are suited to the responsibilities of motherhood: nurturing, educating and raising children by devoting themselves to home and family. In short, 'biology is destiny'. Feminists, however, typically challenge such thinking by drawing a sharp distinction between sex and gender. 'Sex', in this sense, refers to biological differences between females and males. 'Gender', on the other hand, is a cultural term; it refers to the different roles that society ascribes to women and men. Gender differences are typically imposed through contrasting stereotypes of 'masculinity' and 'femininity' and feminists argue that there is no reason for these distinctions, in fact different cultures attribute different values to masculinity and femininity, which shows they are no more than behaviours instilled in men and women through society. As French feminist **Simone de Beauvoir (1908–86)** pointed out, '*One is not born, but rather becomes, a woman.*' By this, **de Beauvoir** rejected the idea that women were born 'feminine', arguing instead that it was learnt behaviour imposed by society. In denying that there is a link between sex and gender, feminists therefore emphasize that gender differences are socially, or even politically, constructed. Writing earlier than de Beauvoir, **Charlotte Perkins Gilman (1860–1935)** argued that male aggressiveness and maternal roles for women were artificial. She wrote, '*There is no female mind. The brain is not an organ of sex. Might as well speak of a female liver.*'

Feminists argue that encouraging women to conform to 'femininity' is a key aspect of female oppression in society. Femininity is to be subordinate and submissive, sympathetic and considerate, docile and composed. In other words, to taking a secondary, passive role in society, usually behind men, who are encouraged to be assertive, aggressive and vocal. Women who display such tendencies are criticized as bossy and pushy. As Sheryl Sandberg, former COO of Meta argued, '*I want every little girl who's been told she is bossy to be told she has leadership skills.*'

The vast majority of feminists believe that human nature is characterized by androgyny. All human beings, regardless of sex, possess the genetic inheritance of a mother and a father, and therefore embody a blend of both female and male attributes. Such a view accepts that sex differences are biological facts of life but insists that they have no other implications. Women and men should thus not be judged by their sex, but as individuals, as 'people'. This implies that the central core of feminism is the achievement of genderless 'personhood'. This is the aim of equality feminists.

Definition

Androgyny: The idea that human nature is 'sexless' and that one's sex is irrelevant to one's social role or political status.

Spec key term

Equality feminism: A form of feminism that spans across liberal, socialist, radical and postmodern feminism which seeks equality for men and women in society and believes that the biological differences between men and women are inconsequential.

COROIMAGE/Getty

Photo 6.2 Women dressed to resemble Rosie the Riveter, a feminist icon who represents the women workers in war industries during the Second World War.

Sex and gender

Summary box

- Sex refers to biological differences between men and women, whereas gender refers to the different roles that society ascribes to men and women.
- Most feminists believe that ones gender is learnt behaviour.
- Feminists believe this distinction to be important in their analysis of society.

Tensions within feminism over sex and gender

AGREEMENT	DISAGREEMENT
✓ All feminists recognize the distinction between sex; biological differences between females and males, and gender; the different cultural roles society ascribes to women and men	✗ While different feminists agree that some aspects of gender are imposed culturally, they also believe that human nature is not androgynous, and that the nature of men and women is innately different
✓ All feminists believe gender roles imposed on women ignore their true nature and believe women can only be truly emancipated when they're encouraged to allow their true nature to evolve	✗ Because of these fundamental differences, women shouldn't seek to replicate male behaviour to emancipate them from the subordination of men; instead, women should be encouraged to value and promote their differences from men
✓ They argue that boys and girls are forced to conform to their gender roles by the clothes they wear, the toys they are bought and by what society expects of them	✗ Cultural feminism also takes an essentialist view of female nature arguing that patriarchal society seeks to impose negative associations with female attributes like childbirth, as it is something only women can do, rather than seeing them as positive values

Patriarchy

This can be included in a discussion of the feminist view of the state, society and the economy.

Definition

Patriarchy: The systematic, institutionalized and pervasive system of male oppression.

Feminists use the concept of patriarchy to describe the power relationship between women and men. The term literally means 'rule by the father'. Feminists believe that the dominance of the father within the family symbolizes male supremacy in all other institutions. Many would argue that the patriarchal family lies at the heart of a systematic process of male domination, in that it reproduces male dominance in all other walks of life: in education, at work and in politics. Radical feminist **Kate Millett (1934–2017)**, described 'patriarchal government' as an institution whereby '*that half of the populace which is female is controlled by that half which is male*'. She suggested that patriarchy contains two principles: 'male shall dominate female, elder male shall dominate younger'. Patriarchy is therefore a hierarchic society, characterized by both sexual and generational oppression. While strides have been made in some countries over the last few decades, it would be naïve to think that Patriarchal dominance is waning, one only needs to look at Afghanistan and Iran, for example, to see how patriarchal values dominate society.

As the concept of patriarchy is so wide-ranging, it is sometimes a difficult topic to grasp. In her 1990 book *Theorising Patriarchy*, Sylvia Walby defined patriarchy as '*a system of social structures and practices in which men dominate and oppress women*' and identified key features prominent in a patriarchal system.

1. **Paid work** – One of the most obvious ways that women have been discriminated against is paid work. Historically, women were denied the opportunity of paid work, and when they had access to some work it was only in industries that men did not dominate. It was argued that a woman (who didn't have the financial responsibility of a family to look after) should not take the job of a man (who did). Even when it was made illegal to discriminate against women, women were still encouraged

(through their education and socialization) to look for work in certain industries and only in roles that were secondary to men, such as an assistant or receptionist.

2. **Patriarchy within the household** – **Kate Millet** called the family '*patriarchy's key institution*'. From a young age, the family is the source of all socialization and where young girls are taught to know their place. This could be through watching gender roles in the home, the toys they are bought to play with (as well as the toys bought for their brothers) and realizing the expectations imposed upon them. By the time they reach secondary school, most girls have already been socialized into a clear understanding of what a patriarchal society expects of them.

3. **Culture** – Patriarchal culture, which promotes specific roles for men and women, is so widespread in society that it has become the norm. Part of that culture is to impose on women the behaviours that keep women in a subordinate position to men – to be sweet, kind, polite, caring and passive while men are encouraged to be powerful, bold, aggressive and dominant. Moreover, society also seeks to encourage women to look a certain way and be a certain size, as American feminist and author of *The Beauty Myth*, Naomi Wolf says, '*dieting is the most potent political sedative in women's history*'. In other words, forcing women to obsess about their bodies distracts them from being able to flourish in society and compete with men.

4. **Sexuality** – There have always been much stricter sexual rules imposed upon women than on men when it comes to sexual activity. Historically, society encouraged women to repress their sexual urges; it was not 'ladylike' to be interested in sex. Prominent radical feminist Germaine Greer argued in *The Female Eunuch* (1970) that women had sexual feelings, but were socialized against doing anything to satisfy them. Any women who showed any interest in sex or dared to have more than one partner was castigated by society, yet this same rule was routinely not applied to men.

5. **Violence** – Violence against women is still commonplace in patriarchal societies, even though nowadays it is recognized as being unacceptable. Up until very recently, however, it was commonly accepted that a husband had as much right to 'discipline his wife' as he did his children, and the Domestic Violence Act only came into force in England in 2005. Figure 6.1 shows a wider societal picture of violence against women – according to the latest UN figures, in 2020 a man kills a woman every three days in the UK and, worldwide, six women an hour are killed by men. Feminists suggest that male violence towards women, including murder, rape and sexual assault, keeps women in a self-imposed curfew in patriarchal societies. Attempts to address this have tended to focus on women's behaviour – 'don't wear short skirts, don't walk alone, always walk with a man' – rather than the culture of male dominance and violence which is the real cause of these appalling statistics.

Share of victims globally by who murdered them

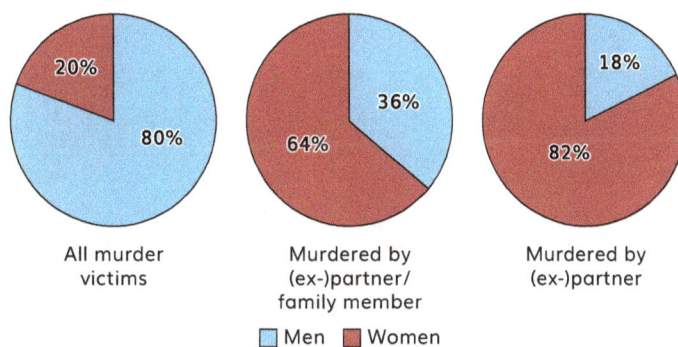

Figure 6.1 **87,000 women and girls were murdered around the world in 2017 – 50,000 of them were murdered by an (ex-) partner or a family member.**

Source: Statista, statista.com/chart/18913/victims-murdered-by-partners-family-femicide

6. **The state** – Historically the state has played its part in the subordination of women by denying them a vote and any legal rights that were commonly given to men. Once women were given the vote, it was still very hard for them to get represented within state institutions. Even now, women only make up a third of the House of Commons and the Lords. The Supreme Court has only two woman out of twelve justices and their representation in the civil service, the cabinet, government and upper echelons of the judiciary are woefully low. Yet women are encouraged to be grateful that things aren't as bad as they were.

Walby's analysis of patriarchy is mainly a radical feminist perspective, as different feminists have different views on patriarchy.

» Liberal feminists, to the extent that they use the term, use it primarily to draw attention to the unequal distribution of rights and opportunities in society. The face of patriarchy they highlight is therefore the under-representation of women in senior positions in politics, business, the professions and public life. Liberal feminists tend to use the word to describe the existence of discrimination in society and don't see it as a widespread system of oppression in the way other feminists do.

» Socialist feminists tend to emphasize the economic aspects of patriarchy. In their view, patriarchy operates in tandem with capitalism, seeing gender subordination and class inequality as interlinked systems of oppression. Some socialist feminists reject the significance of the term altogether, on the grounds that gender inequality is merely a consequence of the class system: capitalism, as the creator of patriarchy, is the main issue.

» Radical feminists, on the other hand, place considerable emphasis on patriarchy. They see it as a systematic, institutionalized and pervasive form of male power that is rooted in society. Patriarchy thus expresses the belief that the pattern of male domination and female subordination that characterizes society at large is, essentially, a reflection of the power structures that operate within domestic life.

» Postmodern feminists agree that patriarchy is a system of female oppression but argue that the analysis of patriarchy by radical feminists focuses exclusively on white, middle-class women. Postmodern feminism argues that patriarchy adapts and mutates in different cultures and classes and manifests itself in many different ways to different women. They argue that any understanding of patriarchy must focus on the ways it manifests itself among different cultures, religions and classes. In Western countries, the social position of women improved significantly during the twentieth century; however, in parts of the developing world, patriarchy still assumes a cruel, even gruesome, form: tens of millions of women are subjected to the practice of female genital mutilation, bride murders still occur and the persistence of the dowry system in India ensures that female children are often unwanted and sometimes allowed to die.

Patriarchy

Summary box

- Society, state and the economy are characterized by systematic, institutionalized and pervasive gender oppression.
- This manifests itself in different ways throughout society.
- The different strands of feminists view it differently.

Tensions within feminism over patriarchy	
AGREEMENT	**DISAGREEMENT**
✓ Radical, socialist and postmodern feminists agree that patriarchy is a pervasive system of oppression	✗ There is clear disagreement between radical and liberal feminists over patriarchy, as liberals (when they use the term) do not recognize it in the same way as a radical feminists, as liberal feminists see discrimination in the private sphere, whereas radical feminists argue that male oppression extends to both public and private realms
✓ They also argue that woman's oppression exists in the public as well as the private sphere	✗ Postmodern feminists criticize other strands of feminism for their lack of recognition of patriarchy as it affects non-white, middle-class, straight women
✓ Nothing less than a radical overhaul of the current system is needed to create an equal society	✗ Socialist feminists disagree with radical feminist about the origins of patriarchy, as they argue it is created by capitalism, whereas radical feminists reject this believing it stands as a form of oppression in its own right

Personal is political
This can be included in a discussion of the feminist view of society and the economy.

The concept behind this slogan is an important one in feminism as it is the notion that the personal experiences of women's oppression are a consequence of their political situation (living in a male-dominated society). It is taken from Carol Hanisch's book of the same name published in 1970. So, for example, if a woman is being abused by her male partner at home or sexually harassed by her male boss at work, it is because of the patriarchal political system and not just her individual experience. Hanisch argued therefore that women's 'personal' problems were in fact 'political' problems, caused by women's subordinate position in society; problems that could only be improved by social change, not by women's individual solutions.

In 1963, leading liberal feminist Betty Freidan published her seminal book, *The Feminine Mystique*. In it, Friedan outlined the problem facing many (white, middle-class) women which she identified as '*the problem with no name*'. This was the deep discontent many women felt with their role as wife, mother and homemaker. All these women felt that their problems were personal to them, it was only on publication of the book that women understood that their problems were widespread and not personal to them, they were political. Her book became a springboard for second-wave feminism.

The idea that the 'personal is political' formed the basis of this next wave of feminism. It sought to encourage women to consider their life and experiences and analyse them through the lens of power-based relationships. This led to the rise of groups for women to share common experiences. These groups empowered women and helped them understand that they were not alone in their struggles and frustrations. This suggested that women's situations were not their fault, but a consequence of wider power relationships and society-based systems of oppression.

Linked to this notion of personal as political is the distinguishing of the public and private spheres. The arena of the public sphere is primarily understood as society, workplace, the political arena – everything outside one's front door. The private sphere is associated with one's domestic and family setup – everything inside one's 'front door'. Hence politics has usually been understood as an activity that takes place within a 'public sphere' of government institutions, political parties, pressure groups and public debate. Family life and personal relationships have normally been thought to be part of a 'private sphere', and therefore to be 'non-political'.

Radical feminists, however, insist that power relations (politics) exist in all social groups and are not confined to the affairs of government; politics exists whenever and wherever social conflict is found. **Kate Millett** defined politics as '*power-structured relationships, arrangements whereby one group of persons is controlled by another*'. The relationship between government and its citizens is therefore clearly political, but so was the relationship in the family, between husbands and wives.

Feminists have therefore sought to challenge the divide between 'public man' and 'private woman' (Elshtain, 1993). However, they have not always agreed about what it means to break down this divide, about how it can be achieved or about how far it is desirable.

» Radical feminists have been the keenest proponents of 'the personal is the political'. Female oppression is thought to operate in all walks of life, and to originate in the family. Radical feminists have therefore analysed 'the politics of everyday life'. This includes the process of conditioning in the traditional family, the distribution of housework and other domestic responsibilities, and the politics of personal and sexual conduct.

» Postmodern feminists believe the personal experiences of women of colour, for example, have been crucial in raising the consciousness of all women. **bell hooks** actively encouraged women to discuss their experiences, explaining how her own experiences as a Black girl left her feeling constrained by her family's views on gender.

» Socialist feminists have also viewed the personal as political, in that they have linked women's roles within the traditional family to the maintenance of the capitalist economic system. Where they disagree with radical feminists is on the political nature of oppression. Whereas radical feminists believe the political system that dominates society to be patriarchy, socialist feminists believe it to be capitalism.

Definition

Second-wave feminism: The form of feminism that emerged in the 1960s and 1970s and was characterized by a more radical concern with 'women's liberation', especially, in the private sphere.

Spec key term

Public sphere: The area in society where relationships are public, specifically life outside the home, particularly society and work.

Private sphere: The area in society where relationships are seen as private, specifically home and domestic life.

» Liberal feminists struggle with the concept of the personal as political. They argue that society should concern itself with the public sphere, correcting historic discrimination by ensuring that it is no longer upheld in discriminatory laws. If women are equal in the eyes of the law and have the same rights as men, they can fight any discrimination through these processes. Liberal feminists have been careful to avoid any restrictions of what they believe are women's choices in their personal life, refusing to see patriarchy as the systematic oppression of women throughout society.

Personal is political

Summary box

- The idea that all relationships between men and women, both in society and in private relationships, are based on power and dominance.
- Many feminists think this goes to the essence of patriarchy.
- Most feminists believe this distinction is crucial.

Tensions within feminism over the personal as political

AGREEMENT	DISAGREEMENT
✓ The 'personal is political' is a radical feminist idea that has been accepted by both socialist and postmodern feminists	✗ Whilst radical and postmodern feminists both agree that the 'personal is political' they disagree over what it identifies. Postmodern feminists argue that the personal experience of different minorities and classes of women has been ignored by radical feminism and seeks to give them a voice
✓ These feminists agree with the notion that the personal experiences of women of oppression are a consequence of their political situation (living in a male-dominated society)	✗ Radical and socialist feminists disagree on what 'political' means, socialist feminists argue that the personal experiences of women are primarily due to capitalism, whereas radical feminists argue it is due to patriarchy
✓ Even liberal feminists like Betty Friedan have recognized that 'the problem with no name' identified women feeling discontented with their personal role as wife, mother, and homemaker	✗ Even though liberal feminists like Friedan recognized that women are confined to a domestic role in society, the solution for them was to improve equality of opportunity

Equality and difference feminism

This can be included in a discussion of the feminist view of human nature.

Traditionally, feminists have demanded equality with men. However, the issue of equality has also exposed a fault line within feminism: feminists have embraced contrasting notions of equality and a very small minority have entirely rejected equality in favour of the idea of difference.

» Liberal feminists champion legal and political equality with men, they are equality feminists. They have supported an equal rights agenda which would enable women to compete in public life on equal terms with men, regardless of sex. Equality thus means equal access to the public sphere.

» Socialist feminists are also equality feminists but in contrast to liberal feminists they argue that equal rights are meaningless unless women also enjoy social equality. Equality, in this sense, must apply to economic power, and so must address issues such as the ownership of wealth, pay differentials and the distinction between waged and unwaged labour.

» Radical feminists are primarily concerned about equality between men and women, for example in family and personal life. Equality must therefore operate, for example, in terms of childcare and other domestic responsibilities, the control of one's own body, and sexual expression and fulfilment.

» Postmodern feminists see equality in terms of the equality of all women in society, seeking to ensure that the voices of women of colour, working-class women and women of different religions' voices are heard in the equality debate.

Despite tensions between the strands, all these feminists believe that women are the same as, and equal to, men, and that society should be reorganized to ensure this is fully reflected in society. These equality feminists link any supposed 'difference' between men and women to socialization under patriarchy, seeing it as a manifestation of oppression or discrimination.

However, there are a small minority of radical feminists who champion difference rather than equality. The term difference feminism is an umbrella term that covers a range of views, from the moderate to the extreme. What unites difference feminism, unsurprisingly, is a belief in fundamental differences between men and women.

At its most simple, difference feminists want women to recognize and embrace their differences from men. They argue that equality feminists have encouraged women to reject their own femaleness. To want to be equal to a man implies that women seek to define their goals in terms of what men are or what men have. The demand for equality therefore embodies a desire to be 'like men'. To idealize androgyny and ignore sex differences is therefore a mistake. Women should recognize and celebrate the distinctive characteristics of the female sex; they should seek liberation *through* difference, as developed and fulfilled women, not as 'persons'.

Thus, although they seek to overthrow patriarchy, they warn against the danger of modelling themselves on men or to adopt the competitive and aggressive behaviour that characterizes patriarchal society.

Difference feminists usually (if not always) subscribe to an essentialist view of feminism. This is the belief that there are certain universal, innate, biologically or psychologically based features of gender that are at the root of differences in the behaviour of men and women. The aggressive and competitive nature of men and the creative and empathetic character of women are thought to reflect deeper hormonal and other genetic differences, rather than the structure of society, as equality feminists would argue.

Cultural feminism is a form of difference feminism which takes an essentialist view of female nature. Cultural feminists seek to reclaim the beauty of 'femaleness' and childbirth from the negativity it has become associated with by equality feminists. Cultural feminists argue that patriarchal society seeks to impose negative associations with female nature rather than seeing them as positive values.

Mary Daly represents a form of difference feminism known as eco-feminism (see page 132 for more details). Some eco-feminists argue that women are a part of nature and the wider ecosystem in a way that men can never be, i.e. they are life creators. In *Gyn/Ecology* (1978), Daly argues that the nature of men is the cause of environmental destruction, something that goes fundamentally against the nature of women. While in earlier work she argued for equality between the sexes, her later works identified fundamental problems with male nature and culture which she saw as the opposite of female nature. Daly contrasted women's life-giving powers with men's death-dealing powers. In a 1999 interview she claimed that '*I don't think about men. I really don't care about them. I'm concerned with women's capacities, which have been infinitely diminished under patriarchy.*'

In *Gyn/Ecology* (1978), Daly criticized the liberal feminist agenda of legal equality arguing that it distracted women from the real goal of abolishing patriarchy, rather than reforming it. She argued that legal equality was irrelevant in a system like patriarchy which is organized to oppress women. Reforms merely tinker at the edges leaving patriarchy largely intact. She also argued that any reformist movement that seeks to work within patriarchy requires women to embody the principles of a patriarchal system rather than overturn them.

However, **Simone de Beauvoir**, writing in the late 1970s, was dismayed by the idea of a separate, mystical 'feminine nature': '*Just as I do not believe that women are inferior to men by nature, nor do I believe that they are their natural superiors either.*' It was dangerous, she argued to imagine an '*eternal feminine nature, in which women were more in touch with the earth and the cycles of the moon*'. This was just another way for men to control women, by imposing unrealistic expectations of women's

Definition

Eternal feminine:
The idea that idealizes woman as solely virtuous – modest, graceful, pure, delicate, civil, compliant, reticent, chaste, affable and polite.

behaviour and also by telling women they are better off in their cosmic, spiritual 'eternal feminine' world, kept away from men's knowledge and left without all the men's concerns like work, careers and power.

There has been a lot written about difference feminism and it is vitally important to understand their message clearly without overstating their significance within radical feminism. Sometimes feminism is defined in its totality by the tiny minority of feminists who see men as the enemy, whereas in fact these are not even the majority within difference feminism. Some might suggest that the inaccurate portrayal of all feminists as 'man-hating women' is part of the patriarchal system that seeks to alienate women (and men) from the importance of feminism.

Equality and difference feminism

Summary box

- Equality feminists seek equality for men and women in society.
- Difference feminists argue that men and women have a fundamentally different nature from one another.
- There are significant differences between these two types of feminism which leads to fundamentally different views of society.

Tensions within feminism over human nature	
AGREEMENT	**DISAGREEMENT**
✓ All feminists believe gender roles imposed on women ignore their true nature and believe women can only be truly emancipated when they're encouraged to allow their true nature to evolve	✗ While equality feminists believe that society should pursue gender equality based on the belief in the androgyny of human nature, difference feminists argue that the nature of men and women is innately different and this needs to be recognized when seeking to emancipate women from the subordination of men
✓ The vast majority of feminists are equality feminists, who believe that human nature is androgynous and that biological differences between men and women are insignificant	✗ Difference feminists believe that women shouldn't seek to replicate male behaviour and should be free to embrace their essentially female selves
✓ They argue that boys and girls are forced to conform to their gender roles by the clothes they wear, the toys they are bought and by what society expects of them	✗ Cultural feminism (a form of difference feminism) takes an essentialist view of female nature arguing that patriarchal society seeks to impose negative associations with female attributes like childbirth as it is something only women can do, rather than seeing them as positive values

Spec key term

Intersectionality:
An idea that challenged the notion that 'gender' was the singular factor in determining a woman's fate, arguing that Black and working-class women's experiences of patriarchy are different from those of white, middle-class women.

Intersectionality

This can be included in a discussion of the feminist view of the economy and society.

Definition

Misogyny:
Ingrained prejudice against women.

The idea of intersectionality within feminism seeks to show how women of different cultures, classes and religions have different experiences of misogyny. It argues that feminism needs to focus on women from a wide range of backgrounds, not just white, middle-class, heterosexual and able-bodied.

Kimberlé Crenshaw, legal scholar and critical race theorist, is generally credited with originating the term in the late 1980s. According to the idea of intersectionality, women do not just have a simple gender-based identity under which they are oppressed, it intersects with other factors like race, social class, ethnicity, age, religion, nationality and sexual orientation. So different women will face different types of oppression based on the factors interconnected with their gender. For example, a white, middle-class, gay woman will experience a different type of misogyny to a Black, working-class, straight woman or a young Muslim woman. This is the essence of intersectionality; a lens through which you can see where

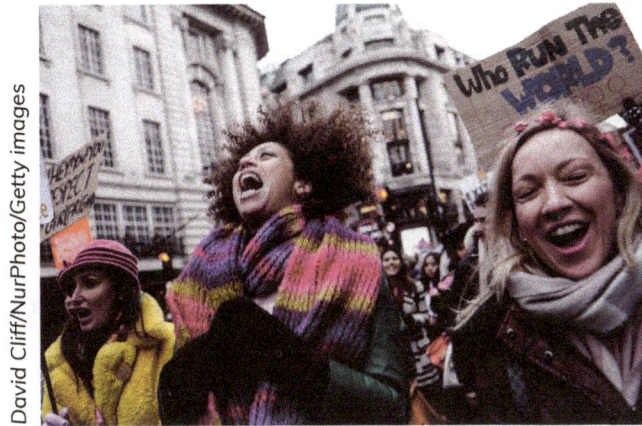

David Cliff/NurPhoto/Getty images

Photo 6.3 The Women's March for Bread and Roses, 2019, was an anti-austerity march that combined feminist and class concerns. Its message was that women of all races, sexualities and backgrounds deserve dignity and joy in addition to basic rights.

power comes and collides, where it interlocks and intersects. Crenshaw went on to argue that '*All inequality is not created equal*', by looking at the way it overlaps, it is possible to see the compounding experiences of oppression: '*We tend to talk about race inequality as separate from inequality based on gender, class, sexuality or immigrant status. What's often missing is how some people are subject to all of these, and the experience is not just the sum of its parts.*' Although Crenshaw came up with the term 'intersectionality', the idea of overlapping systems of oppression was not new. In 1977, the Combahee River Collective, a collective of Black feminists, proclaimed in their manifesto: '*We ... find it difficult to separate race from class from sex oppression because in our lives they are most often experienced simultaneously.*'

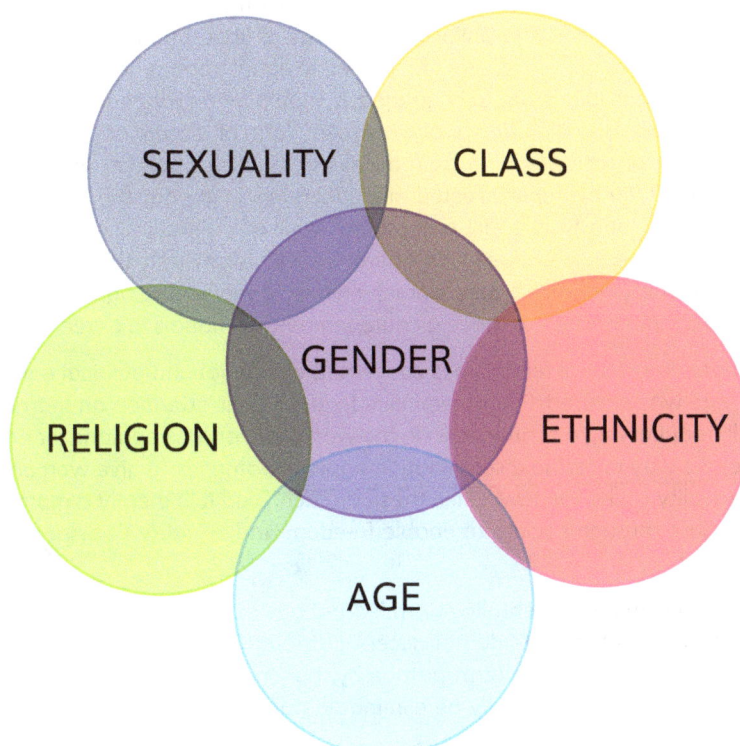

Figure 6.2 Intersectionality in feminism.

The second wave of feminism was primarily defined by educated, middle-class, white women who built the movement largely around their own experiences. Hence feminism, as written about in the 1960s and 1970s, was mainly seen through their lens. This created difficulties for other women who did not recognize the forms of oppression being discussed. When these second-wavers discussed 'women's oppression' the voices of working-class women and women of colour were lost. As a result many Black women had difficulty seeing white women as their feminist sisters. Black women, for example had to work on two fronts; how to get men to think about gender issues and how to get white feminists to think about race. As Toni Cade Bambara said in *The Black Woman: An Anthology* (1970), '*I don't know that our priorities are the same, that our concerns and methods are the same.*' However, many Black women activists agreed that campaigns for affordable day care, abortion, maternity leave, violence were also relevant to Black women.

Intersectionality

Summary box

- The idea that Black and working-class women's experiences of patriarchy are different from white, middle-class women.
- Feminism therefore needs to embrace women's differences and their different experiences of patriarchy.
- Closely linked to postmodern feminism.

> **Definition**
>
> **First-wave feminism:** The early form of feminism which developed in the mid-nineteenth century and was based on the pursuit of sexual equality in the areas of political and legal rights, particularly suffrage rights.

> **Spec key term**
>
> **Political equality:** Equal right to vote and protest.
>
> **Legal equality:** No one is above the law and the law applies equally to all.
>
> **Equality of opportunity:** All individuals have equal chances in life to rise and fall.
>
> **Discrimination:** Less favourable treatment of one group of people compared to other groups.

2. Differences between the feminist strands

Liberal feminism

Early feminism, particularly the 'first wave' of the women's movement, was deeply influenced by the ideas and values of liberalism. The philosophical basis of liberal feminism lies in the principle of individualism. This implies that all individuals are entitled to equal treatment regardless of their gender, race, colour or religion. If individuals are to be judged, it should be on rational grounds, on the content of their character, their talents or their personal worth. Any form of discrimination against women that constrains their ability to participate in, or gain access to, public or political life should therefore be prohibited. Wollstonecraft, for example, insisted that education, in her day the province of men, should be opened up to women. John Stuart Mill argued in favour of political and legal equality. Indeed, the entire suffrage movement was based on liberal individualism and the conviction that female emancipation would be brought about once women enjoyed equal voting rights with men. The aim of liberal feminism is to enable women to thrive as autonomous individuals in a free society.

As well as the right to vote, liberal feminism is concerned with legal and political equality for women. Once the right to vote was secured, liberal feminists focused their attention on marriage and divorce law reform as well as outlawing discrimination in the workplace and campaigns for equal pay. From a liberal perspective, the way to tackle discrimination against women is to give women an equal voice, equal rights and equality under the law. Once these are achieved it is merely a matter of time before these reforms percolate through society to enable freedom and equality of opportunity for women and men.

This makes liberal feminism fundamentally reformist and has many consequences for their views on many core principles. Liberal feminists do not accept patriarchy as 'systematic oppression', the way other feminists do. They may use the term patriarchy, but they attribute discrimination to historic failings. These, they believe, will gradually be eliminated now women have equal opportunities and legal equality.

Liberal feminists focus their concerns on the public sphere, believing that men and women should have the equal opportunity to stay at home or go to work. As more men choose to take a primary role in caregiving, so the gender stereotypes of the past will disappear. In this sense liberal feminists are reformist, believing that, over time, as more women take on traditional male jobs and vice versa, society will remodel on the basis of gender equality.

Second-wave feminism also has a significant liberal component. For instance, Betty Friedan in her best-selling feminist work *The Feminine Mystique* highlighted what she called 'the problem with no name', the sense of despair and deep unhappiness that many women experienced because they were confined to a domestic existence. She argued that society had advanced the cultural myth that women seek security and fulfilment in domestic life and 'feminine' behaviour. This served to discourage women from entering employment, politics and public life in general. Although Friedan's work inspired many radical feminist, she remained firmly committed to removing discrimination in the public sphere, with the aim of giving women equality of opportunity and freedom of choice.

The demand for equal rights and opportunities, which lies at the core of liberal feminism, has principally attracted women whose education and social backgrounds enable them to take advantage of wider educational and career opportunities. For example, the leaders of the suffrage movement were usually educated, middle-class women who had the opportunity to benefit from the right to vote. Female emancipation, in the liberal sense, may mean that other forms of social disadvantage – for example, those linked to social class and race – are ignored. Liberal feminism may therefore reflect the interests of white, middle-class women in developed societies but fail to address the problems of working-class women, Black women and women in the developing world.

Socialist feminism

Although some early feminists subscribed to socialist ideas, socialist feminism only became prominent in the second half of the twentieth century. In contrast to their liberal counterparts, socialist feminists did not believe that women simply face legal disadvantages that can be remedied by equal legal rights or the achievement of equal opportunities. Rather, they argue that the relationship between the sexes is rooted in the social and economic structure of capitalism itself, and that nothing short of profound social change – some would say a social revolution – can offer women the prospect of genuine emancipation.

The central theme of socialist feminism is that patriarchy can only be understood in the light of social and economic factors. The classic statement of this argument was developed in Friedrich Engels' *The Origins of the Family, Private Property and the State* (1884). Engels suggested that the position of women in society had changed fundamentally with the development of capitalism and the institution of private property. In pre-capitalist societies, family life had been community based, and 'mother right' – the inheritance of property and social position through the female line – was widely observed. Capitalism, however, being based on the ownership of private property by men, had overthrown 'mother right' and brought about what Engels called '*the world historical defeat of the female sex*'. Like many subsequent socialist feminists, Engels believed that female oppression operates through the institution of the 'bourgeois family'. The patriarchal character of such a family was ensured by the practice of descent through the male line, together with the inheritance of property.

Most socialist feminists agree that the confinement of women to a domestic sphere of housework and motherhood serves the economic interests of capitalism.

» Some have argued that women constitute a 'reserve army of labour', which is recruited into the workforce when there is a need, but easily shed and returned to domestic life during a depression. In the modern world, women are an increasingly permanent part of the workforce, but are used to lower wages overall due to the gender pay gap.

» Women's paid work is undervalued; women are often socialized into careers which are historically underpaid, such as social care, teaching and nursing as opposed to law, finance and banking.

» Women are more likely to be in part-time work, limiting career progression.

» At the same time, women's domestic labour is vital to the health and efficiency of the capitalist economy; by rearing children, women are producing the next generation of workers.

» Traditionally, women's role as housewives relieved men of this burden, allowing them to concentrate on paid and productive employment. As more women have entered the workforce on a more permanent basis, evidence indicates they still take on the lion's share of domestic responsibilities.

Spec key term

Gender stereotypes: The dominant and usually negative views in society on the different ways men and women should behave.

Reformist: Seeking to change society gradually and peacefully.

Gender equality: The belief that men and women are of equal value in society and should be treated the same.

Spec key term

Reserve army of labour: The idea that women constitute a spare workforce that can be called upon as and when needed.

» Historically, the traditional family provided the worker with a powerful incentive to find and keep a job as he had a family to support.

» The family also provided male workers with a cushion against the alienation and frustrations of life as 'wage slaves'. Male 'breadwinners' enjoyed high status within the family and were relieved of the burden of 'trivial' domestic labour.

Gilman argued that sex and 'domestic economics' went hand in hand. A woman was reliant on pleasing her man sexually and domestically in return for his financial support. She argued that only when society was restructured to give women economic independence, would women be free and equal to men. In *Women and Economics* (1898) she argued that more communal living arrangements could relieve women of the burden of domesticity.

Socialist feminists are divided about the extent of the link between capitalism and patriarchy. Marxist feminists insist on the primacy of class politics over sexual politics. This suggests that class exploitation is a deeper and more significant process than sexual oppression. It also suggests that women's emancipation will be a by-product of a social revolution; women should therefore fight against capitalism, not patriarchy, as patriarchy will only be abolished when capitalism is abolished.

However, many modern socialist feminists have difficulty accepting the primacy of class politics over sexual politics. Many of them support the view which accepts the interplay of economic, social, political and cultural forces in society. They therefore refuse to analyse the position of women in simple economic terms and have also given attention to the roots of patriarchy. Unlike liberal feminists, they argue that oppression occurs in both public and private spheres and agree with radical feminists that domestic expectations around the home are the key area where a woman's role needs to be addressed.

Modern socialist feminists like **Sheila Rowbotham** are critical of the narrow Marxist analysis of history for excluding female oppression through the family, the economy and maternity. The home and family, as well as the economy, are thus key areas of focus for modern socialist feminists. They see women's absence from the economy as caused by society's expectations about women's domestic role and duties. Even as women have been accepted into the workplace, they have still been expected to keep their domestic responsibilities, which, in turn, limits their progression in the workplace. **Rowbotham** argued that capitalism and misogyny are so closely linked that the only way to destroy both is a radical change in the society's expectations regarding women's role in child-rearing, homes, laws and the work.

Juliet Mitchell in *Women's Estate* (1971) argued that the traditional family is an independent source of female oppression as it keeps women hidden away and dependent on their husband. She asserted that women must achieve emancipation in four key areas: work, reproduction, sexuality and the socialization of children. While she recognized that capitalism is responsible for some of these forms of oppression, she argued that the others are unrelated to capitalism. For example, the promotion of women as sex objects seems to run counter to capitalism's requirements for women's fidelity. Mitchell concluded that women should fight both capitalism and patriarchy to create a classless, genderless society where men and women can work alongside each other as equals.

Tensions within feminism over the economy

AGREEMENT	DISAGREEMENT
✓ All feminists agree that the current economic system discriminates against women in different ways and argue that the economy must be organized to enable women to access it on an equal basis to men	✗ Liberal feminists argue that women need equal access and opportunity to the economy, seeking legal and political equality, whereas socialist feminists disagree, arguing that the capitalist economy is at the heart of female oppression, and that economic equality is essential to female emancipation

AGREEMENT	DISAGREEMENT
✓ Feminists agree that the work done at home, usually by women, is devalued and unpaid. They agree that domestic work is not the responsibility of women and that women should be free to choose work which they find satisfying and financially rewarding	✗ Postmodern feminists disagree with both socialist and radical feminists arguing that additional factors like colour, class and religion also affect women's position in the economy
✓ All feminists agree that there are restrictions in women's ability to access well-paid work in comparison to men and that the economy needs to be organized so women should be motivated and encouraged to access work in the same way as men	✗ Socialist feminists argue that patriarchy is promoted by capitalism, whereas radical feminists argue that patriarchy is an independent system of oppression and therefore the abolition of capitalism will not remove patriarchy

Radical feminism

The defining feature of radical feminism is simply the belief that sexual oppression is the most fundamental feature of society and that other forms of injustice – class exploitation, racial hatred and so on – are significant, but secondary. Radical feminism seeks to reshape society which they consider to be inherently patriarchal. They argue that the subservient role of women is too tightly woven into society for simple reforms to be able to change it. Instead, it needs to be replaced with a society removed of the hierarchical structures of patriarchy.

Radical feminists have insisted that society be seen as 'patriarchal' to highlight the central role of gender oppression. Many of the core principles discussed earlier in the chapter are in fact terms and ideas introduced by radical feminists to give language to the typical experiences of women. Where radical feminists differ from liberal and socialist feminists is that they are not seeking to connect the experiences of women to any other ideological tradition. As such they are free to analyse society totally from the perspective of female oppression.

Beyond this, radical feminists don't have a single, all-embracing analysis of society, rather, different radical feminists seek to analyse the different manifestations of patriarchy in society. In recognizing the 'personal' as 'political' radical feminists argue that power relationships exist everywhere. Such thinking is evident in the pioneering work of **Simone de Beauvoir** and was developed by early radical feminists such as Eva Figes, Germaine Greer and **Kate Millett** as well as many others.

» **Simone de Beauvoir's** book *The Second Sex*, published in 1949, became one of the key feminist texts of the second wave. She is famous for two additions to feminist thought. The first is her most famous words that '*One is not born, but rather becomes, a woman.*' These words argued that women are socialized into becoming the 'acceptable' version of a women. Her second addition to the debate is the concept of '**otherness**'. She argued that in a patriarchal society, men are considered the 'norm' and women are therefore the 'other', identified by what they lack in relation to men.

> **Spec key term**
>
> **Otherness:** The idea that women were considered to be fundamentally different from men, who were seen as the 'norm'; women were deviants from this norm.

» **Kate Millet** is a key figure in the radical feminist movement. Like Friedan's *The Feminine Mystique* in the 1960s, **Millet's** *Sexual Politics* (1970) highlighted the ways that women had been treated as appendages to their husbands, rather than people in their own right. **Millett** argued that the different roles of women and men have their origin in a process of 'conditioning': from an early age boys and girls are encouraged to conform to very specific gender identities. This process takes place largely within the family, but is also evident in literature, art, public life and the economy.

» Eva Figes' *Patriarchal Attitudes* (1970) drew attention to the fact that patriarchal values and beliefs pervade the culture, philosophy, morality and religion of society. In all walks of life, women are portrayed as inferior and subordinate to men with the stereotype of 'femininity' being imposed on women by men. She insisted that nurture, not nature, shaped a women's outlook, arguing that men had defined the 'norms' of society throughout history and had defined them in ways that benefited them and undermined women.

» In *The Female Eunuch* (1970), Germaine Greer suggested that women have been 'castrated' by a society which told them that it was unfeminine to enjoy sex. Greer also argued that women must be encouraged to think and speak for themselves: '*I'm sick of pretending that some fatuous male's self-important pronouncements are the objects of my undivided attention.*'

» Susan Brownmiller's *Against Our Will* (1975) emphasized that men dominate women through a process of physical and sexual abuse. Brownmiller argued that sexual violence against women is a deliberate, calculated act aimed at degrading and humiliating them. She argued that rape was not about sex, it was about power. Patriarchy had created an 'ideology of rape' which amounted to a '*conscious process of intimidation by which all men keep all women in a state of fear*'.

» Naomi Wolf's book *The Beauty Myth* (1990) is still highly relevant today. Wolf argued that women were sold the myth that 'beauty' was essential to female happiness as the '*last, best belief system that keeps male dominance intact*'. As a result, women are preoccupied with achieving impossible standards of thinness and 'beauty', with a diet culture that robs women of their quality of life, rather than being able to focus their attention on achieving success in the world. There is, she argued, a direct relationship between women's success and the rise in eating disorders and prevalence of plastic surgery in women. In the era of social media, Wolf's message is more relevant to women and girls than ever before.

» Erin Pizzey did trailblazing work on supporting the victims of domestic violence in the 1970s. Traditionally, it had been assumed that a man could 'punish' his wife however he saw fit. 'Conventional wisdom' said that she had provoked him; maybe she nagged him, or flirted with other men, or withheld sex. He must have had his reasons. In a traditional patriarchal society women had very little choice. They owned very little and had little control over finances, they had nowhere to go and were fearful of the repercussions of leaving. Police largely turned a blind eye when it was 'just a domestic'.

» Kate Figes' book *Life after Birth* (1998) looked at the pressures on women to feel a certain way following the birth of their children. She challenged the assumption that all women immediately felt enormous, unconditional love for their child. She argued that because of this assumption, women were pushed into a cycle of punishment and guilt if they didn't immediately feel this love. In reality, Figes argued, for many women, the love grows as the physical shock of childbirth fades. She argued that motherhood is a huge adjustment for many women, with many contradictory feelings, such as loss of self, confusion and disillusionment, and that women need time to adjust to this without the societal pressure to show 'natural maternal instincts'.

Radical feminists generally agree that the origins of patriarchy lie in the structures of family, domestic and personal life, and therefore that women's liberation requires a sexual revolution in which these structures are reinvented.

Tensions within feminism over society	
AGREEMENT	DISAGREEMENT
✓ Most feminists recognize that in a patriarchal society, the personal experiences of women's oppression are a consequence of their political situation	✗ Postmodern feminists argue that the personal experience of different minorities and classes of women in society has been ignored by radical feminism and seeks to give them a voice; socialist feminists argue that the personal experiences of women in society are based on capitalist oppression

AGREEMENT	DISAGREEMENT
✓ Radical, socialist and postmodern feminists recognize the significance of patriarchy in the oppression of women in society	✗ Liberal feminists reject the radical feminist concept of patriarchy as systematic oppression of women and instead see women as being discriminated against in society. Postmodern feminists also differ in their understanding of patriarchy stressing that patriarchy mutates in society according to class, ethnicity and religion
✓ The vast majority of feminists are equality feminists who believe that biological differences in society between men and women are insignificant	✗ Difference feminists argue that the nature of men and women is innately different and argue that this needs to be recognized when seeking to emancipate women from the subordination of men in society

Postmodern feminism

Postmodern feminism is closely associated with third-wave feminism, a term which was credited to Rebecca Walker. If there is a unifying theme of this strand of feminism it is a wider engagement with the politics of difference, by understanding the differences between women. Postmodern feminism sought to celebrate female differences across race, class and sexual orientations and reject many stereotypes of the feminine ideal. In so doing, postmodern feminists sought to rectify an over-emphasis within second-wave feminism on the aspirations and experiences of middle-class, white women in developed societies.

Postmodern feminism seeks to encourage the voices of, among others, low-income women, women in the developing world, women of colour, women of different religions and LGBTIQ+ people to be heard more effectively. Black feminism has been particularly effective in this respect, challenging the tendency within conventional forms of feminism to ignore racial differences and to suggest that women endure a common oppression by virtue of their gender. Especially strong in the USA and developed in the writings of theorists such as **bell hooks**, Black feminism portrays misogyny and racism as linked systems of oppression, what **hooks** described as '*imperialist white supremacist capitalist patriarchy*' and highlights the particular and complex range of gender, racial and economic disadvantages that confront women of colour.

In *Ain't I a Woman?* (1981) **hooks** argued that Black women have the lowest status of any group in American society. The title of her book was referencing famous abolitionist and women's rights activist Sojourner Truth who questioned why Black women were not entitled to the same considerations and courtesy as white women: '*That man over there says that women need to be helped into carriages, and lifted over ditches, and to have the best place everywhere. Nobody ever helps me into carriages, or over mud-puddles, or gives me any best place! And ain't I a woman?*' **hooks** was showing that more than a hundred years later, feminism had not done enough for women who were non-white and weren't middle class. Like Crenshaw, she believed that the experience of Black women were considerably different and that Black women's voices and experiences had been absent in the second wave of feminism. **hooks** argued in a later book, *In Feminist Theory: From Margin to Centre* (1984), that instead of seeking to create a common understanding of patriarchy, feminism should instead seek to widen its understanding by seeking out as wide a range of experiences as possible from many different women living very different lives. It was only through this process that women's' experiences of patriarchy could be understood.

Postmodern feminism also goes beyond the analysis of **hooks** and Crenshaw to argue that all women's experiences of patriarchy are so different that it was almost impossible to generalize, and it was certainly impossible to clearly define and categorize the forms of exploitation they experience under one simple theory. So, when feminists had previously talked about the patriarchal experiences of 'women' in a general all-encompassing term, they were discussing only the experiences of a small group of women, as it was impossible to speak on behalf of all women, everywhere.

In *Manifesta: Young Women, Feminism, and the Future* (2000), Jennifer Baumgardner and Amy Richards sought to update feminism. They argued that *'feminism wants you to be whoever you are and you want to be a feminist because you want to be exactly who you are'*. They argued that because most women come to feminism through their own personal experiences, the core identity of feminism has to be flexible, as the term needs to represent the huge diversity of individual women's lives. At its heart, postmodern feminism is about being open and fluid about the challenges of being a woman in modern society, about finding the ways women can personally enact feminist ideas in their lives and taking the judgement out of feminism. As Richards suggested in 2020, *'It's not up to any one person or organisation or government to tell you what feminism should look like. It's up to you to take the example that others have given you and apply it to yourself.'*

As a consequence of this, postmodern feminism can often look starkly different from second-wave feminism. Postmodern feminists seek to define feminism for themselves rather than being told how they should address their empowerment. This has been seen by organizations like SlutWalk in Canada and Pussy Riot in Russia. They reclaim words like 'slut' to highlight the double-standards of patriarchal society.

Table 6.1 Tensions within feminism

	Liberal	Socialist	Radical	Postmodern
Patriarchy	Identify 'patriarchy' as discrimination, not oppression	Recognize patriarchy as systematic oppression, but it is primarily caused by capitalism	Patriarchy is a systematic, institutionalized and pervasive form of male power	Patriarchy is pervasive in society and it mutates according to class, ethnicity and religion
Sex and gender	All humans are rational creatures, and so the distinction of sex and gender is artificial. Women should have equal chances in society	Reject and eradicate gender stereotypes, which are required by capitalism as it needs women to do free domestic work and fulfil other functions	Gender roles are created by patriarchy to subjugate women. Women are duped into believing that childcare and household work are their natural roles	Gender roles imposed on Black and working-class women are different to those imposed on white, middle-class women
Personal is political	Reject the term. Their focus is discrimination in the public sphere. They want to see all barriers to entry in the public sphere removed	The personal is political. Women are forced into domesticity to help reproduce the labour force and other functions for capitalism	Women should understand that their experiences of oppression are not personal to them, but part of a wider political oppression of all women.	Support the radical feminist view of society as political but see 'politics' in a wider way than other feminists
Equality vs difference	Equality feminists; all humans are of equal moral worth and entitled to the same rights	Equality feminists; sexual equality is meaningless without class equality and equality must be seen in economic terms	Most are equality feminists. Difference feminists; women should not seek to replicate male behaviour	Equality feminists; the different experiences of women are crucial in understanding the different ways women are oppressed
Intersectionality	All women, no matter what their class, religion or ethnicity should be treated equally	Capitalism oppresses all women and working-class men. They must unite to remove capitalism and patriarchy from society	All women are equally oppressed by patriarchy, albeit in different ways	Different groups of women experience different types of oppression

3. Feminist key thinkers

Key thinkers are an important part of understanding each ideology. The exam board has specified five key thinkers per ideology and TWO must be included in an answer to avoid a cap (please check the Exam Focus chapter (Chapter 9) for lots more discussion of key thinkers). Although key thinkers (and other thinkers) have been discussed throughout the chapter, here we look at each one in detail.

Charlotte Perkins Gilman (1860–1935)

Heritage Images/Contributor/Getty

Charlotte Perkins Gilman was an American author whose writings pre-date what we now understand as feminism. Her best remembered work is her autobiographical short story *The Yellow Wallpaper*, which she wrote after a severe bout of what we would now call post-natal depression.

The Yellow Wallpaper (1892) is a short story describing the experience of a woman who is confined to a room by her husband, in an attempt to cure her 'nervous depression'. Unsurprisingly, the treatment made her condition worse deepening into severe mental illness and psychosis. Gilman wrote it to illustrate how women's lack of independence was detrimental to their mental, emotional and even physical well-being. Gilman believed the domestic environment oppressed women through the patriarchal values it embodied which were upheld by society.

In *Women and Economics* (1898) she argued that sex and domestic responsibilities went hand in hand for women, suggesting that women were required to keep their husbands sexually satisfied so he would provide financially. Women also needed to look after the home and their husband's needs. In this way, women were totally reliant on the good will of their husbands to live a peaceful and decent life. She argued that women were prepared for this role from childhood. Way ahead of her time, Gilman argued that there should be no difference in the clothes that girls wear, the toys they are bought or the activities they do.

In *The Home: Its Work and Influence* (1903) she took her idea even further, focusing her attention on the structure of the home. The theme running through all Gilman's writing was that women were oppressed by their domestic arrangements (something second-wave feminists like Betty Friedan and **Kate Millet** would come to argue sixty years later). Gilman suggested a more communal form of living instead, where men and women, married couples and single people could co-exist together. In this way, they could support each other and enjoy the benefits of friendship and home comforts without absolute reliance of any one of them. She suggested that restructuring the home in this way would allow individuals, especially women, to become an '*integral part of the social structure, in close, direct, permanent connection with the needs and uses of society*'.

It is difficult to give Gilman a label. She clearly sees the structure of the economy as playing a key role in the oppression of women so it is tempting to describe her as a socialist feminist; however, her analysis focuses on women's domestic arrangements, rather than capitalism. This is what radical feminists would focus on half a century later. In essence, the strand she is best associated with is unimportant as her work can be used to discuss many issues that feminists have grappled with.

Simone de Beauvoir (1908–86)

Bettman/Contributor/Getty

A French philosopher, novelist, playwright and social critic, de Beauvoir's work reopened the issue of gender politics and foreshadowed the ideas of later radical feminists. In *The Second Sex* (1949), she developed a complex critique of patriarchal culture.

In the opening line of Book II of *The Second Sex*, de Beauvoir famously wrote that '*One is not born, but rather becomes, a woman.*' She argued that from childhood, through adolescence and beyond, women are forced to adopt and accept a passive role, while men are encouraged to be active. She wrote about how the various roles of women forced them into a monotonous existences by having children, tending the house and being the sexual receptacles of the male libido: '*Few tasks are more like the torture of Sisyphus than housework, with its endless repetition ... Eating, sleeping, cleaning – the years no longer rise up towards heaven, they lie spread out ahead, grey and identical. The battle against dust and dirt is never won.*'

De Beauvoir argued that men and women can be equal without being the same. To equate equality with sameness establishes 'maleness' as the highest ideal for women to aspire to. De Beauvoir insisted, however, that women and men should treat each other as equals. De Beauvoir found it immoral to use sexual differences as an argument for women's subordination.

In her book, de Beauvoir defines women as the 'second sex' because she argued that women are defined in relation to men. She quotes Aristotle who referred to women as being '*female by virtue of a certain lack of qualities*'. So she argued that women are seen as '*the incidental, the inessential, as opposed to the essential. He is the Subject, he is the Absolute – she is the Other.*' De Beauvoir argued that men had made women the 'Other' in society by creating a false air of 'mystery' around them by deeming any experience they cannot have as 'mysterious'. So women's experiences of pregnancy, lactation, and menstruation, foreign to men, contribute to marking women out as different, and therefore subordinate. She also argued that women had 'internalized' their otherness and come to accept it themselves. Thus, women are not just inferior in the eyes of men but inferior in their own eyes too. Women, she argues, are not conscious of having accepted their inferiority. They must first become conscious of their subjugation before they can begin to struggle against it.

Kate Millett (1934–2017)

Barbara Alper/Contributor/Getty Images

In *Sexual Politics* (1970), Millett developed a comprehensive critique of patriarchy in Western society and culture that had a profound impact on radical feminism.

The essence of *Sexual Politics* was a description and analysis of patriarchy. Millet argued that institutional power in a patriarchal society is controlled by men which enables them to exercise dominance over women. Thus the inequality between men and women is socially constructed, not biological. Millet hypothesized that 'every avenue of power within the society, including the coercive force of the police, is entirely in male hands'. She further argued that patriarchal values are so typical that they are considered the 'common sense' of the time. 'In the matter of conformity,' Millett wrote, 'patriarchy is a governing ideology without peer; it is probable that no other system has ever exercised such a complete control over its subjects.' She explained how women are socialized into being part of the very system that seeks to control them, by accepting and even agreeing that their subservient position is natural.

Hence Millet argued that the family was 'patriarchy's chief institution' and undoing the traditional family, with its expectations of female domesticity, was the key to true sexual revolution. The family was both a mirror of and a connection with the larger society, a patriarchal unit within a patriarchal whole. In a patriarchal family, the father was given total control of his wife and children, including the ability to discipline them if he wished.

Millet is clear that one of the most powerful roles of the patriarchal family is the socializing of the next generation into their patriarchal roles. Young girls (and boys) consent to a system of inequality long before they understand the world and their place in it. It is no wonder women consider their subordinate position natural, it was taught to them from the cradle. These roles are taught and learnt via the norms of the family and then reinforced via friends, school and wider society. Millet argued that society supports masculine authority in all areas of life and permits the female none at all. She argued that the relationship between the sexes was one of 'dominance and subordinance'.

The third part of *Sexual Politics* reflects on the literature of famous (male) authors and their portrayal of women in sex scenes. She observed that they reinforced the idea that women should play a passive, subordinate and 'compliant' role during sex. She suggested that the pervasiveness of male dominance in sex was so matter-of-fact as to almost make it unremarkable. She argued that through their language, the male authors displayed misogyny, contempt and disgust for women. In their works, women were never in control of sex, they were 'taken' by men or receivers of sex; there to satisfy the male characters, their own desire always secondary or silent. What made it more shocking, she argued, was that these authors were widely seen as part of the progressive literary set even though their work embodied patriarchal attitudes.

Sheila Rowbotham (1943–)

Simone Padovani/Awakening/Getty

In 1969, Rowbotham published her pamphlet *Women's Liberation and the New Politics*, where she argued that women's oppression is a result of both economic and cultural forces. A dual perspective that examines both is therefore required to liberate women from oppression.

As a socialist feminist, Rowbotham was influenced by Marx's analysis of history. However, she sought to combine this approach with feminism, arguing that capitalism oppresses the working class and women. She argued that working-class women face a duality of oppression; as part of the working class, they are forced to sell their labour to survive, but they are equally forced to use their labour to run a home to support their children and husbands.

Additionally, in her 1973 book *Women's Consciousness, Men's World*, she criticized Marxist analysis for not seeing the oppression of women as a separate but equal form of capitalism oppression. She argued that the Marxist analysis of history neglected areas where women are oppressed, for example, the role of women in supporting the economy, sexuality and maternity. She argued that sexism predates capitalism, and suggested that marriage is a form of feudalism in which wives were required to serve their husbands in much the same way that feudal serfs were expected to serve their masters.

She argued that women's work in the domestic sphere was invaluable to men and to capitalism as it provided men with a place where they could take refuge from capitalism, enabling them to go back to work the next day, physically and spiritually rejuvenated. For Rowbotham, capitalism and sexism are so intertwined that a radical change in humanity's outlook on housework, the world of work and bringing up children is required. She rejected the reformism of liberal feminists by contending that working through the established order would never work in bringing about meaningful change and that only socialist movements have managed to achieve changes.

In *Hidden from History* (1973), she suggested that women could best be understood and defined by both class oppression and sexism, arguing that women's liberation required a '*revolution within the revolution*'. Rowbotham argued that male revolutionaries were willing to accept women as partners for as long as the revolution lasts but, once the revolution is over, expected them to return to their traditional roles. Indeed, one of her best-known lines is '*men will often admit other women are oppressed, but not you*'. In other words, they recognize misogyny in other men, and in society at large, but never in themselves. In her opinion, women and men should stand equally against both capitalism and sexism to achieve radical social reorganization.

bell hooks (1952–2021)

Karjean Levine/Getty

bell hooks (born 1952) was born Gloria Watkins. She took her pen name from her maternal great-grandmother as a way to honour her women ancestors. She chose to use lowercase letters to shift the attention from her identity to her ideas. In her classic *Ain't I a Woman* (1985), she emphasized that feminist theory must take account of gender, race and social class.

In *Feminist Theory: From Margin to Centre* (1984) hooks argued that traditional feminism had marginalized diverse voices. She insisted that feminism could not make men and women equal because women were not equally oppressed and that Black and lower class women do not share the same status as white women.

In *Ain't I a Woman: Black Women and Feminism* (1985), hooks developed the idea that the cultural concerns of African American women must be brought into the mainstream feminist movement. She found that when she looked to feminism to help her understand her plight, she found very little that related to her as a young Black woman as it had focused mostly on the plight of white, college-educated, middle- and upper-class women who had little or no stake in the concerns of women of colour. '*A devaluation of Black womanhood occurred as a result of the sexual exploitation of Black women during slavery that has not altered in the course of hundreds of years.*'

She had to choose whether to focus her attention on the fight for women's equality, ignoring her colour, or the Civil Rights movement, ignoring her gender. Instead, she argued for a feminist theory of empowerment for people of colour. hooks argued that feminism needed to work hard to create solidarity with women of different ethnicities or socioe-conomic classes. She sought to offer a more inclusive type of feminism, to encourage the enduring idea of sisterhood while suggesting that it must both acknowledge and accept women's differences. She was particularly scathing about Friedan's *Feminine Mystique*: '*She did not speak of the needs of women without men, without children, without homes. She ignored the existence of all non-white women and poor white women. She did not tell readers whether it was more fulfilling to be a maid, a babysitter, a factory worker, a clerk, or a prostitute than to be a leisure-class housewife.*'

However, hooks argued that men must be part of the solution. She suggested that patriarchy pushes both boys and girls into clear gender models. From a very young age, boys and girls are told to fit into the characteristics that are expected of them. Boys are taught to deny any emotions and girls are taught that their key role is to please everyone. Girls must change themselves to be as attractive as possible to the opposing sex, by being congenial and passive. As a result of these unacceptable expectations, both boys and girls grow up to deny their true selves.

4. How to apply knowledge to feminism answers

Tensions within feminism over society

Thematic approach

Theme 1: Personal is political

- ✓ The personal experiences of women's oppression are a consequence of their political situation (**Millett**)
- ✗ Postmodern feminists argue that the personal experience of different minorities and classes of women has been ignored by radical feminism (**hooks**)
- ✗ Radical and socialist feminists disagree on what 'political' means: socialist feminists argue that the personal experiences of women in society are primarily due to capitalism (**Rowbotham**), whereas radical feminists argue it is due to patriarchy

Theme 2 – Patriarchy

- ✓ Radical, socialist and postmodern feminists recognize the significance of patriarchy in society, which they define as the systematic oppression of women by men
- ✗ Liberal feminists reject the radical feminist definition of patriarchy and instead see women as being only discriminated against in society
- ✗ Postmodern feminists stress that patriarchy mutates according to class, ethnicity and religion (**hooks**) but socialist feminists recognize patriarchy as playing a role in the oppression of women but argue that it is equally capitalism that oppresses women in society (**Rowbotham**)

Theme 3 – Equality feminism

- ✓ The vast majority of feminists are equality feminists. Liberal, socialist, most radical and postmodern feminists believe that biological differences between men and women are insignificant in society
- ✗ Equality feminists pursue gender equality based on the belief in the androgyny of human nature, difference feminists argue that the nature of men and women is innately different
- ✗ Difference feminists believe that women shouldn't seek to replicate male behaviour in society and should be free to embrace their essentially female selves

Tensions within feminism over human nature

Worked example

Paragraph One – Agreement within feminism

- ✓ All feminists seek to advance the role of women based on their true nature
- ✓ All feminists believe gender roles imposed on women ignore their true nature (**Beauvoir**)
- ✓ Feminists believe women can only be truly emancipated when they're encouraged to allow their true nature to evolve (**Millett**)

Paragraph Two – Agreement within feminism

- ✓ The vast majority of feminists are equality feminists. Liberal, socialist, most radical and postmodern feminists are equality feminists who believe that biological differences between men and women are insignificant

Continued...

✓ Despite disagreements within these strands on many issues, one area they are all in agreement with is the androgynous nature of humanity
✓ They argue that boys and girls are forced to conform to their gender roles by the clothes they wear, the toys they are bought and by what society expects of them (hooks, Gilman)

Paragraph Three – Disagreement within feminism

✗ Difference feminists, however, argue that the nature of men and women is innately different.
✗ They believe there are fundamental differences between the nature of men and women, arguing that women shouldn't seek to replicate male behaviour
✗ Cultural feminism takes an essentialist view of female nature arguing that patriarchal society seeks to impose negative associations with female attributes like childbirth as it is something only women can do, rather than seeing them as positive values

Tensions within feminism over patriarchy

Worked example

Paragraph One – Agreement within feminism

✓ Radical, socialist and postmodern feminists agree that patriarchy is a pervasive system of oppression
✓ They also argue that woman's oppression exists in the public as well as the private sphere
✓ Nothing less than a radical overhaul of the current system is needed to create an equal society

Paragraph Two – Disagreement within feminism

✗ Liberal feminists do not recognize patriarchy in the same way as a radical feminists, seeing only historic discrimination which exists in the private sphere, whereas radical feminists see male oppression in public and private sphere
✗ Liberal feminists are reformist, arguing that women can become equal to men with the correct laws in place, whereas radical feminists believe misogyny is deeply embedded in every aspect of life and would be simply impossible to remove gradually and that within the current structures it is not possible for women to be equal to men (Millett)

Paragraph Three – Disagreement within feminism

✗ Postmodern feminists criticize other strands of feminism for their lack of recognition of patriarchy as it affects non-white, middle class, straight women
✗ They argue that radical feminism doesn't take patriarchy far enough, seeing patriarchy's oppression from too narrow a lens when in fact race, religion and sexuality contribute to how woman experiences in her oppression (hooks)
✗ Socialist feminists argue that patriarchy is promoted by capitalism (Rowbotham), whereas radical feminists (Millett) argue that patriarchy is an independent system of oppression arguing that the abolition of capitalism will not remove patriarchy

Tensions within feminism over the economy

Worked example

Paragraph One – Agreement within feminism

- ✓ All feminists agree that the current economic system discriminates against women in different ways **(Gilman, Rowbotham, Millett)**
- ✓ Feminists agree that the work done at home, usually by women, is devalued and unpaid **(Rowbotham)**
- ✓ All feminists agree that there are restrictions in women's ability to access well-paid work compared to men and that the economy needs to be organized so women should be motivated and encouraged to access work in the same way as men **(Gilman)**

Paragraph Two – Disagreement within feminism

- ✗ Liberal feminists argue that women need equal access and opportunity to the economy, whereas socialist feminists disagree, arguing that the capitalist economy is at the heart of female oppression
- ✗ Liberal feminists argue for seeking legal and political, rather than economic, equality, socialist feminists disagree, arguing that economic equality is essential to female emancipation

Paragraph Three – Disagreement within feminism

- ✗ Postmodern feminists disagree with both socialist and radical feminists, arguing that additional factors like colour, class and religion also affect women's position in the economy **(hooks)**
- ✗ They argue that radical feminism focuses too narrowly on the experiences of white, middle-class women in the economy; however, radical feminism argues that their analysis of women's role in the economy represents all women, who are forced to take responsibility for domestic work, no matter what their class or colour
- ✗ Socialist feminists argue that patriarchy is promoted by capitalism **(Rowbotham)**, whereas radical feminists **(Millett)** argue that patriarchy is an independent system of oppression arguing that the abolition of capitalism will not remove patriarchy

Chapter Summary

- Feminism is a diverse ideology which has evolved and advanced through a number of waves.
- The core principles of feminism were mainly given a voice by radical feminism during the second wave.
- However, many of the strands agree with the ideas of the core principles.
- There is a fundamental conflict between equality and difference feminism.
- There are also significant areas of disagreement between all four strands of feminism.

Exam Style Questions

1. To what extent do feminists agree over the role of the state?
2. To what extent is feminism more divided than united?
3. To what extent do feminists agree that gender distinctions are based on human nature?
4. To what extent do feminists disagree about the nature of the society they wish to create?
5. To what extent do all feminists recognize patriarchy as the key source of female oppression?
6. To what extent do feminists agree about the nature of the economy in a future society?
7. To what extent do feminists believe that the personal is political?
8. To what extent do feminists agree that the distinction between sex and gender is significant?

Further Resources

Adams, I. *Political Ideology Today* (2001). Chapter 10, 'Feminism and Liberation Ideology' is a straightforward read for A-Level students which explores some feminist ideas.

Bryson, V. *Feminist Political Theory: An Introduction*, 3rd edn (2016). A thorough introduction to the development of feminist theory.

Disch, L. and Hawkesworth, M. *The Oxford Handbook of Feminist Theory* (2016). The definitive survey of feminist scholarship across many applications of society and politics.

Elshtain, J.B. *Public Man, Private Woman: Women in Social and Political Thought*, 2nd edn (1993).

Ms. Magazine www.msmagazine.com and the *Feminist Majority* www.feminist.org. Founded in 1971, *Ms.* is one of the longest-running feminist publications, now published by the *Feminist Majority*. Both websites feature news, educational resources, commentary and media on feminist issues, politics and history.

Penguin publishes a range of classic feminist texts (many of which have been mentioned in this chapter) in short form; see https://www.penguin.co.uk/series/VFSE/vintage-feminism-short-editions.

Tong, R. and Botts, T. *Feminist Thought: A More Comprehensive Introduction*, 5th edn (2018). An in-depth survey of the key branches in feminist theory, particularly those emerging in recent decades.

Vincent, R. *Modern Political Ideologies* (1995). Chapter 7 Feminism can be used to stretch and extend a student's knowledge of the content covered in this chapter.

Vox.com. A comprehensive analysis of each wave with recommended reading list for each wave, https://www.vox.com/platform/amp/2018/3/20/16955588/feminism-waves-explained-first-second-third-fourth?fbclid=IwAR0_dcyqcd_2PBxLQoVDEBmgf1brFKKMZel4KY_Tep3_HeDpVwhStoazgfM.

Visit our companion website at https://bloomsbury.pub/essentials-of-political-ideas-2e for more worked examples.

7 MULTICULTURALISM

Historical overview

Multicultural societies have always existed; however, the term 'multiculturalism' is of relatively recent origin. It was first used in Canada in 1965 to describe a distinctive approach to tackling the issue of cultural diversity. Today, events such as the Notting Hill Carnival, which has celebrated the British Caribbean community since the 1960s, highlight the many facets of multicultural society in London.

The 1960s and 1970s witnessed a trend towards growing political assertiveness among minority groups in many parts of the world. This was typically expressed through a quest for cultural or ethnic recognition within a liberal-democratic framework. This was evident among the French-speaking people of Quebec in Canada, in the rise of Scottish and Welsh nationalism in the UK and in the growth of separatist movements in Catalonia and the Basque region in Spain, Corsica in France and Flanders in Belgium. The indigenous people of North America in Canada and the USA, the aboriginal peoples in Australia and the Māori in New Zealand asserted pride in their cultures and identity, in defiance of racism and prejudice.

In response to these pressures, a growing number of countries adopted 'official' multiculturalism policies. The watershed 1988 Canadian Multiculturalism Act acknowledged the freedom of all members of Canadian society to preserve, enhance and share their cultural heritage, and endorsed the principle of bilingualism. A common theme among these emergent forms of ethnic politics was the desire to challenge economic and social marginalization in addition to racial oppression.

Multicultural politics have also been strengthened by trends in international migration since 1945 that have significantly widened cultural diversity in many societies. Migration rates rose steeply in the early post-1945 period, as people tried to escape poverty by looking to economic opportunities abroad, and as Western states sought to recruit workers from abroad to help in the process of post-war reconstruction. More and more societies are characterized by ethnic diversity as a result, meaning that the monocultural nation-state has become very much the exception and not the rule.

By the early 2000s, a growing number of Western states, including virtually all the member states of the European Union, had responded to such developments by incorporating multiculturalism in some way into public policy.

Key Questions

» How did multiculturalism originate?
» What are the main principles that are central to multiculturalism?
» What are the key strands of multiculturalism?
» What are the areas of similarity and difference within multiculturalism?

Specification Checklist

1. Multiculturalism: core ideas and principles:

» Politics of recognition
» Culture and identity
» Minority rights
» Diversity

2. Differing views and tensions within multiculturalism:

» Liberal multiculturalism
» Pluralist multiculturalism
» Cosmopolitan multiculturalism
» The conservative criticism

3. Multiculturalism key thinkers and their ideas:

» Isaiah Berlin (1909–97)
» Charles Taylor (1931–)
» Bhikhu Parekh (1935–)
» Tariq Modood (1952–)
» Will Kymlicka (1962–)

Jack Taylor/Getty

Introduction to multiculturalism and its strands

The term multiculturalism refers to cultural diversity that arises from the existence within a society of two or more groups whose beliefs and practices generate a distinctive sense of collective identity. Multiculturalism is a positive endorsement or celebration of diversity. This is based on the right of different cultural groups to be respected, and recognition of the benefits of cultural diversity.

In this sense, multiculturalism acknowledges that different cultures deserve to be protected and strengthened, particularly when they belong to minority groups. However, there are several competing models of a multicultural society. These draw on the ideas of liberalism, pluralism and cosmopolitanism, each offering a different model of the balance between togetherness and difference.

Multiculturalism is more an ideological 'space' than a political ideology. Instead of advancing a comprehensive world-view which maps out an economic, social and political vision of the 'good society', multiculturalism is an arena for debate, encompassing a range of views about the implications of growing cultural diversity and, in particular, about how cultural difference can be reconciled with civic unity.

Liberal multiculturalism

Liberal multiculturalism developed out of the debate between liberal individualism, and the role of different cultures that were now common in contemporary society. As such, liberal multiculturalism moved beyond the individualistic concepts of liberalism towards a greater understanding of the importance of culture to minority groups. Liberal multiculturalists support shallow diversity, which is the notion that diversity must exist within the values of a liberal society.

Pluralist multiculturalism

Pluralist multiculturalism is a wide-ranging idea, encompassing many different perspectives. The overriding theme of pluralist multiculturalism is that it values diversity in its own right. In this vein, all cultures must be valued and recognized as they form the key identity of many citizens. Pluralist multiculturalists support deep diversity, which argues that cultures need not conform to liberal values to be acceptable. Pluralist multiculturalists also support integration over assimilation in society.

Cosmopolitan multiculturalism

Despite the fact that cosmopolitan multiculturalism supports cultural diversity and recognizes difference, in many ways its aim is to create a 'global citizen'. This citizen may be a 'pick 'n' mix' of many different cultures within which the individual has interacted. The aim of diversity, therefore, is to expose individuals to multiple cultures through which they can develop their own fluid identity. Cosmopolitan multiculturalism is different to liberal and pluralist multiculturalism as it indicates that individuals aren't culturally embedded.

The conservative critique

As the name indicates, the conservative critique is not a strand of multiculturalism at all, instead it is a critique of multiculturalism from a conservative perspective. Conservatives are suspicious of multiculturalism, believing it will undermine the cohesiveness of society and promote divisions. Conservatives believe that humans need to feel safe and secure and a key way of doing that is to embed all members of society into a single, unifying culture, with history and tradition playing a key role in shaping this identity.

1. Multiculturalism: core ideas and principles

» Politics of recognition
» Culture and identity
» Minority rights
» Diversity

Politics of recognition
This can be included in a discussion of the multiculturalist view of state and society.

The politics of recognition is a key starting point for multiculturalism and means that a culture or group must be acknowledged. Multiculturalists argue that minority cultural groups are disadvantaged in relation to majority groups and that remedying this must involve significant changes in society. The politics of recognition aims to move away from ignoring or, even worse, oppressing minority groups, to recognizing them, understanding their culture and heritage, and learning what that means for them living in society. For Canadian academic and philosopher **Charles Taylor (1931–)**, recognition constitutes a '*vital human need*'. He argues that the act of recognition in itself is a powerful validation for minority groups because being ignored makes them feel overlooked. Some argue that one's identity is partly shaped by recognition or its absence, often by the misrecognition of others, and so a person or group of people can suffer real damage and distortion if society around them presents a confining or demeaning picture of themselves. **Taylor** argued that recognition is based on dignity and recognition of minority groups as '*nonrecognition can inflict harm, can be a force of oppression*'; however, different strands of multiculturalism may adopt contrasting approaches to recognition, based on the following ideas.

Equal rights

The notion of the 'politics of rights' is rooted in the ideas of liberalism and is specifically concerned with the denial to certain groups of rights that are enjoyed by their fellow citizens. This thinking was reflected in first-wave feminism, in that its campaign for female emancipation focused on the struggle for votes for women and equal access for women to education, careers and public life in general. This stance can be said to be 'difference-blind': it views difference as 'the problem' (because it leads to discriminatory or unfair treatment) and proposes that difference be removed in the name of equality. They therefore believe that social advancement can be brought about largely through the establishment of formal equality.

Equal redistribution

The idea of the 'politics of redistribution' arose out of the belief that universal citizenship and formal equality are insufficient to tackle the problems faced by minorities. People are held back not merely by legal and political exclusion but also, and more importantly, by social disadvantage – poverty, unemployment, poor housing, lack of education and so on. The key idea of social reform is the principle of equal opportunities, the belief in a 'level playing-field' that allows people to rise or fall in society strictly based on ability and willingness to work. This implies a shift from legal to social egalitarianism, the latter involving a system of that redistributes wealth to reduce poverty and overcome disadvantage. With such an approach, difference is acknowledged as it highlights the existence of social injustice. Nevertheless, this amounts to no more than a limited acknowledgement of difference, in that different groups are identified only to expose unfair practices and structures, to be reformed or removed.

Definition

Social Cohesion: Social cohesion refers to the extent to which people in society are bound together and integrated and share common values.

Spec key term

Formal equality: Equality based on people's status in society, especially their legal and political rights (legal and political equality).

Definition

Citizenship: Membership of a state; a relationship between the individual and the state based on reciprocal rights and responsibilities.

Equality of opportunity: Equality defined in terms of life chances or the existence of a 'level playing-field'.

Equal dignity

The idea of dignity is an important part of recognition. Dignity is the notion that all cultures should be treated with respect and valued as inherent parts of society. Different groups shouldn't just be tolerated, but accepted into society, beyond formal equality, citizenship and social egalitarianism. Recognition therefore requires that states create a legal framework that actively encourages different cultures to flourish. This would mean, for example, the promotion of the Welsh language in Wales as shown in Photo 7.1, or French in Quebec, as well as accommodation of cultural or religious requirements into everyday life, like the wearing of the hijab, kippot or turbans and adaptations around religious observances like Ramadan, Diwali or the Jewish sabbath. Recognition means enabling all different cultures to be treated with dignity and respect, allowing them to continue to observe cultural or religious observances alongside the mainstream culture. The 'politics of recognition' involves a positive endorsement, even a celebration, of cultural difference, allowing marginalized groups to assert themselves by reclaiming an authentic sense of cultural identity.

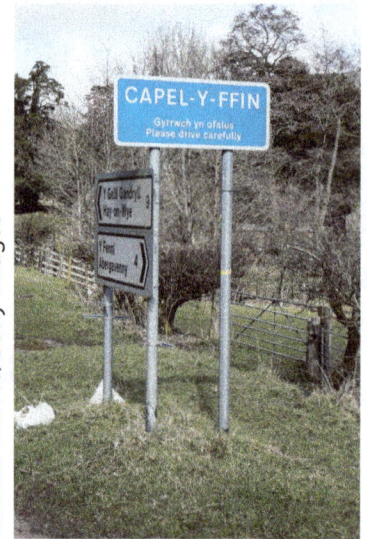

Photo 7.1 **Promotion of the Welsh language is a key part of Welsh culture.**

> **Spec key term**
>
> **Culture:** Beliefs, values and practices that are passed on from one generation to the next through learning; culture is distinct from nature.

> **Definition**
>
> **Communitarianism:** The idea that people are intrinsically shaped by the social, cultural and other structures within which they live and develop.

Politics of recognition

Summary box

- The positive endorsement and celebration of cultural differences.
- Different strands have different approaches to recognition based on rights, redistribution and dignity.
- There is an understanding that recognition affects the way minority communities feel.
- Also an understanding that recognition underpins integration and social cohesion.

Culture and Identity

This can be included in a discussion of the multiculturalist view of human nature and society.

Identity politics (within multiculturalism) is the idea that one's culture is integral to one's identity. Multiculturalism, in that sense, is about cultural self-assertion as pride in one's culture, and especially a public acknowledgement of one's cultural identity gives people a sense of social and historical rootedness. In contrast, a weak or fractured sense of cultural identity can leave people feeling isolated and confused. As **Tariq Modood (1952–)** argued, '*to be among those of different cultures makes us aware of what we are not, and therefore sharpens our understanding of who we are*'. In its most intense form, this can result in what has been called 'culturalism' – as practised by the French political philosopher Montesquieu (1689–1775) and J.G. Herder – which portrays humans as culturally defined creatures. In its modern form, cultural politics has been shaped by two main forces: communitarianism and identity politics.

Communitarianism advances a critique of liberalism and in particular its focus on individualism and universalism – the idea that, as individuals, people in all societies and all cultures have essentially the same 'inner' identity. In contrast, communitarians seek a shift away from universalism to an emphasis on what is distinctive about the groups to which they belong. In this way, it rejects liberal individualism. Identity, in this sense, links the personal to the social, and sees the individual as 'embedded', or rooted, in a particular culture. Multiculturalists therefore accept a communitarian view of human nature, which stresses that people cannot be understood 'outside' society but are intrinsically shaped by the social, cultural and other structures within which they live and develop.

> **Spec key term**
>
> **Identity politics:** Advances a critique of liberal universalism as cultural oppression, where minorities are marginalized and the claiming of an authentic sense of identity by groups is an act of political liberation.
>
> **Universalism:** From a multiculturalist view, universalism is where certain values are applicable to all individuals and all societies, regardless of culture, or any other differences.

Charles Hawes/Getty Images

Communitarian philosophers such as Alasdair MacIntyre, *After Virtue* (1981) and Michael Sandel (*Liberalism and the Limits of Justice*, 1982) portrayed the idea of the abstract individual as a recipe for rootlessness. Only communities can give people a genuine sense of identity and moral purpose. Pluralist multiculturalists, such as UK academic and political theorist **Bhikhu Parekh (1935–)**, argued that humans grow up embedded in a cultural world with their identity formed by the culture they grew up in. This shapes the way they see themselves and the world. One of the consequences of this debate was a growing willingness among many liberal thinkers to acknowledge the importance of culture. This give rise to the tradition of liberal multiculturalism which was more open to the attractions of multiculturalism, than traditional liberalism.

What all forms of identity politics have in common is that they advance a critique of universalism. For pluralist multiculturalism, universalism is a source of oppression, even a form of cultural imperialism, in that it tends to marginalize and demoralize groups and peoples. This is because, behind a façade of universalism, liberal society is constructed in line with the values and interests of its dominant groups: men, white people, the wealthy and so on in this sense it sees a hierarchy of cultures. Subordinate groups and peoples are either consigned an inferior or demeaning stereotype, or they are encouraged to identify with the values and interests of dominant groups (that is, their oppressors). However, identity politics does not only view culture as a source of oppression; it is also a source of liberation and empowerment, particularly when it seeks to cultivate a 'pure' or 'authentic' sense of identity. **Taylor** suggested that one's identity '*is particular to me, and that I discover in myself. This notion arises along with an ideal, that of being true to myself and my own particular way of being ... I will speak of this as the ideal of "authenticity".*'

Identity politics seeks to challenge and overthrow oppression by reshaping a group's identity through what amounts to a process of self-assertion. This reflects two core beliefs.

1. Group marginalization operates through stereotypes and values developed by dominant groups that control how marginalized groups see themselves and are seen by others. These instil a sense of inferiority, even shame.

2. Subordination can be challenged by reshaping identity to give the group concerned a sense of pride and self-respect (e.g. 'Black is beautiful' or 'gay pride'). Embracing or proclaiming a positive social identity is an act of liberation and is therefore a statement of intent, and a form of defiance. This is what gives identity politics its typically combative character and instils it with emotional force.

However, one of the complications of this form of identity politics is that it can create discord between cultures, a sense of competing to be heard and a call for wrongs against their particular culture to be made right. Identity politics can lead to different cultures being inward looking, emphasizing differences, rather than seeking similarities between them and other cultures.

Culture and identity
Summary box
- Culture is crucial to society as it shapes personal, political and social identity.
- Minority cultures should be respected and protected to give a sense of belonging.
- Critics argue it can create discord between cultures.

Minority rights
This can be included in a discussion of the multiculturalist view of the state and society.

The advance of multiculturalism has gone hand in hand with a willingness to recognize minority rights. Minority rights are 'special' rights, specific to the groups to which they belong. This is because each cultural group has different needs for recognition based on the particular character of its religion, traditions and way of life. The most systematic attempt to identify such rights was undertaken by Canadian political philosopher **Will Kymlicka (1962–). Kymlicka** (2000) identified three kinds of minority rights:

» *Self-government* rights belong to those classified as 'national minorities', indigenous or tribal peoples who are territorially concentrated, possess a shared language and are characterized

Definition

Liberal multiculturalism: A form of multiculturalism that is committed to toleration and seeks to uphold freedom of choice in the moral sphere, especially in relation to culture or religion.

Pluralist multiculturalism: A form of multiculturalism that is committed to 'deep' diversity, based on the alleged benefits of cultural entrenchment and the need to resist cultural imperialism.

Cultural imperialism: The imposition by the dominant community of its own culture onto another community.

by a '*meaningful way of life across the full range of human activities*'. Examples include the First Nations, Inuits and Metis peoples in Canada. In these cases, the right to self-government involves the devolution of political power to political units that are substantially controlled by their members, although it may extend to the right of secession and, therefore, to sovereign independence.

» *Polyethnic* rights are rights that help ethnic groups and religious minorities, which have developed through immigration, to express and maintain their cultural distinctiveness. This would, for instance, provide the basis for legal exemptions, such as the exemption of Jews and Muslims from animal slaughtering laws, and the exemption of Muslim girls from school dress codes. These are known as group-differentiated rights.

» Special *representation* rights attempt to redress the under-representation of minority or disadvantaged groups in education and in senior positions in political and public life. **Kymlicka** justified positive discrimination in such cases, on the grounds that it is the only way of ensuring the full and equal participation of all groups in the life of their society, thus ensuring that public policy reflects the interests of diverse groups and peoples, and not merely those of traditionally dominant groups.

Multiculturalists see minority rights as essential to modern societies for a number of reasons:

» First, minority rights have been viewed, particularly by liberal multiculturalists, as a guarantee of individual freedom and personal autonomy. In this view, culture is a vital tool that enables people to live autonomous lives. **Charles Taylor** argues that individual self-respect is bound up with cultural membership. As people derive an important sense of who they are from their cultures, individual rights are entangled with minority rights.

» Second, minority rights are seen as a way of countering liberal 'colour blind' oppression. In this view, liberal societies can 'harm' their citizens by ignoring their cultural identities by being '*inhospitable to difference*' (**Taylor**, 1994). Minority groups are vulnerable because the liberal state, despite its pretence of neutrality, is inevitably aligned with a dominant culture, whose language is used, whose history is taught, and whose cultural and religious practices are observed in public life. So the state is complicit in promoting the majority culture at the expense of others. Of particular importance is the issue of offence and the right not to be offended. This, primarily concerns religious groups who consider certain beliefs sacred and therefore especially deserving of protection. To criticize, insult or ridicule such beliefs is seen as an attack on the group itself.

» Third, minority rights are supported because they redress social injustice. In this view, minority rights are a compensation for unfair disadvantages and for under-representation, usually addressed through a programme of positive discrimination. This has been particularly evident in the USA, where the political advancement of Black people has, since the 1960s, been associated with affirmative action. For example, in the case of *Regents of the University of California v. Bakke* (1978), the Supreme Court upheld the principle of 'reverse' discrimination in educational admissions.

» Finally, multiculturalists such as **Kymlicka** believe that indigenous peoples or national minorities are entitled to rights that go beyond those of groups that have formed as a result of immigration. This can be sustained on the grounds that indigenous peoples have been dispossessed and subordinated through a process of colonization and settlement. In no way did groups choose to give up their culture or distinctive way of life; neither did they consent to the formation of a new state. In contrast, as migration involves some level of choice and voluntary action, immigrant groups can be said to be under an obligation to accept the core values and governmental arrangements of their country of settlement.

However, although the movement on behalf of indigenous peoples shares much in common with anti-colonial nationalism, its political goals are typically more modest. Rather than aspiring to establish sovereign independence, indigenous peoples seek to maintain traditional practices while participating on their own terms in wider social, economic and political arrangements. According to Canadian philosopher James Tully, such a development would involve constitutional remodelling to protect cultural diversity and expand the rights of indigenous peoples. This might apply particularly in areas such as hunting and fishing in specific territories, land ownership on the part of the majority community and the enforcement of traditional family law.

Spec key term

Group-differentiated rights: Rights that belong to a group, in contrast to a right held by individuals, includes self-government rights, polyethnic rights and representation rights.

Positive discrimination: Preferential treatment for groups in society to correct structural inequality or compensate for historical wrongs.

Definition

Affirmative action: Policies or programmes that are designed to benefit disadvantaged minority groups (or, potentially, women) by affording them special assistance.

Nevertheless, controversy surrounds the rights of minority cultural groups which has led to criticism.

» However fair its intentions, positive discrimination is still a form of discrimination. As Chief Justice Roberts of the US Supreme Court argued in 2007 *'The way to stop discrimination on the basis of race is to stop discriminating on the basis of race.'* In other words, you cannot justify one form of discrimination to stop another. It is also suggested that positive discrimination has undermined the achievement of Black people in the US by suggesting that they were less capable.

» Moreover, minority rights can be seen as problematic when it comes to their implications for vulnerable group members, such as women (Okin, 1999). This happens when minority rights and the politics of recognition serve to preserve and legitimize patriarchal and traditionalist beliefs that systematically disadvantage women, an argument that may equally be applied to those of the LGBTQ community. This is sometimes called the 'minorities within minorities' issue. Cultural practices such as dress codes, family structures and access to elite positions may reinforce structural gender biases.

Minority rights

Summary box

- The state should address the specific needs of particular groups in society.
- It should grant special rights to them, based on their different needs as a culture.
- Critics argue that this is a form of discrimination.

Tensions within multiculturalism for minority rights

AGREEMENT	DISAGREEMENT
✓ Multiculturalists believe that minority rights are crucial to integration into society	✗ Liberal multiculturalism supports minority rights based on autonomy and justice and will not accept illiberal practices
✓ Multiculturalists endorse positive discrimination	✗ Some conservatives have criticized positive discrimination
✓ Multiculturalists support polyethnic rights	✗ Some conservatives have criticized polyethnic rights

Diversity

This can be included in a discussion of the multiculturalist view of the state and society.

Diversity is the idea that society should recognize the wide range of different cultures and identities that exist and adapt their systems and policies to accommodate them. The population of non-white people is around 35 per cent in the USA and 15 per cent in Europe. Multiculturalists argue that cultural diversity is compatible with, and perhaps provides the best basis for, social cohesion, emphasizing the capacity of culture to reinforce social unity.

All forms of multiculturalism are based on the assumption that unity and diversity – or 'togetherness in difference' (Young, 1995) – can, and should, be blended with one another: they are not opposing forces. In this sense, multiculturalism accepts that people can have multiple cultural identities and loyalties; for instance, to their country of origin and their country of settlement. Indeed, multiculturalism argues that feeling secure in one's culture underpins stability with 'a common sense of belonging'. **Parekh** argues that people are more willing to participate in society precisely because they have a firm and secure identity, rooted in their own culture. From this perspective, the denial of cultural recognition and forcing conformity results in isolation, powerlessness and oppression, leading to alienation and injustice and providing a breeding ground for extremism and the politics of hate. For pluralist multiculturalist **Tariq Modood**, integration involves bringing communities into relationships of equal respect. This involves

Spec key term

Diversity: Different races and cultures within a state are possible, is positive and should be celebrated.

developing positive group identities, adapting traditional customs and institutions and remaking the national story so that everyone can recognize themselves in it. He believed in unity through diversity, in other words, creating strong multicultural identities but balanced with a national identity that creates a sense of belonging to one's country.

Multiculturalists do not therefore just believe that diversity is possible; they believe it is also highly desirable and should be celebrated.

» Apart from its benefits to the individual – a stronger sense of cultural identity and belonging – multiculturalists believe that diversity is of value to society at large. This can be seen in terms of the vibrancy of a society in which there are a variety of lifestyles, cultural practices, traditions and beliefs. Multiculturalism proposes that cultural diversity is of enormous benefit to any society.

» An additional advantage of diversity is that, by promoting cultural exchange between groups that live side by side with one another, it promotes cross-cultural toleration and understanding, and therefore a willingness to respect 'difference'. Diversity, in this sense, is the solution to polarization and prejudice in society.

Nevertheless, multiculturalism has sometimes been criticized for endorsing diversity at the expense of unity. This has been reflected in the growing interest in what is called interculturalism, seen either as an alternative to multiculturalism or as an updated version of multiculturalism. Viewed as a response to how to live in, rather than with, diversity, interculturalism is based on three key assumptions:

» First, it rejects the idea that cultures are fixed and unchanging, instead emphasizing that they are fluid and internally differentiated. Dialogue thus takes place within cultures as well as between them.

» Second, debate and argument are seen to be intrinsically worthwhile, reflecting an underlying faith in reason.

» Third, cultures are thought to be distinguished more by what they have in common than by what divides them.

However, pluralist multiculturalists hold that interculturalism is a political and moral dead end. This is because they fear that by encouraging cultural exchange and prioritizing mutual understanding, it risks blurring the contours of group identity and creating a kind of 'pick 'n' mix', melting-pot society in which individuals have a 'shallow' sense of social and historical identity.

Spec key term

Toleration: From a multiculturalist view, toleration is a willingness to accept values, customs and beliefs with which one disagrees.

Definition

Interculturalism: An approach to diversity that strongly emphasizes the benefits of dialogue and interaction between cultures.

Diversity

Summary box

- Society should recognize the wide range of different cultures and identities that exist and adapt to accommodate them.
- Different cultures are a positive in society and should be celebrated.
- Critics argue that this can undermine the unity and cohesiveness of society.

Tensions within multiculturalism over support for diversity

AGREEMENT	DISAGREEMENT
✓ Liberal multiculturalists argue that diversity is valuable by bringing variety to society. They endorse shallow diversity	✗ Liberal multiculturalists are supportive of diversity but are unwilling to compromise the principles of liberal democracy, whereas pluralists argue that liberal democracy restricts diversity
✓ Pluralist multiculturalists see individual identity as embedded in cultural context. They endorse deep diversity	✗ Pluralist multiculturalists argue that the shallow diversity is limited, preferring value pluralism and deep diversity
✓ Cosmopolitan multiculturalists view diversity as important in showing and sharing multiple identities	✗ Cosmopolitan multiculturalists support diversity but do not regard it as a value in itself

2. Differences between the multiculturalist strands

All forms of multiculturalism advance a political vision that claims to reconcile cultural diversity with social cohesion. However, multiculturalism is not a single doctrine in the sense that there is no settled or agreed view of how a multicultural society should operate. Indeed, multiculturalism is another example of a cross-cutting ideology that draws on a range of other political traditions and encompasses a variety of ideological stances. Multiculturalists disagree both about how far they should go in positively endorsing cultural diversity, and about how civic cohesion can best be brought about. In short, there are competing models of multiculturalism, each offering a different view of the proper balance between diversity and unity. The three main types of multiculturalism are:

» liberal multiculturalism

» pluralist multiculturalism

» cosmopolitan multiculturalism

In addition, the specification requires knowledge of

» the conservative critique of multiculturalism

Liberal multiculturalism

There is a complex and, in many ways, ambivalent relationship between liberalism and multiculturalism. Some view liberalism and multiculturalism as rival political traditions, the former emphasizing individualism and freedom of choice, while the latter stresses group identity.

The cornerstone of liberalism is an unswerving commitment to toleration and a desire to uphold freedom of choice, especially in relation to matters that are of central concern to cultural or religious traditions. This has contributed to the idea that liberalism is 'neutral' in relation to the moral, cultural and other choices that citizens make. John Rawls championed this belief arguing that liberalism strives to establish conditions in which people can establish the good life as each defines it, but it does not prescribe or try to promote any particular values. Liberalism, in this sense, is 'difference-blind': it treats factors such as culture, ethnicity, race, religion and gender as, in effect, irrelevant, because all people should be evaluated as morally autonomous individuals.

Since the 1970s, however, liberal thinkers have taken the issue of cultural diversity increasingly seriously and have developed a form of liberal multiculturalism. This is seen as reflecting a shift from an emphasis on the individual to group rights. Liberal multiculturalism argues that the traditional liberal focus on human rights is insufficient as they are unable to resolve some of the most pressing questions relating to cultural minorities. For instance, the right to freedom of speech has nothing to say about what an appropriate language policy is for a government to adopt. Liberal multiculturalism is most closely associated with the work of **Will Kymlicka** and looks to develop a form of multiculturalism derived from (but different to) liberalism.

Liberal multiculturalism has a number of features:

1. The first principle of liberal multiculturalism is tolerance, which is the idea that you must allow (and even encourage) views that you may not agree with as all views have equal value. However, liberal multicultural toleration is not morally neutral, and only provides a limited endorsement of cultural diversity, known as shallow diversity. In particular, toleration extends only to views, values and social practices that are themselves tolerant; that is, ideas and actions that are compatible with personal freedom and autonomy. Liberal multiculturalism thus cannot accommodate deep diversity, for example, they may be unwilling to endorse practices such as female genital mutilation, forced marriages and female dress codes, however much the groups concerned may argue that these are crucial to the maintenance of their cultural identity.

Exam Tip – It is worth noting that liberalism and liberal multiculturalism have different values. They should not be used interchangeably.

Definition

Shallow diversity: Diversity that is confined by the acceptance of certain values and beliefs as 'absolute' and therefore non-negotiable.

Deep diversity: Diversity that may be incompatible with liberal values.

Tensions within multiculturalism over tolerance	
AGREEMENT	**DISAGREEMENT**
✓ There is broad agreement within multiculturalism that there should be tolerance afforded to a wide range of cultural beliefs and practices	✗ Liberal multiculturalists would not tolerate practices that are themselves intolerant
✓ Multiculturalists reject the imposition of a dominant culture across the whole of society	✗ Pluralist multiculturalism supports value pluralism, arguing that all practices and beliefs have an equal standing, not just liberal ones
✓ Multiculturalists recognize that this means supporting people's right to behave in ways that they may disapprove of	✗ Multiculturalists' views on tolerance has an impact on their view of diversity

2. The second feature of liberal multiculturalism is that it sees the state as neutral; not seeking to promote any view over any other. The liberal state draws an important distinction between 'private' and 'public' life. It sees the former as somewhere people should be free to express their cultural, religious and linguistic identity. The latter, meanwhile, must be characterized by a shared sense of civic pride. For liberals, cultural identity is a private matter separate from one's public sense of citizenship. Such a stance implies that multiculturalism requires every citizen to accept and support the fundamental values of the state. This is known as individualist-integration. In these circumstances, institutions may make adjustments for individuals, but minority groups are not recognized or given special status in the public sphere.

However, liberal multiculturalism goes beyond liberalism in supporting the politics of recognition and minority rights. **Kymlicka** argues these are consistent with liberalism, and are appropriate in certain situations, arguing that group-differentiated rights have a place within a liberal society alongside formal equality. This is known as multicultural integration. He argues that for the state to be truly neutral it must be responsible for ensuring fair background conditions, including the public recognition of language and culture so that individuals are free to make choices, and are responsible for considering the consequences of their choices. Liberal multiculturalism is focused on the provision of fair opportunities to freely pursue culture-related interests rather than the imposition of duties to maintain any particular identity or way of life. **Kymlicka** insists that group-differentiated rights reflect a liberal, not collectivist outlook.

Some liberals, however, reject these values of liberal multiculturalism arguing that group rights are problematic as they treat individuals as part of a group, rather than individuals. **Kymlicka**, however, draws a distinction between external protection and internal restrictions. He argues that external protections, where rights of minority groups are protected, may be justified to promote foundational equality. Internal restrictions, i.e. a cultural requirement to do or to wear something, however, cannot be justified, insofar as they restrict a person's autonomy. Simply put, the state should protect minorities cultural or religious needs, but an individual from that group cannot be forced to uphold those practices by the group. However, liberals and liberal multiculturalists are very clear that group-differentiated rights can only exist if they conform to the broader liberal-democratic principles of society and are tolerant of others.

3. A third aspect of liberal multiculturalism is that it regards liberal democracy as the sole legitimate political system. In this view, the virtue of liberal democracy is that it ensures that government is based on the consent of the people, and, in providing guarantees for personal freedom and toleration, provides a political space for the expression of diverse views and values. This, nevertheless, does not lead to a free-for-all, in which any views and values can be expressed. Liberal democracy is its own gatekeeper: groups and political movements may be prohibited if their goals and beliefs are incompatible with key liberal-democratic principles. Groups are therefore only entitled to toleration and respect, if they, in turn, are prepared to tolerate and respect other groups.

Spec key term

Individualist-integration: Institutional adjustments for migrants or minorities as those of individual claimants and bearers of rights as equal citizens.

Multicultural integration: The processes of integration are seen as different for different groups and individuals, to create a new national identity, where all citizens have not just rights but a sense of belonging to the whole, as well as to their own group identity/identities.

4. The final principle of liberal multiculturalism is a commitment to communitarianism. This again puts liberal multiculturalism in conflict with liberalism. Communitarianism is the view that people have distinctive values and cultures and are shaped by and understand themselves through the groups to which they belong. This is a clear rejection of liberal individualism and universalism.

Tensions within multiculturalism over integration	
AGREEMENT	**DISAGREEMENT**
✓ Most forms of multiculturalism see the integration of minority cultures as key to a stable society	✗ Liberal multiculturalism supports individualist-integration
✓ Multiculturalism promotes integration by recognizing and supporting difference to create integrated societies	✗ Pluralist multiculturalism supports multicultural integration based on the politics of recognition and minority rights
✓ Multiculturalism's support for tolerance promotes integration, leading to a more integrated society	✗ Cosmopolitan multiculturalism believes in cosmopolitan integration which is the idea that culture is an ongoing, constantly changing aspect of people's lives

Pluralist multiculturalism

Pluralist multiculturalism values diversity and provides firmer foundations for the politics of difference than liberalism. For liberals, diversity is supported only within a framework of toleration and personal autonomy, amounting to a form of shallow diversity. Pluralist multiculturalism, in contrast, believes that cultural recognition is the only way to ensure different cultures fully engage in society. This suggests that liberal values should be challenged. British historian and thinker **Isaiah Berlin (1909–97)** went beyond liberal toleration to endorse the idea of value pluralism. This suggests that people are bound to disagree, which Berlin described as '*an intrinsic, irremovable part of human life*' as it is not possible to demonstrate the superiority of one moral system over another. However, this debate would encourage people to consider other people's cultures resulting in greater understanding and tolerance.

As values clash, he argued, society will be characterized by moral conflict. In this view, liberal beliefs, such as support for personal freedom, individualism, toleration and democracy, have no greater authority than non-liberal beliefs like common humanity, collectivism and communal living. **Berlin's** stance implies a form of live-and-let-live multiculturalism, or what has been called the politics of *indifference*. However, **Berlin** remained liberal to the extent that he believed that value pluralism can be contained only within a society that respects individual liberty. He failed to demonstrate, however, how liberal and non-liberal cultural beliefs could co-exist harmoniously within the same society. In his 1995 book *Isaiah Berlin*, English philosopher John Gray argued that once liberalism accepts moral pluralism, it is difficult to contain it within a liberal framework and argued that pluralism implies a 'post-liberal' stance, in which liberal values, institutions and regimes are no longer seen to enjoy a monopoly of legitimacy.

An alternative basis for pluralist multiculturalism has been advanced by **Parekh**. In **Parekh's** view cultural diversity is, at heart, a reflection of the interaction between human nature and culture. Although humans possess common physical and mental capacities, they are also culturally established in the sense that their attitudes, behaviour and ways of life are shaped by the groups to which they belong. **Parekh** argued that liberalism sees its values and way of life as the highest ideal, and, in so doing, rejects the values of other ways of life. Pluralist multiculturalists instead argue that a person's culture is so deeply embedded within them as to form part of their nature. He argued that humans are culturally embedded in the sense that they grow up, and live within, a culturally structured world, organizing their lives and social relations based on cultural meanings and significance.

As each culture advocates its own version of a 'good life', it is deeply insulting to suggest that it is secondary to another culture. However, **Parekh** and other pluralist multiculturalists argued that being surrounded by other cultures with different values and priorities is an essential part of a human's development as it encourages us to explore different aspects of our humanity. Different cultures

Spec key term

Value pluralism: There is no one absolute conception of the 'good life' but rather multiple, competing and equally legitimate conceptions.

represent different systems of meaning and visions of the good life. Each culture needs other cultures to help it understand itself better, expand its intellectual and moral horizon and stretch its imagination. In other words, the more different views and values we are surrounded by, the more we will grow and develop as humans.

Thus, pluralist multiculturalism rejects the dominance of liberal values as championed by liberal multiculturalism, arguing that on their own they cannot develop people to their full potential. Instead they advocate multiculturalist integration, where the state accommodates different cultures to protect their identities with laws being adapted differently for different cultures. For **Modood**, multiculturalism is crucial to successful integration into society and argues that the state should support multiculturalism by preventing discrimination and inequality and by recognizing difference and minority rights. However, he was also clear that it must also create a '*framework of vibrant, national narratives … to give expression to a national identity*'. **Modood** outlined four different models of integration: assimilation, individualist, pluralist and cosmopolitan. He was clear that no single method fits all groups, but that it was essential that groups were able to choose their own method of integration.

However, this doesn't mean that all cultures are equally rich and deserve equal respect, that they cannot be compared and critically assessed. It simply means is that no culture is wholly worthless, that each deserves at least some respect because of what it means to its members and the creative energy it displays. Pluralist multiculturalists argue that no culture is perfect and has a right to impose itself on others and that cultures are best changed from within.

Cosmopolitan multiculturalism

Cosmopolitanism and multiculturalism can be seen as entirely distinct, even conflicting, ideological traditions. Whereas cosmopolitanism encourages people to adopt an outward, global awareness which emphasizes that moral responsibility should not be confined by national borders, multiculturalism appears to identify a morality focusing on the specific needs and interests of a distinctive cultural group. However, for theorists such as New Zealand philosophy professor Jeremy Waldron, multiculturalism can effectively be equated with cosmopolitanism.

Cosmopolitan multiculturalists like Walden support cultural diversity and identity politics but view them as transitional as we move towards a reorganization. Cosmopolitan multiculturalism celebrates diversity on the grounds of what each culture can learn from other cultures and believes that greater personal self-development is offered by a world of wider cultural opportunities. This results in what has been called a 'pick 'n' mix' multiculturalism, in which cultural mixing is positively encouraged. People, for instance, may eat Italian food, practise yoga, enjoy African music and develop an interest in world religions. Ultimately, cosmopolitan multiculturalists see a process whereby, eventually, cultural groups will fade away as all groups move towards a global cultural identity.

Cosmopolitan multiculturalism is distinct from other forms of multiculturalism as it does not support the idea of communitarianism, rejecting the central role of cultural identity in people's lives. Instead, culture is an ongoing, constantly changing aspect of people's lives as they live amongst and adopt aspects of different cultures. This is known as cosmopolitan integration. Cosmopolitan multiculturalism argues that this is even more relevant in the modern, global age where social media platforms encourage a wide mixing of global cultural phenomena.

Culture, from this perspective, is flexible and responsive to changing social circumstances and personal needs; it is not fixed and embedded, as pluralist multiculturalists would argue. A multicultural society is thus a 'melting pot' of different ideas, values and traditions, rather than a 'cultural mosaic' of separate ethnic and religious groups. In particular, the cosmopolitan stance positively embraces hybridity. This recognizes that, in the modern world, individual identity cannot be explained in terms of a single cultural structure, but rather exists, in Waldron's (1995) words, as a 'melange' of commitments, affiliations and roles. Indeed, for Waldron, immersion in the traditions of a particular culture is like living in Disneyland and thinking that one's surroundings epitomize what it is for a culture to exist. If we are all now, to some degree, cultural 'crossbreeds', multiculturalism is as much an 'inner' condition as it is a feature of modern society. The benefit of this form of multiculturalism is that it broadens moral and political understanding, ultimately leading to the emergence of a 'one world' perspective.

However, multiculturalists from rival traditions criticize the cosmopolitan stance for stressing togetherness at the expense of difference. To treat cultural identity as a matter of self-definition, and to encourage hybridity and cultural mixing, is, arguably, to weaken any genuine sense of cultural belonging.

Tensions within multiculturalism over the state

AGREEMENT	DISAGREEMENT
✓ Multiculturalists agree that the state should act beyond anti-discrimination laws and formal equality to protect minority rights in law	✗ Multiculturalists disagree on how far the state should support diversity
✓ Multiculturalists agree that the state is a useful instrument in protecting minority rights through group-differentiated rights	✗ Multiculturalists disagree on how far the state's role extends in promoting multiculturalism
✓ Multiculturalists agree that the state should promote diversity and integration for minority cultures which are important for people's identity	✗ Multiculturalists disagree on whether or not the state should play a role in redefining national stories to make them more inclusive

The conservative critique

Rather than being a strand of multiculturalism, the conservative critique (as its name implies) sets out a rejection of multiculturalism. Conservatism (see Chapter 2) values the unity of an organic society, one nation, as per the understanding of Disraeli, rather than seeking to encourage differences. As such, conservatives prefer to promote a single cultural understanding of society requiring anyone from different cultures to assimilate and integrate into the dominant culture of society, rather than hold on to any connection to their 'home' culture. In the 1980s, Norman Tebbit highly controversially referred to a 'Cricket Test', arguing that '*a large proportion of Britain's Asian population fail to pass the cricket test. Which side do they cheer for? It's an interesting test. Are you still harking back to where you came from, or where you are?*' It was controversial at the time and would be considered highly offensive today.

The desire for cultural cohesiveness stems from the conservative belief in human imperfection, arguing that humans seek the safe and familiar in order to feel secure and that multicultural societies undermine this cohesiveness. Conservatives hence seek a society where values, customs and lifestyles are familiar and shared by all others; difference leads to insecurity and instability. They argue that the logic of multiculturalism is fundamentally flawed. Encouraging difference in society cannot and will not lead to unity – this is a clear paradox. Encouraging difference has in fact led to different cultural groups leading separate lives in segregated communities.

Conservatives would argue that by not insisting on assimilation and encouraging immigrant communities to instead hang on to their culture, there has been a weakening of identity of the values and culture of the host nation which led to problems. In the UK, the Blair Government (not a conservative one, interestingly) introduced a Life in the UK test (2002) for all people seeking UK citizenship or indefinite leave to remain in the UK. It sought to ensure that applicants had sufficient knowledge of British life and proficiency in the English language. In 2011, David Cameron argued that multiculturalism had failed and argued that the UK needed a stronger national identity to prevent people turning to all kinds of extremism. He argued that a country '*believes in certain values and actively promotes them*' and '*says to its citizens: This is what defines us as a society. To belong here is to believe these things.*' But, he argued, by trying to create a multicultural society, different cultures have been encouraged to live separate lives. He argued that by promoting British values,

> "*common purpose can be formed as people come together and work together in their neighbourhoods. It will also help build stronger pride in local identity, so people feel free to say, 'Yes, I am a Muslim, I am a Hindu, I am Christian, but I am also a Londoner or a Berliner too'. It's that identity, that feeling of belonging in our countries, that I believe is the key to achieving true cohesion.*"

Other European leaders, including Chancellor Merkel and President Sarkozy, also argued a similar view. In 2010 Merkel claimed that the country's attempts to create a multicultural society had '*utterly failed*'. She argued that the idea of people from different cultural backgrounds living happily '*side by side*' did not work. She said the onus was on immigrants to do more to integrate into German society. These Western leaders were recognizing growing resentment among the majority population when immigrants refused to integrate into the values and culture of the host nation.

Spec key term

Segregation: Multiculturalism has led to ethnic and religious groups becoming increasingly separated.

Spec key term

Assimilation: The process through which immigrant communities lose their cultural distinctiveness by adjusting to the values, allegiances and lifestyles of the 'host' society.

Additionally, the conservative critique is deeply unhappy about the adjustments to the 'story of the nation' required by a constantly evolving, multicultural society. The host culture, they believe, is weakened and devalued in order to accept the newly arrived group and to make space for their values and cultures. Additionally, resources are directed and targeted towards this new group, which can reinforce resentment from the majority population.

For conservatives the solution is clear: clear limits on immigration to control the flow of different cultures into the host society and a strong promotion of assimilation to ensure that minorities conform to the dominant culture and adopt the values, customs and beliefs of the majority population.

Table 7.1 Tensions within multiculturalism

	Liberal multiculturalism	Pluralist multiculturalism	Cosmopolitan multiculturalism
Core goal	Cultural diversity within a liberal democratic framework	Deep diversity recognizing both liberal and non-liberal values	Fluid and multiple identities provide the basis for global citizenship
Integration	Equal rights, equality of opportunity plus group-differentiated rights	Value and cherish all cultures equally and reflect this in its structure, policies, conduct of public affairs, self-understanding and self-definition	The maximum freedom to mix and match from different cultures to suit individuals as communal membership can be oppressive
Culture	Communitarianism	Humans are culturally embedded	Hybridity – pick 'n' mix culture
Diversity	Shallow diversity – must exist within the framework of liberal democracy and liberal values	Deep diversity – we must start from the point that all cultures must have some worth	Global citizen – support diversity as it allows freedom of choice to mix and match, as part of the change to a new globalized, cosmopolitan identity
Tolerance	Tolerance can only extend so far but cannot tolerate illiberal group practices that infringe on the autonomy of its members	Based on value pluralism – no ideas are more dominant than any others – and opposition to liberal universalism	Tolerance – in so far as it allows maximum choice, but ultimately it will lead a society made up of a blend of cultures – a 'multiculture' not multiculturalism
State	State to support group-differentiated rights	State functions need to be restructured to facilitate deep diversity	State would support difference, but the goal is the dissolving the concept of groups

3. Multiculturalism key thinkers

Key thinkers are an important part of understanding each ideology. The exam board has specified five key thinkers per ideology and TWO must be included in an answer to avoid a cap (please check the Exam Focus chapter (Chapter 9) for lots more discussion of key thinkers). Although key thinkers (and other thinkers) have been discussed throughout the chapter, here we look at each one in detail.

Isaiah Berlin (1909–97)

Sophie Bassouls/Sygma/Sygma/Getty Images

Isaiah Berlin was a Riga-born British historian of ideas and a philosopher. His best-known political work is *Four Essays on Liberty* (1958), in which he extolled the virtues of 'negative' freedom over 'positive' freedom. Berlin developed a form of 'liberal pluralism' that was grounded in a life-long commitment to reason combined with empirical knowledge.

Berlin adopted the idea of value pluralism, the idea that there is no absolute concept of the 'good' life, but many competing and equally legitimate ideas. He used this to justify diversity in society. Fundamental to Berlin's philosophical stance was the idea that conflicts of values are intrinsic to human life, a position that has influenced 'post-liberal' thinking about multiculturalism.

For Berlin, value pluralism involved conflicts as people were choosing between competing ways of life based on who they were and the way they wanted to live their life. Choice is thus both an expression of an individual personality, and part of what makes that personality; it is essential to the human self. Essentially, Berlin was arguing that it was wrong for humans to try to impose one set of values on others: '*Human nature generates values which, though equally sacred, equally ultimate, exclude one another, without there being any possibility of establishing an objective hierarchical relation among them.*' One person's idea of freedom of speech might be deemed offensive or hate speech by others. He also argued it wasn't possible to rationalize why one set of values were better than others, as these are entirely subjective, based on the different circumstances one was born and brought up in. He also argued that there was no way to resolve these conflicts.

What Berlin was clear about was that to allow these notions to exist and even to flourish, you needed the right type of society, one which encouraged different cultural and moral beliefs and one that promoted open debate and lacked censorship. For Berlin, liberty must be unrestricted to allow individuals to choose between values. Society must not impose the 'right' solution on people. This healthy open debate would promote stability and avoid conflict. For Berlin, this was a liberal society. He recognized that moral conflict and collisions would exist but felt that they could be resolved by compromise and balancing views.

Berlin's views go beyond those of liberal multiculturalism towards pluralist multiculturalism, where different value systems are allowed to exist alongside each other and liberal and illiberal culture and values are equally accepted. His insistence that primary focus of society must be the liberty to choose between any culture, raises questions about how society treats intolerant views.

Charles Taylor (1931–)

Brent N. Clarke/Stringer/Getty

A Canadian academic and political philosopher, Taylor drew on communitarian thinking to construct a theory of multiculturalism as 'the politics of recognition'. Taylor's most influential work in this field is *Multiculturalism and 'The Politics of Recognition'* (1994).

Emphasizing the twin ideas of equal dignity (rooted in an appeal to people's humanity) and equal recognition (reflecting difference and the extent to which personal identity is cultural), Taylor's multiculturalism goes beyond liberalism, while rejecting particularism. For Taylor, the politics of recognition is based on both the equality of all rights and entitlements, as well as the politics of difference.

For Taylor, equal dignity is based, in the first instance, on legal and political equality, i.e. it is difference blind, based on the idea of foundational equality and natural rights. However, in order to ensure equal citizenry, equal dignity may also require tackling the social and economic inequality often affecting minority groups.

Alongside equal dignity, Taylor advanced the principle of equal recognition based on the politics of difference. This is the idea that each minority group should be recognized as unique. Equal recognition may also include support for differentiated rights and positive discrimination. Taylor argued that giving respect and recognition to minority cultures is essential if dominant and minority cultures are to engage in sustained dialogue with a view to developing a shared understanding of the good life.

Taylor argues that the politics of recognition is distinct from traditional ideas of liberalism, which he sees as '*inhospitable to difference, because (a) it insists on uniform application of the rules defining these rights, without exception, and (b) it is suspicious of collective goals*'. For Taylor, the politics of recognition is about what makes a good life, and the role culture has in that judgement.

For Taylor, identity is defined by the commitments and identifications that provide the frame within which people can try to determine what is good or valuable, or how they ought to behave. He argued that humans don't define their identity in isolation from others, instead '*we define our identity always in dialogue with, sometimes in struggle against, the things our significant others want to see in us*'. He was suggesting that the dominant group in society seek to maintain their superior position by creating a negative image of minority groups and imposing a false image upon minority groups leading to them feeling insecure and vulnerable. '*A person or a group of people can suffer real damage, real distortion, if the people or society around them mirror back to them a confining or demeaning or contemptible picture of themselves.*'

Bhikhu Parekh (1935–)

SAM PANTHAKY/Stringer/Getty

An Indian-born political theorist, successful UK academic and Labour member of the House of Lords, Bhikhu Parekh has developed an influential defence of cultural diversity from a pluralist perspective. Parekh sees liberalism as an inadequate basis for multiculturalism. He also chaired the Commission on the Future of Multi-Ethnic Britain, and its report, commonly known as the Parekh Report (2000).

In *Rethinking Multiculturalism* (2005), Parekh rejected universalist liberalism, arguing that the individual is culturally embedded. He claimed that what individuals believe to be reasonable and moral is embedded in and mediated by their culture, which, in turn, helps people to make sense of their lives and the world around them. He therefore argued that it was important for people to be treated equally but also to understand cultural differences. Respect for the individual must therefore include respect for their cultures and values.

Parekh rejected attempts by liberals to 'absolutize' liberalism, making their values the central frame of reference and assuming that all individuals relate to their culture and to themselves in the same way that they do. This can be seen in the tendency to divide all ways of life into either liberal or non-liberal, and to equate the latter as being illiberal, also to talk of tolerating other cultures rather than respecting or cherishing them.

Parekh argued that different treatment, including exemptions from laws that apply to the wider society, are required to put ethnic, cultural or religious minorities on an equal footing with the majority community. In this vein, Parekh has advocated state funding in the UK for Muslim schools though, interestingly, positive discrimination was rejected for the UK in the Parekh Report.

Parekh argues that all cultures are important, but that each culture encapsulates only one idea of a good life and no culture is perfect. As such, it is important for different cultures to talk to each other to enhance understanding. He also believed that different cultures should learn from each other and encouraged cross-cultural dialogue. In this way, diversity enhances unity in society.

The Parekh Report (2000) argued that, while cherishing cultural diversity, Britain must remain a cohesive society with a shared national culture. This is based on shared values like tolerance, mutual respect, dialogue and the peaceful resolution of differences. Human dignity should be respected and all should be worthy of equal life opportunities: '*A community of citizens and a community of communities*'. However, the report also recognized that the traditional view of history needed to be reconsidered and opened up to new sensibilities and aspirations. Parekh argued that national identity cannot and should not be preserved as if it were an antique piece of furniture. Parekh suggested that we should think of the UK as a looser federation of cultures held together by common bonds of interest, affection and a collective sense of belonging. The aim of this is to ensure equal opportunity, to secure fair treatment and respect for differences, and to create a cohesive and self-confident country.

Tariq Modood (1952–)

A British Pakistani sociologist and political scientist, Professor Tariq Modood has defended multiculturalism as a theory and as a series of policies. He is the founding Director of the Bristol University Research Centre for the Study of Ethnicity and Citizenship. His particular focus is the importance of multiculturalism for social cohesion.

In works such as *Multicultural Politics* (2005) and *Multiculturalism* (2007), he has portrayed liberal or ideological secularism, which seeks to exclude religion from the state, as an obstacle to multicultural integration. Instead, he champions 'accommodative secularism' which aims to foster multi-faith inclusivity by recognizing organized religion as a potential public good or national resource.

Modood rejected David Cameron's view that multiculturalism had failed, arguing that it had in fact been successful and that the many cultures in existence in the UK are now better represented as part of the UK's national story. He argued that the multiculturalist concept of integration is not one-way but interactive which inevitably involves a redefinition of Britishness.

Highlighting the benefits of strong cultural identities, Modood argued that there is no fixed model for integration, all cultures are different and each should be able to find their own model of integration. By allowing this, the best chance of an integrated society is possible. Modood identified four views of integration:

1. *Assimilation* – which demands conformity on the part of minorities. This is when the newcomers do little to disturb the society they are settling in, becoming as much like their new compatriots as possible. Modood suggested this could be thought of as one-way integration.

In the remaining three modes of integration, he argued that social interactions are seen as two-way, where members of the majority community as well as immigrants and ethnic minorities are required to do something.

2. *Individualist-integration* – this leaves minorities free to cultivate their own identities in private and as individuals. Institutions in society may adjust migrants or minorities as individuals and as equal citizens. Minority communities may exist as private associations but are not recognized or supported in the public sphere.

3. *Multiculturalism* – this involves a remaking of citizenship and national identity to include group identities. Here, integration is seen as two-way, involving groups as well as individuals. The process might work differently for different groups, recognizing that each group is distinctive and integration cannot consist of a single template. This is different from individualist-integration because it explicitly recognizes the social reality of groups, not just of individuals and organizations.

4. *Cosmopolitanism* – this fosters unity across cultural/national boundaries and accepts the concept of difference while dissolving the concept of groups. Neither minority nor majority individuals should think of themselves as belonging to a single identity. Instead, people should be free to unite across communal and national boundaries and should think of themselves as global citizens.

Modood argued that all four models may serve as a useful model of integration and it should be left to the group or individual to choose which is most beneficial.

Will Kymlicka (1962–)

A Canadian political philosopher, Will Kymlicka is often seen as the leading theorist of liberal multiculturalism. Influenced by the ideas of John Rawls, he sought to find ways in which people with diverse beliefs could live together without any imposing their values on each other. His experiences in Canada gave him a clear understanding of multiculturalism, in relation to both the French Canadians of Quebec and the indigenous Inuit people.

Kymlicka developed the most influential liberal theory of multiculturalism by marrying the liberal values of autonomy and equality with an argument about the value of cultural membership. In works such as *Liberalism, Community and Culture* (1989) and *Multicultural Citizenship* (1995), Kymlicka argued that certain 'collective rights' of minority cultures are consistent with liberal-democratic principles but acknowledged that no single formula can be applied to all minority groups, particularly as the needs and aspirations of immigrants differ from those of indigenous peoples.

One of his main concerns is providing a framework for the fair treatment of minority groups. He identified two types of minorities: immigrant communities and ethnic groups that were already present when nations were founded. He lists criteria for such national minorities as:

» present at founding of the state

» prior history of self-government

» common culture

» common language

» governing selves through institutions

Kymlicka argues that these groups deserve clear and unique rights from the state by the nature of their unique role and history within the national population. He champions additional protections for such groups' cultural heritage, while at the same time arguing that individual rights must be universal across the whole of society. He has also argued that immigrant communities shouldn't be given the same level of protection as national minorities as they had chosen (to some extent) to become part of the host community. Nonetheless, he also argued that migrant community cultures must be respected.

For Kymlicka, cultural identity and minority rights are closely linked to personal autonomy. He argues that '*if a culture is not generally respected, then the dignity and self-respect of its members will also be threatened.*' Seeing people as 'cultural creatures' but rejecting the communitarian assertion that identity is constituted through culture, Kymlicka argues that culture constitutes an inescapable context for freedom and autonomy. For example, culture provides the 'contexts of choice' by helping people make intelligent decisions about what is valuable.

As such, he supports group-differentiated rights, believing that personal autonomy can only be achieved in this way. He argues that differentiated rights takes three forms:

» Self-government rights for national minorities when they live in self-contained areas.

» Polyethnic rights so minorities can maintain their cultural integrity, for example, exemption from some laws.

» Representative rights to redress the under-representation that most minorities face. He also supports positive discrimination for minorities to correct historic wrongs.

4. How to apply knowledge to multiculturalism answers

Tensions within multiculturalism over the state

Worked example

Paragraph One – Agreement within multiculturalism

- ✓ Multiculturalists agree that the state should act beyond anti-discrimination laws and formal equality to protect minority rights in law **(Kymlicka)**
- ✓ Multiculturalists agree that the state is a useful instrument in protecting minority rights **(Kymlicka)** through group-differentiated rights
- ✓ Multiculturalists agree that the state should promote diversity and integration for minority cultures which are important for people's identity **(Taylor)**

Paragraph Two – Disagreement within multiculturalism

- ✗ Multiculturalists disagree on how far the state should support diversity
- ✗ Liberal multiculturalists are clear about the state setting clear limits to what can be tolerated, e.g. intolerant or harmful views in according with the principles of shallow diversity
- ✗ Pluralist multiculturalists believe in deep diversity and value pluralism **(Berlin)** or opposition to the idea of liberal universalism **(Parekh)**

Paragraph Three – Disagreement within multiculturalism

- ✗ Multiculturalists disagree on how far the state's role extends in promoting multiculturalism
- ✗ Liberal multiculturalism argues that the state should promote the politics of recognition **(Taylor)** and/or group-differentiated rights **(Kymlicka)**
- ✗ Pluralist multiculturalists on the other hand, see the role of the state as much wider, arguing that social and economic inequality must be tackled to promote multiculturalism **(Parekh)** – all aspects of the state must be redesigned in the light of multiculturalism

Tensions within multiculturalism over society

Worked example

Thematic approach

Theme 1 – Integration

- ✓ Most multiculturalists support integration in society. They oppose assimilation, which they believe ignores the importance of culture and identity and undermines the unity of society
- ✗ Unlike most multiculturalists, cosmopolitan multiculturalists encourage individuals to 'pick 'n' mix' from different cultures till cultural differences dissolve into one single identity and culture

Theme 2 – Diversity

- ✓ Multiculturalists promote tolerant and diverse societies which are enriched by the different cultures that co-exist within them
- ✗ Multiculturalists disagree over tolerance. Specifically, the limits of tolerance in a liberal multiculturalist society might not extend to intolerant views or those which oppose liberal democracy

× Liberal multiculturalists therefore support shallow diversity whilst pluralist multiculturalists support deep diversity, opposing liberal universalism **(Parekh)**

Theme 3 – Minority rights

✓ Many multiculturalists support minority rights in society, supporting the politics of recognition **(Taylor)** and group-differentiated rights **(Kymlicka)**

× Different forms of multiculturalism support minority rights, but for different reasons. Liberal multiculturalism, for instance, emphasizes creating societies that support minority rights and promote justice and individualism **(Kymlicka)**

× Pluralist multiculturalism, by contrast, supports minority rights as they believe that diversity in society is a cultural good in its own right **(Parekh)**

Tensions within multiculturalism over support for diversity

Worked example

Paragraph One – Agreement within multiculturalism

✓ All multiculturalists recognize the value of a diverse society

✓ Liberal multiculturalists believe that diversity is valuable in creating a vibrant society **(Kymlicka)**

✓ Pluralist multiculturalists see individuals as embedded in their culture and hence believe diversity is essential in society **(Parekh)**

✓ Cosmopolitan multiculturalists view diversity as important in enabling individuals to experience many different cultures

Paragraph Two – Disagreement within multiculturalism

× Liberal multiculturalists are supportive of diversity as it enhances autonomy **(Kymlicka)** but are unwilling to compromise the principles of liberal democracy, whereas pluralists argue that liberal democracy provides a framework that restricts diversity and difference

× Liberal multiculturalists endorse shallow diversity, but many pluralist multiculturalists argue that the shallow diversity is too limited, supporting value pluralism instead **(Berlin)**

× Pluralist multiculturalists support deep diversity, which argues that cultures need not conform to liberal values to be acceptable and starts from the basis that all cultures must have some value **(Parekh)**

Paragraph Three – Disagreement within multiculturalism

× Cosmopolitan multiculturalists do not agree with liberal or pluralist multiculturalists in supporting diversity in itself

× Instead, cosmopolitan multiculturalists support diversity because it promotes a wider awareness of other people's cultures, where individuals should be free to 'pick 'n' mix' from different cultures to create new identities for themselves

× Liberal and pluralist multiculturalists argue that this can lead to the weakening of cultural distinctiveness and undermine diversity

Continued...

Tensions within multiculturalism over tolerance

Worked example

Paragraph One – Agreement within multiculturalism

✓ Multiculturalists promote tolerance between different cultures, positively embracing different cultures in societies

✓ Most multiculturalists reject the view that a single dominant culture should be imposed upon society, rejecting the need for newly arriving groups to assimilate

✓ Most multiculturalists believe that an essential element of a free society is to support and be tolerant of individuals' cultural practices, all of which have validity

Paragraph Two – Disagreement within multiculturalism

✗ Liberal multiculturalists would not tolerate practices that are themselves intolerant. For example, they would not tolerate practices that are harmful or oppressive, such as FGM

✗ Pluralist multiculturalism supports value pluralism which argues that the state and society should allow different values to exist **(Berlin)**

✗ Pluralist multiculturalism rejects the tolerance of only liberal values, arguing that this cannot allow people to develop to their full potential **(Parekh)**

Paragraph Three – Disagreement within multiculturalism

✗ Multiculturalists' differences over toleration lead to rifts in their views on diversity

✗ Liberal multiculturalists endorse shallow diversity, but many pluralist multiculturalists argue that the shallow diversity is too limited, supporting value pluralism instead **(Berlin)**

✗ Pluralist multiculturalists support deep diversity instead. This argues that cultures need not conform to liberal values to be acceptable and starts from the basis that all cultures must have some value **(Parekh)**

Chapter Summary

- As multiculturalism has developed, so different strands emerged with distinct attitudes and approaches to multiculturalism.
- While liberal and pluralist multiculturalism accepts the idea that people are culturally embedded, cosmopolitan multiculturalists do not.
- The conservative critique is not a strand of multiculturalism, but instead a criticism, even rejection of multicultural values.

Exam Style Questions

1. To what extent does multiculturalism agree over the role of the state?
2. To what extent is multiculturalism more divided than united?
3. To what extent do multiculturalists disagree about the nature of the society they wish to create?
4. To what extent do multiculturalists support diversity?
5. To what extent do multiculturalists' views of minority rights support integration?
6. To what extent do multiculturalists agree over toleration?

Further Resources

Cordeiro-Rodrigues, L. and Simendic, M. *Philosophies of Multiculturalism: Beyond Liberalism* (2017). Diverse commentaries on how multiculturalism interacts with other political ideologies, particularly in non-Western contexts.

Ivison, D. *Ashgate Research Companion to Multiculturalism* (2016). A broad collection of essays from leading scholars on multiculturalism and its wider philosophical and political implications.

Modood, T. 'The strange non-death of multiculturalism', https://cadmus.eui.eu/bitstream/handle/1814/26814/MWP_LS_2013_03_Modood.pdf

Murphy, M. *Multiculturalism: A Critical Introduction* (2012). An accessible general introduction to multiculturalism as a societal philosophy.

Okin, S.M. *Is Multiculturalism Bad for Women?* (1999).

Parekh, B. *Rethinking Multiculturalism: Cultural Diversity and Political Theory*, 2nd edn (2005). A comprehensive defence of the pluralist perspective on cultural diversity that also discusses the practical problems confronting multicultural societies.

Tremblay, A. *Diversity in Decline? The Rise of the Political Right and the Fate of Multiculturalism* (2019). A timely book exploring the place of multicultural ideas in the context of increasingly right-leaning politics.

Young, I. *Justice and the Politics of Difference* (1995).

Visit our companion website at https://bloomsbury.pub/essentials-of-political-ideas-2e for more worked examples.

8 NATIONALISM

Historical overview

The idea of nationalism was born during the French Revolution as the revolutionaries in France rose up in 1789 in the name of the 'French nation'. The rising tide of nationalism re-drew the map of Europe in the nineteenth century as the autocratic empires of Turkey, Austria and Russia started to crumble in the face of liberal and nationalist pressure. By the end of the nineteenth century, nationalism had become a popular movement, with the spread of flags, national anthems, patriotic literature, public ceremonies and national holidays. Nationalism also came to stand for social cohesion, order and stability and sought to integrate the increasingly powerful working class into the nation, to preserve the established social structure against the powerful message of socialism. Patriotism was encouraged and became associated with the commemoration of past national glories and military victories. The end of the First World War in 1918 saw the completion of the process of nation building in Europe. At the Paris Peace Conference, Woodrow Wilson advocated the principle of national self-determination and eight new states were created, including Finland, Hungary, Czechoslovakia, Poland and Yugoslavia.

During the twentieth century nationalism spread throughout the globe as the peoples of Asia and Africa rose in opposition to colonial rule. Nationalist uprisings took place in Egypt in 1919 and quickly spread throughout the Middle East. The collapse of the world's last major empire, the Soviet empire, which took place against the backdrop of the fall of communism during 1989–91, encouraged many to believe that the task of nationalism had been completed: the world had largely become a world of nation-states.

However, the twenty-first century has been marked by a resurgence of nationalism fuelled primarily as a reaction against globalization but also due to intensifying rivalries between great powers, primarily the USA, Europe, China and Russia.

Key Questions

» How did nationalism originate?
» What are the main principles that are central to nationalism?
» What are the key strands of nationalism?
» What are the areas of similarity and difference within nationalism?

Specification Checklist

1. Nationalism: core ideas and principles:

» Nations
» Self-determination
» Nation-state
» Culturalism
» Racialism
» Internationalism

2. Different types of nationalism:

» Liberal nationalism
» Conservative nationalism
» Expansionist nationalism
» Anti-/postcolonialism nationalism

3. Nationalist key thinkers and their ideas:

» Jean-Jacques Rousseau (1712–78)
» Johann Gottfried von Herder (1744–1803)
» Giuseppe Mazzini (1805–72)
» Charles Maurras (1868–1952)
» Marcus Garvey (1887–1940)

Mitch Diamond/Getty

Introduction to nationalism and its strands

Nationalism can be defined broadly as the belief that the nation is the central principle of political organization. As such, it is based on two core assumptions, that:

» Humankind is naturally divided into distinct nations.

» The nation is the most appropriate, and perhaps only legitimate unit of political rule.

Traditional nationalism sets out to bring the borders of the state into line with the boundaries of the nation. However, nationalism is a complex and highly diverse ideology. Not only are there distinctive political, cultural and ethnic forms of nationalism, but the political implications of nationalism have also been wide-ranging and sometimes contradictory. Although nationalism is associated with a principled belief in self-determination, based on the assumption that nations are equal, it has also been used to defend traditional institutions and the established social order, as well as to fuel programmes of war, conquest and imperialism. Nationalism has been described as a chameleon ideology because of its many varieties and strands. The key ones addressed in this chapter are as follows.

Liberal nationalism

The essence of liberal nationalism is to take all the principles of liberalism that have been applied to the individual and apply them to the nation. So, if individuals have the right to self-sovereignty and are of equal moral worth, so are individual nations. Liberal nationalism is also the only strand to support nationalism and internationalism in a complementary way.

Conservative nationalism

Conservative nationalism can be seen as an extension of the conservative ideology expressed by Edmund Burke and Benjamin Disraeli. Here, nationalism is seen as a way to create a sense of unity within society, to identify the areas people share in society, not the issues that divide them. It is not by accident that the term *One Nation* was coined by conservatism.

Expansionist nationalism

> **Definition**
>
> **Chauvinism:** Unreasonable belief in the superiority or dominance of one's own group.

Expansionist nationalism is almost always based on the idea that One Nation is superior to others, known as national chauvinism. Because of this belief, these nations tend to act in a predatory fashion and seek to take other nations under their control, with or without their consent.

Anti- and postcolonial nationalism

Anti- and postcolonial nationalism are forms of nationalism unique to countries who have been colonized. Anti-colonialism is the first stage in the process, where countries develop the desire for independence, based on the principles of liberal nationalism, and postcolonial nationalism is the process of nation building and seeking a new identity, free from oppression.

1. Nationalism: core ideas and principles

Nations

This can be included in a discussion of the nationalist view of society and human nature.

The basic belief of nationalism is that the nation is at the heart of political organization. However, much confusion surrounds what nations are and how they can be defined. In everyday language, words such as 'nation', 'state', 'country' and even 'race' are often confused or used as if they are interchangeable. A nation can be defined as a group of people who consider themselves to be a nation and are therefore self-defined. However, just because a group consider themselves a nation, does not mean that others recognize them, and these differing opinions can often lead to conflict. This applies, for instance, to the Tibetans, the Kurds, the Palestinians, the Basques, the Tamils and so on. It is useful therefore to consider the different ways that nations identify.

» On the most basic level, nations are *cultural* entities, collections of people bound together by shared values and traditions. However, to define a nation simply as a group of people bound together by a common culture and traditions raises some questions. Although particular cultural features are commonly associated with nationhood (notably language, religion, ethnicity, history and tradition), there is no objective criteria that can establish if and when a nation exists.

» *Language* is often taken to be a clear symbol of nationhood. A language embodies distinctive attitudes, values and forms of expression that produce a sense of familiarity and belonging. Nevertheless, at the same time, there are peoples who share the same language without having any conception of a common national identity: Britons, Americans, Australians and New Zealanders may speak English as a first language, but certainly do not think of themselves as members of an 'English nation'.

» *Religion* is another major component of nationhood. Religion expresses common moral values and spiritual beliefs. In Northern Ireland, people have traditionally been divided along religious lines: most Protestants regarding themselves as Unionists and wishing to preserve their links with the UK, while many in the Catholic community have favoured a united Ireland. On the other hand, religious beliefs do not always coincide with a sense of nationhood, countries such as Poland, Italy, Brazil and the Philippines share a common Catholic faith but do not feel that they belong to a unified 'Catholic nation'. Equally, Islam is the religion in much of Northern Africa and the Middle East, without them sharing a common sense of nationhood.

» Nations have also been based on a sense of *ethnic* or, in certain circumstances, *racial* unity. An extreme version of this was evident in Germany during the Nazi period. However, nationalism usually has a cultural rather than a biological basis; it reflects an ethnic unity that may be based on race, but more usually draws on shared values, common cultural beliefs and descent. Black nationalism in the US, for example, is based on colour as well as a distinctive history and culture.

» Nations usually share a common *history*. Not uncommonly, national identity is preserved by recalling past glories such as national independence, the birthdays of national leaders or important military victories. The USA celebrates Independence Day and Thanksgiving; Bastille Day is commemorated in France; in the UK, ceremonies continue to mark Armistice Day and jubilees of the monarchy.

The unity that expresses itself in nationhood is therefore very difficult to pin down. It reflects a varying combination of factors, rather than any precise formula. Ultimately, therefore, nations can only be defined by their members, not by any fixed set of factors. In this sense, the nation is a group of people *who regard themselves* as a natural community, considering themselves connected together, distinguished by shared loyalty in the form of patriotism.

Difficulties such as the absence of land, a small population or lack of economic resources are of little significance if a group of people insists on demanding what it sees as 'national rights'. Latvia, for example, became an independent nation in 1991 despite having a population of only 2.6 million, no source of fuel and very few natural resources. Likewise, the Kurdish peoples of the Middle East have nationalist aspirations, even though the Kurds have never enjoyed formal political unity and are at present spread over parts of Turkey, Iraq, Iran and Syria.

Spec key term

Ethnicity: The sense of belonging to the social group that shares a common and distinctive culture, religion, language or descent.

Spec key term

Black nationalism: A reaction to white oppression originating in the mid-twentieth century.

Definition

Patriotism: A psychological attachment to one's nation, literally a 'love of one's country'.

Nations

Summary box

- People who identify themselves as a cohesive group based on shared values in society.
- There are many different ways of defining a nation.

Self-determination

This can be included in a discussion of the nationalist view of society and human nature.

To be self-determined is to govern oneself, to have agency and independence. Therefore the idea of self-determination refers to the desire of a nation to rule itself. Nationalism is usually (but not always) bound up with the notion of self-determination as each nation believes itself to be distinct and therefore seeks to express its own unique characteristics in its own state. Also, they believe that only the nation can define their own national interest and make decisions to benefit themselves.

Nationalism as a political ideology only emerged when the idea of a national community encountered the doctrine of popular sovereignty. This occurred during the French Revolution and was influenced by the writings of French philosopher **Jean-Jacques Rousseau (1712–78)**, sometimes seen as the 'father' of modern nationalism. Although Rousseau did not specifically address the question of nationalism, his stress on popular sovereignty, expressed in the idea of the general will, was the seed from which nationalist doctrines sprang. **Rousseau** came to believe that sovereignty was instilled in a culturally unified people and that government should be based not on the absolute power of a monarch, but on the indivisible collective will of the entire community. During the French Revolution, these beliefs were reflected in the assertion that the French people were 'citizens' possessed of inalienable rights, not merely 'subjects' of the Crown. Sovereign power thus resided with the 'French nation'. The form of nationalism that emerged from the French Revolution was therefore based on the vision of a nation governing itself – national self-determination.

While self-determination sounds relatively uncontroversial, this simple idea has been at the heart of many conflicts throughout history. More recently, conflicts in Northern Ireland, the Balkans, Crimea, Ukraine, Catalonia, Scotland and even Brexit can be associated with the notion of national self-determination. Sometimes these conflicts are to do with the definition of a nation; are Catalans an independent nation or are they part of the Spanish nation? The same question applies to Scots. In other cases, self-determination is denied, or threatened; in the case of the Ukraine for example, who see themselves as a distinct nation, whereas Russian President Putin believes that Ukraine is part of Russia. This disagreement over the definition of the Ukrainian nation led to the invasion of Ukraine in 2022.

Definition

Popular sovereignty: Supreme authority lies with the people.

General will: The genuine interests of a collective body, equivalent to the common good; the will of all, provided each person acts selflessly.

Self-determination

Summary box

- The belief that nations should decide how they are governed.
- Based on the idea that the nation is a genuine political community capable of self-government.

The nation-state

This can be included in a discussion of the nationalist view of the state and society.

When a nation achieves their ambition of self-determination, they become a nation-state, i.e. a nation that rules itself in its own sovereign, geographical borders. For many, this is a theoretical ideal, where the political concept of the state meets the cultural identity of a nation. To date, this has been achieved in one of two ways:

» It may involve a process of unification for example when East Germany and West Germany were reunited in 1990.

» Nation-states can be created through the achievement of independence from another nation. For example, when the many nations achieved independence from the USSR in the 1990s as seen in map 8.1.

Although in the modern world and particularly Europe, the nation-state is a familiar concept, it is a relatively new invention and is still not a universally accepted ideal.

For many nationalists, the nation-state is the highest and most desirable form of political organization. The great strength of the nation-state is that it offers the prospect of both cultural and political

Definition

State: A sovereign geographical territory with a permanent population considered as an organized political community under one government, with clear borders.

Map 8.1 **Post-USSR territories.**

unity. When a people who share a common identity gain the right to self-government, nationality and citizenship coincide. Moreover, nationalism legitimizes the authority of government, as political sovereignty in a nation-state resides with the people of the nation, as suggested by **Rousseau**. Consequently, nation-states represent the notion that government is carried out in accordance with their 'national interest'. Hence it has been the aim of many nationalists to create a world of independent nation-states, believing that the right to self-determination is universal. However, other forms of nationalism, specifically expansionist nationalism, reject this idea, believing that only some nations should enjoy nation-statehood, while other nations should accept their position as colonies of 'stronger' nations.

It would also be misleading to suggest that nationalism is always associated with the nation-state or is necessarily linked to the idea of self-determination. Some nations, for instance, may be satisfied with a measure of political autonomy that stops short of statehood and full independence. This can be seen in the case of Welsh nationalism in the UK.

Nation-state

Summary box

- A nation that rules itself in its own state.
- While this belief is supported by most nationalists, it is not universally supported.

Tensions within nationalism over the role of the nation-state

AGREEMENT	DISAGREEMENT
✓ All nationalists agree that the nation-state is built around people identifying as a nation with shared values	✗ Most nationalists support the creation of a world of nation-states; however, others are expansionist in character
✓ Liberal, anti and postcolonial nationalists support the principle of the nation-state as a universal right for all nations	✗ Some nationalists approach the idea of a nation-state in a rational way, whereas others base it on emotional and mystical ways
✓ Liberal, anti and postcolonial nationalists agree that a world of nation-states promotes peace and order by allowing nations to decide what is in their own best interests	✗ Some nationalists base their nation-state on an inclusive basis, whereas others seek a more exclusive or even racial basis

Culturalism

This can be included in a discussion of the nationalist view of society and human nature.

Culturalism is a way that some nations identify, believing that the emotional link people have with their nation is based on mystical ties which draw them together; that a nation's essence is tied up in its music, art, folklore and language, drawing on popular rituals, traditions and legends. Cultural nationalism is therefore a form of nationalism that emphasizes the strengthening of cultural identity over overt political demands. Its principal stress is on the regeneration of the nation as a distinctive cultural entity, with statehood being viewed as secondary or even irrelevant. Cultural nationalism tends to be emotional or irrational, as it is based on a belief in the nation as a unique historical and organic whole.

Whereas **Rousseau** is commonly seen as the 'father' of political nationalism, **Johann Herder (1744–1803)** is usually viewed as the architect of cultural nationalism. **Herder**, together with writers such as Johann Fichte (1762–1814) and Friedrich Jahn (1778–1852), highlighted what they believed to be the uniqueness of German culture. **Herder** believed that each nation possessed a Volksgeist which revealed itself in songs, myths and legends, and provided a nation with its source of creativity. For **Herder**, no nation was like any other, and each nation's culture was as valuable as any other's. The role of **Herder's** form of cultural nationalism is to develop an awareness and appreciation of national traditions and collective memories rather than to provide the political quest for statehood. As he argued, *'the most natural state therefore is also one people, with a national character of its own'*. The tendency for nationalism to be expressed through cultural regeneration was particularly marked in nineteenth-century Germany, where it was reflected in the revival of folk traditions and the rediscovery of German myths and legends. The Brothers Grimm, for example, collected and published German folk tales, and the composer Richard Wagner (1813–83) based many of his operas on ancient myths.

Although cultural nationalism has often emerged within a European context, cultural nationalism has been found in many parts of the world. It was, for instance, evident in Black nationalism in the USA, as articulated by figures such as Jamaican political activist **Marcus Garvey (1887–1940)** and by groups such as the Black Panthers and the Nation of Islam. Similarly, it has been apparent in India, in forms of nationalism that have been based on the image of India as a distinctively Hindu civilization, as advanced by the Bharatiya Janata Party, which has been in power since 2014 under the leadership of Narendra Modi. It is also evident in modern China in the increasing prominence given by party and state officials to the idea of 'Chineseness', expressed, among other things, in a revival of traditional cultural practices and an emphasis on 'Chinese' principles and moral values.

However, there has been disagreement about the implications of viewing nations primarily as cultural rather than political communities. Political nationalism is linked to a civic understanding of nationalism, where nationhood is based on shared values, in which new members can participate virtually instantly. This form of nationalism is recognized as inclusive as it allows, even invites, new people to become part of an existing nation. Cultural nationalism, on the other hand, indicates that becoming part of a nation takes time, immersing oneself in the culture of a nation and understanding the unique Volksgeist of a nation is not something that can happen quickly. As such, these forms of nationalism are considered exclusive.

At the most extreme end of cultural nationalism is the darker idea that One Nation's culture is superior to all others. This may be based in biological or racial ideas or in feelings of superiority or chauvinism, which in turn may lead to domination or imperialism. However, it is clear that **Herder** rejected this interpretation of culturalism arguing that *'notwithstanding the varieties of the human form, there is but one and the same species of man throughout the whole earth'*.

Definition

Cultural nationalism: A form of nationalism connected to an awareness and appreciation of national traditions and collective memories.

Irrational: Thinking based on emotion rather than reason.

Political nationalism: A form of nationalism that regards the nation as a natural political community, usually expressed through the idea of national self-determination.

Spec key term

Volksgeist: The 'spirit' of a nation, the unique identity of a people based on a culmination of their own unique experiences, history, culture and language.

Civic nationalism: A form of nationalism based on the active participation of its citizens and a shared vision of equal citizens.

Culturalism

Summary box

- The idea that nationalism is based on shared cultural societal values.
- Some forms of nationalism are grounded in more mystical, emotional ties to the nation.

Tensions within nationalism over society

AGREEMENT	DISAGREEMENT
✓ All nationalists agree that the nation is the most significant divide in society	✗ Some nationalists seek a society on an inclusive basis, whereas others seek a more exclusive or even racial basis
✓ Nationalists argue that society is built around people identifying as a cohesive nation	✗ Some nationalists seek a society with progressive ideals, whereas others are more regressive
✓ Most nationalists seek societies where nations decide how they are governed	✗ Some nationalists reject self-determination for all, supporting expansionist goals instead

Racialism

This can be included in a discussion of the nationalist view of human nature and society.

Racialism (a term now generally treated as synonymous with 'racism') is the highly controversial and dubious belief that political or social conclusions can be drawn from the idea that humankind is divided into biologically distinct races. Racist theories are thus based on two assumptions:

» The first is that there are fundamental genetic, or species-type, differences among the peoples of the world.

» The second is that these racial differences matter, and are reflected in cultural, intellectual and/or moral differences, making them politically or socially significant.

Racialism thus implies that there are meaningful biological or genetic differences among humans. While it may be possible to change one's citizenship, it is impossible to change one's race, determined as it is at birth, by the racial identity of one's parents. The symbols of race – skin tone, hair colour, physiognomy and blood – are thus fixed and unchangeable. Political racism manifests itself in calls for racial segregation (for example, apartheid) and in doctrines of 'blood' superiority or inferiority (for example, Aryanism). Within nationalism, race becomes, for some, the defining quality of the nation. The nation is not defined by history, language or shared culture, but simply by a biological link to the race.

A form of implicit racism has long been associated with conservative nationalism. This is based on the belief that stable and successful societies must be bound together by a common culture and shared values in an organic society. For example, Enoch Powell in the UK in the 1960s and the 2022 presidential candidates Eric Zemmour and Marine Le Pen in France have argued against 'non-white' immigration into their countries on the grounds that the distinctive traditions and culture of the white 'host community' would be threatened. We also see this in the white supremacists of the USA.

However, more systematic and developed forms of racism are based on explicit assumptions about the nature, capacities and destinies of different racial groups. These biologically based racial theories, as opposed to those that are linked to culture or religion, are particularly militant because they make claims about the essential and inescapable nature of a people that are supposedly backed up by the certainty and objectivity of scientific belief.

The growth of a 'science of race' in the nineteenth century which applied pseudo-scientific ideas to social and political issues led to Jewish people being thought of as a race rather than a religious, economic or cultural group. Thereafter, they were defined inescapably by biological factors and anti-Semitism was elaborated into a racial theory by the Nazis, which assigned to the Jewish people a pernicious and degrading racial stereotype. All good cultural development was ascribed to the German way of life, while Jewish people were used as a universal scapegoat for all of Germany's misfortunes and were described as 'physically, spiritually and morally degenerate'. The Nazis blamed the Jews for Germany's defeat in 1918; they claimed they were responsible for Germany's humiliation in the Treaty of Versailles (which removed land from Germany and made them pay war reparations to other countries), that they were behind the banks and big businesses that enslaved the lower middle classes

Spec key term

Exclusive nationalism: A form of nationalism that believes that it takes time to be a part of the nation, as membership is based on shared history and language.

Inclusive nationalism: A form of nationalism that believes that joining a nation is straightforward and quick, as it is not based on shared previous experiences.

Imperialism/ colonialism: The extension of control by one country over another by settlement or economic domination.

and that their influence was exerted through the working-class movement and the threat of social revolution. In Hitler's view, the Jews were responsible for an international conspiracy of capitalists and communists, whose prime objective was to weaken and overthrow the German Aryan race.

Although racial segregation was prevalent in South Africa before the 1940s, it wasn't until 1948, after the passing of a number of laws by the all-white government, that it was made legal. Apartheid in South Africa enforced racial segregation where the majority non-white South Africans were forced to keep a strict separation from the white minority. Interracial relationships were banned, and the population was divided into four categories: Black, Indian, coloured and white. Millions of Black citizens were forcibly removed from their homes while the white population took over all aspects of politics and society. Black people were denied the vote or any role in politics and were forced to work as cheap labour for the white population.

When the Black population fought back against their white oppressors, it was met with brutal armed repression and long imprisonment. Infamous demonstrations took place in Sharpeville in 1960, when the authorities opened fire and killed 69 Black protestors and the Soweto riots in 1972 where it is estimated that 575 people were killed. Many were also imprisoned.

The most famous prisoner of Robben Island was Nelson Mandela. Mandela, joint head of the African National Congress (ANC), had spent his life fighting, legally at first, against apartheid and his anti-apartheid activism made him a frequent target of the authorities. It was after Sharpeville that he turned away from non-violent protest to advocating sabotage and more direct action. Eventually after a number of periods in prison, he was imprisoned for life in 1964. As apartheid was eventually dismantled in the 1990s, Mandela was released from prison in 1990. Free elections took place in 1994 and Mandela because the first president of the post-apartheid era.

More recently, China has been accused of segregating and oppressing its 12-million-strong Uyghur community and accused of committing crimes against humanity in Xinjiang.

Racialism

Summary box

- The highly controversial and dubious belief that humankind can be meaningfully divided into separate 'races', which each possess different natures.
- This view is held by a very small group of nationalists who believe that nationhood is determined purely by biological factors.

Internationalism

This can be included in a discussion of the nationalist view of society and the economy.

Internationalism is the idea that people across the world should connect with each other above and beyond their national boundaries. It is characterized by the belief that the ties that bind the peoples of the world are stronger than those that separate them. This vision has been most clearly associated with liberalism and socialism, each of which has developed a particular brand of internationalism.

Liberal internationalism

Liberals have usually been prepared to accept that nations are natural entities that provide the most appropriate units of political rule while at the same time acknowledging that unchecked national power has very much the same drawbacks as unrestrained individual liberty. There are, broadly, two bases of liberal internationalism.

The first is a fear of an international 'state of nature'. Liberals have long accepted that national self-determination is a mixed blessing. While it preserves self-government and forbids foreign control, it also creates freedom to pursue one's own national interest, possibly at the expense of other nations. Hence liberals have generally proposed two means of preventing this:

» The first is national interdependence, aimed at promoting mutual understanding and cooperation. Liberal nationalists have traditionally supported free trade as economic interdependence means that the economic cost of international conflict is so great that warfare becomes virtually unthinkable. Not only would it promote prosperity, but it would also draw people of different nationalities, faiths and languages together.

» Liberals have also proposed that national ambition should be checked by the construction of supranational bodies seeking to bring order to an otherwise lawless international scene as well as the growth of global governance and international law. This argument draws on precisely the same logic as social contract theory: government is the solution to the problem of disorder. This explains Woodrow Wilson's support for the first experiment in world government, the League of Nations, set up in 1919, and its successor, the United Nations, in 1945. Liberals have looked to these bodies to establish law-governed states system to make possible the peaceful resolution of international conflicts.

It is worth noting that the EU was set up specifically with the intention of achieving both these aims. The EU's mission statement is 'Promoting peace and security and respecting fundamental rights and freedoms'.

The second basis for liberal internationalism stems from an overriding commitment to the individual and the principle of individualism.

This implies that all human beings, regardless of race, religion, social background and nationality, are of equal moral worth. While liberals endorse the idea of national self-determination, by no means do they believe that it entitles nations to treat their people, however they choose. Respect for the rights and liberties of the individual outranks the claims of national sovereignty. Liberal internationalism is thus characterized not so much by a desire to supersede the nation as a political formation, but rather by the demand that nations conform to a higher morality embodied in the doctrine of human rights. Such beliefs have led to the drawing up of documents such as the UN Declaration of Human Rights in 1948 and the European Convention on Human Rights and Fundamental Freedoms in 1956.

Socialist internationalism

Socialists are more likely than liberals to reject nationalism in principle, believing that it breeds resentment and conflict and that it has an implicitly right-wing character. Marxism has traditionally embraced a form of internationalism rooted in the idea that class solidarity is more powerful and politically significant than national identity. The Communist Manifesto expresses this graphically in its famous final words: 'Working men of all countries, unite!' Socialism therefore has an intrinsically internationalist character. Not only does proletarian class solidarity inevitably cut across national borders, but the emergence of world markets had turned capitalism into a global system that could only be challenged by a genuinely international movement.

Socialist internationalists aim, through an international class struggle, to establish harmony and cooperation amongst all the world's peoples. Socialist internationalism is therefore ultimately based on a belief in a common humanity. This is the idea that humankind is bound together by mutual sympathy, compassion and love, based upon the belief that what human beings share with one another is greater than what divides them. From this perspective, socialists usually reject nationalism not only as part of bourgeois ideology, which conceals the contradictions upon which capitalism and all other class societies are based, but also because it encourages people to deny their common humanity. Internationalism, for a socialist, may imply not merely cooperation amongst nations within a framework of international law, but the more radical goal of the dissolution of the nation and the recognition that there is but one world and one people.

Definition

Supranational: Having power or influence that is above national boundaries or governments.

Spec key term

Liberal internationalism: The idea that sovereign nations should cooperate and create a level of interdependency to avoid international conflict.

Socialist internationalism: The idea that class solidarity is more powerful and politically significant than national identity. As Marx said, 'Working men of all countries, unite!'

Internationalism

Summary box

- The belief that the world should unite across national boundaries to advance their common interests.
- Some forms of nationalism have an internationalist perspective, whereas other forms of internationalism reject nationalism.

Tensions within nationalism over internationalism	
AGREEMENT	**DISAGREEMENT**
✓ Liberal and anti-postcolonial nationalism believe in the independence of and interdependence between nations	✗ Expansionist nationalism rejects both independence and interdependence between nations, focusing more on self-sufficiency and autarky
✓ Liberal and anti-postcolonial nationalism argue that nations who trade with each other build up bonds of mutual dependency which makes war between these nations unlikely	✗ Conservative nationalism rejects the idea of supranationalism, believing that it removes sovereignty from the host nation
✓ Liberal and anti-postcolonial nationalism believe that independent nation-states need to be protected from an international state of nature	✗ Most forms of nationalism reject the socialist idea of internationalism, that the idea of nations should be rejected in favour of class

2. Differences between the nationalist strands

Nationalism is a highly complex phenomenon, characterized more by ambiguity and contradictions than by a single set of values and goals. For example:

» Nationalism has been both liberating and oppressive; it has brought about self-determination but has led to conquest through expansionism.

» Nationalism has been progressive, regressive and reactionary: it has looked forward to a future of national independence or national greatness, and it has been backward-looking, celebrating past national glories and entrenched established identities.

» It has sought to be inclusive in its understanding of the nation, encouraging multiculturalism and a civic understanding of nationhood as well as exclusive, seeking a monoculture or even a racial or ethnic definition of nation.

» Nationalism has also been both rational and irrational: it has appealed to rational views, such as national self-determination, and it has bred from irrational drives and emotions, including ancient fears and hatreds.

Figure 8.1 looks at these important ways of analysing the nationalism strands.

This ideological shapelessness is a product of several factors. Nationalism has the capacity to fuse with and absorb other political doctrines and ideas, thereby creating a series of rival nationalist traditions. The most significant of these traditions are:

» liberal nationalism

» conservative nationalism

» expansionist nationalism

» anti-colonial and postcolonial nationalism

Liberal nationalism

Liberal nationalism is the oldest form of nationalism, dating back to the French Revolution and embodying many of its values. Its ideas spread quickly through much of Europe and were expressed most clearly by **Giuseppe Mazzini (1805–72)**, often thought of as the 'prophet' of Italian unification. US President Woodrow Wilson's 'Fourteen Points', proposed as the basis for the reconstruction of Europe after the First World War, were also based on liberal nationalist principles.

The ideas of liberal nationalism were clearly shaped by **Rousseau's** defence of popular sovereignty, expressed by the notion of the 'general will'. As the nineteenth century progressed, the aspiration for self-government was linked with liberal principles. This fusion was brought about by the fact that the empires against which nationalists fought were autocratic and oppressive. **Mazzini**, for example, wished the Italian states to unite, but this also entailed throwing off the influence of autocratic Austria. For many European revolutionaries in the mid-nineteenth century, liberalism and nationalism were virtually indistinguishable. Indeed, their nationalist creed was largely forged by applying liberal ideas, initially developed in relation to the individual, to the nation and to international politics.

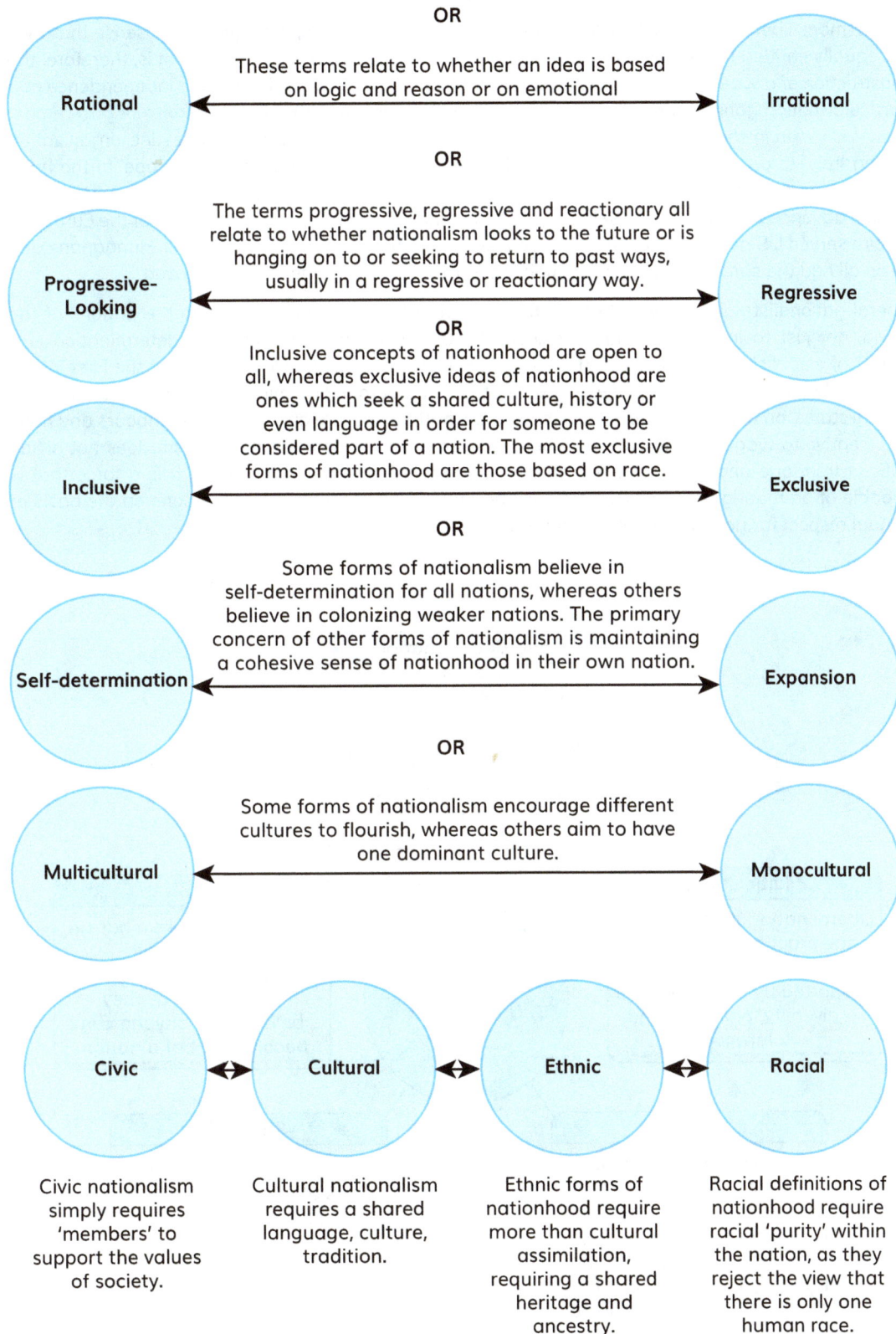

Rational

OR

These terms relate to whether an idea is based on logic and reason or on emotional

Irrational

Progressive-Looking

OR

The terms progressive, regressive and reactionary all relate to whether nationalism looks to the future or is hanging on to or seeking to return to past ways, usually in a regressive or reactionary way.

Regressive

Inclusive

OR

Inclusive concepts of nationhood are open to all, whereas exclusive ideas of nationhood are ones which seek a shared culture, history or even language in order for someone to be considered part of a nation. The most exclusive forms of nationhood are those based on race.

Exclusive

Self-determination

OR

Some forms of nationalism believe in self-determination for all nations, whereas others believe in colonizing weaker nations. The primary concern of other forms of nationalism is maintaining a cohesive sense of nationhood in their own nation.

Expansion

Multicultural

OR

Some forms of nationalism encourage different cultures to flourish, whereas others aim to have one dominant culture.

Monocultural

Civic ↔ **Cultural** ↔ **Ethnic** ↔ **Racial**

Civic nationalism simply requires 'members' to support the values of society.

Cultural nationalism requires a shared language, culture, tradition.

Ethnic forms of nationhood require more than cultural assimilation, requiring a shared heritage and ancestry.

Racial definitions of nationhood require racial 'purity' within the nation, as they reject the view that there is only one human race.

Figure 8.1 **Nationalism definitions.**

Liberalism was founded on a defence of individual freedom, traditionally expressed in the language of rights. Nationalists believed nations to be sovereign entities, entitled to liberty and in possession of rights, the most important being the right of self-determination. This is seen as rational and progressive. Liberal nationalism is therefore a liberating force in two senses:

» First, it opposes all forms of foreign domination and oppression by colonial powers.

» Second, it stands for the ideal of self-government. Woodrow Wilson, for example, argued in favour of a Europe composed not only of nation-states, but also democratic.

Furthermore, liberal nationalists believe that nations, like individuals, are equal in the sense that they are equally entitled to the right of self-determination. The goal of liberal nationalism is, therefore, the construction of a world of independent nation-states, not merely the unification or independence of a particular nation. John Stuart Mill expressed this as the principle that 'the boundaries of government should coincide in the main with those of nationality'. **Mazzini** formed the clandestine organization 'Young Italy' to promote the idea of a united Italy, but he also founded 'Young Europe' in the hope of spreading nationalist ideas throughout the continent. At the Paris Peace Conference, Woodrow Wilson advanced the principle of self-determination not simply because the break-up of the European empire served US national interests, but because he believed that the Poles, Czechs, Hungarians and so on all had the same right to political independence that Americans already enjoyed.

Liberal nationalists also believe that the principle of natural harmony applies to the nations of the world, not just to individuals within society. The achievement of national self-determination is a means of establishing a peaceful and stable international order. Wilson believed that the First World War had been caused by an 'old order', dominated by autocratic and militaristic empires. Democratic nation-states, on the other hand, would respect the national sovereignty of their neighbours and have no incentive to wage war or subjugate others. For a liberal nationalist, nationalism does not divide nations from one another, promoting distrust, rivalry and possibly war. Rather, it is a force that is capable of promoting both unity within each nation and alliances among all nations on the basis of mutual respect for national rights and characteristics.

So, in summary, Liberal nationalism can be categorized as shown in Figure 8.2:

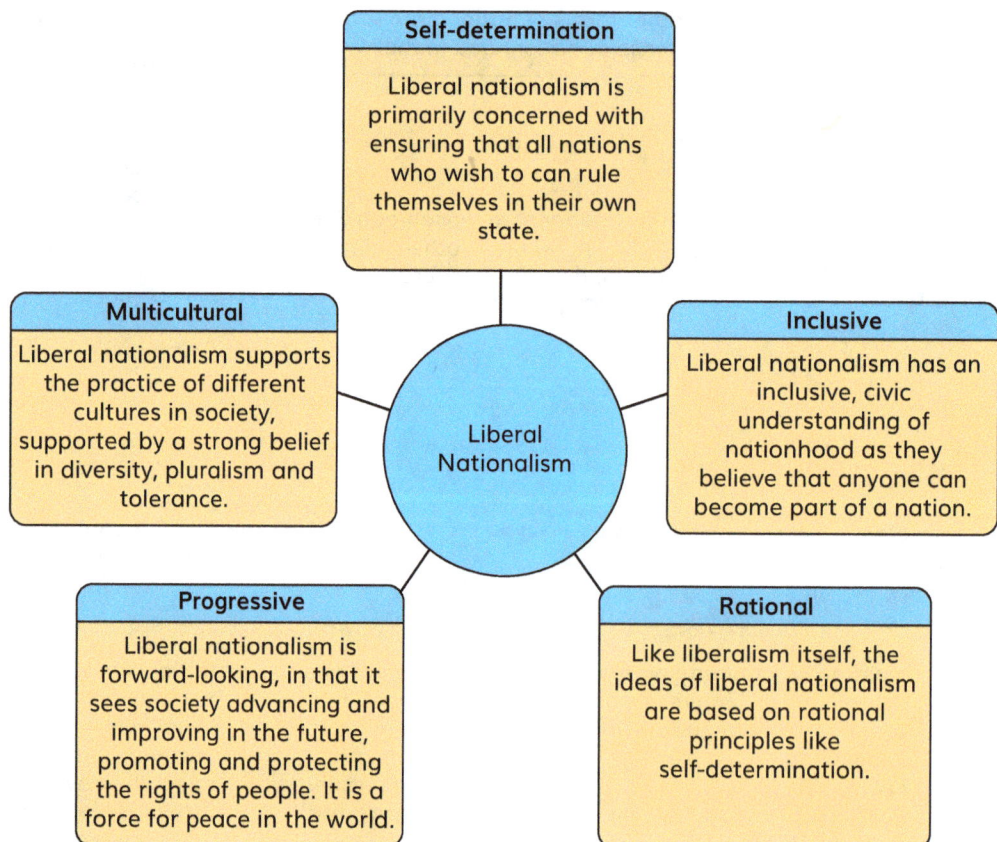

Self-determination

Liberal nationalism is primarily concerned with ensuring that all nations who wish to can rule themselves in their own state.

Multicultural

Liberal nationalism supports the practice of different cultures in society, supported by a strong belief in diversity, pluralism and tolerance.

Inclusive

Liberal nationalism has an inclusive, civic understanding of nationhood as they believe that anyone can become part of a nation.

Liberal Nationalism

Progressive

Liberal nationalism is forward-looking, in that it sees society advancing and improving in the future, promoting and protecting the rights of people. It is a force for peace in the world.

Rational

Like liberalism itself, the ideas of liberal nationalism are based on rational principles like self-determination.

Figure 8.2 **Liberal nationalism.**

Tensions within nationalism over progressiveness

ARE PROGRESSIVE	AREN'T PROGRESSIVE
✓ Liberal, anti- and postcolonial nationalism promote mutual respect for nations and seek independence for all showing strong support in both strands for progressive values	✗ Expansionist forms of nationalism breed feelings of intense patriotism, often leading to war, they cannot be seen as progressive as their main aim seeks to repress others
✓ Civic forms of nationalism like liberal and anti-colonial nationalism see nations in rational and broadly inclusive terms, showing agreement on a common progressive goal	✗ Conservative and expansionist nationalism believes that nations are forged by having a shared history looking back at past national greatness showing that they do not look forward and are not progressive
✓ Liberal and anti-colonial nationalism both seek international harmony, believing nation-states should be regulated by international law showing them both as a liberating, progressive force	✗ Some forms of nationalism base their understanding of nationhood on culture, or biologically distinct 'races', showing that they exclusive which is not progressive

Conservative nationalism

Early conservatives regarded nationalism as a radical, if not revolutionary, force, a threat to order and political stability. However, conservative statesmen like Benjamin Disraeli became increasingly sympathetic towards nationalism, seeing it as a natural ally in maintaining social order and defending traditional institutions. Hence conservative nationalism developed as a form of inward-looking nationalism, simply concerned with promoting the cohesion of its own nation, unconcerned with the nationalism of self-determination, but more with the promise of social cohesion embodied in patriotism. For conservatives, society is organic and they understand nationhood in cultural terms, as people who share common traditions, history and heritage. As such, they believe that nations emerge naturally from the desire of humans to live with others who possess the same views, habits, and ancestry as themselves. Humans are thought to be limited, irrational and imperfect creatures, who seek meaning and security within the national community.

Conservative nationalism tends to develop in established nation-states, rather than in those that are in the process of nation building. Having a shared sense of purpose is easy in new nation-states, but in existing ones, it can be more difficult. Conservatives have therefore harnessed nationalism to maintain a sense of national unity by fostering patriotic loyalty and pride in one's country, especially in the face of the divisive idea of class solidarity preached by socialists. Indeed, by incorporating the working class into the nation, conservatives have often seen nationalism as the antidote to social revolution by reminding people of what they have in common and using nostalgia to create unity. This has been referred to as 'One Nation' conservatism.

The conservative character of nationalism is further maintained by an appeal to tradition and history; nationalism becomes a defence of traditional institutions and a traditional way of life. Conservative nationalism is essentially irrational, nostalgic and backward-looking, reflecting on a past age of national glory or triumph. This is evident in the widespread tendency to use ritual and commemoration to present past events as defining moments in a nation's history, to appeal to people's deep cultural connections with their nation.

Politicians like Margaret Thatcher, UK Prime Minister from 1979–90, used nationalism and patriotism to promote British identity and create a sense of national purpose and independence within Europe, with the promise of strong government and firm leadership. They have also sought to use traditional British institutions and ceremonies as key symbols of national identity. Nowhere is this clearer than with the British monarchy. The United Kingdom's national anthem is 'God Save the King', and the royal family plays a prominent role in national celebrations such as Armistice Day, and on state occasions such as the opening of Parliament.

Due to their belief in human imperfection, conservatives believe that humans seek security and are drawn to the familiar, in this case, drawn towards people 'like them'. As a result, conservative nationalism seeks to promote an understanding of nationhood based around a common language, culture, values and customs. They reject multiculturalism as undermining the stability and cohesiveness of society. Conservative nationalism is therefore particularly prominent when the sense of national identity is felt to be threatened or in danger of being lost.

The issue of immigration has helped to keep this form of nationalism alive. Conservative reservations about immigration stem from the belief that cultural diversity leads to instability and conflict. Anti-immigration sentiment is often fuelled by the perceived lack of integration of an immigrant population. As stable and successful societies must be based on shared values and a common culture, immigration, particularly from societies with different religious and other traditions, should either be firmly restricted, or minority ethnic groups should be encouraged to assimilate into the culture of the 'host' society. If this does not happen, conservative nationalism can become hostile and xenophobic. This can be seen in the form of conservatism espoused by President Trump in America (2017–21), where immigrants are blamed for the loss of power and a desire to 'Make America Great Again'. Consequently, conservative nationalism is more exclusive than liberal nationalism, one cannot 'join' the nation automatically, it requires time to be immersed in the culture, values and history before one can be accepted.

Conservative nationalists have been concerned about the threat that supranational bodies, such as the EU, pose to national identity and so to the cultural bonds of society. This is expressed in the UK in the form of 'Euroscepticism', particularly strong within the Conservative Party. Eurosceptics not only defend sovereign national institutions and a distinctive national currency on the grounds that they are vital symbols of national identity, but also warn that the 'European project' is fatally misconceived because a stable political union cannot be forged out of such national, language and cultural diversity. In the UK, the growing strength of such sentiments contributed to the decision to hold an in/out referendum on EU membership in 2016, resulting in the UK leaving the EU in January 2020.

So, in summary, conservative nationalism can be categorized as shown in Figure 8.3.

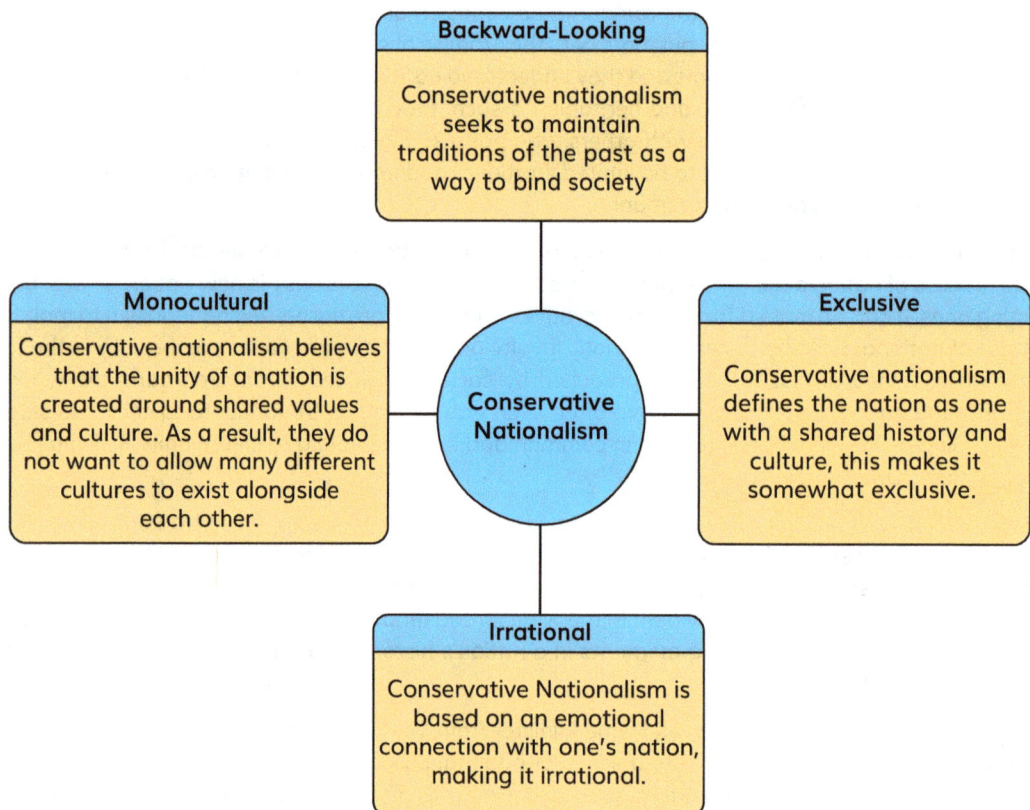

Backward-Looking

Conservative nationalism seeks to maintain traditions of the past as a way to bind society

Monocultural

Conservative nationalism believes that the unity of a nation is created around shared values and culture. As a result, they do not want to allow many different cultures to exist alongside each other.

Conservative Nationalism

Exclusive

Conservative nationalism defines the nation as one with a shared history and culture, this makes it somewhat exclusive.

Irrational

Conservative Nationalism is based on an emotional connection with one's nation, making it irrational.

Figure 8.3 **Conservative nationalism.**

Expansionist nationalism

In many countries the dominant image of nationalism is one of aggression and militarism, quite the opposite to a principled belief in national self-determination. The aggressive face of nationalism became apparent in the late nineteenth century as European powers indulged in what was called the 'scramble for Africa' in the name of national glory. The imperialism of the late nineteenth century differed from earlier periods of colonial expansion in that it was supported by a climate of popular nationalism. National prestige was linked to the possession of an empire and each colonial victory was greeted by demonstrations of public approval. Aggressive and expansionist nationalism reached its high point in the interwar period when the authoritarian or fascist regimes of Japan, Italy and Germany embarked on policies of imperial expansion and world domination, eventually leading to war in 1939.

Photo 8.1 **The Berlin conference 1884–85.**

What distinguished this form of nationalism from earlier forms of nationalism was its chauvinism. Nations were not thought to be equal in their right to self-determination; rather, some nations were believed to possess characteristics or qualities that made them superior to others. Such ideas were clearly evident in European imperialism, which was justified by an ideology of racial and cultural superiority. In nineteenth-century Europe the racist belief that the white people of Europe and America were intellectually and morally superior to the people of Africa and Asia was widespread. Indeed, Europeans portrayed imperialism as a moral duty: colonial peoples were the 'white man's burden'. Imperialism, they argued, brought the benefits of civilization, and in particular Christianity, to the less fortunate and less sophisticated peoples of the world.

More particular varieties of national chauvinism have developed in the form of pan-nationalism. After unification in 1871, German nationalism developed a pronounced chauvinistic character. German chauvinism found its highest expression in the racialist and anti-Semitic doctrines developed by the Nazis. The Nazis adopted the expansionist goals of pan-Germanism with enthusiasm but justified them in the language of biology rather than politics.

In Russia this took the form of pan-Slavism in the nineteenth century. The Russians are Slavs and enjoy linguistic and cultural links with other Slavic peoples in eastern and south-eastern Europe. Pan-Slavism was defined by the goal of Slavic unity, which many Russian nationalists believed to be their country's historic mission. The chauvinistic character of pan-Slavism derived from the belief that the Russians are the natural leaders of the Slavic people, and that the Slavs are culturally and spiritually superior to the other peoples of Europe. Pan-Slavism is therefore both anti-Western and anti-liberal. This has been most apparent in the adoption of a more assertive and expansionist foreign policy under Vladimir Putin, including the annexation of Crimea in 2014 and the invasion of Ukraine in 2022. Putin has been clear that he believes Ukraine to be a part of Russia and not a separate nation.

Chauvinistic and expansionist forms of nationalism bred from feelings of intense, even hysterical, nationalist enthusiasm which was anti-democratic, anti-individualist, irrational and highly regressive. The individual as a separate, rational being is rejected and replaced by one swept away on a tide of patriotic emotion, expressed in the desire for aggression, expansion and war. **Charles Maurras (1868–1952)** called such intense patriotism integral nationalism, which is where individuals lose their identity within an all-powerful 'nation', which has an existence and meaning beyond the life of any single individual. Such nationalism is often accompanied by militarism. This is when military glory and conquest are the ultimate evidence of national greatness and generate intense feelings of nationalist commitment. The civilian population is, in effect, militarized: it is infected by the military values of absolute loyalty, complete dedication and willing self-sacrifice. When the honour or integrity of the nation is in question, the lives of ordinary citizens become unimportant. As Hitler argued, '*What is life? Life is the nation. The individual must die anyway.*' These forms of nationalism seek to promote more than mere patriotism; they wish to establish an intense and militant sense of national identity; they offer the prospect of national regeneration and the rebirth of national pride.

In practice, national regeneration meant the assertion of power over other nations through expansionism, war and conquest. Influenced by social Darwinism and a belief in national and

Definition

Militarism: The achievement of ends by military means, or the extension of military ideas, values and practices to civilian society.

Spec key term

Imperialism: Extending the power of a state beyond its boundaries through the establishment of an empire.

Chauvinistic nationalism: A form of nationalism that believes its nation is superior to others, seeing them as a threat to their survival.

Definition

Pan-nationalism: A style of nationalism that is dedicated to unifying a disparate people either through expansionism ('pan' means 'all' or 'every').

sometimes racial superiority, expansionist nationalism became inextricably linked to militarism and imperialism. Nazi Germany looked to construct a 'Greater Germany' by building an empire stretching into the Soviet Union – a 'Lebensraum in the East'. Fascist Italy sought to create an African empire through the invasion of Abyssinia in 1934. Imperial Japan occupied Manchuria in 1931 in order to found a 'co-prosperity' sphere in a new Japanese-led Asia. These empires sought autarky, the idea of strict economic self-sufficiency and self-reliance. In this view, economic strength is based on the capacity of the nation to rely solely on resources and energies it directly controls. Conquest and expansionism are therefore a means of gaining economic security as well as national greatness. National regeneration and economic progress are therefore intimately tied up with military power.

So, in summary, expansionist nationalism can be categorized as shown in Figure 8.4.

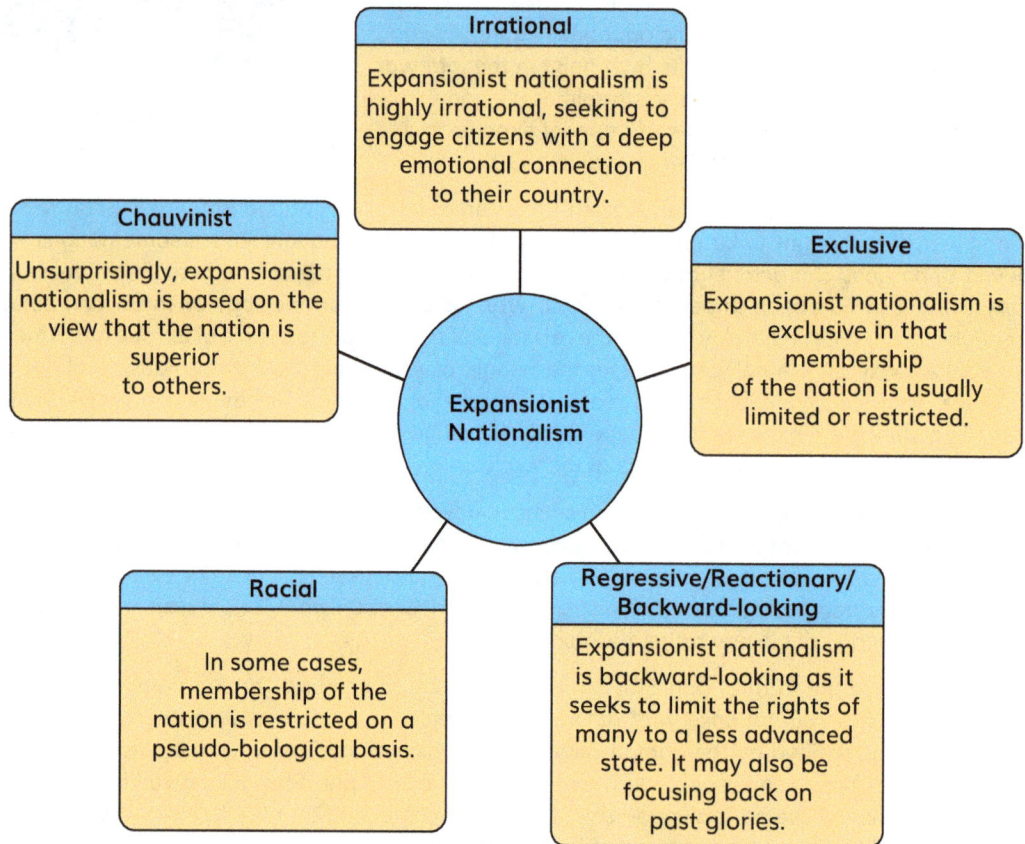

Figure 8.4 **Expansionist nationalism.**

Tensions within nationalism over expansionism	
ARE EXPANSIONIST	**AREN'T EXPANSIONIST**
✓ Some forms of nationalism are expansionist, believing their nation to be superior to other nations	✗ Expansionism is not a feature shared by most nationalists. Liberal, anti- and postcolonial and conservative nationalism do not have expansionist tendencies
✓ These forms of nationalism deny the right of other nationalists to sovereignty and independence	✗ Most forms of nationalism are committed to the notion of self-determination, believing that nations have the right to rule themselves
✓ These forms of nationalism often lead to conflict and war	✗ Conservative nationalism, while more exclusive and backward-looking than liberal, anti- and postcolonial nationalism, has at its core the desire to forge a cohesive and united society and is not expansionist

Anti-colonial and postcolonial nationalism

Anti-colonial nationalism relates to countries which have experienced colonial rule. In the 1880s, Africa and Asia were invaded and annexed by European countries. By 1914, 90 per cent of Africa was under colonial rule.

One of the key reasons behind colonialism was simple: Africa and Asia were an untapped economic resource which could be exploited by European countries who wanted to exploit their economies and natural resources. Indigenous populations were expected to work for a pittance, with profits going to colonial rulers. As well as economic exploitation, colonialism sought to impose Western culture to Africa and Asia. Colonized countries were forced to adopt the language of their oppressors, as well as their culture and religion.

For these nations the quest for political independence was closely related to their awareness of their economic under-development and their subordination to the industrialized Western states. Anti-colonialism thus came to express the desire for 'national liberation' in both political and economic terms.

After the Second World War these colonies gained momentum in challenging their colonial oppressors, seeking to govern themselves, to exercise their right to national self-determination. For the peoples of Africa and Asia, their desire for national identity was reinforced by their desire for liberation from their imperialist oppressors. Anti-colonial nationalists looked to Marxist or socialist analysis to understand their experience of colonialism. Socialist ideas appealed powerfully to anti-colonial nationalists, because socialism embodies values such as community and cooperation that were deeply entrenched in traditional, preindustrial societies. More importantly, socialism, and in particular Marxism, provided an analysis of inequality and exploitation through which the colonial experience could be understood and challenged, as an extended form of class oppression. In his 1917 pamphlet, *Imperialism, The Highest Stage of Capitalism*, V.I. Lenin provided the basis for such a view by portraying imperialism as an essentially economic phenomenon, a quest for profit by capitalist

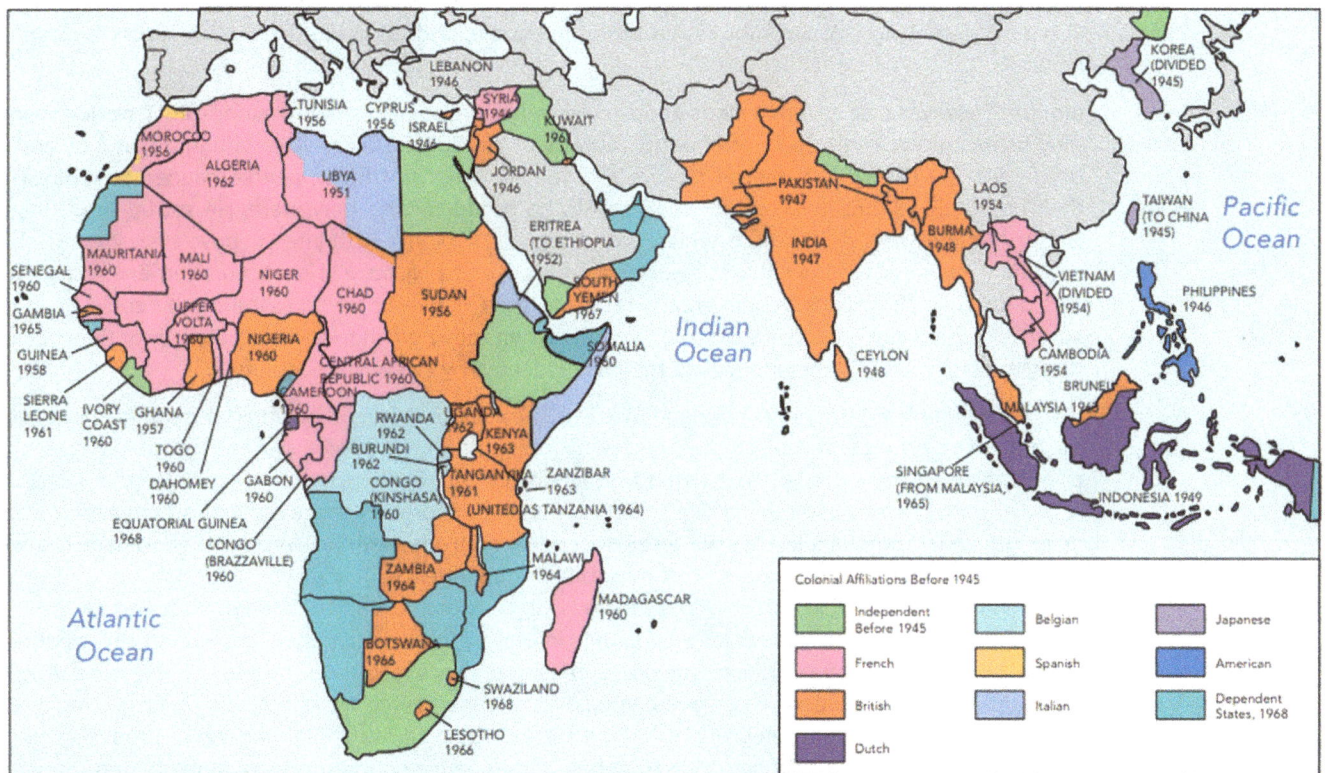

Map 8.2 **Colonial affiliations in Africa and Asia before 1945 with the dates that various countries gained independence.**

countries seeking investment opportunities, cheap labour and raw materials, and secure markets. The class struggle thus became a struggle against colonial exploitation and oppression. The overthrow of colonial rule therefore implied not only political independence but also a social revolution offering the prospect of both political and economic emancipation.

In the post-war era, the political geography of much of the world was transformed by the power of anti-colonial nationalism. The population of the colonies recognized the power of new media, where stories from around the globe could be heard by an international audience and utilized this to showcase the brutal suppression of the colonial powers. One example of this was the Salt March in India in 1930 where thousands of peaceful protestors, led by Mahatma Gandhi, were subject to brutal beatings and arrest. This led to negative stories around the world, shaming the colonial rulers.

Postcolonial nationalism refers to the experience of countries after the colonies gained independence. Many previously colonized nations sought to express their autonomy not by replicating Western-liberal society but by rejecting it. This meant looking to ideologies that were more in keeping with their traditional pre-colonialized existence. As such, most of the leaders of Asian and African anti-colonial movements were attracted to some form of socialism, ranging from the moderate and peaceful ideas represented by Gandhi and Nehru in India to the revolutionary Marxism espoused by Mao Zedong in China, Ho Chi Minh in Vietnam and Fidel Castro in Cuba.

Frantz Fanon actively supported and participated in the Algerian Revolution (1954–62) for independence from France, and wrote extensively on postcolonialism. In *The Wretched of the Earth* (1961), Fanon argued that colonialism imposed a colonial identity on the indigenous peoples of the colonies, destroying their true identity. In *Black Skins, White Masks* (1952), Fanon argued that colonialism ruled every aspect of colonized people's lives. They had to speak a language and adopt and participate in the very civilization which oppressed them; they were participating in their own oppression. Such dehumanization was achieved with physical and mental violence, by which the colonist aimed to instil a submissive mentality upon the colonial people. Hence for Fanon, colonized people must violently resist colonial subjugation. Fanon believed that years of colonial rule had created a paralysing sense of inferiority and impotence amongst the Black peoples of Africa, which could only be purged by the experience of revolt and violence. He argued that the violent resistance was liberating, removing colonial submission from the people, and restoring their self-respect. '*Violence,*' he wrote, '*is man re-creating himself.*'

Marcus Garvey is also linked to ideas of postcolonialism. Although, in many minds, **Black nationalism** may be associated with the US civil rights movement of 1960s, **Garvey** was writing about it as early as the 1920s. The main thrust of **Garvey's** argument was that Black people needed to maintain their unique Black ancestry and identity, and to be proud of who they were. He set up the United Negro Improvement Association which was '*organised for the absolute purpose of bettering our condition, industrially, commercially, socially, religiously and politically*'. He encouraged emigration to Africa, arguing that Black people should return to their native homeland where they could build a successful Black nation. **Garvey** argued that only when they had shown white people that they could be successful in their homeland, would they be respected by the white population.

Kwame Nkrumah led Ghana to independence in 1957 declaring that Ghanaian independence marked the birth of a new African '*ready to fight his own battles and show that after all, the Black man is capable of managing his own affairs*'. He insisted that Ghanaian independence was '*meaningless unless it is linked up with the total liberation of the African continent*'. He argued that even though the Africa was no longer under colonial rule, they were still dependent on trade with the West which had huge global economic power. He acknowledged that even after independence, '*practically all our natural resources, not to mention trade, shipping, banking, building … remained in the hands of foreigners seeking to enrich alien investors, and to hold back local economic initiative*'. Instead Nkrumah envisioned the creation of a United States of Africa which was self-sufficient and not reliant on the West. Nkrumah's vision of a pan-African federation would overcome colonial dependence by establishing a larger regional market. Through economic integration, African states would create a huge market of producers and consumers which would release Africa from their dependence on international markets and reorient their economic relationships toward each other.

So, in summary, anti- and postcolonial nationalism can be categorized as shown in Figure 8.5.

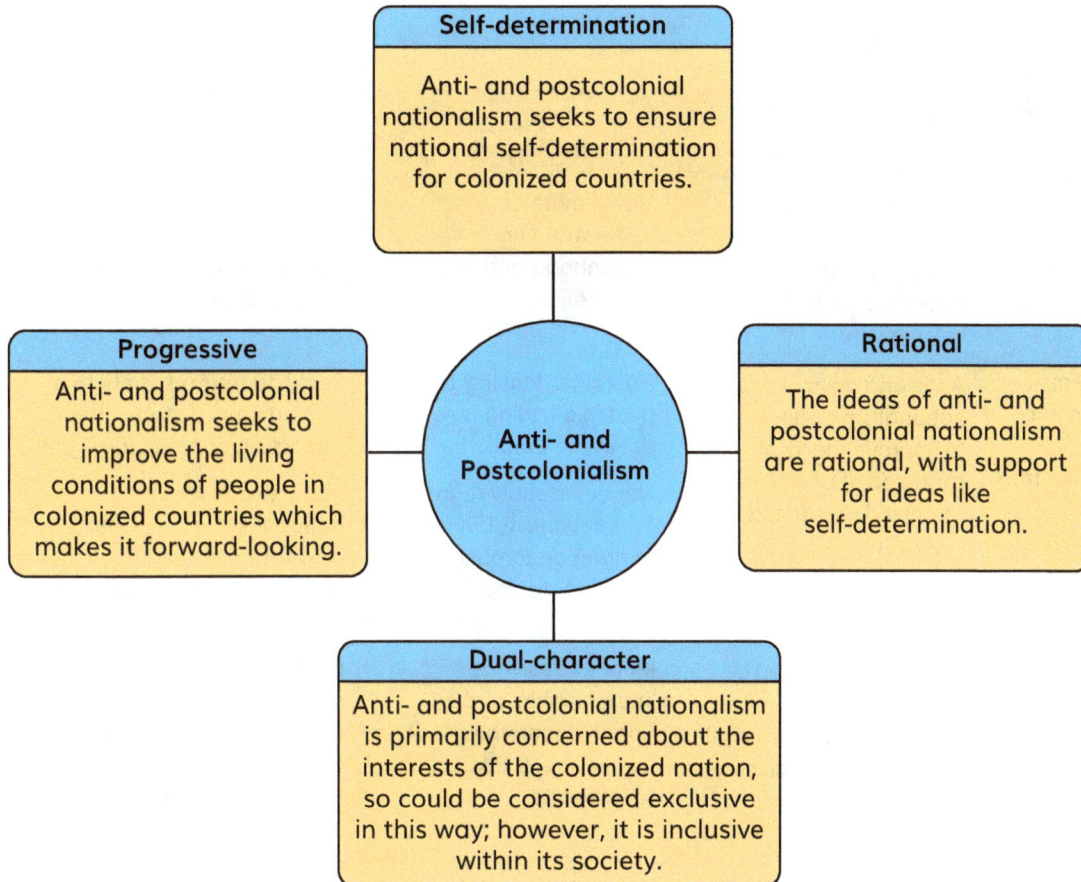

Figure 8.5 **Anti- and postcolonial nationalism.**

Tensions within nationalism over inclusivity

ARE INCLUSIVE	AREN'T INCLUSIVE
✓ Liberal and anti-colonial nationalism has an inclusive understanding of nationhood	✗ The civic, inclusive view of what forms a nation is very different from the view of other nationalists, which have a more exclusive character
✓ Liberal and anti-colonial nationalism is based on a civic understanding of nationalism believing that an active commitment to the values of the nation is all that is required to be a part of a nation	✗ Conservative nationalists and postcolonial nationalism reject a civic understanding of nationalism, believing instead in a more exclusive view of nationalism, based on shared culture, history, tradition and values
✓ Liberal, anti- and postcolonial nationalism view the 'nation' as a sovereign political unit where members of the community are encouraged to accept those wishing to join the nation	✗ Expansionist nationalists have a highly exclusive, chauvinistic view of the nation based on ethno-cultural or even racialist views of what constitutes the nation. This often leads to expansionism and war

Table 8.1 **Tensions within nationalism**

	Liberal	Anti- and postcolonial	Conservative	Expansionist
Rational	They can be seen to be the most rational, based on liberal values	Rational to an extent but also has an emotive response to the oppression faced under colonialism	Has a more emotive understanding of nationhood and nationalism	The most irrational, adopts an integral form of nationalism to heighten emotional understanding
Progressive	A progressive form of nationalism which is forward-looking, seeking to improve, free and advancing society	Anti- and postcolonial nationalism seeks to improve the living condition of people in colonized countries which makes it forward-looking	Nostalgic, looking to the past in deciding how to act in the future. Not necessarily regressive or reactionary, but seeks to hang on to past experiences and tradition	Seeks to return society to a less advanced state, often restricting or removing rights. Many expansionist nationalists were driven by a future aim of world domination, so cannot solely be seen as backward-looking
Inclusive	Inclusive understanding of nationhood, associated with civic nationalism	Primarily concerned with the interests of the colonized nation, so could be considered exclusive in this way; however, it is inclusive within its society	More exclusive as 'membership' of the nation cannot be immediate; it takes time to integrate	Believe their nation is superior to others and therefore membership is highly exclusive. Only racial understandings of nationhood are more exclusive
Self-determination	They strongly believe in the concept of self-determination for all nations; it is a fundamental value	Seeks to ensure national self-determination for colonized countries	Unconcerned with the status of other nations, being solely interested in the cohesiveness of their own nation	Does not support the right of self-determination for other nations, believing instead that they are superior and should conquer and control other nations
Multi or monocultural	Support a diverse society. However, these diverse views cannot challenge the overall values of society	Postcolonial nationalism seeks a society without Western influence hence may reject the idea of a multicultural society	Believe all members of the nation must fit in with the dominant culture by assimilating and dropping their past customs and traditions	They revere their superior culture, believing all other cultures are degenerate cultures
Civic or cultural	Have a civic understanding of nationhood. The only requirement for 'membership' is to want to be part of the nation, accepting their values	Postcolonial countries promote a civic understanding of nationhood, combined with a strong cultural postcolonial identity	Has a cultural approach, believing a single culture is essential to promote cohesiveness. Some may support an ethnic approach, believing that ancestry is also important	Sees ancestry as significant in defining nationhood. The most extreme forms of expansionist nationalism take a racial (biological) understanding of race

3. Nationalist key thinkers

Key thinkers are an important part of understanding each ideology. The exam board has specified five key thinkers per ideology and TWO must be included in an answer to avoid a cap (please check the Exam Focus chapter (Chapter 9) for lots more discussion of key thinkers). Although key thinkers (and other thinkers) have been discussed throughout the chapter, here we look at each one in detail.

Jean-Jacques Rousseau (1712–78)

Hulton Archive/Stringer/Getty

Jean-Jacques Rousseau was a Geneva-born French moral and political philosopher. Rousseau is commonly viewed as the architect of political nationalism.

Rousseau is best associated with the idea of a general will. In *The Social Contract* (1762), Rousseau argued that humans could only throw off the corruption, exploitation and domination imposed by society and regain the capacity for choice through a radical form of democracy, based on the 'general will' of the people. He thus proposed that government be based on the 'general will', as opposed to the 'particular', or selfish, will of each individual citizen.

Rousseau was suggesting that *the people* were the sovereign entity from which the state gained its legitimacy. '*The law is the expression of the general will.*' This is highly significant for nationalism because he was one of the first thinkers who articulated the idea that 'the people' had a collective 'will' and collective values. As such, it is suggested that he was the first person to identify the idea of a nation as a group of people who share common views and values. The general will is therefore the will of the nation, the people bound together by patriotism or a sense of national *esprit de corps*.

For Rousseau, nationalism was therefore inextricably linked to citizenship, democracy and the belief that the state's legitimacy derives from the active participation of its citizens. This is closely associated with the idea of civic nationalism, the belief that an active commitment to the values of the nation is all that is required to be a part of a nation. Moreover, by arguing that these communities should govern themselves, he was supporting the idea of national self-determination. Lastly, Rousseau believed that the function of the government is to enforce the general will of the people and not to direct it.

Johann Gottfried von Herder (1744–1803)

Nastasic/Getty

Johann Gottfried von Herder was a German poet, critic and philosopher, often portrayed as the 'father' of cultural nationalism. Herder's major work was *Reflections on the Philosophy of the History of Mankind* (1784–91). He was a powerful intellectual opponent of the Enlightenment and a crucial influence on the romantic movement.

Herder placed an emphasis on the nation as an organic group characterized by a distinctive language, culture and 'spirit', which both helped to found cultural history and gave rise to a form of nationalism that stresses the intrinsic value of national culture. He argued that the state develops its legitimacy from the culture of the nation which must be preserved and upheld from one generation to the next.

Specifically, Herder placed particular importance on the power of language on each nation's culture, arguing that 'A poet is the creator of the nation around him, he gives them a world to see and has their souls in his hand to lead them to that world.' He believed that language was uniquely placed to foster a nation's history and identity and consequently, creating greater unity. Language was a source of all that is precious to a nation.

Herder rejected the enlightenment, and civic forms of nationalism, believing instead that each nation or *Volk*, has its own culture, spirit, known as their *Volksgeist*, which develops naturally. As such, each nation will be imbued with its own *Volksgeist*. 'Each nationality contains its centre of happiness within itself.' In seeking and enhancing one's own national spirit and identity, nations would continue to be different. Nations should respect and admire each other's distinct culture and there was no need for comparison between nations as 'every nation bears in itself the standard of its perfection, totally independent of all comparison with that of others'. It is important to note that Herder did not think that some nations were superior to others.

Herder attached a great deal of importance to the nation and argued that 'He that has lost his patriotic spirit has lost himself and the whole worlds about himself.' He rejected other ideas which sought to divide the nation, like socialism, arguing instead that 'there is only one class in the state, the volk, and the King belongs to this class as well as the peasant'.

Giuseppe Mazzini (1805–72)

duncan1890/Getty

Giuseppe Mazzini is often portrayed as the founder of Italian unification. After spells in France and Britain, Mazzini returned to Italy during the 1848 Revolutions, helping to liberate Milan and becoming head of the short-lived Roman Republic.

Mazzini's nationalism had a profound influence across Europe in strengthening the idea that freedom entails the creation of one's own nation-state. Mazzini championed two principles, which he believed to be universally applicable: 'every nation a state' and 'only one state for the entire nation'. This can be seen as a distinctly liberal and rational concept of nationalism, the belief in self-determination for all nations. Mazzini was very clear that the nation was the key group in any society, he argued that a country was much more than a group of individuals, it was a united community of people and he called on people around the world to unite around the idea of the nation-state. He was clear that the nation-state was the best form of government as it forged a community with a clear purpose, out of free and equal humans.

Despite having clearly liberal nationalist principles, it would be wrong to categorize Mazzini as wholly liberal. He argued that the search for individual liberty had led to a weakening of common bonds of nationhood. In Essays on the Duty of Man (1844–58) he asked people to place duty to their country above individual interests, arguing that rights should come second to one's wider duty towards humanity. In other words, individuals needed to cooperate towards common aims; they needed to be part of a nation. Mazzini argued that greater liberty had not been matched by improvements in workers living and working conditions, even though wealth had increased overall, liberty was therefore an 'illusion and bitter irony'. He believed that genuine human freedom rested primarily on the creation of each nation's own state. 'Every nation is destined, by the law of God and humanity, to form a free and equal community of brothers.'

He nevertheless distrusted abstract thinking generally, arguing that thought must always be harnessed to action, an idea he expressed through the concept of 'thought and action'. His motto was Dio e Popolo – 'God and People' – as he believed that God had created separate countries and nations, 'the home wherein God has placed us, among brothers and sisters linked to us by the family ties of a common religion, history and language.'

Charles Maurras (1868–1952)

Photo 12/Universal Images Group/Getty Images

A French political thinker and leading figure within the political movement *Action Française*, Maurras was a key exponent of right-wing nationalism and an influence on fascism.

Maurras believed in 'goddess France' as a marvel unequalled in the entire world, he believed it had a pronounced beauty and deep philosophical character. He nevertheless warned that France needed to be protected from its enemies within and without, influenced by the instability of losing the Franco-Prussian War in 1870, and subsequently the Paris Commune of 1871. His insular and exclusionary nationalism articulated hostility towards Protestants, Jews, Freemasons and foreigners in general, blaming France's decline on these 'anti-France' forces.

His key idea was integral nationalism, which emphasized the organic unity of the nation with a stress on hierarchy and traditional institutions. Integral nationalism was a form of right-wing nationalism that influenced the ideas of fascism. Individuals should not place their interests first, their interests were best served by serving the nation. Integral nationalism was anti-rational in character, believing that the individual had to immerse themselves completely within the state and subsume themselves into the interests of their nation. As Maurras said, '*A true nationalist places his country above everything*'. As such, integral nationalist societies were usually totalitarian in nature, with the state dominating every aspect of people's lives. As Mussolini argued, '*everything within the state, nothing outside the state, nothing against the state*'. Strong government was essential to counteract the decadence of previous societies; Maurras believed that France had lost its way during the revolution so he sought an aggressive nationalist strategy that would change French history.

Maurras' nationalism resembled fascism most clearly in its emphasis on militarism. In his view, the mission of the nation was intrinsically linked to aggressive expansionism and war, grounded in the belief that, while some nations are destined for conquest and glory, others were weak and subordinate. Mussolini's Italy was the first example of such a society, followed by Nazi Germany and Japan in the 1940s. In these nations, military expansionism and war were a key part of the militarization of the whole of society. As Mussolini argued, '*War alone brings up to its highest tension all human energy and puts that stamp of nobility upon the people who have the courage to meet it.*' For Maurras, the whole of society should be organized in preparation for expansionism and war.

Maurras' support for the Church and monarchy was connected to his view of social order and hierarchy. He believed that strong state religion was the best way of maintaining public order. He also valued the role it had played throughout French history, believing it was the glue that held society in place and fused French people together.

Marcus Garvey (1887–1940)

A Jamaican political thinker and activist, and an early advocate of Black nationalism, Garvey was the founder of the Universal Negro Improvement Association (UNIP) in 1914. He left Jamaica for New York in 1916, where his message of Black pride and economic self-sufficiency gained him a growing following.

Garvey wanted to establish a sense of Black pride among the Black community and urged Black people to be proud of who they were and their ancestry rather than to try to fit in with white society. He spoke to Black communities, talking of a 'new negro' who was proud of being Black and attracted thousands of supporters. In order to promote these ideas, he set up a newspaper, *Negro World*, which wrote of the exploits of Black heroes and highlighted many examples of Black and African culture connecting Black communities on three continents.

His brand of Black nationalism had three components: unity, pride in the African cultural heritage and complete autonomy. Garvey believed people of African descent could establish a great independent nation in their ancient homeland of Africa. He believed that the African people constituted one nation and that they needed to set aside cultural differences in order to unite and progress in the world. He argued that Black people would only be respected when they were economically self-sufficient and believed that there needed to be an autonomous Black economy in Africa.

Bettman/Contributor/Getty

He argued that the purpose of separatism was to free the Black community from the negativity of white culture and to find their true Black identity, of which they could and should be proud. To that end he set up the Negro Factories Corporation to develop industries of African descent as well as a chain of restaurants and grocery stores, laundries and a hotel. In 1919 Garvey founded the Black Star Line, to provide transportation to Africa and to encourage trade among Black businesses of Africa and the Americas. The Black star on the flag of Ghana was a symbol of African unity and anti-colonialism.

Garvey's idea of Africa for the Africans was associated with a call to unite the continent from Cairo to the Cape. This had a profound impact on emerging pan-Africanism, which is the idea that peoples of African descent have common interests and should be unified, and inspired figures such as Kwame Nkrumah, the first prime minister and president of Ghana. Garvey wished to inspire a global mass movement and his ultimate dream was the creation of a United States of Africa.

Rastafarianism is also based largely on Garvey's ideas. Garvey made a prophecy saying '*Look to Africa where a Black king shall be crowned, he shall be your Redeemer.*' The prophecy was followed by the crowning of Emperor Haile Selassie I in Ethiopia. Rastafarians see this as the fulfilment of Garvey's prophecy.

4. How to apply knowledge to nationalism answers

Tensions within nationalism over the role of the nation-state

Worked example

Paragraph One – Agreement within nationalism

- ✓ All nationalists agree that the nation-state is built around people identifying as a nation with shared values
- ✓ Liberal, anti- and postcolonial nationalists support the principle of the nation-state as a universal right for all nations **(Mazzini)**
- ✓ Liberal, anti- and postcolonial nationalists agree that a world of nation-states promotes peace and order by allowing nations to decide what is in their own best interest

Paragraph Two – Disagreement within nationalism

- ✗ Most nationalists support the creation of a world of nation-states; however, others are expansionist in character **(Maurras)**
- ✗ Anti- and postcolonial nationalists believe that all nations should be free to rule themselves and be self-determined, and hence reject expansionism
- ✗ However, chauvinistic forms of nationalism are expansionist in nature rejecting the idea of universal nation-states

Paragraph Three – Disagreement within nationalism

- ✗ Some nationalists approach the idea of a nation-state in a rational way, whereas others base it on emotional and mystical ways **(Herder)**
- ✗ Liberal nationalists see the nation in rational terms, believing in civic forms of nationalism, whereas conservative and postcolonial nationalism sees the nation in irrational, cultural terms
- ✗ As a consequence, liberal nationalism is inclusive in its approach to nation stales, whereas conservative and postcolonial forms of nationalism can be exclusive

Tensions within nationalism over society

Worked example

Theme 1 – Inclusive society

- ✓ Liberal nationalism seeks an inclusive society, based on a civic understanding of nationalism **(Rousseau)**
- ✗ Conservative nationalists reject a civic understanding of nationalism, believing instead in a more exclusive society, based on shared culture, history, tradition and values **(Herder)**
- ✗ Expansionist nationalists seek a highly exclusive society, based on a chauvinistic view of the nation based on ethno-cultural or even racialist views of a nation **(Maurras)**

Continued...

Theme 2 – Progressive society

✓ Liberal, anti- and postcolonial nationalism seek a progressive, forward-looking society, seeking improvements in society and by protecting the rights of people

✗ Expansionist forms of nationalism do not seek a progressive society, as a key aim is to repress others. Instead they seek a society based on intense patriotism **(Maurras)**

✗ Conservative nationalism seeks to build a society by looking backwards, seeking to maintain traditions of the past to bind society together **(Herder)**

Theme 3 – Self-determined society

✓ Liberal, anti- and postcolonial nationalism seeks a society based on mutual respect for all nations and seeks self-determination for all

✗ However, chauvinistic forms of nationalism are expansionist in nature rejecting the idea of universal nation-states

✗ Conservative nationalism tends to value cultural homogeneity in society **(Herder)**, but is not concerned with the independence, or otherwise, of other nations. It has the desire to forge a cohesive and united society but is not expansionist

Tensions within nationalism over principle of inclusiveness

Worked example

Paragraph One – Agreement within nationalism

✓ Liberal and anti-colonial nationalism have an inclusive understanding of nationhood

✓ Liberal and anti-colonial nationalism are based on a civic understanding of nationalism **(Rousseau)** believing that an active commitment to the values of the nation is all that is required to be a part of a nation

✓ Liberal, anti- and postcolonial nationalism view the 'nation' as a sovereign political unit where members of the community are encouraged to accept those wishing to join the nation

Paragraph Two – Disagreement within nationalism

✗ Conservative nationalism disagrees with liberal nationalism, believing instead in a more exclusive view of nationalism, based on shared culture, history, tradition and values. This is more exclusive as 'membership' of the nation cannot be immediate, it takes time to fully integrate into a nation's culture, customs, etc.

✗ While postcolonial nationalism is inclusive within its own community, it seeks to exclude its oppressors from being part of its future nation

✗ This form of cultural nationalism views the 'nation' in terms of a distinctive civilization rather than in political terms and tend towards a mystical or romantic view of the 'nation' **(Herder)**

Paragraph Three – Disagreement within nationalism

✗ Expansionist nationalists also disagree with liberal nationalism and have a highly exclusive view of the nation based on ethno-cultural or even racialist views of what constitutes the nation

✗ This form of nationalism is also chauvinistic as it believes its nation is superior to other nations

✗ This often leads to expansionism and war **(Maurras)**

Tensions within nationalism over progressiveness

Worked example

Paragraph One – Agreement within nationalism

- ✓ Liberal and anti-/postcolonial nationalism promotes mutual respect for nations and seeks independence for all **(Rousseau)** showing strong support in both strands for progressive values
- ✓ Civic forms of nationalism like liberal and anti-/postcolonialism see nations in rational and inclusive terms showing agreement on common progressive goal
- ✓ Liberal nationalism and anti-/postcolonialism both seek international harmony, believing nation-states should be regulated by international law. This shows them both as a liberating, progressive force

Paragraph Two – Disagreement within nationalism

- ✗ Expansionist forms of nationalism breed feelings of intense patriotism, often leading to war **(Maurras)**, they cannot be seen as progressive as their main aim seeks to repress others
- ✗ These forms of nationalism base their understanding of nationhood on culture **(Herder)**, or biologically distinct 'races', showing that they exclusive which is not progressive
- ✗ These forms of nationalism promote an irrational view of nationhood, encouraging the view that not all nations have the right to self-determination

Paragraph Three – Disagreement within nationalism

- ✗ Conservative and expansionist nationalism believes that nations are forged by having a shared history and culture looking back at past national greatness. This shows that they do not look forward and are therefore not progressive
- ✗ Conservative nationalism is based on a nostalgic view of the past, seeking to hold on to traditions and learning from the past, and expansionist nationalism seeks to re-establishment national greatness by militarizing the whole of society **(Maurras)**
- ✗ Within some forms of nationalism there is a desire to subjugate other nations, showing no interest in working towards a better future for all nations. This cannot be seen as progressive

Chapter Summary

- Nationalism is a diverse ideology which has many different, often contradictory views within it.
- Despite this, the overriding principle of all nationalism strands is the fundamental importance of the nation as a political or cultural unit.
- Nationalism can be characterized as being inclusive or exclusive, rational or irrational, progressive or regressive.
- Anti-colonial nationalism is based on the liberal nationalist principles of national self-determination, but postcolonial nationalism has evolved from these ideas.
- There is a fundamental conflict between liberal nationalism and expansionist nationalism.

Exam Style Questions

1. To what extent do nationalists agree over the role of the nation-state?
2. To what extent does nationalism agree more than it disagrees?
3. To what extent does nationalism support self-determination for all nations?
4. To what extent can nationalism be seen as inclusive?
5. To what extent does nationalism have a common understanding of what forms a nation?
6. To what extent can nationalism be seen as progressive?
7. To what extent are nationalists irrational?
8. To what extent can nationalism be seen as expansionist?

Further Resources

Adams, I. *Political Ideology Today* (2001) 'Chapter 4, 'Nationalism and Internationalism' is straightforward read for A-Level students which explores the ideas of nationalism.

Baradat, L. *Political Ideologies* (2003) 'Chapter 3, Nationalism' has a short review of the history of nationalism, a useful companion to understanding the evolution of the ideology.

Bruilly, J. *The Oxford Handbook of the History of Nationalism* (2013). Leading scholars in a variety of fields present the latest research on nationalism across a broad array of areas.

Coakley, J. *Nationalism, Ethnicity and the State* (2012). A broad and comprehensive overview of nationalism, and its expression across many spheres of public and political life.

Greenfeld, L. *Nationalism: A Short History* (2019). A concise overview of the evolution of nationalism and its ongoing presence in a globalized world.

Kelly, P. et al. *The Politics Book* (2013). A clearly written, student-friendly book which covers some of the thinkers discussed in this chapter.

Özkirimli, U. *Theories of Nationalism*, 3rd edn (2017). A clear and genuinely international account of classical and modern contributions to debates.

Vincent, R. *Modern Political Ideologies* (1995). Chapter 9, 'Nationalism', and Chapter 5, 'Fascism', can be used to stretch and extend a student's knowledge of the content covered in this chapter.

Visit our companion website at https://bloomsbury.pub/essentials-of-political-ideas-2e for more worked examples.

EXAM FOCUS

Introduction

The 2017 Politics A-Level specification made Political Ideas a compulsory part of the course, with all students studying three core ideas of Conservatism, Liberalism and Socialism and then choosing an additional non-core idea to study from a choice of Anarchism, Ecologism, Feminism, Multiculturalism and Nationalism. The aim of this chapter is to help you understand how to approach the Ideas section of your exams and to learn how to write great answers by incorporating the demands of all three Assessment Objective (AOs).

The exam

The Ideas content of the course is examined in two separate exams. Component One is the core ideas element (9PL01) and Component Two is the non-core ideas (9PL02).

» In Component One you will have to answer one 24-mark core ideas essay from a choice of two. The exam board have also advised that in some years, the two questions may be from the same core idea, i.e. a choice from two Conservatism questions, etc.

» In Component Two you will have to answer one 24-mark non-core ideas essay from a choice of two. There will always be a choice of two questions for your non-core idea; in this way, you can consider the non-core topic to be 'compulsory' as there will always be a question on your chosen non-core idea.

What types of questions can be asked in the Ideas part of the exam?

» Both core and non-core ideas questions are identical in structure and the way they should be answered; in other words, there is only one 'type' of question.

» They will ALWAYS begin with the stem 'To what extent …'.

» They will ask about similarities and differences, or agreements and disagreements between the strands within an ideology as outlined in the specification.

» They will never ask you to compare two different ideologies.

Ideas questions (core and non-core)

As identified above, questions for Ideas Essays will begin with the stem 'To what extent …' and follow with an area of disagreement or difference within the ideology. The question is therefore asking you to identify whether the similarities within the Idea are greater than the differences. You will do this by comparing the strand's views (or characteristics) on the issue that has been asked. For example, in the Edexcel Pearson 2020 9PL01 A-Level exam, one Ideas Essay question was 'To what extent do modern liberals accept the ideas of classical liberals?' Ideas Essay questions are marked out of 24 which are allocated as follows: AO1 – 8 marks, AO2 – 8 marks. AO3 – 8 marks.

An introduction to the AOs

AO1

> 'Demonstrate knowledge and understanding of political institutions, processes, concepts, theories and issues.'

AO1 is probably the AO that everyone is most familiar with as it relates to 'knowledge and understanding'. This is the bread and butter of what is taught in classrooms day in, day out. Everything in the chapters of this book begins with AO1; knowledge and the understanding that flows from it. Without good knowledge and understanding, there is a limit to how to effectively you can utilize the other two AOs.

AO2

> 'Analyse aspects of politics and political information, including in relation to parallels, connections, similarities and differences.'

AO2 is about analysis, but what does this actually mean? The dictionaries define it as 'detailed examination' or 'the process of examining' something. So, let's work out what we have to do to improve our AO2 marks.

» First, we have to be solid in our AO1 as AO2 flows from and is grounded in AO1.

» Second, we have to explore our AO1 point in more detail, probing, investigating and exploring the knowledge we have stated as AO1.

» Third, AO2 also required 'comparative analysis' which means exploring AO1 points to tease out similarities and differences between the strands.

AO3

> 'Evaluate aspects of politics and political information, including to construct arguments, make substantiated judgements and draw conclusions.'

To evaluate, according to dictionary definitions, is to 'judge the importance or value of something' or 'make a judgement about them, for example about how good or bad they are'. AO3 is all about judgements; it requires you to not just know information (AO1) and to explore and compare information (AO2), AO3 requires you to consider all of that and then decide which side of the argument is stronger, i.e. judge.

So that's an introduction to the AOs. Later in the chapter we will be exploring ways to incorporate them into answers and looking at good (and not-so-good) practice.

Questions

Unlike in other parts of the specification, Ideas questions are structured in a relatively uniform way. Ideas questions will ask you to compare differences or similarities between the strands within an ideology. This may, however, take a variety of forms, as follows:

1. Theme

This is what we might call the standard Ideas question; one which asks you to identify the similarities or differences within an ideology over a named theme: state, society, human nature or economy:

» To what extent do liberals agree over the role of the **state**?

» To what extent do feminists agree on **human nature**?

» To what extent do anarchists agree on the nature of a future anarchist **society**?

2. Strands-specified question

A variation is when a question is asked using only some of the strands. In questions like these, the answer needs to focus specifically on the strands referenced. Discussion of other strands not mentioned in the question will likely be ignored.

» To what extent are the views of **One Nation conservatives** on the economy consistent with the **New Right**?

» To what extent do **deep green** ecologists and **shallow green** ecologists agree over the economy?

However, it is worth noting that sometimes, a question looks like it is only referencing two strands when in fact it is still asking for a discussion of the whole ideology.

» To what extent do **individualist and collectivist anarchists** agree about human nature?

Here individualist and collectivist anarchists are the only strands of anarchism referenced in the specification, so this question includes all anarchists.

» To what extent do **modern and classical liberals** agree over the role of the state?

Here modern and classical liberals are the only strands of liberalism referenced in the specification, so this question includes all liberals.

3. More general questions

Another type of question is one where you can be asked about similarities and differences within an ideology in a much more general fashion, without specifying a particular area of focus. While often feared by students who find it quite vague, actually it means you don't have to be restricted in what you discuss. Any areas of similarity or difference can be discussed.

» To what extent do modern liberals accept the ideas of classical liberals?

» To what extent is there more to unite rather than divide the New Right from One Nation conservatives?

» To what extent is nationalism a coherent ideology?

4. Core principles

Questions can also be asked on an ideology's core principles. These are the four to five key ideas outlined in the first section of the Idea's specification and in each chapter of the book for each ideology.

» To what extent does multiculturalism's support for **minority rights** promote divisions in society?

» To what extent does nationalism support **self-determination** for all nations?

» To what extent are different socialists committed to **equality**?

5. Key terms

The last type of question is when questions are asked on a key term from the specification. Key terms for each ideology are listed in the spec. We have also used them and defined them throughout the chapters of the book, like this.

» To what extent is nationalism **progressive**?

» To what extent do multiculturalists disagree over the limits of **tolerance**?

» To what extent is ecologism a clear rejection of **anthropocentrism**?

What caps exist in the Ideas questions?

In the exam paper, below your Ideas question, is the following wording '*You must use appropriate thinkers you have studied to support your answer and consider differing views in a balanced way.*' This wording relates to two caps:

1. The first one is about key thinkers. You must include two of the named key thinkers referenced in that particular ideology to avoid being capped at L2 (9/24).

2. The second one is about 'balancing' the 'differing views'. In Ideas questions, this means that it's important to ensure you are looking at both agreements and disagreements within the strands and also, therefore, that you are looking at the different viewpoints of the different strands. That is why in Ideas questions it refers to 'differing views'. This cap is also at L2, i.e. 9/12.

'Consider differing views in a balanced way'– how to achieve in your answers

The 24-mark Ideas questions ask students to '*consider differing views in a balanced way*'. So, what does this mean?

» First, it means that your answer must include the different views of the strands within the ideology. Also, these differing views must be 'balanced', which means that you shouldn't let one strand dominate your answer. While it's not necessary to ensure that you have an even word count for each strand, it is important to ensure that all relevant strands have been fairly considered.

» It also means that you must consider agreement *and* disagreement; although, again, it doesn't mean a 50:50 split, you must give reasonable consideration to both agreement and disagreement within an ideology.

» Another issue which students find difficult is the requirement to reconcile the need for 'balance' with the AO3 need to 'make a substantiated judgement'. The answer to this conundrum is not as complicated as it may first appear. If you are answering a question on the extent of agreement within liberalism over the state, and you are taking the viewpoint that there is more disagreement than agreement, you must still ensure that your answer is exploring agreement within liberalism over the state in enough detail before you go on to reject this to justify your view.

Thinkers and Key Thinkers

An important aspect of the Ideas course is the key thinkers. For each ideology, there are five named key thinkers in the specification. These key thinkers have a special status, as two of them must be used in every Ideas answer, otherwise it will be capped at L2 which is 9/24.

It is important to understand, however, that only the named key thinkers for each ideology has this special status. For example, Betty Friedan is a key thinker in the liberalism part of the course (see Chapter 1) and so she can be used to lift the thinkers cap in Liberalism ONLY. While it is absolutely fine to use Friedan in a feminism essay (see Chapter 6), she is not a feminist key thinker and will not count towards the two named key thinkers cap. The same is true of Disraeli in conservatism (see Chapter 2). It would be very difficult to discuss One Nation conservatism without reference to Disraeli, but he is NOT a named key thinker in conservatism and so won't count towards your two named key thinkers.

Sometimes students think that they need to incorporate all five key thinkers from an ideology into a single answer. This is simply not correct. You should choose any relevant key thinker, making sure you have two to remove the cap. Sometimes, students try to shoehorn less relevant thinkers into their answer in the mistaken belief that this is how you achieve high levels of AO1.

So, what about other thinkers, should you use them and why? The answer to this is absolutely YES! As identified above, there are many thinkers who are either used across two ideologies, like Friedan, or others who are not included at all as a key thinker, who have an awful lot to contribute towards the various debates like Disraeli. By using other thinkers *in addition* to your two key thinkers (or more if you so choose), you are enhancing your AO1 knowledge and hence AO1 marks.

However, a word of caution. While key thinkers are an essential part of your answer, your answers should not be thinker-driven. In other words, you shouldn't answer questions from the perspective of what key thinkers' views are. **You must discuss and compare the views of strands, not key thinkers.** You will never be asked a question referencing a key thinker or asking you to incorporate a specific key thinker. The role of key thinkers is to exemplify and reinforce the thinking of the different strands. There are examples of this throughout the chapter.

STUDENT EXTRACT – 'To what extent is socialism more divided than united?' – looking at thinker-driven vs strand-driven answers

✖

Marx and Engels believe that society is dominated by ideas of the ruling class, known as bourgeois hegemony. These ideas work to divide the workers, therefore they need to be eradicated to create a classless society. On the other hand, more modern thinkers such as Crosland, believe in not eradicating class, but attempting to minimize the divide and close the gap between rich and poor.

✔

Revolutionary socialists believe that class control of society is a consequence of who owns the means of production. This control is exercised by the dominant class over the working class. Marx and Engels believe that society is dominated by ideas of the ruling class, this is known as bourgeois hegemony. These ideas work to divide the proletariat, therefore they need to be eradicated to create a classless society. On the other hand, social democrats, like Crosland, believe in not eradicating class, but attempting to minimize the divide and close the gap between rich and poor.

One very common issue raised is to which strand do thinkers 'belong'. The truth is, there is no easy answer. Some key thinkers are very clearly connected to the strands included in the specification; for example in socialism, Marx and Engels are clearly revolutionary socialists, Antony Crosland is clearly a social democrat and Tony Giddens is easily associated with the Third Way. However, many other thinkers in different ideologies don't fit neatly into a strand, so how can they be used? The simple answer is to associate their views with a strand rather than labelling them as part of that strand. For example, Robert Nozick is not a New Right thinker, he is a libertarian thinker, but he is in the conservatism specification and can be used to illustrate neoliberal (but not neoconservative) thinking.

From this ...

New Right conservatives like Nozick believe in full economic freedom and therefore advocate pure laissez-faire capitalism and free-market economies where state functions are privatized and deregulated and where levels of taxation and state spending are significantly reduces.

To this ...

New Right conservatives believe in full economic freedom and therefore advocate laissez-faire capitalism and free-market economics where state functions are privatized and deregulated and where levels of taxation and state spending are significantly reduced, this view connects the neoliberal element within the New Right conservatives to Robert Nozick who argued that ...

STUDENT EXTRACT – 'To what extent do conservatives agree over the economy?' – looking at thinkers

Agreement in the views of the economy between traditional conservatives and the New Right arise over their view of ownership and control. Both strands are enthusiastic supporters of individual enterprise and a free market and we can see echoes of this in the works of Burke, Rand and Nozick.

> Here the student is making very minimal use of thinkers, merely name-checking them. It is debatable if this would even lift a student out of the cap

STUDENT EXTRACT – 'To what extent do conservatives agree over the economy?' – looking at thinkers

Agreement in the views of the economy between traditional conservatives and the New Right arise over their view of ownership and control. Both strands are enthusiastic supporters of individual enterprise and a free market and we can see echoes of this in the works of Burke, Rand and Nozick. These thinkers supported the enterprise of individuals to be the motor of wealth creation. As a traditional conservative, Burke looked at enterprise from working in a community spirit and driving an organic type of society and the more libertarian element like Rand supported a free economy but had little altruistic impulses and felt that society benefited from the innate greed and the acquisitive drive in humans as a free market operated. Hence both traditional and One Nation conservatives have similar views over the economy but for different reasons.

> Here, however, the student is continuing by elaborating on what each thinker's view is and how it relates to the issue of the economy
>
> Importantly, note how the answer is being driven by considering the strands, not thinkers

STUDENT EXTRACT – 'To what extent to conservatives disagree over human nature?' – looking at key thinkers

One Nation conservatives have an imperfect view of human nature, contrary to this, New Right conservatives recognize human rationality and therefore, uphold a more positive view of human nature. The One Nation position, however, can be understood by looking at Oakeshott who identifies a somewhat negative view as he believes human nature is 'fallible not terrible'. He focuses on intellectual imperfection arguing that decisions should be grounded in empiricism not rationalism whereas Rand reflects the New Right view arguing that humans are capable of rational thought and should be 'objectivist' in pursuing self-interest which supersedes the state and society.

> Note how the thinkers are linked informally with a strand, rather than being labelled
>
> Also note that the answer is driven by looking at strands and exemplified by thinkers

Assessment Objectives in detail

AO1 in detail

> **'Demonstrate knowledge and understanding of political institutions, processes, concepts, theories and issues.'**

We introduced the AOs at the beginning of the chapter, but now were going to look at them in more detail. To recap, AO1 is about what you know, what you've been taught and how well you understand it.

When answering a question, you have to begin with AO1 and the crucial issue is to carefully select the information you think will best help you answer the question, i.e. what are the key points you need to discuss. Knowledge selection is a much-underrated skill when considering AO1, but it's right there in the exam board mark scheme for AO1. This means you must choose very carefully the information you are going to write about in your answer. Sometimes, students write 'everything they know' about an ideology and hope their teachers can sift the important bits from the unimportant bits. It's worth noting that higher AO1 marks require students, not their teachers, to do the sifting!

Using key terms can also really help to elevate an answer as they add sophistication. Using terms like 'negative freedom', 'class consciousness', 'hierarchy' or 'atomism' identify students as having a deeper understanding of AO1.

Another area where AO1 can cause issues is if students focus predominantly on AO1 to the exclusion of the other two AOs. An outstanding student, who can write reams of detail about an idea, can only ever get 8/24 for it as there are only 8 marks available for AO1 knowledge and understanding. Remember the key to writing a really good answer is to balance all three AOs.

A final aspect of AO1 is the use of key thinkers. As discussed above, thinkers and key thinkers are an important part of AO1; when used well, they lift an ordinary AO1 to a really good AO1. Sometimes, students do little more than reference a thinker, punctuating an answer with little more than 'e.g. John Locke'. Ideally, you want to use your thinker knowledge to expand and enhance your knowledge and understanding of an ideology's views.

STUDENT EXTRACT – 'To what extent do socialists have a consistent view of the state?' – looking at AO1

All socialists disagree over what type of state there should be, if any state at all. Revolutionary socialists like Marx and Engels saw the state as a 'managing committee for the Bourgeoisie'; therefore, the state had to be overthrown in order to deliver any sort of real change. Furthermore, they saw parliament as part of the superstructure and hence rejected the parliamentary road, so favoured by evolutionary socialists like social democrats. Therefore, for revolutionary socialists there should not be any state at all, apart from a temporary state made up of the proletariat designed to collectivize ownership of property, which would eventually wither away to create a communist society.

> This is part of a paragraph looking at the different views of socialists on the state

> This is high level AO1 showing excellent understanding of the revolutionary socialist view of the state with excellent use of Marxist terminology

STUDENT EXTRACT – 'To what extent do liberals agree over individualism?' – looking at AO1

Classical liberals believe that an individual's main motivation should be egoistical individualism, which is the belief that individual freedom is associated with a rational sense of self-reliance and self-interest. This emphasizes classical liberals' view on human nature as they believe that they are able to make decisions for themselves without the state intervening. Unlike modern liberals, classical liberals believe that the state should promote negative freedom, linked to J.S. Mill's idea of the harm principle, which is the idea that the state should only intervene to prevent harm to others.

> The student uses key terms like 'egoistical individualism', 'negative freedom' and 'harm principle' very effectively

> They make good use of different pieces of knowledge – individualism, freedom, state, social contract

> They use a key thinker, J.S. Mill, effectively

AO2 in detail

> 'Analyse aspects of politics and political information, including in relation to parallels, connections, similarities and differences.'

AO2 requires students to analyse in two distinct ways:

» First, to examine and explore AO1 in more detail, to make 'logical chains of reasoning'

» Second, to make 'comparative analysis' by 'drawing on similarities and differences' within the ideology to make 'cohesive and convincing connections'.

The first type of AO2 requires students to explore and probe AO1 points that they have raised. This is often a challenge to understand. Sometimes, students add AO1 detail, thinking this is the same as analysing a point.

STUDENT EXTRACT – 'To what extent do socialists agree over the role of the state?' – looking at AO2

Collectivism is seen to involve making the state bigger, and an increase in state spending. Evolutionary socialists advocate raising taxes so that a bigger state can be provided. Socialists would like to see a bigger welfare state providing benefits like pensions and unemployment child and housing benefit, as well as

> This answer is providing too much unnecessary detail on what welfare means, rather than exploring why socialists support welfare

free healthcare. They would also like to pursue collectivism by nationalizing industries like gas, electricity, British telecom and the railways. Also, they would like to provide housing for people, as they did in the 1950s and 1960s through the building of council houses.

Often, students make the same point in different ways, rather than develop their point.

STUDENT EXTRACT – 'To what extent do liberals disagree with the state?' – looking at AO2

Modern liberals disagree with the idea of a minimal state. They think a state should be larger to help people and argue against a minimal state. They believe all individuals should have equal opportunity as the state would intervene, helping everyone gain equal life chances. The state will help people to improve their life.

> This paragraph doesn't really move on from the initial point that modern liberals disagree with a minimal state

One way of ensuring you get good analysis into your paragraphs is by using some phrases which naturally lend themselves to analysis:

- » this means that
- » therefore
- » this leads to
- » this is because
- » this shows that
- » as a consequence
- » as a result

You can try to use one of these phrases after you've written a couple of sentences at the beginning of your paragraph to help you analyse your point. Using 'signposts' like this helps to flag to your teacher that you are analysing.

STUDENT EXTRACT – 'To what extent does liberalism agree over the state?' – looking at AO2

Classical liberals support laissez-faire capitalism, this means that the state limits its involvement in the economy as much as possible and allows any issues to resolve themselves. This is the theory of the 'invisible hand' identified by Adam Smith, which suggests that a lack of state involvement will lead to a healthy economy. The lack of state involvement will allow individuals to express their individuality, as well as promoting meritocracy through the economy.

> Here the student is developing the concept of laissez-faire capitalism and why it is so favoured by classical liberals

STUDENT EXTRACT – 'To what extent is there more to unite rather than divide the New Right from One Nation conservatives?' – looking at AO2

Although some traditional conservative thinkers like Burke supported the free market believing that trade should involve organic free markets and laissez-faire capitalism, mostly, however, traditional conservatives, like One Nation are sceptical about free market capitalism. This is because they are cautious that its dynamic

> In this response, the student is developing and probing conservative views of free-market capitalism

effects amplify inequality, which is a threat to one nation and fuel support for socialism. They are fearful that a free market promotes a more liberal and universal society which could destroy the idea of a shared national identity and common culture. Subsequently, one-nation conservatives were willing to approve state intervention by subscribing to a more keynesian approach to economics, which included higher public spending on state welfare.

While key thinkers (as well as thinkers) are primarily a feature of AO1, the way they are used can allow them to improve a student's AO2.

STUDENT EXTRACT – 'To what extent do liberals agree on individualism?' – looking at AO2

Classical liberals believe in negative freedom which is the idea that freedom is defined by an absence of constraint which Isaiah Berlin described as 'freedom from' rather than 'freedom to'. This is because classical liberals believe that negative freedom encourages individuals to take responsibility for themselves. J.S. Mill advocated the harm principle which suggested that the state should be restrained from intervening unless it was to prevent harm to others. Mill was arguing that freedom was of key importance in liberalism and individuals should be left alone to do anything, other than harm others.

> Here the student is developing the concept of negative freedom explaining what it is and why classical liberals support it and using a thinker and a key thinker to develop the point

The second aspect of AO2 requires students to apply comparative analysis. Comparative analysis is a key part of essay writing. This means to look at two different features and then to compare them to see where there might be similarities and/or differences. Students often don't understand how to construct comparative analysis, as opposed to just writing about two different things. A very useful way to enhance comparative analysis is by using comparative language. This will enable you to draw comparisons and contrasts between different arguments. Some simple ways to incorporate comparative analysis is by using words like:

» whereas	» not only	» instead
» despite	» but also	» no longer
» however	» in contrast	» still
» similarly	» both	
» although	» as well as	

As discussed earlier, using 'signposts' like this helps to flag to your teacher that you are comparing.

With ideas, as you may be comparing the ideas of three (or sometimes even four) strands, it is essential to understand how to do this. There is a simple way to understand the difference. Here are three bottles, let's start off describing them all.

'This bottle is red, holds water and is designed in a way to keep the liquid fresh. It is made from acrylic, with a rubber coating to make it easy to grip. This bottle is cylindrical and has a lid which incorporates the spout to allow easy drinking of the liquid. It has a rubber hand strap.'

This is knowledge – AO1

'This bottle is blue, holds water and is made of metal. It has been designed to keep liquid fresh. It has a rubber opaque finish and a different coloured lid which incorporated a handle. The lid needs to be twisted off and there is no drinking spout. This bottle is cylindrical in shape. This bottle is insulated to keep the water cold and can also be used to contain hot water.'

This is knowledge – AO1

'This bottle is black, holds water and is made of plastic. It has been designed to keep liquid fresh. It has a plastic opaque finish. It doesn't have a handle, but is shaped in a way that makes it easy to carry. The lid includes a drinking spout which needs to be lifter to drink. This bottle is mainly cylindrical in shape.'

This is knowledge – AO1

Above are correct facts about the bottles but there is no comparison. If the question was asked 'To what extent are the bottles the same?', and students answered with three separate paragraphs on each bottle they would NOT be answering the question. They would be answering the question 'Can you tell me about each bottle?'!

Instead, students need to compare different characteristics of the bottles to be able to come to a judgement about whether the similarities are greater than the differences.

'All the bottles are designed to hold water and to keep the water fresh. They also all have straightforward ways of accessing the water to drink it. All three bottles are broadly cylindrical in shape.

While all three water bottles are designed to make them easy to hold, they all do this in different ways. Both the red and blue bottles are designed with a handle whereas the black bottle has no handle but is shaped in a way that is easy to hold, unlike the red and blue bottles.

One clear way they are different is that one is made of acrylic, one plastic and the last one metal. This also means that while the red one is semi-transparent, the other two are opaque. Also, the one made of metal will be considerably heavier than the other two. However, the metal bottle also insulates both hot and cold drinks, which neither of the other two do.

One final comparison is how easy it is to drink from them. The red and black bottles both have easily accessible spots which makes them very easy to drink from, however, the blue metal bottle requires the whole lid to be screwed off to drink from, which is not very accessible.'

This is comparative analysis – AO2

This type of technique can be used in Ideas answers when discussing the differing views of two or more strands' views on an issue. In order for comparative analysis to be effective, it is essential to ensure you are discussing different strands' views in the same paragraph.

If you look at the example paragraphs above, the comparisons are made between related themes of the containers; lids are compared with lids, shape is compared with shape and so on. The comparison would not be effective if we compared the lid of one with the shape of the other, it would be an inadequate comparison. This is true when comparing strands within a paragraph, students need to be discussing their view on the same thing.

STUDENT EXTRACT – 'To what extent do conservatives agree over the state?' – looking at comparative analysis AO2

One Nation conservatives believe that the state has a natural ruling class that paternalistically governs for the benefit of all. Burke believes in an aristocratic government that saves humans from themselves. Traditional conservatives are pragmatic about the extent of the state and are prepared to enlarge it to achieve social stability. This is associated to Burke's idea of changing to conserve which continued to develop through early One Nation conservatism. On the contrary, the New Right has mixed opinions on state intervention as they wish to 'roll back the frontiers of the state'.

> Although this answer includes all three strands in one paragraph, there is still very little comparison of the different views – this is side-by-side comparison. It would be better if there was some interplay between the strands' views

STUDENT EXTRACT – 'To what extent do socialists agree over the economy?' – looking at comparative analysis AO2

However, socialists accept capitalism to varying degrees highlighting a fundamental discrepancy in their views on class. Third Way socialists accept capitalism, considering it to be a permanent part of society that can be utilized, embracing it due to its capacity to create economic growth. Whereas revolutionary socialists completely reject this, asserting that capitalism is an instrument of the bourgeoisie which creates the condition for class divisions, which they reject as a basis for a socialist society. However, the Third Way accept a degree of class division as they seek to accommodate capitalism whereas revolutionary socialists seek to eradicate class completely along with capitalism which they assert enables it, whereas Third Way socialists don't.

> In this answer, the student is interlinking the views of the two strands throughout the paragraph rather than a block of writing on each

STUDENT EXTRACT – 'To what extent do conservatives agree over society?' – looking at comparative analysis AO2

Both traditional and One Nation conservatives agree on human imperfection in respects to humans being morally, psychologically and intellectually flawed. However, the New Right oppose this view because humans to them are rational beings. They therefore believe in a more atomistic and individualistic approach than traditional or One Nation conservatives. This is backed up by Ayn Rand's ideas on objectivism. This outlines that individuals are rational to reach the goal of happiness and self-reliance, they are 'motivated by the desire to achieve, not by the desire to beat others'. While the traditional and One Nation conservative's view of human imperfection leads to a belief in an organic society, hierarchy and authority from above, the New Right, however, believe that society consists of self-interested and self-sufficient individuals.

> Here the student is looking at differences, comparing views and making effective use of comparative language

AO3 in detail

'Evaluate aspects of politics and political information, including to construct arguments, make substantiated judgements and draw conclusions.'

This AO requires you to evaluate. This means weigh up the evidence and come to a reasoned judgement. In Ideas, all questions will start 'To what extent ...' and be asking about agreements/disagreements similarities/differences within an ideology, hence the nature of the 'judgement' is different. You are being required to judge whether the agreements are MORE SIGNIFICANT than the disagreements or vice versa. Hence it is not enough to show that there ARE disagreements and or similarities, **you are required to identify which one is greater**. You must come down on one side; you must conclude that the agreement is more significant than the disagreement or vice versa. It doesn't matter which side you land on, as all perspectives are equally valid; additionally, your judgement can be that the agreement is so much stronger than the disagreement (or vice versa) or that it is very finally balanced, but agreement just 'wins' (or vice versa).

Source: Scales by Maxim Kulikov from Noun Project (CC BY 3.0)

It may be useful to think of this in terms of a weighing scale. You put all the agreement on one side of the scale and all the disagreement on the other side and one side will be 'heavier' than the other. The heavier side may be made up of lots of small agreements (or disagreements) or it may be that the there are fewer, very significant or 'heavier' arguments. Equally the heavier side may be significantly heavier or just heavier, but one side 'wins'.

It is also important to understand that you are required to make a 'substantiated judgement', in other words you can't just present agreement and disagreement equally throughout the essay and then, in your conclusion, argue that agreement is stronger than disagreement. A substantiated judgement is one which is argued throughout the answer. This should begin in the introduction, continue throughout the essay and be reasserted in the conclusion. This means that answers need to be carefully thought out and planned to ensure that AO3 is embedded throughout your answer.

In addition, AO3 marks can be improved by weighing up the importance of the point you are making: 'this is one of the most important arguments that shows', 'this argument is very significant', 'this point may be of less importance than others'. Think about adjectives that could go before the words agree or disagree to emphasis their significance. Doing this will help to identify their importance, for example:

» superficial

» fundamental

» clear

» strong

» underlying

» weak

» central

» core

Using introductions to begin the AO3 journey

STUDENT EXTRACT – 'To what extent do socialists agree over human nature?' – looking at AO3 in introductions

Socialism is built upon the idea that humans are social creatures and a positive view of human nature. This goes for all three strands of socialism: revolutionary, social democracy and the Third Way. However, when evaluating all strands of socialism, it is clear that there are differences between their views of human nature.

> In this introduction, the student outlines generally that there are agreements and disagreements but, crucially, not which one is more significant

STUDENT EXTRACT – 'To what extent do conservatives agree over society?' – looking at AO3 in introductions

This essay will evaluate the extent to which conservatives believe in an organic society, it will look at whether there are similarities between the views of traditional, One Nation conservatives and the New Right and it will consider the differences between their views. It will evaluate whether there are more agreements than disagreements.

> This student is giving all the possible options of what they might think in their introduction and crucially, not coming to a judgement. This should be avoided

STUDENT EXTRACT – 'To what extent do socialists agree over the state?' – looking at AO3 in introductions

Socialists' view of the state differs to a large extent. Revolutionary socialists completely oppose the state, believing it is a tool of the ruling classes; therefore, it can never be harnessed for socialist means. Social democrats reject this view, opposing revolution and instead supporting the view that the state can be used to create equality, though this will take time. The Third Way differs even further, viewing the state in a very positive light, seeing it as key in making the UK more competitive. Thus, it is clear that there is more disagreement than agreement over the state.

> Although this introduction unnecessarily outlines all the views, rather than framing the debate, it sets the context for the question and sets out clearly the way it is going to argue to answer the question

Incorporating AO3 throughout the essay

One of the most important things to understand about all three AOs is that they don't work in isolation. AO2 feeds off AO1 and AO3 feeds off AO2 and hence in turn, AO1. In other words, in order to enhance AO3, it is necessary to, firstly, know the views of all the strands of the ideology (and related key thinkers) (AO1), and then to have developed and compared them with each other (AO2). If this has been done, you are then able to come to a 'substantiated judgement' about whether you think the agreement is more significant or the disagreement.

While it's important for AO3 to top and tail answers with effective introductions and conclusions, this is not enough. To achieve a Level 5 in AO3, the Pearson Level Based Mark Scheme requires students to

> *Construct fully relevant evaluation of political information, constructing fully effective arguments and judgements, which are consistently substantiated and lead to fully focused and justified conclusions.*

This can be interpreted to mean that your AO3 must exist throughout the answer. We're now going to look at ways this can be achieved.

We have discussed the idea that all paragraphs should include a discussion of more than one strand to ensure effective comparative analysis. As we will see later there are two different ways that paragraphs can be organized to accommodate this. Irrespective of which essay structure is used, AO3 needs to be incorporated into all the paragraphs of an answer.

In the paragraph below the student is identifying areas of agreement (and in the following two paragraphs they would reject those agreements by arguing that the disagreements are more significant). This extract shows how to consistently argue that the disagreements are more significant in a paragraph identifying agreements.

STUDENT EXTRACT – 'To what extent do liberals agree on individualism?' – looking at AO3 judgements incorporated into paragraphs

Despite the fact that this essay will argue that, overall, there are more differences than similarities within liberalism over individualism, that does not mean that there is no agreement. All liberals agree on the primacy of the individual above any claims by the state or groupings within society. This is because the individual should not be defined by what the government says they are or whatever group they may be a part of. Additionally, all liberals believe in foundational equality which is the belief that all individuals are born with natural rights that entitles them to 'life, liberty and the pursuit of happiness'. They also believe in formal equality, where all individuals are treated equally, and no one is above the law ...

The extract above shows how the student is evaluating by incorporating their view into their paragraph. With this method, they explain at the outset that even though they are looking at agreements, it does not change their overall judgement that there are more disagreements within liberalism. If they did not explain this, it may look as if they were arguing both sides equally, which would limit their AO3 marks.

STUDENT EXTRACT – 'To what extent do liberals agree on freedom?' – having discussed agreement in previous paragraph, looking at AO3 judgements incorporated into paragraphs agree/disagree approach

However, despite this agreement, there is significantly more disagreement between classical and modern liberals as they have different views over the nature of the freedom that individuals should have. This is because classical liberals believe in negative freedom which is the idea that freedom is defined by an absence of constraint, which is, as liberal philosopher Isaiah Berlin describes it, 'freedom from' rather than 'freedom to'. Modern liberals reject negative freedom as the only understanding of freedom due to the fact that they argue that individuals who are disadvantaged through no fault of their own need help to overcome these obstacles, they cannot become free without it, which is why modern liberals advocate positive freedoms instead ... Thus, it is clear that due to their fundamental differences in the understanding of freedom, which is the central principle of liberalism, there is clearly more disagreement than agreement over liberty.

Here, the student begins by reaffirming their view, that there is more disagreement, then the paragraph goes on to identify the differences in their views. They end the paragraph by highlighting that they have showed that the disagreements are more significant than the agreements.

STUDENT EXTRACT – 'To what extent is there more to unite rather than divide conservatives?' – looking at AO3 judgements incorporated into paragraphs – thematic approach

One area where it could be argued that there is more to divide conservatives than unite them is with regards to the economy, specifically free-market capitalism. Although there is agreement between traditional and One Nation conservatives, this does not diminish the overall view that the divisions are greater. These strands are both sceptical about free market capitalism, this is because they are cautious that its dynamic effects can amplify inequality, and become a threat to the stability of society. Conservative thinkers like Burke supported the free market, but Conservatives recognized the damage it did to the stability of society and were willing to support a larger role for the state …

However, despite this agreement, the more compelling view is that the divisions far outweigh the areas of unity. This is because there is a very clear divide between the pragmatic acceptance of capitalism which underlies the traditional and One Nation view and the ideological commitment to it which is supported by the New Right. New Right conservatives believe in economic freedom and therefore advocate laissez-faire capitalism and free-market economies where state functions are privatized and deregulated, a view echoed by Nozick …

One Nation conservatives reject this ideological commitment to the free market, preferring instead to adapt and adjust their approach to the economy depending on the circumstances and the needs of society. The New Right, however, arguing instead that individuals should rely on themselves rather than the state and that larger state intervention to provide welfare, resulted in individuals becoming dependent on welfare rather than relying on themselves. This significant disagreement clearly shows that there is more to divide conservatives than unite them.

In the extract above, the student is incorporating agreement and disagreement within a longer section. Here there are evaluative statements throughout the paragraph, making their view clear, that there is more to divide than unite conservatives. Note also the use of terms like 'clear divide' and 'significant agreement'.

Using conclusions to end the AO3 journey

While your introductions begin the process of AO3, your conclusion should simply bring your whole argument together and end the journey. What a conclusion should not do is contain **all** your evaluation in one place; evaluation must be spread throughout your essay.

STUDENT EXTRACT – 'To what extent is there more to unite rather than divide the New Right from One Nation conservatives?' – looking at AO3 in conclusions

In conclusion, One Nation and New Right conservatives agree on the fundamental need of a state in order to provide economic security. They disagree on the amount of state intervention as neoliberals argue that the state is just a service provider whereas One Nation conservatives argue that the state should pursue a paternalistic role. Thus, there are many disagreements between them.

> Here the student is bringing their essay to a close with a summary of their points. They argue that there are disagreements, but they don't resolve the issue of whether there are MORE disagreements than agreements

STUDENT EXTRACT – 'To what extent do socialists agree over the state?' – looking at AO3 in conclusions

In conclusion, there are very few similarities on the state within socialism. It is arguably the area where socialists disagree the most, due to the division between evolutionary and revolutionary socialists. The state, for Marx and Engels, is intolerable; they believed that the state would inevitably come to an end and be replaced with communism. Whereas social democrats disregard a lot of what Marx advocated, claiming that in modern day society revolution is unnecessary, the state is vital to providing equality. This is taken one step further by the Third Way which argues the state's role is to harness the success of capitalism and redirect it through targeted welfare. Therefore, ultimately socialists do not have a consistent view of the state.

> This is a rather long conclusion where the student outlines the views of the different strands before concluding (just!) that disagreement is more significant. It would be better to summarize these arguments in a more general way

STUDENT EXTRACT – 'To what extent do different socialists agree over the role of the state?' – looking at AO3 in conclusions

In conclusion, it is evident that there are more areas of disagreement within socialism regarding the state's role in creating collectivism and equality within a socialist society, than agreement. For example, Third Way call for a limit on state intervention, whilst social democrats maintain that gradual change and increased state intervention is essential when achieving a socialist society and revolutionary socialists reject the state outright, seeing it as unnecessary in a socialist society. Thus, demonstrating there is more disagreement than agreement over the role of the state.

> This is a good conclusion which reinforces at the beginning and the end of the paragraph what it has been arguing throughout the answer. It also summarizes the views of the different strands without going into detail

STUDENT EXTRACT – 'To what extent do conservatives agree about the economy?' – looking at AO3 in conclusions

Although there are some areas of agreement within conservatism such as their united views on private property and ownership, which could lead to agreement with the statement, there is also a clear divide between One Nation and New Right conservatives which could lead to disagreement with the statement. There is clear agreement between traditional and One Nation conservatives but despite their agreement, clearly contrast with the views of the New Right on a majority of factors. Also the New Right is formed of two strands: neoliberalism and neoconservatism – the neoliberal part of the New Right heavily contrasts to all of the opinions of the other conservative strands, especially the more traditional ones, whereas neoconservatism agrees with it.

> This is a very confusing conclusion which doesn't resolve a great deal. It is always best to keep conclusions simple and simply restate the view argued through the essay

How do I structure Ideas answers?

Over the next few pages, you will see many ideas of how to, and not to structure your answers. It is important to note that the Exam board does not prescribe any fixed way of structuring answers. However, it is essential to hit all Assessment Objectives, which is what these suggestions are based on.

Introductions and conclusion

Although we have discussed introductions and conclusions in the AO3 section, they play an important role in ideas answers beyond AO3 judgements. **Introductions** should usually fulfil two to three functions.

» First, they should **outline** the ideology, briefly.

- For example on a question about disagreement on the liberal view of the state, it could outline that liberalism is an ideology that is primarily concerned with freedom of the individual and consist of two strands, modern and classical liberalism.

» The second purpose an introduction should serve is to provide **context** to the question/answer.

- This is usually a summary of the different strands perspectives of the debate. It's important to note the word 'summary'. Too often students spend too long explaining too much in their introduction. This is unnecessary and a waste of precious words (and hence time). A couple of sentences which sum up the key views of the strands is more than sufficient.

» Lastly, a final, but key function of an introduction is to express a **view**.

- This is crucial to your AO3 analysis. It needs to be clear.

- Often students end their introduction by stating their intention to identify the agreements and disagreements within the ideology. However, it is better, at this stage to outline the view that

STUDENT EXTRACT – 'To what extent do New Right conservatives differ from One Nation conservatives?' – looking at AO3 in introductions

It can be argued that there is more to unite rather than divide the New Right from One Nation conservatives as they are both strands of conservatism. Therefore, they both have the same opinion and beliefs on the core conservative principles. An example of this would be the importance of individualism and tradition. However, the more convincing argument is that there is more to divide rather than unite. This is because originally, New Right conservatism emerged as the main rival to One Nation and was formed in the 1970s as a reaction to One Nation. Therefore, this means that there will be contrasting views as it is a much more modern view of the world and was formed after One Nation conservatism. So, there will be a division as otherwise there wouldn't have been a reason to form the New Right.

> This is quite a long, narrative introduction – it includes clear statements of its judgement in the middle of the paragraph but doesn't frame the debate in an effective way. Ideally introductions should be brief and just provide context

STUDENT EXTRACT – 'To what extent do liberals support equality?' – looking at AO3 in introductions

This essay will argue to what extent liberals support the principle of equality, concluding that there is more disagreement than agreement due to the fact that modern and classical liberals both advocate different types of equality.

> While this one is very short, too short, even though it outlines a view, it does nothing else

STUDENT EXTRACT – 'To what extent do socialists agree over the state?' – looking at AO3 in introductions

Socialism traditionally opposed a capitalist society whilst supporting common ownership of economic and social systems to promote an egalitarian society. To achieve these goals, different socialists introduce different ways that the state can provide to create a more equal society. This leads to a disagreement amongst socialists, regarding the size of the state and whether it should exist at all. Therefore, this essay will illustrate that there is more disagreement than agreement amongst socialists regarding the state's role within a socialist society.

> This introduction frames the debate that is to come in the essay and provides a judgement at the end

you are going to take, to signal that you are fully aware of the AO3 demands. This is why it is so important to plan your answer fully before you start writing – you need to know your destination.

Conclusions are crucial as they play a parallel role to introductions. The role of a conclusion should not be underestimated.

- A good conclusion should be brief, it should not be rambling.

- It is the culmination of your essay and the last thing to be read, so its objective is to reassert your view.

- You need to briefly bring all the arguments together and clarify your line of argument by making your point of view clear.

- You need to be convincing and persuasive without being overly strident or dismissive. It's ok to argue that the ideologies are more different than similar, but only just.

- Remember, the conclusion is your last chance to convince the reader of your view.

STUDENT EXTRACT – 'To what extent do socialists agree over the state?' – looking at AO3 in conclusions

In conclusion, this essay has displayed the ways in which socialists come to an agreement over the state's role but essentially it has been made evident that there are more areas of disagreement than agreement regarding the state's role within a socialist society. For example, some socialists call for an eradication of state intervention as it creates a dependency culture, whilst others maintain that gradual change and increased state intervention is essential when achieving a socialist society. Thus, demonstrating there is more disagreement than agreement over the role of the state.

> This conclusion sums up all the points made throughout the essay, reasserting its view that there are more disagreements than agreements

STUDENT EXTRACT – 'To what extent does conservatism agree over human nature?' – looking at AO3 in conclusions

Thus, to conclude whilst there is agreement among conservatives, with traditional and One Nation in particular agreeing on human imperfection, and the subsequent need for tradition and that society should be organic, ultimately there is more disagreement than agreement between the different strands of conservatism as the New Right believe that humans are rational support radical ideas which reject tradition. Therefore, this outlines how conservatism does not agree over human nature due to the extent the different strands of conservatism disagree over it.

> A really good conclusion which summarizes the key area of difference between the strands and gives a clear view

How to organize paragraphs to hit as many AOs as possible

One of the most challenging aspects of A-Levels answers is bringing everything you've learnt together to answer the question asked of you while making sure you are hitting the requirements of all three AOs. Here we are going to look at ways you can organize your answers to be as effective as possible.

First, it goes without saying that you need to know your stuff. No amount of organizing of paragraphs can drastically improve the quality of a student's answer if it doesn't have good knowledge and understanding of the content. As was outlined on page 234, AO1 is the foundation of everything else; without it, there is a limit to what can be achieved. On the assumption that AO1 knowledge is solid, it's important to know how you can ensure that the structure of your answer is set up to address the different needs laid out in this chapter.

So, we've covered introductions and conclusions, which leaves the main body of the essay. The first step when considering the content you need to answer a question is to select the best arguments to discuss. Once you've decided on the best content, how then do you organize this? One option is considered below.

Structure one

Introduction	
Strand 1	Here you look at one strand's view on the issue being asked in the question.
Strand 2	Here you look at another strand's view on the issue being asked in the question.
Strand 3	Here you look at another strand's view on the issue being asked in the question.
Conclusion	

The problem with this structure (above) is that while it covers AO1, it is very difficult to achieve any AO2 comparative marks as it is hard to compare the views of different strands if they aren't being discussed in the same paragraph. Additionally, if strands aren't compared, it is hard to make substantiated judgements, AO3, throughout the essay.

Overall, therefore, we can see that this structure is not ideal as it limits your ability to access two of the three AOs. **This is NOT an advisable structure.**

So, what structure would best enable an answer to address all three AOs? The answer is clearly one which discusses different strands in each paragraph, which facilitates comparative analysis and consequently enables substantiated judgements to be made.

There are two different effective structures for Ideas answers. The first one is outlined in the table below.

Structure two – Agree/Disagree

This structure consists of three paragraphs, each one divided into 'agree' or 'disagree' paragraphs. If you are going to argue that there are more agreements than disagreements as your overall view, then you should have two agree and one disagree paragraphs. If you're arguing that there are more disagreements than agreements within an ideology, then you should do one agree and two disagree paragraphs.

There are two things to remember here:

» Make sure you are always discussing more than one strand in each paragraph.

» Make sure, even in your opposing paragraph to maintain your overall AO3 view.

Let's look at how you can do this.

Option A: if you are arguing more disagreement than agreement

Introduction	
Agree	In this paragraph you outline areas of agreement within the strands of the ideology.
Disagree	In this paragraph you outline areas of disagreement within the strands of the ideology and explain that they are more significant than the agreement outlined in P1.
Disagree	In this paragraph you outline areas of disagreement within the strands of the ideology and explain that they are more significant than the agreement outlined in P1.
Conclusion	

Option B: if you are arguing more agreement than disagreement

Introduction	
Agree	In this paragraph you outline areas of agreement within the strands of the ideology.
Disagree	In this paragraph you outline areas of disagreement within the strands of the ideology.
Agree	In this paragraph you outline areas of agreement within the strands of the ideology and explain that they are more significant than the disagreement outlined in P2.
Conclusion	

STUDENT EXTRACT – 'To what extent to conservatives agree over pragmatism?' "Agree/Disagree structure"

While this essay will argue that there are more disagreements than agreements within conservatism over pragmatism, there are still clear areas of agreement. Specifically, there is agreement between One Nation conservatism and traditional conservatism who both see pragmatism as a key value, agreeing that change should be made gradually with practical solutions instead of radical change. Their attitude of 'change to conserve' is rooted in pragmatism, so change should be gradual, and organic instead of drastic and catastrophic which could destabilize and undermine society, which is a key value of conservatism. These ideas are supported by Burke who rejected the abstract ideas and 'rational' thought of enlightenment thinkers on political and social issues; he viewed revolution as dangerous, as they caused unrest as conservatism believe society should be stable. In addition, One Nation and traditional conservatives view radical change as counterproductive as humans do not have the capability to understand the world, let alone change it, as they are intellectually imperfect. Hobbes believed that humans are imperfect and selfish with the only rational capability being that of seeking order and naturally a sovereign body/individual. This shows clearly that humans seek order and pragmatic response due to their flawed natures in which pragmatism is a shared belief and core principle.

> Here in the opening paragraph the student is identifying areas of agreement. Their overall judgement is that there is more disagreement than agreement, but they begin their answer by identifying agreements

STUDENT EXTRACT – 'To what extent is there more to unite rather than divide the New Right from One Nation conservatives?' "Agree/Disagree structure"

Despite the agreement identified above, the more compelling argument is that there is clearly more to divide than unite conservatives. One area which shows this division between the New Right and One Nation conservatives is their contrasting views on the state. One Nation conservatives are pragmatic about the role of the state and are prepared to use it to achieve social stability. This is the idea of changing to conserve which continued to develop with Disraeli. On the contrary, the New Right has rejected this pragmatic approach as they stand very firmly against any unnecessary state intervention and wish to 'roll back the frontiers of the state'. Rand and Nozick can both be associated with these views as both objected to state intervention which they perceived as undermining individual freedoms. Conversely, One Nation conservatives have been prepared to use the state to provide welfare for those who find themselves in difficult circumstances as they understand that discontent among the working class destabilizes society. As Disraeli said, 'the palace is not safe when the cottage is not happy', however, the New Right reject this idea believing that a welfare state is not an effective way of supporting the poor as they argue it creates a dependency culture. Thus, it is very clear, that when it comes to their view of the state, there is more to divide than unite One Nation and New Right conservatives.

> Here in a second paragraph, the student is outlining areas of disagreement between One Nation and New Right conservatives over the state

> Throughout the paragraph, they are identifying and exploring differences between the two strands

> They mention two relevant key thinkers, although it would be better if they elaborated more

> Finally, they reiterate their judgement

In this extract, the student is ticking all three AOs in a highly effective and clear way.

STUDENT EXTRACT – 'To what extent do liberals agree on freedom?' – "Agree/Disagree structure" having discussed agreement in the previous paragraph

As this essay has identified, there are more agreements than disagreements within liberalism over freedom, there is still some disagreement between classical and modern liberals as they have different views over the nature of the freedom that individuals should have. This is because classical liberals believe in negative freedom which is the idea that freedom is defined by an absence of constraint which as liberal philosopher Isaiah Berlin describes it as 'freedom from' rather than 'freedom to'. Modern liberals reject negative freedom as the only understanding of freedom since they argue that individuals who are disadvantaged through no fault of their own need help to overcome these obstacles, they cannot become free without it, which is why modern liberals advocate positive freedom …

Thus, it is clear that despite their fundamental differences in the understanding of freedom, there is fundamental agreement within liberalism over the central principle of liberty.

> Here a student's overall argument is that there is more agreement, but they are still including one paragraph on disagreement

Structure three: thematic approach

An alternative structure is shown in the table below. This is a thematic approach. In this structure, each paragraph addresses a different theme and discusses agreement and disagreement within each paragraph, as well as coming to a view. Because this might take longer, it might be that you can only manage two themes in the time allowed.

Introduction	
Theme 1	Here you address agreement and disagreement within the strands over a theme while coming to a judgement about which one is greater.
Theme 2	Here you address agreement and disagreement within the strands over a theme while coming to a judgement about which one is greater.
Theme 3	Here you address agreement and disagreement within the strands over a theme while coming to a judgement about which one is greater.
Conclusion	

STUDENT EXTRACT – 'To what extent is there more to unite rather than divide conservatives?'

One area where there is more to divide than unite conservatives is with regards to society. Even though this is the case, there are still superficial areas of agreement about society. Traditional and One Nation conservatives agree that tradition is the bedrock of society. Conservatives like Burke say that because humans only know what they observe, tradition and the past is the best place to turn to find an answer. This is why they rely on empiricism rather than ideology. This will preserve the organic society that evolves gradually with no rush to change. However, there is disagreement between New Right and One Nation conservatives how society should be structured.

> Here they begin the section by outlining the theme they are going to discuss, in this case, society

> Then they address agreement within the strands over society

> Before rejecting this and arguing that there is greater disagreement over society

One Nation and Traditional conservatives believe in hierarchy and paternalism because they believe that the aristocracy were born to rule and so they will make the most pragmatic decisions that will lead to social cohesion. Whereas, New Right conservatives believe that the your position in society should be decided by the effort and talent you have, thus they believe in a meritocracy. Nozick says that these individuals have no social responsibility or allegiance to the state's rule so they will make the best decisions to preserve order. Overall, whilst there is some agreement on society, there is fundamental disagreement on the make-up of society's upper class.

> They end with a restatement of their overall view

STUDENT EXTRACT – 'To what extent do different socialists agree over the role of the economy?'

All socialists can agree that the economy should be structured in such a way that promotes economic justice and greater equality in society. Socialists argue that inequality in a capitalist society creates social divisions whereas equality encourages humans to work together. Socialists tend to agree that the differences in humans' abilities are relatively small and yet the differences in wealth are very much larger, suggesting that inequality is structural and hence changes need to be made to the structure of society. However, despite this agreement on the values promoted by a more equal society, social democrats advocate reform to the existing system, whereas revolutionary socialists advocate the overthrow of the economy via revolution showing significantly more disagreements than agreements. Social democrats seek to offset the worst excesses of capitalism whilst taking advantage of the prosperity it creates, whereas, revolutionary socialists seek to dismantle capitalism entirely, replacing it with a system of collectivism and worker's control. Social democrats and revolutionary socialists disagree entirely when it comes to solving the problems that arise from capitalism. Social democrats attempt to reconcile free-market capitalism with more socialist aims via state intervention. Antony Crosland believed that capitalism is a reliable creator of wealth but the distribution of this wealth produces inequality and poverty. Social democrats argue that state intervention in the economy is the remedy to the inherent weaknesses of capitalism, chiefly through the welfare state, progressive tax and nationalized industries. However, this view is vehemently rejected by revolutionary socialists like Marx and Engels who argued that the underlying driver of capitalism is inequality and exploitation and thus any attempt to humanize it will fail. They therefore seek to replace capitalism, based on class division and exploitation, with a new society based on collective ownership. Thus, it is clear that these two strands of socialism are irreconcilable with regards to the structure of the economy, with social democrats seeking to improve capitalism whilst revolutionary socialists seek to replace it entirely.

> Again this answer starts by outlining areas of agreement

> Before moving on to disagreement between two of the strands. Note how the answer is going back and forth between the two views, clearly showing disagreement

Putting this all together

We have now looked at all the different elements of an answer to an essay. Let's now finally look at a whole essay and how to combine these to make a good answer.

'To what extent do liberals agree on the economy?' #1

This essay will argue to what extent liberals agree on the economy, concluding that there is more disagreement than agreement due to classical liberals and modern liberals disagreeing over the extent to which the state should intervene in the economy.

> ✓ This introduction is outlining the view it will take
>
> ✗ It isn't doing much else. It needs to frame the debate by putting these differences into context

All liberals agree that the economy should be a capitalist economic system based on private ownership and market forces. This is due to the fact that this type of economy complements liberal individualism through economic self-striving. All liberals also support the pursuit of competition and profit, providing humans the freedom and opportunity to fulfil their potential. However, there is disagreement as classical liberals would advocate for a laissez-faire, free-market economics associated with Adam Smith. This would be where markets would be subject to the 'invisible hand' controlling supply and demand. Classical liberals also believe that in a free market the state should adopt a 'hands-off' approach to the economy, and thus limited state intervention. Conversely, modern liberals would instead promote government intervention, similar to keynesianism. This is a capitalist economy but would not be self-regulating as not intervening would lead to cyclical slump and unemployment for individuals. Therefore, instead, the state should guide the economy and provide some form of welfare to those that need it to enable equality of opportunity and allow individuals an equal chance of fulfilling their potential.

> ✓ This section includes agreement and disagreement between the strands
>
> ✗ It would better to have more discussion of agreements and for the disagreements to be more comparative
>
> ✗ It lacks any judgement as to whether agreements of disagreements are greater

Similarly, there is agreement among all liberals on the role of the state on the lives of individuals and the economy. This is because all liberals believe that the state is a necessary evil and without a state society would descend into the war of 'each against all' as described by Hobbes. The 'state of nature', a stateless society where individuals live without laws and protection and where existence would be bleak and life would be 'solitary, poor, nasty, brutish and short'. Thus, showing agreement among liberals on the state and the economy. However, there is fundamental disagreement among liberals over the extent to which the state should intervene. This is because classical liberals believe that the state is more evil than necessary, and therefore believe in a minimal state. Mill had the idea of the 'harm principle' which was the principle that the state should only intervene if an individual was causing harm to someone. This is similar to classical liberal's view of the state in the economy as they believe there should be no state intervention as it would infringe on their individual freedoms. Having said that, modern liberals would argue that the state is more necessary than evil and therefore would prefer an enabling state. This is because the state should be able to intervene in order to help individuals fulfil their potential. Additionally, the state should provide 'cradle to grave' welfare for individuals in order to ensure equality of opportunity allowing individuals equal opportunity to succeed.

✓ This section has correctly identified the role of the state in the economy as an area of discussion

✓ It makes good use of a key thinker (Mill) and connects them to a relevant strand

✗ However, it is paying lip service to the issue of the economy, in reality it is about the role of the state, although the reference to the welfare state is welcome

✗ It uses a conservatism thinker which wouldn't be recognized here as a key thinker

✗ It would better for the disagreements to be more comparative

✗ Again, it lacks a judgement

Finally, all liberals agree on the primacy of the individual above any claims by the state or groupings within society. This is due to the fact that the individual should not be defined by what the government says they are or whatever group they may be part of. This idea extends to the economy as well with individuals being able to achieve their potential. However, classical liberals are in favour of egoistical individualism which is the belief that individual freedom is associated with a rational sense of self-reliance and self-interest. They believe that in order to achieve egoistical individualism, the state must be limited so that it does not infringe on individual freedom and respects formal equality to ensure that individuals can have the freedom to undergo self-regarding acts. Hence, illustrating classical liberals view of laissez faire economics with limited government intervention. On the other hand, modern liberals disagree with egoistical individualism as without state intervention individuals who are disadvantaged would not have the opportunity to change the status quo because of structural inequalities and obstacles blocking them to fulfil their potential. Instead, they advocate for developmental individualism which is the belief that the state, by intervening, can assist in individuals' development. Modern liberals believes that the state should enable equality of opportunity for individuals and this is done through keynesian economics and welfare provision by the state.

✓ There is good discussion of the agreement and disagreement within liberalism over individualism

✓ The last part on modern liberalism does compare back to classical liberalism

✗ As above, it isn't really addressing the issue of the economy

✗ It could be more detailed about agreement

✗ The disagreements section could still be more comparative

✗ Again, it lacks a judgement

Thus, to conclude, whilst all liberals agree that the economy should be based on a capitalist economic system, the state is a necessary evil and the primacy of the individual, there is more disagreement between the different strands of liberalism. This can be seen by classical liberals preferring laissez-faire economics with limited state intervention whereas modern liberals would advocate for keynesian type of economics. Thus overall, there is more disagreement than agreement over the issue of the economy among liberals.

✓ This concludes by summing up the key points made and restating the view outlined in the introduction

✗ It isn't enough to leave judgements to introductions and conclusions

'To what extent do liberals agree on the economy?' #2

Liberalism is an ideology which values freedom and individualism, with the two main strands being classical and modern liberals. While all liberals agree on the importance of a capitalist economy, there are considerable differences on the extent to which they promote it, for example on the extent of the role of the state within the economy. Hence this essay will argue that there is more disagreement than agreement within liberalism over the role of the state.

✓ Now this introduction is introducing liberalism and its strands as well as identifying a key area of dispute before coming to a view

While there is significantly more disagreement than agreement within Liberalism over the economy, there is also some agreement. All liberals have been supportive of the capitalist system, recognizing the role it could play in supporting and upholding individual liberty and meritocracy. They believe that a capitalist economic system based on private ownership and market forces complements liberal individualism through economic self-reliance. All liberals also support the pursuit of competition and profit, providing humans the freedom and opportunity to fulfil their potential. For liberals, the free market encouraged individuals to make rational choices about how they worked, what they bought, sold, saved or spent. The market therefore upholds the key principle of free choice. They also accepted that capitalism would result in some inequality, which they argued would play an important role in incentivizing individuals.

However, despite these agreements, there are significant and fundamental disagreements between the strands as classical liberals would advocate for a laissez-faire, free-market economics associated with Adam Smith, whereas modern liberals like Rawls support a form of capitalism based on keynesianism. Classical liberals support a form of economic liberalism where markets would be subject to the 'invisible hand' of supply and demand, where markets were the key decider on what and how much was produced, and what it was priced at. The state should adopt a 'hands-off' approach to the economy, and there should be limited state intervention. Modern liberals reject this model, arguing that laissez-faire economics does not result in genuine freedom for all, as wealthy capitalists have significantly more power than others and are able to manipulate the market in their own best interests. Instead they argue that governments must intervene to limit the extreme booms and slumps of the capitalist economic cycle, supporting the overall demand in the economy at times of recession and ensuring employment stayed high. This is known as keynesianism. Keynes argued that economic growth and employment levels are largely determined by the level of demand in the economy, and that government can and should encourage demand through economic and tax policy, to deliver full employment. However, Classical Liberals reject such extensive government intervention in the economy arguing that the larger the state, and accompanying tax rises, the less free individuals are. This identifies the clear irreconcilable differences between Modern and classical Liberals over the economy.

✓ This section includes agreement and disagreement between the strands

✓ It has a more thorough analysis of the agreements within liberalism and approaches the disagreement section in a more comparative way

✓ It makes judgements throughout the disagreement paragraph, being clear it sees these as more significant

✓ Note, it uses thinkers which aren't part of the five key thinkers defined by the specification. This is absolutely fine as long as two key thinkers are also included in the whole essay

Another area of some agreement among liberals is the role of the state in the economy. In accordance with their view of the state in society, all liberals believe that the state is a necessary evil in the economy too. As Locke argued, the fundamental values that the state should protect were 'life, liberty and property'. It is this last one that indicates the values of all liberals in seeing the role of the state to protect property rights as well as contracts between individuals in the economy are upheld. For Locke, the right to private property is key. He argues that all individuals own their bodies and hence their labour power belongs to them too. Individuals can thus use their labour power to create goods (property) which belong to them. The role of the state in the economy was to ensure property was secure and contracts were honoured to allow free trade and market competition to flourish.

However, despite this agreement, there is fundamental disagreement among liberals over the extent to which the state should intervene in the economy. While all liberals support the protection of property and contracts by the state, modern liberals see the role of the state in the economy as significantly greater than that, which is rejected by classical liberals. This is because classical liberals believe that the state is more evil than necessary, and therefore believe in a minimal state. Classical liberals would endorse Mill's 'harm principle' which argued that the state should only intervene to prevent harm to others. This suggests that the state has a very limited role in the economy which would not infringe on their individual freedoms. However, modern liberals reject this idea arguing instead that the role of the state in the economy should be significantly greater and instead prefer an enabling state based on a belief in positive freedom. This is because the state should be able to intervene in order to help individuals fulfil their potential. This it is clear one again that there are significant and fundamental differences between modern and classical liberalism over the extent of state intervention in the economy.

✓ This section has correctly identified the role of the state in the economy as an area of discussion

✓ It makes good use of a liberal key thinker in both the agreement and disagreement section and, in the case of J.S. Mill, connects him to a relevant strand

✓ Disagreements are now more comparative

✓ Judgements are clear throughout

Finally, despite overall there being more disagreement than agreement, all liberals also recognize the capitalist system as the clearest embodiment of the liberal principle of individualism and agree on the primacy of the individual above any groupings within society. This is due to the fact that the individual should not be defined by what the government says they are or whatever group they may be part of. Individualism also implies that the economy should be constructed so as to benefit the individual, giving moral priority to individual rights, needs or interests, not the other way round. This is best summed up by Mill when he suggested that 'Over himself, over his own body and mind, the individual is sovereign'. Moreover, each individual is thought to know their own best interests. Hence the capitalist economy best fits this idea as it does not rely on the state acting as a paternal authority to make decisions on behalf of the individual.

However, despite this agreement, classical and modern liberals fundamentally disagree over the role of individualism in the economy. Whereas classical liberals support egoistical individualism, which is based on the belief of negative freedom and is associated with a rational sense of self-reliance and self-interest, modern liberals reject this, and support the idea of developmental individualism, based on a positive view of freedom. This idea prioritizes human flourishing, focusing on the potential individuals have and how to help them achieve it. Whereas egoistical individualism relies on a limited role for the state in the economy, so that it doesn't infringe on individual freedom, developmental individualism relies on state intervention in the economy to help individuals to become free. Specifically, this is based on tax funded welfare to tackle the 'five giants'. Rawls argued that only a capitalist economy with strong social institutions like welfare, education and healthcare were the key to distributive justice. In other words, the creation of a welfare state was necessary to create genuine equality of opportunity. Classical liberals would totally reject this reasoning in two ways: firstly, welfare is funded from taxes which is, for many classical liberals, legalized theft of an individual's hard-earned property; secondly, classical liberals argue that welfare creates a dependency culture which goes against the key principles of self-reliance and self-sufficiency. This once again shows clearly that there are fundamental differences between liberals on the economy.

- ✓ There is good discussion of the agreement and disagreement within liberalism over how individualism impacts their view of the economy
- ✓ It has good comparisons between classical and modern liberals in the disagreement section
- ✓ Makes good use of key thinker Rawls, linking him to the modern liberal perspective
- ✓ Makes clear the view being followed; that there are more disagreements than agreements

Thus, to conclude, whilst all liberals agree that the economy should be based on a capitalist economic system, with good protection of private property, there is more disagreement between the different strands of liberalism. This can be seen by classical liberals preferring laissez-faire economics with limited state intervention whereas modern liberals would advocate for keynesianism alongside a welfare state. Thus, overall, there can be no doubt that there is more disagreement than agreement over the issue of the economy among liberals.

- ✓ This concludes by summing up the key points made and restating the view outlined in the introduction
- ✓ As there are constant judgements throughout the answer, the conclusion merely needs to reiterate them

Index

Note: Page locators in **bold** refer to tables and page locators in *italic* refer to figures.

www.ingramcontent.com/pod-product-compliance
Lightning Source LLC
Chambersburg PA
CBHW080415270326
41929CB00018B/3040